A M E R I C A N  C L A S S I C S

# THE LITERATURE OF THE MIDDLE WESTERN FRONTIER

*Ralph Leslie Rusk*

## VOLUME I

FREDERICK UNGAR PUBLISHING CO.
*NEW YORK*

Republished 1962

First published 1925

*Printed in the United States of America*

Library of Congress Catalog Card No. 61-13639

*To Clara Gibbs Rusk*

# PREFACE

Almost a century has passed since James Hall, Timothy Flint, and William D. Gallagher attempted to create a literature of the West which should be marked both by excellence of artistic achievement and by a distinctly Western quality. Their failure to realize any large measure of artistic achievement may be granted without debate. There remains, however, the question of whether they and the great number of obscure authors who were their unconscious collaborators did not succeed in creating a body of literature invaluable for the record it contains of the growth of civilization during a unique epoch. The epoch was indeed unique; and its literary expression, with which the present book has to do, is, one may believe, a no less significant memorial of this pioneer era than are the facts of economic and political history which recent writers have so diligently explored.

Upon the literature of the West before the end of the year 1840, the date which I have somewhat arbitrarily chosen to regard as marking the close of the pioneer period, two more or less comprehensive works have already been written — William T. Coggeshall's *The Poets and Poetry of the West* (1860) and William H. Venable's *Beginnings of Literary Culture in the Ohio Valley* (1891). Coggeshall's book is an anthology with biographical sketches which are for the most part undiscriminating eulogies. Venable's much more notable work, written some thirty years ago, remains a valuable popular miscellany of biographical and critical fact and anecdote. It was my reading of these early chroniclers which first suggested to me the need of such a study as I have here undertaken.

In the course of gathering my materials I have incurred a large debt to the many librarians who have placed their collections at my disposal and have aided me in searching out a mass of forgotten books and pamphlets, and, later, in verifying quotations and citations.   Special acknowledgment of this kind of aid is due to Mr. W. H. Cathcart, of the Western Reserve Historical Society; Miss Mary Foster and Miss Lillian Beecroft, of the State Historical Society of Wisconsin;  Miss G. B. Krum, of the Burton Historical Collection; Miss Winifred Ver Nooy, of the University of Chicago Libraries; Miss Stella M. Drumm, of the Missouri Historical Society; Miss Esther McNitt, of the Indiana State Library; Miss Florence Dillard, of the Lexington Public Library, Lexington, Kentucky; Dean Thomas Macartney and Mrs. Charles F. Norton, of Transylvania College; Miss Mary Hirst, of the Cincinnati Public Library; Miss L. B. Hamlin, of the Historical and Philosophical Society of Ohio; Mr. W. W. Bishop and Mr. F. L. D. Goodrich, of the general library of the University of Michigan; and Dr. F. K. Farr, of the Lane Theological Seminary. Various other officials and assistants of the same libraries, as well as of the library of Columbia University, the New York Public Library, the Library of Congress, the library of Indiana University, the Newberry Library, the St. Louis Mercantile Library, the St. Louis Public Library, the Young Men's Mercantile Library of Cincinnati, and numerous other libraries, have given me liberally of their time.   Mr. Samuel M. Wilson, of Lexington, Kentucky, and Mr. William Clark Breckenridge, of St. Louis, have generously allowed me the use of rare imprints in their private libraries.

It is a pleasure to express my gratitude to those who have made valued suggestions regarding the general plan or the mechanical detail of this book — to Professor H. H.

Carter, of Indiana University, who has read the proof of
Chapter I; to Professor A. C. Judson, of the same faculty,
who has read the proof of Chapters I-IX; to Professor A.
H. Thorndike and other members of the Department of
English in Columbia University, who have examined the
proof of both volumes; and, especially, to Professor W. P.
Trent and Dr. Carl Van Doren, who have not only read
the manuscript but given invaluable advice regarding the
conduct of this study from the time of its inception.

I wish also to express my thanks to Professor Thorndike
and Dean Frederick J. E. Woodbridge, of the graduate
faculties, and to Mr. Frederick Coykendall and Mr. Alfred
Hartog, of the Columbia University Press, for their generous interest in many important matters pertaining to
publication.

Finally, I wish to acknowledge my great indebtedness
to my wife, to whom I have dedicated this book as very
inadequate recognition of her patient and sympathetic collaboration.

R. L. R.

INDIANA UNIVERSITY
*February, 1925*

## PREFACE TO THE SECOND IMPRESSION

In its present form this book differs from the original
issue only in three or four mechanical details of slight
importance and in the account (Volume I, page 423) of
the plays of Caroline Lee Hentz. Her *De Lara*, though not
performed in the Middle West, so far as I have been able
to discover, and not published until after 1840, was probably written during the author's residence in Kentucky.
It seems clear, at any rate, that Pelby's prize was awarded
at that time (*De Lara; or, the Moorish Bride*, 1843,

"Note by the Publishers"). The prefatory note also records the success of the play as performed "in the eastern cities." This tragedy, which is in blank verse, has its setting in a Spanish castle on the frontier of Granada during the Moorish wars and is interesting chiefly because of its resemblance to the earlier Elizabethan type of revenge play: the ghost of a murdered father urges upon a vacillating son the duty of revenge, and there are other clear echoes of *Hamlet* both in plot and in phrasing. *Werdenberg, or the Forest League,* another tragedy which Mrs. Hentz wrote for Pelby, apparently about the same time, was produced at the Park Theatre, New York, on April 24, 1832, and was, according to an observer's account published the following day, "all but damned." The play, the critic conceded, was indeed deficient in stage effect and would probably never obtain much favor with the public; but it did not want merit as a literary production and its failure on the stage had been due principally to the weakness of the company, who were incapable of performing tragedy. (*Morning Courier and New-York Enquirer,* April 25, 1832.) I have found no evidence that *Werdenberg* was seen in any Western theatre or that it was ever printed.

The anonymously published *Tales of the Northwest; or, Sketches of Indian Life and Character,* the account of which given below (Volume I, page 286) is based entirely upon a review, was the work of William Joseph Snelling, who later, during his residence in Boston, gained notoriety as a journalist and writer of satirical verse. The facts regarding his earlier years, however, seem to be somewhat obscure. Some entries relating to his brief and not very favorable record at West Point are to be found in the *Official Register of the U. S. Military Academy* for June, 1819, and for June, 1820; and his adventures from 1821 to

1827 among the Indians, soldiers, explorers, and traders about Fort St. Anthony (the name of which was changed in honor of the author's father) are casually noticed in Edward D. Neill's *Fort Snelling, Minnesota, while in Command of Col. Josiah Snelling, Fifth Infantry*, 1888, and in *Collections of the Minnesota Historical Society, passim*. The "seven years' intimate acquaintance with the tribes in the northwest" mentioned in the preface to *Tales*, 1830, may, therefore, have been completed more than two years before the book was issued. But I have not been able to determine whether Snelling had removed to the East before he wrote the ten tales which make up this collection.

The *Union List of Serials in the Libraries of the United States and Canada*, now in course of publication, will doubtless reveal the location of a number of early Western periodical files which I was unable to discover.

R. L. R.

COLUMBIA UNIVERSITY
   *March, 1926*

# CONTENTS OF VOLUME I

## CHAPTER I

### Cultural Beginnings

## CHAPTER II

### Travel and Observation

## CHAPTER III

### Newspapers and Magazines

## CHAPTER IV

### Controversial Writings

## CHAPTER V

### Scholarly Writings and Schoolbooks

## CHAPTER VI

### Fiction

# CHAPTER VII

## POETRY

# CHAPTER VIII

## DRAMA

# CHAPTER I

## CULTURAL BEGINNINGS

Had a new planet dropped at once alongside of the old, Europe could not have been more astonished than when she opened her eyes, at the first discovery of America, on the unknown companion which had been sleeping for ages at her side. It was the heroic age of Geography. The outline, too, of this new nature, seemed struck with a bolder hand. The contemporaries of an event so marvellous, may well be excused, if, amidst the novelty of such excitements, their expectations were turned more towards an El Dorado, and a Fairy Land, than to any mere variety and modification of their own worn and 'work-a-day world.' — *The Edinburgh Review*, June, 1829.

I started the subject of emigration. JOHNSON. 'To a man of mere animal life, you can urge no argument against going to America, but that it will be some time before he will get the earth to produce. But a man of any intellectual enjoyment will not easily go and immerse himself and his posterity for ages in barbarism.' — Boswell, *The Journal of a Tour to the Hebrides.*

## I

For more than three centuries after America was discovered, the West cast a spell of romance. Many generations of explorers, missionaries, and immigrants turned their faces toward it hopefully. Drayton's verses "To the Virginian Voyage" sounded the authentic note of the appeal of this new country to the adventurous:

> You brave heroic minds,
> Worthy your country's name,
>   That honour still pursue,
>   Go, and subdue;

1

> Whilst loitering hinds
> Lurk here at home with shame.

For with the settlement of the Atlantic seaboard, the farther West, beyond the mountains, became in its turn the frontier of the imagination. The legend of the West, already well established, drew new life from the teachings of Rousseau, whose noble savage was to be found, if anywhere, in the valley of the Mississippi. And later writers, who, like Chateaubriand, had in fact seen little or nothing of the frontier country, supplied with the aid of imagination the details which served to give an air of reality to this exotic dream. Romancers would have it that the primitive and the ideal were the same; and the vastness of the new country, its strange aboriginal inhabitants, its mysterious forests and prairies, and its great rivers and lakes were the very stuff of romance. To Blake, who saw America only in radiant vision, the unspoiled wilderness of the West was a symbol of spiritual regeneration:

> Tho' born on the cheating banks of Thames,
> Tho' his waters bathèd my infant limbs,
> The Ohio shall wash his stains from me:
> I was born a slave, but I go to be free!

Byron, whose aristocratic nature would have revolted at actual contact with the squalor of frontier life, glorified the rough backwoodsman Boone as "happiest amongst mortals anywhere," and his race as "tall, and strong, and swift of foot":

> Motion was in their days, rest in their slumbers,
>   And cheerfulness the handmaid of their toil;
> Nor yet too many nor too few their numbers;
>   Corruption could not make their hearts her soil;
> The lust which stings, the splendour which encumbers,
>   With the free foresters divide no spoil;
> Serene, not sullen, were the solitudes
> Of this unsighing people of the woods.

Usually, it is true, travellers who had seen for themselves were not altogether flattering in their reports, yet the more imaginative yielded to the glamour of the legend. Even to the end of the pioneer period there were some who, like Alexis de Tocqueville, found the extreme frontier a flowery wilderness in which the enthusiast might yield himself to romantic reverie.[1] As for actual settlers, no doubt the great majority were men of an extremely practical kind who had come with no other desire than to acquire land or

[1] One of the best of the later examples of this type of travel books is Alexis de Tocqueville's ''Quinze jours au désert,'' written in 1831 in the month following his excursion into the wilderness between Detroit and Saginaw. Tocqueville, who visited the West determined to see the extreme frontier, was disappointed with the Indians he found in close contact with whites — ''J'étais plein des souvenirs de M. de Chateaubriand et de Cooper, et je m'attendais à voir dans les indigènes de l'Amérique des sauvages sur la figure desquels la nature aurait laissé la trace de quelques-unes de ces vertus hautaines qu'enfante l'esprit de liberté.'' But when he reached the extreme frontier and found the Indian in something near his original state, he felt for him a much higher regard. As for the Michigan wilderness, it was very nearly a paradise: ''Les seules sentiments qu'on éprouve en parcourant ces déserts fleuris, où, comme dans le *Paradis* de Milton, tout est préparé pour recevoir l'homme, c'est une admiration tranquille, une émotion douce et mélancolique, un dégoût vague de la vie civilisée, une sorte d'instinct sauvage qui fait penser avec douleur que bientôt cette délicieuse solitude aura cessé d'exister.'' And, though this enthusiastic traveller found the practical-minded Americans of the settlements strangely unappreciative of his romantic sentiments, he discovered many white men beyond the line of the frontier who had yielded to the spell of these solitudes: ''ce sont les Européens qui, en dépit des habitudes de leur jeunesse, ont fini par trouver dans la liberté du désert un charme inexprimable.'' ( *Œuvres*, 1861, I, 175, 207, and 213.) Little less romantic and much more influential in luring immigrants to the West was Gottfried Duden's glowing account in his *Bericht über eine Reise nach den westlichen Staaten Nordamerika's und einen mehrjährigen Aufenthalt am Missouri, (in den Jahren 1824, 25, 26 und 1827)*, 1829. See, for example, pp. 224 and 230-231.

to speculate in it.  But the legend nevertheless had its victims (as witness the French colony at Gallipolis); and many a credulous emigrant who, like Wordsworth's Solitary, bent his way "westward, tow'rd the unviolated woods" of the Mississippi Valley or of the shores of the Great Lakes was disenchanted when he failed to find "Primeval Nature's child" to be "that pure archetype of human greatness" which had been pictured to him.  And, too often, he found the European settlers, if not the sentimental "heart-sick exiles" whom Scott imagined in "Kentucky's wood-encumber'd brake" singing songs that recalled their native country, men nevertheless broken prematurely by the ravages of disease and intellectually dwarfed by the stern necessity of devoting themselves continuously to the struggle against the wilderness.

But the romantic legend of the West, fostered by enthusiasts and dreamers, was hardly more misleading than the hostile tradition which was given vogue by those writers who, because of private interest or national prejudice, lost no opportunity to pour out their contempt upon the incipient civilization of the frontier.[2]  This hos-

[2] The bitter prejudice against all things American conceived by such men as Dr. Samuel Johnson, had, no doubt, some part in the growth of an intolerant attitude toward the settlers on the Western frontier, upon whom fell the taunts which had been at first directed against the people of the older states.  Boswell reports that as early as 1769 Johnson had said of the Americans: "Sir, they are a race of convicts, and ought to be thankful for any thing we allow them short of hanging" (*Boswell's Life of Johnson*, ed. G. B. Hill, 1891, II, 356-357).  As for the romantic fiction of the felicity of life among the savages in the wilds of America, Johnson dismissed it contemptuously.  When a gentleman of learning quoted an officer who had lived for some time with an Indian woman as being perfectly happy, Johnson rejoined: "Do not allow yourself, Sir, to be imposed upon by such gross absurdity.  It is sad stuff; it is brutish.  If a bull could speak, he might as well exclaim, — Here am I with this cow and this grass; what being can enjoy greater felic-

tile tradition, like the romantic one, colored the reports of
actual observers; and in the early decades of the nineteenth century many Europeans, especially British, who
saw much of the West at first hand added thoroughgoing
condemnation of the people to disgust for the country.

The real West of pioneer days offers, however, a com-
plexity utterly impossible to summarize in the convenient
formula of either the romancer or the cynic. In order to
draw its outlines even faintly, one must reckon with a
number of important, but often intangible, influences.[3]

---

ity?'' (*Ibid.*, II, 262.) In the following century this hostile tradition of America found some of its most effective defenders in the
British reviews. ''We cannot reason from history in regard to these
people,'' declared a writer in *Blackwood's* (IV, 547, Feb., 1819);
''the experiment, now performing in some parts of the new world,
is the first, which ever exhibited man under precisely similar circumstances — intellectually and morally savage, and at the same time
powerful as a perfect knowledge of all the artificial means of increasing physical strength can make him.'' ''The back settlers,'' though
acknowledged to be useful as pioneers, were characterized by a contributor to *The Quarterly Review* (II, 331, Nov., 1809) as ''a worse
race than the Indians upon whose border they trespass; in as much
as they have been better taught, possess greater power of doing mis-
chief, and are without principle.'' A decade and a half later, the
tone of the same magazine was only slightly more hopeful. ''This
state of things,'' declared the reviewer, ''will unquestionably improve by time; but long ages must pass away before the population,
now thinly spread over the immense vale of the Mississippi, will
become sufficiently dense to render any part of it a desirable habitation for civilized beings; . . . then, and not till then, . . .
can the present race of emigrants, however sanguine, contemplate
even the future happy condition of their descendants'' (*ibid.*, XXIX,
368, July, 1823). Even *The Edinburgh Review* could foresee no
cultural achievement by Americans for hundreds of years: ''Literature the Americans have none — . . . Prairies, steam-boats,
grist-mills, are their natural objects for centuries to come.'' (XXXI,
144, Dec., 1818.)

[3] The purely economic and political aspects of the problem are,
for obvious reasons, omitted, so far as possible, from this study.

## II

In exploration and settlement of the Middle West, the French were beforehand with the British, who were busy on the Atlantic coast. From the third quarter of the seventeenth century, when La Salle appeared on the Ohio and Marquette on the Mississippi, till a hundred years later, when the English took possession of the country to the east of the latter river, the French explored, built forts, and traded in this region. But, in spite of the early beginnings of their settlements, they were, in the long run, to exert a scarcely perceptible influence on the growth of European culture in the West.

Their towns in Upper Louisiana — Detroit, Kaskaskia, Cahokia, Vincennes, St. Genevieve, St. Louis, and a few others — effectually isolated from the mother country,[4] were little more than trading posts until they were transformed by the Westward movement of English-speaking colonists more than half a century after their establishment. The inhabitants of these early posts were generally, with the exception of the priests and officers, of the most ignorant class;[5] and it seems almost certain that there was not so much as a printing press in any of these places until the end of the eighteenth century. Nor was the French element which endured through the American pioneer period to contribute much of importance to cultural achievement. From the time of the earliest settlements, there had taken place in many quarters a process of assim-

---

[4] A. Levasseur, who visited the old French towns in the American Bottom in company with La Fayette in 1825, found that the inhabitants were acquainted with France only by tradition from the reign of Louis XIV; that they knew nothing at all about the French Revolution; and that they had scarcely heard the name of Napoleon, whose importance he was obliged to explain to them (*Lafayette in America*, Philadelphia, 1829, II, 132).

[5] *Cf.* C. M. Burton, "Early Schooling in Detroit," in *The City of Detroit*, 1922, I, 702.

ilation to savage life. Unlike the English and their descendants, the French mingled easily with the Indians, usually maintaining friendship and social intercourse. The contrast between the backwoodsman of French descent and the pioneer of English stock affords an insight into two interesting racial phenomena: the Frenchman, always more quick to adapt himself to his environment, succumbed to the charm of savage life; the Englishman, uncompromising and stolid, ended by conquering the wilderness.[6] Intermarriage between French and Indians was common.[7] And, as this process of amalgamation proceeded, the men of French descent became closely identified with the savages, not only in sympathies, but in their pursuits. They became less enterprising, so that economically their achievement contrasted strangely, as Volney noted, with that of

[6] The Frenchman who lived in the Michigan wilderness in 1831 is pictured thus by Tocqueville: ''Dans le premier moment, vous le prendrez peut-être pour un Indien. Soumis à la vie sauvage, il en a adopté volontairement les habits, les usages et presque les mœurs: il porte des mocassins, le bonnet de loutre et le manteau de laine. Il est infatigable chasseur, couche à l'affût, vit de miel sauvage et de chair de bison. . . . L'Européen le plus civilisé est devenu l'adorateur de la vie sauvage. Il préférera les savanes aux rues des villes, la chasse à l'agriculture. Il se jouera de l'existence, et vivra sans nul souci de l'avenir.'' As for the pioneer of English blood, ''celui-ci est froid, tenace, impitoyable argumentateur. Il s'attache à la terre, et arrache à la vie sauvage tout ce qu'il peut lui ôter. Il lutte sans cesse contre elle, il la dépouille chaque jour de quelques-uns de ses attributs. Il transporte, pièce à pièce, dans le désert ses lois, ses habitudes, ses usages, et, s'il se peut, jusqu'aux moindres recherches de sa civilisation avancée.'' (Op. cit., I, 240-242.) Cf. also Edmund Flagg, The Far West, 1838, II, 155; and Anna B. Jameson, Winter Studies and Summer Rambles in Canada, 1839, II, 72.

[7] C. F. Volney, View, 1804, p. 370; Tocqueville, loc. cit.; J. H. Lanman, History of Michigan, 1839, p. 299; and Wisconsin in Three Centuries, n. d. (1906), II, 213-214, based on the authority of James W. Biddle, a contemporary observer.

pioneers of other nationalities. While the American
settlers prospered, the French were generally dull and
indolent, and, consequently, poverty-stricken and ill-con-
ditioned. Discouragement, apathy, and wretchedness pre-
vailed in the towns of the latter.[8] Such energetic individuals as the Chouteaus, the Ménards, and Dr. Saugrain
were the rarest exceptions among them. The economic
failure of their towns was supposed by some to be partly
attributable to their misfortunes under American rule;[9]
but their poverty at an earlier date, as well as during the
period of American control, is shown by the nicknames
which were given to several of them by the inhabitants
themselves.[10]

A much later attempt at colonization by the French,
at Gallipolis, on the Ohio, met with an even more serious
reverse, though from somewhat different causes. To this
place came an ill-assorted company from Paris and Lyons,
chiefly artisans unfit for life in the wilderness.[11] Such
high festival proceedings as Marnezia's dinner to the queen

---

[8] Volney, *op. cit.*, pp. 369-377; and Calvin Colton, *Tour of the
American Lakes*, 1833, I, 61. *Cf.* also Estwick Evans, *A Pedestrious
Tour*, 1819, p. 118; and Flagg, *op. cit.*, I, 117-122, and II, 19 and
140. "Les français des Illinois," wrote André Michaux in 1795
(printed in *Proceedings of the American Philosophical Society*,
XXVI, 122, Jan.-July, 1889), "ayant toujours été élevés et habi-
tués au commerce des Pelleteries avec les sauvages sont devenus les
plus paresseux et les plus ignorants de tous les hommes. Ils vivent
et ils sont habillés la pluspart en partie à la manière des Sauvages."

[9] *Cf.* Victor Collot's account of Vincennes in 1796 or 1797 (*A
Journey in North America*, 1826, p. 179).

[10] St. Louis, for example, was called Paincourt; and the neighboring village of Carondelet was known as Vide Poche (Philip Pittman,
*The Present State of the European Settlements on the Missisippi*,
1770, p. 49; Levasseur, *op. cit.*, II, 121; Flagg, *op. cit.*, I, 147; and
John Bradbury, *Travels in the Interior of America*, 1817, p. 262).

[11] H. M. Brackenridge, *Recollections of Persons and Places in the
West*, n. d. (1834), p. 42.

of the Hurons[12] gave place to poverty and sickness for those unable to leave the colony. Most of the people of culture who had had a part in the ill-fated enterprise succeeded in getting away. The settlers who remained were shortly reduced to a deplorable condition; and in this state the town seems to have remained until the arrival of American immigrants, who quickly transformed it.[13] Difficulties regarding title to their lands and trouble with the Indians after St. Clair's defeat had, it must be admitted, a considerable share in the disaster which befell the original French settlers at Gallipolis; but it is equally true that they were the dupes of their own imagination and of too much admiration for Bernardin de Saint-Pierre.[14]

Throughout the West, communities of Frenchmen, living under such conditions as those which have been described, retained, it is true, an almost inalienable social charm, but soon lost nearly every trace of the mental alertness characteristic of their race. They seem to have taken little interest in the political and civic affairs with which their neighbors of English stock busied themselves.[15] Public

---

[12] Lezay-Marnezia, "Lettre à M. Le Chevalier de Boufflers," dated Marietta, Nov. 15, 1790, in *Lettres écrites des rives de l'Ohio,* Fort-Pitt, an IX de la République, pp. 1-10. Eloquent proof that Marnezia was a willing victim of the exotic dream of America is to be found in another letter published in the same volume, addressed to Bernardin de Saint-Pierre a year later.

[13] Volney, *op. cit.,* pp. 355-366; Brackenridge, *op. cit.,* pp. 41-42, 47, and 220-221; Levasseur, *op. cit.,* II, 178.

[14] *Cf.* Henri Carré, "Les émigrés français en Amérique — 1789-1793," in *La revue de Paris,* III, 311-340 (May 15, 1898).

[15] See a report of a committee of the Detroit Lyceum in the *Detroit Gaz.,* Jan. 29, 1819. *Cf.* also a list of men who voted in the Detroit city election of Apr. 4, 1825, given in *Journal of the Proceedings of the Common Council,* n. d., pp. 18-19. The list of 115 names contains only fifteen which seem to be French. For an account of the same situation in the Illinois and Missouri towns, see Flagg, *op. cit.,* II, 161-162.

notices issued by the authorities at Detroit were for years
given in French as well as in English;[16] but it is certain
that the majority of the French population there as well
as in other parts of the West were so illiterate that they
could not even write their own names.[17]  It is not surprising to find that literary activity of any kind was rare
among even the most intelligent members of such communities.  It seems likely, indeed, that there was not so much
as a single newspaper in the French language which was
wholly a matter of French enterprise;[18] and of books there

[16] See *Corporation of the Town of Detroit Act of Incorporation
and Journal of the Board of Trustees 1802-1805*, ed. C. M. Burton,
1922, pp. 9-79, *passim*. *Cf.* also various broadsides issued by the
American authorities; e.g., one headed "Par William Hull, gouverneur du territoire de Michigan," dated Oct. 19, 1809.

[17] See, for example, the *Translation of a Memorial in the French
Language, of Sundry Citizens of the County of Wayne, in the Indiana Territory*, dated Jan. 17, 1805, and printed at Washington the
same year.  Of the 241 owners or claimants of land in or near Detroit who united in this petition, 104 were unable to sign their own
names, and of these all but one seem to have been Frenchmen; while,
of the 137 who signed their names, 40 seem to have been at least
partly of English or other European extraction.  If such was the
condition of French property owners, it is not difficult to believe
that almost universal illiteracy obtained among the poorer class of
French settlers.  *Cf.* also Charles Fenno Hoffman, *A Winter in the
West*, 1835, I, 121; and John T. Blois, *Gazetteer of the State of
Michigan*, 1838, p. 156.

[18] In American newspapers intended primarily for readers of English descent, a considerable amount of space was often given to
articles or advertisements in the French language.  See, for example,
*Louisiana Gazette*, for 1810, *passim*.  The *Michigan Essay*, a short-
lived paper which was published at Detroit in 1809, contained about
a column of French, with some advertisements of books in that language.  And the *Detroit Gazette*, which followed it in 1817, began
by devoting about one-eighth of its space to editorials, news, and
advertisements in the same language; but before the end of the
year this practice was discontinued (see issue for Nov. 28, 1817),
and from that time only scattering paragraphs, mostly advertise-

must have been almost none except the few, mostly translations of religious works, which Father Richard caused to
be published at Detroit.[19]  It is, of course, much more

ments, were printed in French.  In 1823 a prospectus was issued of
a weekly journal to be printed in French, in Detroit (see *Detroit
Gaz.*, June 13, 1823); but it is likely that nothing came of this project until late in 1825, when *La gazette française* appeared (see
*Detroit Gaz.*, Nov. 15, 1825; Silas Farmer, *The History of Detroit*,
1884, p. 672; and N.-E. Dionne, *Galerie historique VI Gabriel Richard*, 1911, p. 89).  But this paper, which is said to have continued
for only a few issues after the initial number of Oct. 31, 1825, was
plainly an American enterprise, subsidiary to the *Detroit Gazette*;
and the editor, it seems, was Ebenezer Reed, who was also from time
to time part owner or editor of the *Detroit Gazette*.  I have been
unable to discover a copy of this paper.  At St. Louis, in 1810, a
prospectus was issued for a French paper to be called *Gazette de la
Louisiane,* which was to begin publication as soon as one hundred
subscribers were secured (*Louisiana Gazette*, Apr. 12, 1810).  The
subscription lists were to be returned before May 1 of that year.  I
have been unable, however, to discover any evidence that this paper,
which seems to have been projected as an adjunct to the *Louisiana
Gazette*, ever made its appearance.  For the prospectus cited above,
I am indebted to Miss Stella M. Drumm, of the Missouri Historical
Society.

  [19] James Miller, the founder of the ill-fated *Michigan Essay*, published in 1809 what may have been the first French book printed in
Detroit, *L'ame penitente ou le nouveau pensez-y-bien*, a reprint of
216 pages.  In the same year, it is said (MS. note by Judge B. F. H.
Witherell in copy of *Les ornemens de la memoire* in Burton Collection, Public Library, Detroit) that Father Gabriel Richard went to
Canada and the Eastern states, bringing back with him Coxshaw, a
Boston printer.  At least two extant volumes, *Neuvaine a l'honneur
de St. François Xavier* (Detroit, 1810) and *Les ornemens de la
memoire; ou les traits brillans des poetes francois les plus celebres*
(Detroit, 1811), bear the name of this printer on the title-page.  The
latter book is asserted to have been the work of Father Richard himself (see MS. letter of R. Elliott, Nov. 24, 1902, in Burton Collection),
giving his views on the French poets available when he wrote.  But
there seems to be no internal evidence of the authorship, and the fact
that a much earlier Paris edition of the same work has recently come

difficult to determine the contribution which the descendants of these Frenchmen later made in English; but it is

to light is against the claim for Richard. In 1812 Théophile Mettez
printed at Detroit at least three books with French and English on
alternate pages: *Epitres et evangiles; pour tous les dimanches et
fetes*; a *Petit catachisme historique*; and *The Family Book, or
Children's Journal. Consisting of Moral & Entertaining Stories*
(the French title-page of the only copy I have seen is missing), by
M. Berquin. All of these books are badly printed; and S. R. Brown,
who visited Detroit sometime between 1809 and 1814, describes this
unique publishing house (*Views on Lake Erie*, 1814, p. 96) as ''a
wretched printing office in which religious French books are printed
in a rude style.'' Lezay-Marnezia's *Lettres écrites des rives de
l'Ohio*, only partly written in Ohio, has already been mentioned.
Father Stephen T. Badin's *Origine et progrès de la mission du
Kentucky* (Paris, 1821), a pamphlet in French and Latin, contains
a small section written by two Kentucky friars; but Badin's own
share is dated from Paris. In the same year a bulky volume called
*Officia propria pro Diœcesi Ludovicenensi*, by Bishop Du Bourg,
appeared at St. Louis. No doubt there were other books which are
now difficult to discover or which have disappeared altogether, but the
titles here enumerated very likely give a correct idea of the characteristic content of such publications and of their total bulk as compared with the thousands of titles which were issued by American
presses in the West during the same period. For evidence that there
were at an early date some Frenchmen in Detroit who were keenly
interested in the literary contribution of their race in America, see
MS. The Constitution of the French Moral and Benevolent Society
of the City of Detroit and its Vicinity, dated 1818 (in Burton Collection; the minutes of the society also appear in *Supplement to
Library Service Published by the Detroit Public Library*, Vol. 4, No.
11). It was proposed by this society to keep a list of ''all productions whatever, about to emanate from the American Press in the
French language.'' In citing above the titles of Detroit imprints,
I have attempted, as in all titles and quotations throughout the
present study, to reproduce the originals without correction of any
sort. But it has, of course, been necessary to disregard both capital
letters and italics in title-pages. It should perhaps be added that I
have not indicated omissions at the beginning or end of quotations;
and that the context has often been allowed to determine the use of
a capital for the first word of a quoted passage. In quotations, except

clear that it must have been small, and that up to the end of the pioneer period the impress of this element of the population upon the culture of the West was extremely slight. The great French names in the early annals of the West are those of travellers and adventurers who remained but a short time within its borders; and these were men of action who furnished themes for books but did not write them.

## III

The second stage in the colonizing of the West, in which Americans were the chief actors, with newcomers from several European countries appearing in numbers comparatively small until late in the period, began during or shortly after the Revolutionary War; and by the first decade of the nineteenth century the stream of immigration had become a flood tide. In general the immigrants moved Westward in roughly parallel columns.[20]

The first widely used routes of ingress were the wilderness trails over the Alleghenies from Virginia and the Carolinas into Kentucky. Near the vanguard of the throng which poured into the West from this direction, following closely upon the heels of Boone and other such hunters and adventurers, came large numbers of disbanded Revolutionary soldiers,[21] many of them armed with land warrants as a reward for their services in the war.[22] Many

those used as chapter headings, all capitals are printed large, without regard to their original size.

[20] This striking characteristic of the Westward movement before 1840, which was noted by many contemporary observers, is graphically described by "R. B." in his *View of the Valley of the Mississippi*, second ed., 1834, pp. 100-101.

[21] *Cf.* N. S. Shaler, *Kentucky a Pioneer Commonwealth*, 1885, p. 21. According to this authority, the pension returns showed that as late as 1840 there were about nine hundred of these veterans still living in Kentucky, their ages varying from seventy to one hundred and nine years.

[22] See Grant Books, Land Office, Richmond, Virginia.

were turbulent spirits bent on gaining a competence by
no matter what means.  With them began the era of the
speculation in lands which occupied the attention of a large
part of the population of the West until long after the
pioneer period had come to a close.  In the wake of the
soldiers came the long column of what might be called professional emigrants, made up of Scotch-Irish[23] and other
racial elements drawn mostly from the upland districts of
Virginia and the Carolinas.  In 1790, before any other
section of the Middle West had more than a mere handful
of settlers, Kentucky had over seventy thousand inhabitants, and at the beginning of the next century, over two
hundred thousand.

Soon the new state not only became a thoroughfare for
emigrants to the farther West, but supplied a large part
of the migratory stream from settlers within its own
borders.  The southern parts of Indiana and of Illinois lay
in the path of this current of population[24] and took much

[23] For a study of racial elements in southern Illinois, which early
received a part of the overflow population of Kentucky, see S. J.
Buck, *Illinois in 1818*, 1917, pp. 93 ff.

[24] *Cf.* Timothy Flint, *The History and Geography of the Mississippi Valley*, second ed., 1832, I, 136; and F. Marryat, *A Diary in
America*, Philadelphia, 1839, II, 25.  *Niles' Weekly Register*, for
Apr. 9, 1825, reported that of forty-four members of the general
assembly of Indiana whose places of nativity were tabulated, over
half had been born in North Carolina, Virginia, and Kentucky, and
only five in New England and two in New York.  It is likely that
the great majority of the North Carolina-Virginia-Kentucky group
had come to Indiana from Kentucky.  In 1832 or 1833 the legislature of Illinois included among its ninety members, clerks, and
other officers, fifty-eight persons born in Kentucky or in the South,
nineteen natives of New York and Pennsylvania, and only four
natives of New England (*The Western Monthly Magazine*, I, 199-
200, May, 1833).  For immigration into southern Illinois about
1834, see *ibid.*, II, 662 (Dec., 1834).  According to Buck, *op. cit.*,
pp. 93-95, more than two-thirds of the people of Illinois in 1818
were from Southern states or from Kentucky.  *Cf.* also William

of their permanent character from the flotsam and jetsam left along its course. Until after 1840, Missouri, which received its settlers very largely from the same source, partly by way of Tennessee,[25] was the Western limit of this migration. Here, shortly before the admission of the territory into the Union as a state, the inrush of Southern people, bringing with them many slaves, was especially noticeable; and, after a lull which followed this event, the current of immigration again set in strongly in the same direction.[26] As a result of priority in settlement,

Cullen Bryant, *Prose Writings*, ed. Parke Godwin, 1884, II, 22. In a letter from Jacksonville, Illinois, June 19, 1832, Bryant describes the people among whom he has been travelling. "Short," he says, "was also from Kentucky, or Kaintucky, as they call it, as indeed was every man whom I saw on my journey, except the Virginian, the Quaker family, who were from Pennsylvania, and Shurtliff, who is from Massachusetts, but who has a Kentucky wife." Ohio, on the other hand, received a very small contingent from Kentucky, though perhaps a fifth of her population came directly from Virginia and North Carolina (see *Picture of Cincinnati*, for 1839, p. 72). According to *Niles' Weekly Register*, Feb. 2, 1822, there were at that time, among the 102 members of the Ohio legislature, forty-nine persons born in the group of states including Pennsylvania, New York, New Jersey, and Maryland; twenty-five in New England; and only twenty-two in Kentucky and the whole of the South together.

[25] See, for example, "R. B.," *op. cit.*, p. 101; Charles Latrobe, *The Rambler in North America*, London, 1835, I, 121; and Gustave Koerner, *Memoirs*, ed. T. J. McCormack, 1909, I, 296 and 322. *Niles' Weekly Register*, July 29, 1820, shows that of the forty-one members of the Missouri constitutional convention of that year, only one was a native of New England, and none of New York; only eight were born in Pennsylvania and Maryland together. Almost three-fourths of the total were of Kentucky or Southern stock. For both Northern and Southern elements in Western immigration, see also F. J. Turner, "The Colonization of the West, 1820-1830," in *The American Historical Review*, XI, 303-327 (Jan., 1906).

[26] *Niles' Weekly Register*, Oct. 19, 1816, Dec. 25, 1819, Oct. 27, 1821, and Dec. 24, 1825; and *Niles' National Register*, Nov. 30, 1839.

Kentucky was the political and cultural leader of the West until late in the period — it was not until 1820 that Ohio gained a clear superiority in population — and the racial stock of early Kentucky, mostly lovers of pioneer life with little ability for either cultural or economic achievement, but with a sprinkling of daring and capable political leaders,[27] was to determine to no small extent the character of the frontier until after 1840.

When the Westward movement from the Northern states commenced, about 1788, the Ohio River, heretofore used but little by immigrants to Kentucky, became an important highway. And, along this route or directly overland from western Pennsylvania and Maryland, a second great migratory column made its way, first into Ohio, its chief destination, and later, and in much smaller volume, into Indiana and Illinois. After 1810 the increase of Ohio's population was phenomenal, amounting in the next thirty years to a million and a half of which New England and Pennsylvania had furnished not quite a majority, perhaps, but at all events the dominant element.[28]

A large proportion of the Northern immigrants, however — especially of those from New England and New York —

[27] According to Buck, *op. cit.*, p. 101, most of both political and economic leaders in early Illinois were from the South, but from the tide-water districts, and not from the uplands, which supplied the larger portion of the migratory stream.

[28] The *Picture of Cincinnati*, for 1839, p. 72, estimates the New England element in Ohio at that time as 23% of the whole, while Pennsylvania's share is put at 20%, and Virginia's, the third largest, at 13%. *Cf.* Henry Caswall, *America, and the American Church*, 1839, p. 50, where New York is ranked with New England and Pennsylvania as a source of emigration to Ohio. Timothy Flint (*op. cit.*, I, 136), whose remarks are usually based on careful observation, thought that New England and New Jersey were the chief moulding influences in early Ohio; Hoffman (*op. cit.*, II, 139) found New England characteristics clearly predominant.

formed a third great division in the movement toward the frontier, reaching Ohio, and later Michigan, by way of the Great Lakes or along their shores; and from these states there was a constantly increasing overflow into the northern parts of Indiana and Illinois, and finally into Iowa and Wisconsin. No doubt the Western Reserve in Ohio attracted a more nearly pure New England population than any other section of the new country, but the influence of both New England and New York was strongly felt from the Reserve westward over a broad area.[29] The inrush of population along this northernmost route, which had received considerable stimulus from the inauguration of steamboat service on the Lakes in 1818, was vastly increased by the opening of the Erie Canal through the state of New York in 1825.[30] It was supposed that in the

[29] Michigan, for example, was very largely settled from New York and New England. See Chandler Gilman, *Life on the Lakes,* 1836, I, 51; *North-Western Journal,* Sept. 15, 1830; and Blois, *op. cit.,* p. 157. Nearly two-thirds of the white population, says Blois, ''is from New England and Western New York, and the larger part from the latter.'' *Cf.* also G. N. Fuller, *Economic and Social Beginnings of Michigan,* 1916, p. 482. Late in the pioneer period central and northern Illinois began to show a marked New England influence. Flagg (*op. cit.,* II, 53) thought that the state might then be considered the New England of the West. Had he travelled in northern Indiana at that time, he would probably have formed the same opinion of that state. For emigration from New England into northern Illinois, as well as for the influence of both New England and New York in Michigan, see *The Western Monthly Magazine,* II, 662 (Dec., 1834). A discussion of New England settlements in several states of the Middle West, with citation of numerous city, county, and state histories, is to be found in Lois K. Mathews, *The Expansion of New England,* 1909, pp. 171-249.

[30] See *Niles' Weekly Register,* June 29, 1822; May 14, 1825; June 12, 1830; June 18, 1831; May 25, 1833 (by this time as many as 2610 immigrants were arriving at Detroit alone in a week); and Oct. 25, 1834. *Cf.* also *Detroit Journal and Michigan Advertiser,* May 23, 1832, and May 15, 1833.

parts of the frontier, especially Michigan and Missouri, was also now of considerable volume.[39]  But this element in the population, though it was by 1840 numerically out of all proportion to what remained of the early French villagers, exerted an important influence upon only economic and political life.  Up to that time it had made a very slight impression upon the growth of literary culture in the new country.  Among the authors of thousands of pamphlets and books in English which poured from the Western press, very few belonged to this racial group; and, in spite of the conventions of 1837 and later years, in which an attempt was made to devise means of maintaining the German language and of training teachers who would propagate it, publications in German were not numerous.[40]

*Picture of Cincinnati*, for 1839, p. 72.  It was, of course, impossible to make an accurate estimate.

[39] Blois (*op. cit.*, p. 155) names the Germans first in his list of foreign nationalities in Michigan's population at that time.  According to Flagg (*op. cit.*, II, 19), a flood of German immigrants poured into the neighborhood of St. Charles, Missouri, from about 1830 to 1836, when he visited that region.  *Cf.* also Koerner, *Memoirs*, 1909, I, 307 and 314.  Koerner found that the Germans on the Missouri River had been influenced to migrate to that part of the West by Duden's too favorable description.  For some account of the spread of German immigration over the Middle West as a whole, with notices of many individuals of prominence among this racial group, see Albert Bernhardt Faust, *The German Element in the United States*, 1909, I, 357-490.

[40] For the period before 1830, see Oswald Seidensticker, *The First Century of German Printing in America, 1728-1830*, 1893, pp. 169-245, *passim*.  The books and pamphlets here noted are a German almanac (1807), translated from one printed in English; a collection of songs used by the United Brethren; a similar collection used by the Dunkers; and a history of martyrs, apparently taken for the most part from John Fox.  Five newspapers are also mentioned: *Der westliche Adler von Lancaster* (1807), later called *Der Ohio Adler; Der westliche Beobachter*, Canton (1823); *Die Ohio Chronik*, Cincinnati (1826); *Die National-Zeitung der Deutschen*, German-

The necessary adjustment of various racial elements and
the establishment of such social equilibrium as would make

town (1826); and *Vaterlandsfreund und Geist der Zeit,* Canton
(1830). All of the publications mentioned above appeared in Ohio.
For the years 1818-1840, see especially Körner, *Das deutsche Element
in den Vereinigten Staaten von Nordamerika, 1818-1848,* 1880, pp.
181-184 *et passim.* Additional books cited by Körner are Friedrich
Reese's *Geschichte des Bisthums Cincinnati,* which was published at
Vienna in 1829, but was perhaps written in the West; and Adolf
Wislizenus' *Ein Ausflug nach den Felsen-Gebirgen,* St. Louis, 1840.
The same author mentions three religious papers, all published at Cincinnati: *Wahrheitsfreund,* a Catholic organ (1837); *Der Protestant;*
and a Methodist journal, *Der christliche Apologet* (1838). And he
also lists several newspapers of political significance: *Der Weltbürger,*
Cincinnati (1834), later changed to *Der deutsche Franklin;* the
*Volksblatt,* Cincinnati (1836); *Der Freiheitsbote für Illinois,* Belle-
ville — but printed at St. Louis — (1840); and the remarkable
periodical called *Das Westland,* which was written in St. Louis, but
issued (1837-1838) at Heidelberg in order to encourage German
emigration to the Mississippi Valley. In addition to these lists, the
following papers, either incompletely named or not noticed by the
authorities referred to above, may be mentioned: *Deutscher Anzeiger
des Westens,* St. Louis (1835); *Ohio Staats-Zeitung,* Columbus
(1839) — so badly supported that in 1840 it became half English
(see *Cinc. Daily Gaz.,* Mar. 7, 1840); *Der westliche Merkur,* projected
and apparently published by German partisans of Harrison at
Cincinnati in 1840 (see *Cinc. Daily Gaz.,* Feb. 22, Mar. 7, and Nov.
17, 1840); and *The Tribune,* a German and English paper, which
appeared at St. Louis in 1838 (see *Mo. Rep.,* May 10 and July 13,
1838). A few books not noticed by Seidensticker or Körner have
also come to light. At Harmonie (later New Harmony), Indiana,
there was printed in 1824 a songbook significantly called *Eine kleine
Sammlung harmonischer Lieder als die erste Probe der anfangenden
Druckerey anzusehen;* and in the same year there appeared at this
place a series of religious leaflets called *Hoher Zweck und Bestim-
mung der Harmonie* (the title varies). To Mr. William Clark
Breckenridge, I am indebted for a· copy (not, however, from the
original) of the title-page of a schoolbook said to have been the
first German book printed in St. Louis, the *Erstes Uebungsbuechlein
fuer Kinder welche schnell und gruendlich lesen lernen wollen,* by
Friedrich Steines, 1837.

possible the production of literature of some value, might
have proceeded more rapidly had the settlers left in the
wake of the migratory columns remained fixed.  Throughout the period, however, the population of the West was
an extremely unsettled one; and few cultural groups
struck root deeply.  The life of the typical Westerner was
a succession of leaps further Westward.[41]  But a certain
kind of progress toward civilizing the wilderness was in
this way accomplished with remarkable rapidity.  The
extreme line of the frontier was carried before 1840 to the
upper waters of the Mississippi and of the Missouri; and
the Indians had been pushed back so rapidly that Captain
Marryat, who travelled through the West in 1838 or 1839,
saw no savages in their primitive state until he had gone
as far north as Fort Snelling.[42]  In the meantime the new
possessors of the land had grown to such numbers that,
according to the census of 1840, the Middle Western states
and territories alone contained over four millions of people,
nearly one-fourth the population of the whole Union.
For the greater part of the new country afterwards comprised within the boundaries of the states of Kentucky,
Ohio, Indiana, Illinois, Missouri, Michigan, Wisconsin,
Iowa, and Minnesota — which is the territory here arbitrarily defined as the Middle West — the year 1840 may

---

[41] The Westerner in Paulding's *John Bull in America; or, the
New Munchausen*, 1825 (p. 186), who describes himself to an astonished English tourist as ''born in New-Hampshire; raised in the
western part of the state of New-York; married in Ohio; and  . . .
now settled, for the present, in the state of Missouri'' was scarcely
overdrawn.  The characteristic restlessness of the frontiersmen was
often noticed both by writers of fiction and by travellers before 1840.
See, for instance, James Hall, *Tales of the Border*, 1835, p. 159; and
Tocqueville, *Democracy in America*, second ed., 1836, II, 209 and
212-213.  Boone and Lincoln are examples of the pioneer migratory
habit.

[42] Marryat, *op. cit.*, I, 204.

be regarded as the end of the pioneer period. The growth
in population and the rapidly increasing facilities for
intercourse between East and West were soon thereafter to
bring about a transformation which would destroy in large
measure the distinct national character of the old frontier.

## IV

In spite of the constant Westward drift of a great body
of population, the means of communication, though always
improving, were primitive enough throughout the pioneer
period to have a considerable influence in checking the
spread of intelligence and preventing close intellectual
contact with the outside world. It was not until about the
end of the eighteenth century that travellers in Kentucky
and Ohio were free from the menace of the Indians;[43] and
this danger continued, of course, until much later in more
remote parts of the West, especially during the War of 1812
and again during the Black Hawk War. Early travellers
on the wilderness trails usually attempted long journeys
only in large companies, well armed against the savages;
and public notice of the rendezvous at Crab Orchard or
other frontier points was often given weeks in advance.[44]
Companies travelling on the Ohio were organized in much
the same way, and in some cases only armed passengers
were allowed on the keel boats.[45] In 1793 a regular line

[43] As late as 1795 "Indian News" was a common heading in the
Kentucky Gazette.

[44] Asbury, op. cit., II, 75 (May 24, 1790) and 164 (May 8, 1793).
See also Ky. Gaz., May 14, 1791; Mar. 30, Aug. 24, Nov. 2, 1793;
Jan. 18, Apr. 26, and May 3, 1794; and for 1795, passim. For a
notice of a rendezvous at Cincinnati for a journey by way of Chillicothe to Pittsburg, see Cent. N.-W. Ter., Sept. 26, 1795.

[45] Nathaniel Allen and William M'Donald inserted the following
notice in the Ky. Gaz. for May 7, 1791: "TWO large keel bottom
boats will start up the Ohio, the 25th day of May next, at which time
all those who are inclined to go, will meet precisely at that time at

of armored packet boats was established between Pittsburg and Cincinnati, intended to convoy other boats and to carry passengers.  These craft, constructed for sailing or rowing, were provided with portholes for musketry; and each carried six one-pounders.[46]  Within a short time the Ohio was covered with a multitude of craft, many of them makeshift conveyances for immigrant families — skiffs, keel boats, house-rafts, flatboats, and other nondescript varieties.  Even after 1811, when the "New Orleans," the first steamboat on Western waters, made the voyage from Pittsburg down the Ohio and Mississippi,[47] communications were difficult.  It was not until 1817 that a steamboat reached the port of St. Louis;[48] and for years afterwards the river steamers were mostly so primitive that the voyage up stream was painfully slow.[49]  Steam transportation on Lake Erie did not begin until 1818, when the "Walk-in-the-Water" arrived at Detroit from Buffalo after a voyage of slightly more than forty-four hours;[50] but by 1830 a daily line of such vessels had been established to accommodate the rapidly growing throng of immigrants

Limestone landing; and as the depredations of the savages have been excessively bad this spring, none but those who may be well armed need expect a passage."

[46] *Cent. N.-W. Ter.*, Nov. 23, 1793; and *Ky. Gaz.*, Feb. 15, 1794. The first boat of this line was to start from Cincinnati on the return trip to Pittsburg on Nov. 16, 1793.  A month was required for going and coming.  The equipment, consisting at first of only two boats, was to be increased shortly to four, which would provide weekly service.

[47] For the progress of the steamboat from Pittsburg to Natchez, where it arrived late in Dec., 1811, see *Ky. Gaz.*, Nov. 5, 1811, and Jan. 28, 1812.

[48] Charles Keemle, *The St. Louis Directory, for the Years 1838-9*, 1838, p. iv.

[49] *Cf.* N. M. Ludlow, *Dramatic Life as I Found it*, 1880, pp. 182-183.

[50] *Detroit Gaz.*, Aug. 28, 1818.

over this route.[51]  During the last decade before 1840 the
number of steamboats on both the Great Lakes and the
Ohio River grew to remarkable proportions.[52]

Meantime, a slow, but convenient, means of intercourse
was being provided for inland communities by a rapidly
growing system of canals, the future importance of which
was greatly overestimated by their builders, unable to
foresee the vast expansion of railways soon to come; and
during the latter part of the pioneer period numerous
lines of stagecoaches were established, affording frequent
service over the main-travelled roads.[53]  Before 1840 it
was possible to travel from St. Louis to New York in
about eight or nine days by the northern route, while
the same journey by the Ohio required ten or twelve days.[54]

Railroad communication, which, had it come earlier,
might have exercised a strong influence toward intersec-

[51] *Niles' Weekly Register*, June 12, 1830.

[52] By 1837 there were said to be thirty steamboats running
between Detroit and Buffalo (*Detroit Daily Advertiser*, Jan. 20,
1837).  The steamboat arrivals at Cincinnati about the same year
were reported as 1276 (*Picture of Cincinnati*, for 1839, p. 37).  The
rapid growth of river traffic is shown by the increase from 1476
steamboat arrivals at St. Louis in 1839 to 1721 at the same port in
1840 (Keemle, *The St. Louis Directory, for the Years 1840-1*, p. vi).
About the end of the period, a passage from Cincinnati to Pittsburg
could be purchased for $12, and one from Cincinnati to New Orleans
for from $30 to $50 (*Picture of Cincinnati*, for 1839, pp. 49-50).

[53] As early as 1831 there were two daily lines of post coaches
between Detroit and Ann Arbor (*Detroit Journal and Michigan
Advertiser*, May 11, 1831).  By 1833 the village of Chicago had become
the meeting place of stages from Fox River and those from Detroit;
and thus was completed a line of stage travel from St. Louis to
Albany, New York (*Sangamo Journal*, June 15, 1833).  At Cincinnati,
by 1838, there were, during the greater part of the year, somewhat
fewer than a hundred stage arrivals each week (*Picture of Cincinnati*,
for 1839, p. 37).

[54] *Daily Mo. Rep.*, July 11, 1839.

tional solidarity, was established too late and in too small
measure to have an important effect on the pioneer country.
As early as 1830 there was a project for a great railroad
to connect East and West through northern Ohio, Indiana,
Illinois, and what later became Iowa;[55] and within a few
years the most influential citizens of Cincinnati were
enthusiastic in their support of the project for a railroad
connecting that town with the Southern seaboard.[56] But
nothing of the sort was realized until long after the pioneer
period, and by 1840 only a few short lines of railroad were
actually in operation in the Western country.[57]

Until near the end of the period there were continual
complaints regarding the unsatisfactory handling of the
mails. In 1794 the arrival of a post at Cincinnati was an

[55] See *Sketch of the Geographical Rout [sic] of a Great Railway,
by which it is Proposed to Connect the Canals and Navigable Waters,
of New-York, Pennsylvania, Ohio, Indiana, Illinois, Michigan, Missouri, and the Adjacent States and Territories*, second ed., 1830.

[56] See *Rail-road from the Banks of the Ohio River to the Tide
Waters of the Carolinas and Georgia*, 1835; and E. S. Thomas,
*Reminiscences*, 1840, II, 101 ff.

[57] A railroad from Toledo, Ohio, to Adrian, Michigan, was completed in 1836; and the same year cars commenced running between
the two towns (*Niles' Weekly Register*, Dec. 24, 1836). The Detroit-
Ypsilanti road began operation in Feb., 1838 (*Detroit Free Press*,
May 3, 1838); and in the same year the Detroit and Pontiac
road was operated for twelve miles from Detroit (*ibid.*, May 17,
1838). By this time, however, there had been incorporated no less
than twenty-six railway companies in Michigan alone (Blois, *op. cit.*,
pp. 89-95). In Kentucky, the Lexington-Louisville railway had
attained a length of fourteen miles in 1834 (*The Western Monthly
Magazine*, II, 532, Oct., 1834), and was operating horse cars over a
part of its course before the end of the period (Frederick Hall,
*Letters from the East and from the West*, n. d. (1840), pp. 127-128;
*cf.* Julius P. B. MacCabe, *Directory of the City of Lexington*, 1838,
p. 28). At the same time railroads were projected or in process of
construction in many parts of the West.

event worthy of special comment by a newspaper editor.[58]
In the early years of the nineteenth century, the government undertook to dispatch mail once or twice a week over
a number of Western routes; but long delays were numerous, and it was not uncommon in Kentucky and Ohio to
receive letters and papers from Eastern states from one to
two months after they had been sent.[59] By 1810, however, the regular time of the post to Lexington in fair
weather was two weeks from Philadelphia, not quite a
month from New Orleans, and from seventeen days to a
month from the Southern seaboard states;[60] and similar
schedules remained in effect, not only for Kentucky and
Ohio, but for other places in the West, until many years
later.[61]

## V

Of such literary activity as the frontier could boast, the
towns were the centers; but of these there were fewer than

[58] *Cent. N.-W. Ter.*, July 12, 1794.

[59] *Ky. Gaz.*, Mar. 16 and June 22, 1801, and June 4, 1802; *Liberty
Hall*, Jan. 27, 1806; *The Reporter*, Dec. 19, 1808. In 1809 the Post-
master General refused a request of the people of Lexington for
three deliveries of mail each week (*Ky. Gaz.*, Aug. 1, 1809).

[60] *Ky. Gaz.*, Oct. 9, 1810.

[61] Cincinnati and Lexington experienced approximately the same
delay in mails. News of the declaration of war against Great
Britain on June 18, 1812, reached Cincinnati on the 29th of the same
month (*Liberty Hall*, June 30, 1812); the deaths of Jefferson and
Adams, on July 4, 1826, were announced in *Ky. Gaz.*, July 21.
In the last decade of the pioneer period the improvement was, however, very rapid. In 1838 Cincinnati received usually sixty-four
mails a week (*Picture of Cincinnati*, for 1839, p. 37). In Detroit,
where, in 1823, the post arrived but once a week, Washington papers,
which should have been received in eleven days, frequently required
six weeks for delivery; but by 1826 the number of mails received had
risen to three a week, and in 1837 there were daily mails with the
time from Baltimore and Philadelphia reduced on some occasions to

a score which attained a population of more than five thousand by 1840, and there were only a few of smaller size which were notable for cultural influence. To Lexington, permanently settled in 1779, the acknowledged supremacy belonged until the second or third decade of the nineteenth century, when it passed to Cincinnati. In Lexington the first newspaper of the West was established (1787) ; and to this town somewhat later Transylvania University, by far the most influential college of the pioneer country, drew a number of distinguished scholars and a student body representing several states and territories. Many travellers record the town's early fame: it was the Athens of the West, where literature was a common topic of conversation; its streets and buildings had a charm not to be found in most of the Atlantic coast cities; its wealth was equalled by that of few towns of its size in any part of the world. Such, at any rate, was the all but unanimous opinion of travellers from about 1810 to 1840, of this first metropolis of the backwoods, which had less than seven thousand inhabitants at the latter date.[62]    No other Kentucky town, however, attained during the period any such cultural prominence as was for a time possessed by Lexington. Louisville, which had over twenty thousand people in 1840, had outstripped Lexington in population shortly after 1820, and soon became perhaps the most important theatrical center in the West; but it had already been surpassed by Cincinnati both in size and in general cultural influence.    The old towns of Harrodsburg, Maysville (earlier called Limestone), and Danville were of some importance; while Frank-

less than a week (*Detroit Gaz.*, Feb. 14, 1823, and Feb. 7, 1826; *Detroit Daily Advertiser*, Apr. 25 and May 3, 1837).

62 See, for example, John Melish, *Travels*, 1812, II, 185-190; Timothy Flint, *op. cit.*, I, 353-354; Samuel R. Brown, *The Western Gazetteer*, 1817, pp. 91-93; Caswall, *op. cit.*, p. 221; and Koerner, *Memoirs*, 1909, I, 347.

fort, with less than two thousand inhabitants at the
end of the period, was made the seat of the state government
in 1792, six years after it was founded, and gained, for
that reason, some prominence as a publishing center.

But the leadership in the early West passed from Kentucky to Ohio; and Cincinnati, before 1830, had become the
cultural as well as the commercial capital of the frontier.[63]
Though on the dividing line between the southern and
central columns of immigration, Cincinnati, like Ohio in
general, was settled largely by people from New England,
Pennsylvania, New Jersey, and New York; and there was
probably no time during the pioneer period when the
population drawn from the South was more than about
one-third as great as that drawn from the North.[64] As late
as 1825 the foreign-born residents were mostly from the
British Isles; but by the end of the period the great influx
of Germans had begun, and people of that nationality
then formed about one-fourth of the total population.
The situation of the town on the river highway between
East and West and its phenomenal growth, spread its
fame throughout America; and even the not wholly unjust
ridicule of Mrs. Trollope served only to raise up defenders
for the Western capital. Aside from the commercial
distinction which its citizens no doubt too noisily proclaimed, Cincinnati could, in fact, boast of being, before
1840, one of the great publishing centers of the continent;
had made some creditable attempts to establish an adequate

---

[63] Founded as Losantiville in 1788-1789, Cincinnati had a population of about 750 in 1800, but in 1810 had 2540, and increased so
rapidly from that time that in 1840 the number was not far short of
fifty thousand, more than twice as great as was to be found in any
other Western town at that time.

[64] Harvey Hall, *The Cincinnati Directory, for 1825*, 1825, p. 7;
David Shaffer, *The Cincinnati, Covington, Newport and Fulton
Directory, for 1840*, n. d. (1839), p. 484; Charles Cist, *Cincinnati in
1841*, 1841, p. 39.

educational system; and had given some encouragement to drama and the fine arts.

Among other Ohio towns, Marietta is conspicuous as the oldest permanent settlement in the state — it was founded in 1788, a few months earlier than Cincinnati — and was from the first an outpost of New England culture. For a time the place dreamed of commercial importance. At the beginning of the nineteenth century Marietta built ships that voyaged from Ohio to Europe, and thus gained unique fame as a backwoods seaport.[65] But the shipbuilding soon ceased and the importance of the town declined. In 1840 the population was still less than two thousand. Chillicothe, founded in 1796 on the site of one of the several Indian villages of that name, represented the encroachment of Southern culture in Ohio. It was the capital of the North-West Territory from 1800 to 1803, and the state capital from 1803 to 1810 and again from 1812 to 1816. At the end of the pioneer period, it had about four thousand people. Another entering wedge from the South was the western tier of counties above Cincinnati, which were colonized by Kentuckians.[66] Dayton, Cleveland, and Columbus, each with a population of about six thousand, were, except Cincinnati, the only Ohio towns of considerable size in 1840. Columbus, which had become the state capital in 1816, was from that time notable for its activity in publishing.

In the Indiana of the pioneer period the few towns capable of important cultural influence were nearly all in the southern third of the state. Vincennes, on the Wabash, one of the oldest settlements in the West, was made the

[65] See Henry Howe, *Historical Collections of Ohio*, 1854, p. 513. A Marietta ship is said to have been seized at St. Petersburg because the authorities, unaware of the existence of such a seaport as Marietta, thought the captain was sailing under forged papers.

[66] See Archer B. Hulbert, *The Ohio River*, 1906, pp. 319-320.

capital (1800-1813) of Indiana Territory, though its inhabitants when it first gained this distinction numbered only
about seven hundred.[67] Indeed its growth thereafter was
small; but, in spite of the fact that its straggling population
was made up of a remarkable complex of Americans,
French, Canadians, and negroes,[68] it became, through force
of circumstances, the place of publication of one of the first
and longest-lived of pioneer newspapers north of the Ohio.
New Albany, opposite Louisville, and Madison, also on the
Ohio, were the largest towns in the state as late as 1840.
Indianapolis, which had a few hundred inhabitants when
it became the state capital in 1824, had less than three
thousand at the end of the period. Richmond, with about
two thousand, was the fourth city of the state, and early
became the center of activity of a distinct cultural group.

For cultural influence, however, the most notable town
of early Indiana was New Harmony, on the lower Wabash,
a mere village of no commercial importance, which, during
the brief Owenite régime, afforded a stimulus to intellectual
activity such as the West had not known before and was
not to know again during pioneer times. Even before
the coming of Owen, the place had gained fame as the
scene of a communistic experiment.[69] The town, first called
Harmonie, was founded by a German religious society
who had left their native country because of opposition
to their scheme of forming a community according to
what they thought the primitive Christian pattern.[70] In

[67] See Clarence Alvord, *The Illinois Country 1673-1818*, 1920, p.
407.

[68] Morris Birkbeck, *Notes on a Journey*, 1817, p. 112.

[69] ''Rapp the Harmonist'' does not escape the fate of the thousand
and one other eccentrics who are caught in the dragnet of Byron's
*Don Juan* (Canto XV, xxxv-xxxvii).

[70] An enthusiastic, but somewhat vague, account of the doctrine of
this sect is to be found in *Thoughts on the Destiny of Man*, published
by the Society in 1824.

1815, after ten years in Pennsylvania, George Rapp, spiritual leader and dictator of the colony, was established with his followers (they numbered about a thousand) at Harmonie.[71] The subjection of the members of the colony to the rule of Rapp and their eccentricities of conduct were incomprehensible to their American neighbors as well as to travellers.[72] But the prosperity of the community was remarked by all observers. In the division of the society into bands, each consisting of those belonging to a single trade,[73] Rapp had anticipated the Harmonists of the Owenite period. Very few in the town, however, could speak English;[74] and the influence of the colony, which was bodily removed within about ten years, must have been negligible.

But the period of the town's real significance as an intellectual seminary began when the Harmonie settlement was purchased by Robert Owen, the Scotch philanthropist and social theorist. New Harmony (for so he rechristened the place) was rapidly filling with the followers of Owen in the summer of 1825 — by the end of July of that year nearly a thousand[75] had been attracted there by Owen's prospectus for his communistic establishment. For the basis of this régime was communism; and, though the founder succeeded in retaining title to the property, he allowed

[71] *Niles' Weekly Register*, Oct. 28, 1815.

[72] William Tell Harris, *Remarks Made during a Tour*, 1821, pp. 134-135; *Niles' Weekly Register*, Sept. 7, 1822; and William Faux, *Memorable Days in America*, 1823, p. 265.

[73] Thomas Hulme, "Journal," in William Cobbett's *A Year's Residence*, second ed., 1819, p. 486.

[74] Adlard Welby, *A Visit to North America*, 1821, p. 132; and W. N. Blane, *An Excursion through the United States and Canada*, 1824, p. 248.

[75] *Niles' Weekly Register*, July 9 and 23, 1825. For an account of an attempt to found, in Ohio, a second community on Owenite principles, see *ibid.*, July 23, 1825.

the members of the society great freedom, and they adopted constitution after constitution to serve as the basis of self-government. Discussion was encouraged, absolute freedom of religious thought was a primary principle, and education was regarded as an important duty.[76] During its most fortunate days the experiment brought together a group of persons whose achievements were remarkable for a backwoods community: besides the members of the Owen family, a number of whom distinguished themselves, there were such famous intellectuals as William Maclure, Thomas Say, Charles Lesueur, and Frances Wright. But as early as 1826 visitors to this unique colony were convinced that its dissolution could not be long delayed.[77] The nightly meetings for discussion of policy developed sharp differences of opinion; and already a considerable part of the communists, unable to secure the adoption of their own proposals, were chafing under what seemed to them to be the betrayal of the society's ideals.[78] The division into trades and professions was succeeded by a breaking up into separate communities, and, finally, by the practical

[76] See *The New-Harmony Gazette*, I-III (Oct. 1, 1825-Oct. 22, 1828), *passim*.

[77] The best travel account is in Bernhard, Duke of Saxe-Weimar's *Travels through North America*, 1828, II, 106-123. For a contemporary observer's discussion of the causes of the failure of the scheme, see S. A. Ferrall, *A Ramble of Six Thousand Miles*, 1832, pp. 97-108.

[78] See Paul Brown, *Twelve Months in New-Harmony*, 1827, *passim*. This angry and incoherent recital well illustrates the temper of the more turbulent spirits among the colonists. Brown was especially bitter against Owen because of the latter's refusal to give up his private ownership of the property used by the community. *Cf.* also the same author's *A Dialogue, on Commonwealths*, 1828, p. 5. For a somewhat idealized picture containing many valuable details of the life of the New Harmony community, see Caroline Dale Snedeker, *Seth Way*, 1917.

abandonment of the scheme within about four years of its inception.

The oldest towns of Illinois — Kaskaskia, Cahokia, and other villages of the American Bottom — belong, in their origins, like Vincennes, to the early French period. After the English took the country from France in 1763, the economic decline of these towns, which had never been prosperous, was rapid. During the early years of American sovereignty, from the close of the Revolutionary War to 1790, they went through a period of chaos.[79] Kaskaskia's decay was retarded for a time when it was made the capital of Illinois (1809-1820) ; and it probably had nearly a thousand people when Illinois became a state, in 1818.[80] But after the capital was removed to Vandalia, its final decline began. Bellefontaine and Eagle, each with a population of less than three hundred at the end of the eighteenth century, were then the chief American villages; but a little later they were outstripped by Shawneetown, on the Ohio. Albion, founded in 1818, soon gained some prominence as the center of the English Prairie settlements, and as such was of considerable cultural importance. Its inhabitants took an active and effective interest in the political, social, and economic problems of early Illinois. As late as 1830 the southern half or two-thirds of the state was more densely populated than the remainder; and, although near the end of the period the heretofore thinly peopled northern section included the larger part of the settlers,[81] the shift in population came too late to be significant in an estimate of the cultural potentiality of the pioneer state. By 1840, Springfield, Alton, and Quincy were towns of between two and three

---

79 Cf. Alvord, op. cit., pp. 358-378.

80 Buck, op. cit., pp. 75-77.

81 Theodore Pease, The Frontier State, 1818-1848, 1918, maps opposite pp. 174 and 384.

thousand. Chicago, then containing a population of over four thousand, was the new marvel of the West because of its rapid growth, which had begun only after the Black Hawk War.[82] But, though a tribe of Indians gathered about it waiting for a treaty might supply color to contrast with the dinginess of the frontier post, it was at best a "mushroom town" and an "upstart village," a "chaos of mud, rubbish, and confusion."[83] By 1838 it was the scene of excited speculation, from which, it was rumored, the most fortunate were able to make almost incredible sums.[84] The atmosphere of the place was, however, unfriendly to cultural ideals.[85]

In Missouri, as in Indiana and in Illinois, the oldest towns owed their origin to the French; but as late as 1810, some years after the Americans had secured control, there were less than two thousand inhabitants in St. Louis, the only one of any size. In 1825 it had grown to something near five thousand; but there was little increase thereafter until 1834,[86] when a flow of immigration com-

[82] *Illinois in 1837*, 1837, p. 135; and Hoffman, *op. cit.*, I, 236-244.

[83] Latrobe, *op. cit.*, II, 202-209.

[84] See, for example, James Logan, *Notes of a Journey*, 1838, p. 104. Harriet Martineau, who visited Chicago in 1836, thus describes the feverish speculation then in progress: "The streets were crowded with land speculators, hurrying from one sale to another. A negro, dressed up in scarlet, bearing a scarlet flag, and riding a white horse with housings of scarlet, announced the times of sale. At every street-corner where he stopped, the crowd flocked round him; and it seemed as if some prevalent mania infected the whole people. The rage for speculation might fairly be so regarded. As the gentlemen of our party walked the streets, store-keepers hailed them from their doors, with offers of farms, and all manner of land-lots, advising them to speculate before the price of land rose higher." (*Society in America*, 1837, I, 259-260.)

[85] Joseph Balestier, *The Annals of Chicago*, 1840, p. 18.

[86] Keemle, *The St. Louis Directory, for the Years 1840-1*, pp. v-vi.

menced which gave the place within the next six years a
population of over sixteen thousand. Until late in the
pioneer period St. Louis was noted for its mean houses and
its narrow and dirty streets,[87] as well as for the variety of
its inhabitants and the air of adventure which belonged to
the large portion of them who were engaged in the fur
trade with the Far West.[88] By 1840 Jefferson, the state
capital, had only slightly over a thousand inhabitants.
Columbia was at the same time laying the foundations for
its later distinction as an educational center. Independence was important as the extreme Western white settlement on the way to the Rocky Mountains.

In Michigan, the fringe of French population along the
straits was the earliest outpost of civilization; and Detroit,
founded by Cadillac in 1701, was the oldest settlement
in the Middle West. American immigrants did not arrive
in considerable numbers until after 1805; but by 1834 they
had increased to such an extent that the French population
was outnumbered about five to one.[89] The new inhabitants
of Detroit, as of the rest of the state, were largely from
New England and New York. By 1840 the population
was over nine thousand; but, although the total number
of people in the state of Michigan rose from less than
thirty-two thousand in 1830 to over two hundred thousand
in 1840, there were no other towns of considerable size.

[87] Timothy Flint, *op. cit.*, I, 306; Ludlow, *op. cit.*, pp. 183-184.
Sir Charles Augustus Murray (*Travels in North America*, 1839, II,
69) found the town, only a few years before 1840, an extremely dull
and dingy place, with miserable accommodations for travellers.

[88] Hoffman (*op. cit.*, II, 76) records his impressions of the
"Engagés (as they are called) of the fur-trade — fellows that talk
of a trip to the Rocky Mountains as you would speak of a turn on
the Battery."

[89] Fuller, *op. cit.*, pp. 122 and 148. Until comparatively late, the
majority had been French (*cf.* Samuel Brown, *Views on Lake Erie*,
1814, p. 96; and *Detroit Gaz.*, July 25, 1817).

In Wisconsin, the whole population in 1840 was only slightly over thirty thousand. Milwaukee was the chief place; but, though German immigration was already noticeable, it had less than two thousand people. Madison was chosen as the capital in 1836, before it was actually in existence as a town. Iowa, closed to white immigration until 1833,[90] had by 1840 a population of over forty thousand. A printing press was at work within about three years after the beginning of white immigration. Minnesota, by far the latest of the Middle Western group to be settled, had within its borders little more than a military post until after 1840.

Toward the end of the period the contrast between the life of the larger towns, like Cincinnati and Louisville, and that of the extreme frontier posts in Missouri and Iowa and Wisconsin was no doubt greater than between life in Cincinnati and that in New York or Philadelphia. But even the largest Western towns could boast of few municipal improvements worthy of their size. In 1834 Louisville considered a project for water works, but it was decided that such an improvement could not be realized for years to come.[91] It was not until the end of the year 1839 that the same city introduced street lights, a novelty at that time unknown in either St. Louis or Cincinnati.[92] With the exception of a very few theatres and churches erected late in the period, there were no buildings of architectural distinction. Mrs. Trollope, in her attempt to give Cincin-

[90] John Plumbe, *Sketches of Iowa and Wisconsin*, 1839, p. 5.

[91] *Lou. Pub. Adv.*, Nov. 7, 1834. At Cincinnati a primitive water supply system was established by private enterprise in 1819, becoming municipal property in 1839 (Cist, *op. cit.*, pp. 147-148). For the St. Louis water works in 1835, see *The Revised Ordinances of the City of Saint Louis*, 1836, pp. 138-143.

[92] *Lou. Pub. Adv.*, Jan. 1, 1840; *Cinc. Daily Gaz.*, Nov. 17, 1840; *Daily Mo. Rep.*, Mar. 9 and Dec. 18, 1840.

nati something of the kind, had succeeded only in creating a discord of what passed for Egyptian, Turkish, Greek, and Gothic.[93] The account which a citizen of Cincinnati wrote for an Eastern periodical in 1831 was generally true for the whole of the pioneer era and for all towns of the West: "I have said nothing of our literary institutions, because they are yet in embryo or in infancy. I have not praised our public works and buildings, because we have none that entitle us to distinction."[94]

## VI

Probably the most pervasive cultural influence in the early West was religion. At a time when the population was characterized by its large number of distinct racial elements, it was equally remarkable for its confusion of religious creeds.

Roman Catholicism followed in the steps of the French explorers and traders, and was thus the first religious creed to influence Western culture. Among its early representatives were leaders, like Marquette, whose chief energies were directed toward conversion of the Indians. But little of permanent value resulted from the work of the early missionaries, and the growth of the church in the settlements was very slow. At Detroit, for example, where the Church of St. Anne was founded about the beginning of the eighteenth century, there seem to have been, nearly a hundred and twenty years later, but two priests;[95] and the Diocese of Detroit was not established till 1832. During the third quarter of the eighteenth century Father Gibault travelled the West from Michilimackinac to the Illinois towns and Vincennes, but his sect was as yet poorly organized and must have been largely ineffective.

[93] Martineau, *Retrospect of Western Travel*, 1838, II, 54.
[94] *The New-England Magazine*, I, 34 (July, 1831).
[95] *Detroit Gaz.*, Jan. 29, 1819.

Of the more important early French towns, St. Louis had, near the beginning of the American period of occupation, a Catholic church; but it was only occasionally opened, and there was no regular priest.[96] The first considerable accession to Catholicism in the migratory period was the body of adherents who came from Maryland to Bardstown, Kentucky, in 1785. A priest was sent out two years later; and in 1811 Flaget arrived as the first Bishop of Kentucky, and the first in the West.[97] A group of Trappist monks who migrated from Europe to Kentucky shortly before this time presently moved to the neighborhood of the French towns along the Mississippi, and a few years later returned to Europe.[98] Within the fourteen years following 1820 the Dioceses of Cincinnati, St. Louis, Detroit, and Vincennes were established; but the expansion of the church during pioneer times was not at all in proportion to that of the stronger Protestant organizations. Toward the end of that period the Catholic population of Kentucky may have amounted to between twenty and thirty thousand,[99] and that of Illinois to about five or six thousand (mostly in the old French towns).[100] In Indiana, where the whole Diocese of Vincennes is said to have contained less than two thousand Catholics in 1834,[101] when Bishop Bruté arrived, there could not have been a very considerable body of adherents by 1840. The Catholic population of Michi-

[96] Artemas Bullard, *Historical Sketch*, 1839, p. 8.

[97] Lewis Collins, *Historical Sketches of Kentucky*, 1847, pp. 140-142. According to the account here given (by M. J. Spalding), the whole Catholic population of Kentucky was estimated, as late as 1793, at three hundred families.

[98] Flagg, *op. cit.*, I, 169-172.

[99] Collins, *op. cit.*, pp. 141. The estimate of thirty thousand here given is presumably for about the year 1847.

[100] J. M. Peck, *A Gazetteer of Illinois*, second ed., 1837, p. 74.

[101] Charles Blanchard, *History of the Catholic Church in Indiana*, 1898, I, 56-59.

gan, however, seems to have been much greater, and was perhaps larger than the membership claimed by any of the Protestant churches.[102]   Throughout the West the rapid growth of the church began only near the end of the pioneer period [103] with the great increase in Irish and German immigration.

Another religious movement, later in origin than the Catholic, but belonging entirely to the early part of the pioneer period, was the missionary work of the Moravians in Ohio and Michigan.[104]   But, in spite of its spectacular struggle of many years against misfortune and persecution, the community which grew up about Post and Heckewelder and Zeisberger was to disintegrate without having exerted any permanent cultural influence.

The Shakers, after establishing a number of societies in New York and New England, penetrated the West immediately following the great religious upheaval of 1800-1801. The first missionary bands to arrive received financial

[102] Blois, *op. cit.*, pp. 148-150.

[103] According to *The American Almanac*, for 1841, p. 157, the Dioceses of Bardstown, Cincinnati, Vincennes, St. Louis, Detroit, and Dubuque, contained together only 201 ministers.

[104] See John Heckewelder, *A Narrative*, 1820, *passim*; and Randall and Ryan, *History of Ohio*, 1912, II, 17 ff.   By 1762 both Christian Post and Heckewelder were at work among the Delaware Indians on the Muskingum.   Zeisberger became the third member of this notable group of leaders, and in 1772 he and Heckewelder founded Schoenbrunn near the Muskingum.   All went well until the time of the Revolutionary War, when the missionaries and their charges found themselves on the direct road between the hostile camps of Pittsburg and Detroit.   Then began the series of remarkable sufferings and wanderings of the community which ended with their return to eastern Ohio in 1798.   But, after surviving the extremes of persecution, the Moravians were to fail through the loss of their leaders.   After the death of Zeisberger, in 1808, and the return of Heckewelder to Pennsylvania in 1810, the settlement gradually disappeared.

aid from the older communities in the East;[105] and, in spite of political difficulties and opposition that caused a pamphlet war, they settled at Pleasant Hill and elsewhere in Kentucky, and at Watervliet and Whitewater in Ohio. Their greatest leader and chief pamphleteer was Richard McNemar, earlier a preacher in the great Kentucky Revival, but one of the first converts[106] of the Shakers after their arrival in 1805 at what was soon to be famous as Union Village, near Lebanon, Warren County, Ohio. This settlement soon aroused the suspicion of more orthodox religionists, and curious travellers who visited it brought back conflicting reports: in the eyes of some the industry and prosperity which, as in the case of Rapp's Harmonie, were evident to all observers suggested that, in spite of their odd behaviour, these might be children of light;[107] but to others the villagers seemed blasphemous, acting like madmen in their worship.[108] The number of Shakers, however, was always very small. From something more than a hundred in 1805 they increased in Ohio alone to perhaps about five hundred in 1825,[109] most of whom must have been at Union Village.[110] Save for an unsuccessful attempt to found a community near Vincennes, in the Wabash Valley,[111] the movement probably did not extend beyond Ohio and Kentucky. Intellectually, the character of the members of this sect was peculiarly low; and they looked

[105] J. P. MacLean, *Shakers of Ohio*, 1907, p. 14.

[106] *Ibid.*, p. 61.

[107] Asbury, *op. cit.*, III, 393.

[108] Harris, *op. cit.*, pp. 121-122.

[109] MacLean, *op. cit.*, pp. 11 and 70.

[110] Bernhard, Duke of Saxe-Weimar, *op. cit.*, II, 140. According to this authority, the Shakers of Union Village alone numbered six hundred.

[111] See MS. account book of the Shaker settlement at Busseron Creek, for the period from Feb. 23, 1815, to Apr. 8, 1822, in Indiana State Library; *cf.* also *The Western Sun* (Vincennes), July 1, 1815.

with strong dislike upon all literary, scientific, and kindred achievements.[112]

A much later sectarian invasion of the West, and a very spectacular one, was that of the Mormons, or Latter Day Saints, whose advance made them for a time the center of bitter controversy in Ohio, in Missouri, and in Illinois. In 1831, shortly after the first missionary campaign had begun, Joseph 'Smith, their chief, moved from the state of New York to Kirtland, Lake County, Ohio, to establish the New Jerusalem; and a temple was actually dedicated in 1836. There were at one time nearly three thousand Mormons in the community; but persecution soon caused the leaders to leave for Missouri, where members of the church had long been forming a colony. The harsh treatment which the now rapidly growing settlements of the Saints suffered at the hands of the citizens and the militia of that state, presently forced a large company of the new sect to seek refuge in Illinois, where, in 1840, they founded Nauvoo, the last important stronghold which they possessed before the exodus of their main body to the Far West. Their number was great enough to arouse the interest of politicians, to cause widespread alarm among orthodox religious bodies, and to add slightly to the sum of controversial writings; but they left no permanent mark upon the pioneer community.

The most widely effective religious programs of the early West were those of the Methodists, the Baptists, the Disciples of Christ, and the Presbyterians. The Methodists, who adapted themselves with remarkable success to frontier conditions, were, on the whole, the prevailing sect; but none of the churches, even in the older communities, exerted

---

[112] MacLean, *op. cit.*, p. 70. Both for lack of intellectual achievement by the Shakers and for their economic success, *cf.* also an account of their village near Lexington, Ky., in *The Western Monthly Magazine*, II, 591 (Nov., 1834).

more than a feeble and sporadic influence until near the
end of the period. On the extreme fringe of civilization
the church bell was seldom heard, and formal religious
observance was rare enough to be regarded as the occasion
of a holiday season.[113]

In Kentucky, the Baptists, who were the first religious
sect to enter in numbers, had attained a membership of
perhaps five thousand by 1800,[114] when the total population
of the state was considerably over two hundred thousand.
During the same period the Methodists, probably second in
strength, had increased to about one-third the number of
the Baptists,[115] while the Presbyterians, whose organization
was from the first torn by dissension, probably had many
less. Protestants and Catholics together thus formed an
extremely small part of this earliest Western community.
Even after allowance has been made for a larger number
of irregular adherents, it seems impossible that these
religious sects could have had a very great effect on pioneer

[113] Tocqueville (*Œuvres*, 1861, I, 201), in his account of a conversation with his host at Pontiac in 1831, epitomizes the religious
life of the isolated settlers along the whole line of the frontier: "La
voix de la religion parvient-elle quelquesfois jusqu'à eux? — Très-
rarement. On n'a encore rien pu faire pour assurer dans nos bois
l'observation publique d'un culte. Presque tous les étés, il est vrai,
quelques prêtres méthodistes viennent parcourir les nouveaux éta-
blissements. Le bruit de leur arrivée se répand avec une incroyable
rapidité de cabane en cabane: c'est la grande nouvelle du jour.
A l'époque fixée, l'émigrant, sa femme et ses enfants, se derigent à
travers les sentiers à peine frayés de la forêt vers le rendez-vous
indiqué. On vient de cinquante milles à la ronde."

[114] Collins, *op. cit.*, p. 109; and B. F. Riley, *History of the
Southern Baptists*, 1898, p. 119, as quoted in C. C. Cleveland, *The
Great Revival in the West*, n. d. (1916), p. 19.

[115] *Minutes of the Annual Conferences of the Methodist Episcopal
Church, for the Years 1773-1828*, 1840, I, 93. The membership for
Kentucky is here given as 1741 and that for the whole North-West
Territory as 257.

life; but no doubt they touched a far greater portion of the population than was reached by any educational propaganda or by books or even newspapers.

From such beginnings these churches grew during the first forty years of the next century more rapidly in proportion than did the population of the West. The Baptists retained their early superiority in Kentucky; but elsewhere the Methodists, with their remarkable organization of circuit riders, held the allegiance of the largest numbers. From a total of almost two thousand members recorded in 1800,[116] the church had grown by 1820 to a membership of over forty thousand;[117] and by 1840 the whole number had risen to nearly 225,000 [118] in a total population for the Middle West of something over four millions. At the same time the Baptists probably had a membership of about half that number.[119] The Presbyterians, of all kinds, must have been still less numerous.[120] The Disciples of Christ, a church formed by the union of the followers of Alexander Campbell and Barton Warren Stone, and confined to a greater degree than any other

[116] *Ibid.*

[117] *Ibid.*, I, 346.

[118] *Cf. Minutes of the Annual Conferences of the Methodist Episcopal Church, for the Years 1839-1845*, III, 87, 90, 94, 96, 99, 102, 104, and 109.

[119] See I. M. Allen, *The Triennial Baptist Register. No. 2.-1836*, p. 307. According to this authority the membership of Baptist churches in the states of Kentucky, Ohio, Indiana, Illinois, Missouri, and Michigan was 79,560 in the year 1835. Of these, over thirty-five thousand were in Kentucky, with something over fourteen thousand of the remainder in Ohio, and about thirteen thousand in Indiana.

[120] *Cf. Minutes of the General Assembly of the Presbyterian Church in the United States of America. 1840*, 1841, pp. 63-64. The membership here reported for thirty-three presbyteries in the Middle West is slightly over twenty-six thousand. This number does not, of course, include the membership of other branches of the church, which were entirely independent.

important sect to the West, grew with such rapidity that
in 1840 its membership may have equalled that of the
Baptists.[121]

Of the many other sects represented in the new country,
only a few exerted a perceptible influence. Early in the
nineteenth century the Friends had established two main
groups of colonies — one on the eastern border of Ohio,
with Mountpleasant as its center, and another near the
eastern boundary of Indiana, in the Whitewater district,
of which Richmond later became the chief town. Among
the members of this church were leaders who carried on an
energetic sectarian controversy as well as notable antislavery agitation, but the number of the Friends was so
small and their distribution so limited that they had no
great part in the evolution of Western culture.

The Protestant Episcopal Church, less adapted to frontier conditions than many other religious organizations,
and handicapped by the popular fear of English political
propaganda,[122] had only a comparatively small body of
adherents at the close of the period.[123] The Unitarians,

[121] *Cf.* W. T. Moore, *A Comprehensive History of the Disciples of
Christ*, n. d. (1909), p. 341. As many churches kept no record of
their membership, the total number of members is largely a matter
of conjecture.

[122] Caswall (*op. cit.*, pp. 45-46) quotes an old Ohio farmer's
opinion of the attempt of the Episcopalians to found a college in
that state: " 'I have fought the British,' said he, 'in the revolutionary war; I have again encountered them in the last war; and
I know something of their character. . . . I am, therefore, convinced that Bishop Chase is an agent employed by them to introduce
British domination here. . . . when you think you have an
opportunity, you will throw off the mask, and proclaim the king of
England.' "

[123] According to *The American Almanac*, for 1841, p. 158, there
were only 132 ministers of this church in the entire Middle West at
that time, fifty-four of these being in Ohio. Caswall (*op. cit.*, pp. 32-
33 and 224) estimated that there were not more than three thousand

who, between 1830 and 1840, began to wage a notable campaign in the West with the aid of some of the most distinguished New England men of the time,[124] remained numerically negligible.

In general it may be said that, with the exception of extremists such as the Mormons and Shakers, Protestant sects succeeded in the pioneer West in inverse ratio to their intellectual attainments, and in direct ratio to their emotional appeal. The methods used were primitive. The most successful preachers were extremely vehement in their discourses, and sought to arouse their hearers to a frenzy of emotion. "Frequently," wrote F. A. Michaux, the French scientist, who visited the frontier in 1802, "in the middle of these sermons, the heads of some of the congregation are lifted up, their imaginations exalted, and they fall down, inspired, exclaiming, *Glory! Glory!*"[125]

Nothing was more characteristic of the religious activity of the pioneer community than the camp meetings, which became popular after the great Kentucky Revival in the opening years of the nineteenth century. At the union meeting of Presbyterians and Methodists at Cain Ridge in August, 1801, which was the climax of that revival, many thousands of people were gathered, and there was exhorting and singing without intermission for not quite a week, six or seven preachers addressing the throng at the same time. The number of those who fell was estimated at about

---

people in Ohio in 1830 who acknowledged Bishop Chase as their ecclesiastical head, and that Kentucky did not have that number of Episcopalians until some years later.

[124] See *The Western Messenger*, I-VIII (1835-1841).

[125] *Travels to the Westward*, 1805, p. 242. *Cf.* also James Flint, *Letters from America*, 1822, p. 169. For an account of extreme eccentricity of conduct in a minor religious sect of the time, see R. H. Taneyhill, "The Leatherwood God," in *Ohio Valley Historical Series Miscellanies*, 1871.

a thousand.[126] From this time for many years such gatherings were holiday occasions for the population of the back parts of the country. By 1808 hundreds of meetings were being held, some in almost every corner of the backwoods that had been reached by the immigrants.[127] It was common for the excitement to continue unabated for a greater part of the night or even, as at Cain Ridge, for days together. Many fell to the ground, sometimes in a trance that lasted for hours, with no apparent signs of life. Jerking, shouting, barking, and dancing were common manifestations of the intense excitement; and in some cases people who had gone through these experiences were subject to peculiar nervous disorders the rest of their lives. Pens were at times constructed in the tents for the more violent of those who came under the influence of the exhorters. A few of the less emotional leaders were alarmed at such extraordinary proceedings; but the majority, especially the Methodists, had long been accustomed to regard extreme religious enthusiasm as indispensable. For thousands the wild scenes of the camp meeting afforded simply a brutal form of entertainment, while, on the edges of the throng, the politicians were wont to take advantage of the unusual opportunity. Perhaps no more graphic account is to be found than that of James Finley, a Methodist preacher who was an enthusiastic participant in Western camp meetings during the period of greatest religious excitement:

These meetings began to follow one another in quick succession, and the numbers which attended were almost incredible. While the meetings lasted, crowds were to be seen in all directions, passing and repassing the roads and paths, while the woods seemed to be alive with people. Whole settlements appeared to be vacated, and only here

---

[126] Cleveland, *op. cit.*, pp. 75-81. I have followed Miss Cleveland's spelling of the name Cain Ridge.

[127] Asbury, *op. cit.*, III, 249, 276, 333-334, *et passim.*

and there could be found a house having an inhabitant. All ages, sexes, and conditions, pressed their way to the camp meeting. . . . At these meetings thousands fell under the power of God, and cried for mercy. The scenes which successively occurred . . . were awfully sublime, and a general terror seemed to have pervaded the minds of all people within the reach of their influences. . . . Twenty thousand persons tossed to and fro, like the tumultuous waves of the sea in a storm, or swept down like the trees of the forest under the blast of the wild tornado, was a sight which mine own eyes witnessed, but which neither my pen nor tongue can describe.

During the religious exercises within the encampment, all manner of wickedness was going on without. . . . Men, furious with the effects of the maddening bowl, would outrage all decency by their conduct; and some, mounted on horses, would ride at full speed among the people. I saw one, who seemed to be a leader and champion of the party, on a large, white horse, ride furiously into the pray-ing circle, uttering the most horrid imprecations. Sud-denly, as if smitten by lightning, he fell from his horse. At this a shout went up from the religious multitude, as if Lucifer himself had fallen. I trembled, for I feared God had killed the bold and daring blasphemer. He exhib-ited no signs whatever of life; his limbs were rigid, his wrists pulseless, and his breath gone. Several of his com-rades came to see him, but they did not gaze long till the power of God came upon them, and they fell like men slain in battle.[128]

In spite, however, of the extreme emphasis upon emo-tional appeal, the sects which met with greatest popular favor showed, near the end of the period, a friendly atti-

---

[128] For detailed accounts of the camp meetings by contemporary observers, see James B. Finley, *Autobiography*, ed. W. P. Strickland, 1872, pp. 362-368; Ferrall, *op. cit.*, pp. 71-78; L. Garrett, *Recollec-tions of the West*, 1834, p. 29; James Flint, *op. cit.*, pp. 231-238; and Timothy Flint, *op. cit.*, I, 144-146. For a recent study of psychological and other aspects of these meetings, see Cleveland, *op. cit.*, *passim*.

tude toward intellectual attainment. As early as 1800 the Methodist General Conference had made the circuit riders agents for books published under the direction of the church;[129] and somewhat more than thirty years later the conference of one of the Middle Western states had taken independent action, instructing its preachers to address the people throughout its territory expressly on the subject of education, demanding the establishment of both common schools and institutions of higher learning.[130] The Presbyterians had from the first paid a great deal of attention to education; and even the Baptists, who were in earlier years sharply opposed to it,[131] began to interest themselves, some years before the end of the period, in the matter of providing schools for the training of their preachers.[132]

But, for the most part, the preachers who carried on the religious campaigns among the backwoodsmen were men of more zeal than culture. No doubt a great number of them, including some of the most successful, were only one stage removed from illiteracy. Many, like John Colby, who "felt the impression renewed, to arise and go to the state of Ohio, and to cry against it,"[133] began as preachers with no preparation but emotional fervor and conviction. Men of no greater intellect than Lorenzo Dow, famous for "his outlandish exterior, his orang-outang features, the beard that swept his aged breast," and "the piping, treble voice, in which he was wont to preach what

[129] W. W. Sweet, *The Rise of Methodism in the West*, n. d. (1920), pp. 68-69.

[130] See the program adopted by the Illinois Conference, quoted in *The Western Monthly Magazine*, II, 443 (Aug., 1834).

[131] Cleveland, *op. cit.*, p. 48.

[132] *Proceedings of the General Convention of Western Baptists at Cincinnati . . . 1835*, reviewed in *The Western Monthly Magazine*, III, 255 (Apr., 1835).

[133] John Colby, *The Life, Experience, and Travels of John Colby, Preacher of the Gospel*, third ed., 1829, p. 27.

with surveying[143] sometimes added as a practical training
for backwoodsmen. Of modern foreign languages, French
alone received any considerable attention.[144] Schools on
the Lancastrian plan were early to be found in the principal
towns;[145] and there were, here and there, as at New Harmony, intelligent experiments in educational theory. Public schools, however, were hardly known until the second
decade of the nineteenth century; and even nominally free
public schools were not introduced into the largest of the
cities until about 1830, when Cincinnati, Louisville, Lexington, and Detroit established institutions of that kind.[146] St.
Louis was much later.[147] For some years after such public

---

[143] *Cent. N.-W. Ter.*, Dec. 20, 1794, and Dec. 5, 1795.

[144] Mary Estelle Delcamp in her list for Lexington (1787-1820),
*op. cit.*, includes five French schools. When LaFayette visited that
town in 1825 he was greeted with speeches in Latin, English, and
French by students at Transylvania (Levasseur, *op. cit.*, II, 168).

[145] See, for example, *Mo. Gaz.*, June 1, 1816; *Lou. Pub. Adv.*,
June 19, 1819; *Detroit Gaz.*, Oct. 16, 1818.

[146] In Cincinnati the session of 1840 was the twelfth for the common schools of the city (*Cinc. Daily Gaz.*, July 17, 1840); the City
Free School of Louisville was also opened in 1829 (*Lou. Pub. Adv.*,
June 10 and Aug. 15, 1829; and *An Account of the Louisville City
School*, 1830, p. 5); and Lexington was not far behind — the sixth
session of its City School began in Sept., 1836 (*Ky. Gaz.*, Aug.
18, 1836, and Feb. 23, 1837; *cf.* MacCabe, *op. cit.*, p. 16). The
Free School at Detroit, which was opened about 1832, was founded
by a group of women and intended only for those children whose
parents were unable to pay for their education, and its capacity was
soon found to be inadequate (*Detroit Courier*, Dec. 10, 1834); high
school instruction in that town, which began as early as 1833, was
not free (*ibid.*, Aug. 21, 1833; and *Detroit Journal and Michigan
Advertiser*, Oct. 9, 1833). In 1834 the number in school in
Detroit, in this and other institutions, was equal to about one-
tenth of the total population (*Niles' Weekly Register*, Apr. 19,
1834).

[147] Two public schools were established about 1837, but could
accommodate less than three hundred pupils, and employed only four

schools had been provided in the cities, the private institutions continued to attract a large proportion of pupils.[148]

Not until near the end of the pioneer period was there a successful attempt to establish free schools under the direct supervision of the state. Nothing is more significant of the cultural atmosphere of the early West than the long and arduous campaign necessary to secure the beginnings of this system. From the time of the Ordinance of 1787, it was a matter of good form for governors and legislatures to mention the subject of popular education with great respect; but it was long before officials had the courage to urge the raising of taxes and the appropriation of funds necessary to put such a scheme into effect. Individual protests were heard from time to time, and a number of influential newspapers attempted to arouse public sentiment. In Ohio, committees of correspondence were formed at Cincinnati and in other parts of the state about the year 1816; and the cause of popular education was for several years thereafter effectively advocated in an almanac issued by Nathan Guilford.[149]

The first important results of the campaign were seen in the enactment of a state law in 1825 providing for a system of schools; but so large a section of public opinion was still hostile that the law was in great measure inoperative for many years. Not until 1837 was the system brought under the control of a state superintendent, whose first report showed that there were at about that time

teachers (Keemle, *The St. Louis Directory, for the Years 1838-9*, p. vii). Even these schools were not entirely free (J. T. Scharf, *History of Saint Louis*, 1883, I, 837).

[148] According to Caleb Atwater (*The Writings of Caleb Atwater*, 1833, pp. 182-183) Cincinnati had, in 1833, twenty-four private schools, with 1230 pupils; and twenty public schools, with 2000 pupils.

[149] *The North American Review*, XLVII, 47-48 (July, 1838).

something over a hundred thousand children in the public schools, while less than half that number were in private schools.[150] Within a year or two, it was estimated that about half the children of the state were in school.[151]

In other Western states the progress toward free public education was much slower. Michigan, though not admitted to the Union until 1837, was the only one of them which established an effective system before 1840; and even in this state the schools were not, for many years after that date, wholly free. In Kentucky there was early recognition of the unsatisfactory state of education. By 1820 most communities of the state had occasionally some kind of school; but conditions were primitive,[152] and a state system of free schools, though much discussed,[153] was not established during the pioneer period. In 1840, Kentucky, though it had the largest number of private schools, ranked lowest of all the Middle Western states in the proportion of persons of school age actually in school. Indiana, whose scanty population at the end of the eighteenth century was reputed the most ignorant in the world,[154] bore a reputa-

---

[150] *Niles' Weekly Register*, Mar. 3, 1838. *Cf. First Annual Report of the Superintendent of Common Schools, . . . Ohio*, 1838.

[151] *Picture of Cincinnati*, for 1839, p. 62.

[152] *Ky. Gaz.*, Mar. 12, 1819, *et passim*.

[153] *Cf.* William Pitt, *Letters to the Honorable James T. Morehead*, 1837, reviewed in *The North American Review*, XLIX, 262 (July, 1839); and *Report of the Committee on Education, of the House of Representatives of Kentucky, on so Much of the Governor's Message as Relates to Schools and Seminaries of Learning*, second ed., 1830. According to the latter work (p. 3), "The aggregate number of children in the 34 counties, as returned" was, at this time, "51,702, and the whole number at school" (including, of course, those attending both private and public schools) "10,945."

[154] Of the inhabitants of the Wabash Valley in 1790, Governor St. Clair said, "There is not a fiftieth man that can either read or write" (James Albert Woodburn, *Higher Education in Indiana*, 1891, p. 36).

tion only slightly more favorable during the early decades
of the nineteenth century. Travellers familiar with
frontier conditions were struck by the illiteracy of the
population which entered the southern half of the state as
part of the first great wave of migration.[155] From the time
of Indiana's admission as a state in 1816 (when a law was
enacted to authorize township schools, but without any
provision for the necessary revenues) until long after
1840, the measures brought forward for the encouragement
of education were largely ineffective.[156] In Illinois, where
a state law providing a source of funds had been passed as
early as 1825, but repealed, there were by 1834 some free
schools supported by local levies and the proceeds of land
sales; but provision for a state system through taxation was
not made until many years afterwards. As late as 1832, it
was estimated that not more than about one-fourth of the
children received any instruction during the year, while a
great proportion of the entire population were wholly
unable to read.[157] Missouri had an even less enviable record.
Doubtless the influence of Kentucky was the cause of the

[155] For an observer's account of the schools and general cultural
conditions in Indiana about 1826, see Isaac Reed, *The Christian Traveller*, 1828, *passim*. A valuable picture of the rude state of culture
in one of the chief centers of higher education in the state about the
same time and somewhat later is to be found in Baynard Rush Hall,
*The New Purchase*, 1843, *passim*.

[156] Woodburn, *op. cit.*, pp. 40-42. The difficulty of obtaining
funds for the support of public schools, though more marked in some
states than in others, was general in the early Middle West; a careful investigation showed that as late as 1835 there was not a county
in the whole West in which the funds raised for public instruction
amounted to $1.50 a year for each pupil (Samuel Lewis, ''Report
on the Best Method of Establishing and Forming Common Schools
in the West,'' in *Transactions of the Fifth Annual Meeting of the
Western Literary Institute and College of Professional Teachers*,
1836, p. 152).

[157] *The American Almanac*, for 1832, p. 265.

relatively large number of private academies and similar
institutions, which were notorious for their inefficiency.[158]

In the entire Middle West, according to the census of
1840, the number of persons attending "primary and
common" schools was equal to slightly more than one-
eleventh of the whole population, as compared with an
average of considerably more than one-sixth for the states
of New York, Pennsylvania, and Massachusetts at the
same time.[159]   The proportion of persons in attendance
upon such schools varied among states of the Middle
West from about one-seventh for Ohio and Michigan to
about one-twenty-third for Missouri and somewhat more
than one-thirty-second for Kentucky.[160]   The most striking
fact made clear by an analysis of the census figures is the
much greater attention given to elementary schooling by
the states largely populated from New England, New York,
and Pennsylvania than by the states whose population was

[158] Cf., for example, "Senex," in Mo. Rep., Oct. 11, 1827.

[159] The total population of the Middle West was now, according
to this census, 4,131,370, while that of New York, Pennsylvania, and
Massachusetts was 4,890,653.   In the Middle West the number of
persons attending primary or common schools was 376,241, while in
the three Eastern states named the number was 842,613.

[160] Of the total for the Western states, Ohio had over half—218,609,
or slightly more than one-seventh of a population of 1,519,467;
Indiana was next with 48,189, or not quite one-fourteenth of a population of 685,866; Illinois had 34,876, or somewhat more than the
same fraction of a population of 476,183; Michigan had 29,701, or
about one-seventh of a population of 212,267; Kentucky had 24,641,
or slightly over one-thirty-second of a population of 779,828; Missouri had 16,788, or a little more than one-twenty-third of a population of 383,702; Wisconsin had 1937, or over one-sixteenth of a
population of 30,945; while Iowa had 1500, or something less than
one-twenty-eighth of a population of 43,112.   In the case of Wisconsin and Iowa, especially the latter, settlement had so recently
begun that the number of children in the territory must have been
exceptionally small in proportion to the whole population.

derived chiefly from the Southern migratory column. The large number of negroes in the latter group had some effect upon the remarkable disproportion, but the omission of their number from the totals of population would only slightly lessen the contrast between the two bodies of white settlers. Indiana and Illinois, which by 1840 contained a large admixture from the Northern streams of immigrants as well as a great body of population derived from the Southern one, stand, as might be supposed, midway between the two extremes in the matter of attention to elementary schooling. Iowa and Wisconsin, which remained territories at the end of the period, were too recently settled to admit of comparison with the states of the same section.[161] It is clear, however, that in no part of the West was the general attention to elementary schooling early enough to have a great effect upon literary activity during the pioneer period. Here the advantage lay with such of the older communities as had established secondary schools or colleges near the beginning of the nineteenth century.

Academies and grammar schools, which, though of very irregular quality, sought recognition as institutions of higher rank than the primary and common schools, had early appeared in considerable numbers, so that there were by 1840, according to the census, between three and four hundred of them in the Middle West, almost exactly one-third of the whole being in Kentucky. Of the more than sixteen thousand persons attending such schools, Kentucky had not quite the same proportion; and, likewise, Indiana, Illinois, and Missouri had a greater proportion of the whole number of these institutions than of the total of primary and common schools. The best of the academies,

---

[161] Before 1840, however, Iowa had made legal provision for a free common school in each county (John Newhall, *Sketches of Iowa, or the Emigrant's Guide*, 1841, p. 66).

or seminaries, as some were called, afforded training for teachers in the lower schools; and in some cases the state undertook to establish such a training center in every county.[162]

Among the numerous colleges and universities of the early West, two of the older ones had a great influence upon the cultural achievement of the frontier country. By far the most influential of them all was Transylvania University, which, at the end of the eighteenth century, emerged from what was known as Transylvania Seminary (1783). From the time of its existence as a seminary, it had done much to uphold the dignity of higher education. Under the presidency of Harry Toulmin, a Unitarian minister and disciple of Priestley, who had emigrated from England, it offered instruction not only in reading, writing, arithmetic, and English grammar, but also in Latin, Greek, moral philosophy, history, and "some of the Fine Arts, as Oratory and Criticism."[163] Transylvania, though it became nominally a university in 1798-1799, remained, in fact, an excellent grammar school until 1818,[164] when Horace Holley, a Boston Unitarian clergyman who had graduated from Yale, came to Kentucky resolved to make Transylvania known as the center of higher education in the

---

162 Indiana, in which the first county seminary was established in 1825, made legal provision in 1831 for a seminary in each county; and by 1840 twenty-one such schools had been incorporated (Woodburn, *op. cit.*, pp. 46-47).

163 *Ky. Gaz.*, July 5, 1794.

164 Charles Caldwell, *A Discourse on the Genius and Character of the Rev. Horace Holley*, 1828, p. 70, *et passim*. *Cf.* also Thomas Ashe, *Travels in America*, Newburyport, 1808, pp. 191-192. One of the few American institutions which Ashe found worthy of praise was Transylvania University, which, he said, gave a course much like that of English grammar schools, and graduated "young men, who are far from being contemptible scholars."

West.[165] Within half a dozen years this ambition had been achieved, for in 1824 the faculty of fifteen members contained such eminent men as Charles Caldwell and Daniel Drake, the leaders of the medical profession in the West; James Blythe, later president of Hanover College; Robert Hamilton Bishop, first president of Miami University; Mann Butler, the second historian of Kentucky; and Constantine Rafinesque, the celebrated scientist and cosmopolite. These men were not only eminent teachers but the editors of magazines, and authors of scores of books and pamphlets which formed no small part of such Western pioneer literature as was of solid value. The student body of over four hundred were drawn from fifteen different states, more than a third of them from outside Kentucky.[166] When Holley resigned, in 1827, the University, now embracing schools of medicine and of law together with the older departments of liberal studies, had graduated between six and seven hundred students.[167] And, though the sectarian and professional quarrels which helped force Holley's withdrawal were renewed from time to time until the final ruin of the old Transylvania was accomplished, the institution continued throughout the pioneer period to exercise a remarkable influence; perhaps the majority of Kentuckians of note during these years

[165] "This whole Western country," he wrote in 1818, "is to feed my seminary, which will send out lawyers, physicians, clergymen, statesmen, poets, orators, and *savans*, who will make the nation feel them" (Caldwell, *op. cit.*, p. 162).

[166] *A Catalogue of the Officers and Students of Transylvania University, Lexington, Kentucky, January, 1824.* This catalogue shows that nearly half the students were enrolled in the medical school, which remained, until near the end of the period, one of the best-known in the United States. Only twenty-seven students in a total of 404 were listed as members of the preparatory department.

[167] Caldwell, *op. cit.*, p. 210.

were at one time or another connected in some way with Transylvania.[168] By 1838, the medical college alone, which, soon after its establishment, or revival, by Holley in 1819-1820, had become the most prominent part of the University, had graduated over a thousand students and had given instruction to a total of not far from four times that number.[169]

Miami University at Oxford, Ohio, probably the second most influential institution of higher learning in the West during the period, did not rise to the rank of a college until 1824, when Robert Hamilton Bishop, a graduate of the University of Edinburgh, resigned his professorship in Transylvania to become the first president of the new institution. William Holmes M'Guffey, later famous as the author of a series of readers used throughout the Western and Southern states, was for some time one of its professors. Within five years the faculty had been increased to thirteen members.[170] Before 1840 the University had graduated more than two hundred and fifty students, representing a number of states.[171]

Other universities and colleges founded early in the period were too small to exert a marked influence on the life of the West of pioneer days. Ohio University, at Athens, though originally provided for in Congressional

[168] Thomas Speed, in preface to Robert Peter's *Transylvania University*, 1896.

[169] *Transylvania Catalogue of Medical Graduates, with an Appendix, Containing a Concise History of the School*, 1838, p. 3. The school of law had also prospered: according to the *Catalogue of the Transylvania Law Class; Session of 1839-40*, it had sixty-six students at that time.

[170] *Catalogue of the Officers and Students of Miami University*, 1829, p. 4.

[171] *Third Triennial Catalogue of the Officers and Graduates of Miami University, March A.D. 1840*, 1840, pp. 26-29. *Cf.* also *The Alumni and Former Student Catalogue of Miami University*, 1892.

grants to the Ohio Company and legally established in 1802 by the legislature of the North-West Territory as the American Western University, did not actually come into corporate existence until 1804 and was not opened until 1809. Thereafter its growth was small: at the end of the first twenty-five years of the century it had graduated not more than twenty-five students; and by 1840 the total was only 113.[172] The Territorial University at Vincennes, opened for instruction in 1810, soon lost its rank and its financial support through the action of the state legislature, which transferred its rights to the Indiana Seminary, at Bloomington, established in 1820.[173] The latter institution, opened in 1824, became Indiana College in 1828 and Indiana University ten years later. Its growth was so slow that in 1840 it had a student body, not counting persons enrolled as irregular or as in the preparatory department, of only thirty-three,[174] though the number of its alumni was then about sixty.[175] No other state universities were opened before the end of the period. Though the curiously pedantic scheme for what was at first called the Catholepistemiad, or University of Michigania,[176] was proclaimed by an act of the governor and judges of the Territory in 1817, the act which in reality established the Uni-

[172] George W. Knight and John R. Commons, *The History of Higher Education in Ohio*, 1891, pp. 13-25.

[173] Woodburn, *op. cit.*, pp. 33 and 75-76.

[174] *Catalogue of the Officers and Students in Indiana University, 1840-41*, p. 8.

[175] *The American Almanac*, for 1841, p. 153. By the end of 1840 there were sixty-four graduates (*Indiana University Bulletin*, IX, No. 5, June 1, 1911, *Register of Graduates*).

[176] Andrew C. McLaughlin, *History of Higher Education in Michigan*, 1891, pp. 29-40; and *Detroit Gaz.*, Sept. 12, 1817, and Jan. 22, 1819. There were to be thirteen didaxum, or professorships, ranging from that of anthropoglossica, or literature and philology, to that of catholepistemia, or universal science.

versity of Michigan was not passed until twenty years later, and the doors of the institution were not opened until 1841. The Detroit Branch of the University of Michigan had, however, been opened in 1838;[177] and about the same time other branches went into operation at Pontiac, Kalamazoo, and Monroe.[178] The University of Missouri was in 1840 legally established [179] but not yet open for students.

Near the end of the period, denominational colleges, which from that time were a striking feature of higher education in the West, were established in considerable numbers, usually upon endowments or current contributions wholly inadequate to make possible a high grade of collegiate instruction. Western Reserve College, opened in 1827, at Hudson, was controlled for many years by ministers of the Presbyterian or Congregational Church. Kenyon College, founded about the same time by Bishop Chase for the training of ministers of the Protestant Episcopal Church, represented the missionary zeal of prominent Englishmen. Illinois College, Presbyterian, founded in 1829 by a remarkable group of Yale men who were fired with missionary enthusiasm,[180] had grown within a decade to a faculty of five and a regular student body of thirty-nine.[181] Perhaps the most noted of the many Presbyterian colleges which were begun in the West during this period was the Lane Theological Seminary, also founded in 1829, of which Lyman Beecher was president from 1832. By

---

[177] *Detroit Free Press*, Apr. 24 and June 2, 1838.

[178] Blois, *op. cit.*, p. 131. For details of the history of the branches as well as of the University proper, see *University of Michigan Regents' Proceedings . . . 1837-1864*, 1915, *passim*.

[179] "University Report. Columbia, 29th October, 1840" (in *Journal of the Senate, . . . of the State of Missouri*, 11th General Assembly, 1841, pp. 427-428).

[180] Theron Baldwin, *Historical Sketch of the Origin, Progress, and Wants, of Illinois College*, 1832, p. 7; and Flagg, *op. cit.*, II, 55.

[181] *Catalogue of the Officers and Students of Illinois College*, 1838, pp. 4-6.

1840 it had about thirty students.[182] A secession from this school, occasioned by a bitter dispute on slavery, was an important influence in the growth of Oberlin Collegiate Institute, which was notable for its admission of negroes, and for the activities of its faculty in opposition to slavery. Hanover College, which had grown from a log cabin school founded by Presbyterians in 1827, had about forty students of college grade by 1840.[183] A remarkable feature of the growth of higher education in the West during the last decade of the period was the tendency of such religious bodies as Baptists and Methodists, who had earlier exhibited little interest in education and whose appeal had been seldom directed to the more intellectual part of the population, to equip themselves with colleges and seminaries intended primarily for the training of their ministers. The awakening of Baptist interest in an educational program was marked by the founding of Georgetown College (1829) and of the Granville Literary and Theological Institution (1831), which became Denison University. Indiana Asbury University, later DePauw, the first important Methodist college founded in the West, was not chartered till 1837 and had perhaps a dozen students of collegiate rank at the end of the period.[184] St. Louis University, which had its origin in a small Catholic seminary founded while Missouri was still a territory, was the result of Jesuit participation in higher education in the West. From 1829 to 1839, however, it had graduated only twelve students.[185]

Even the best of both non-sectarian and sectarian insti-

---

[182] *The American Almanac*, for 1841, p. 156.

[183] *Catalogue of the Officers and Students of Hanover College,* 1839, p. 9.

[184] *First Annual Catalogue of the Officers and Students of Indiana Asbury University*, 1839, pp. 8 and 12.

[185] Scharf, *op. cit.*, I, 861.

tutions of what was called higher education were in fact
seriously handicapped by frontier conditions; and the great
majority of the forty-eight colleges and universities which,
according to the census, were to be found in the Middle
West in 1840, were wholly incapable of giving instruction
of a high grade.  With a few exceptions they were very
nearly what Karl Postl, the German novelist and traveller,
called the best of them — nothing but names.[186]  The average establishment of the sort was justly described by
Henry Caswall, a sympathetic English observer, as

the infant college, just rising in the backwoods, with its
two or three teachers, themselves perhaps but lately
released from school; its twenty or thirty students sustain-
ing themselves by mechanical or agricultural labour, its
log buildings, its scanty salaries, and its library barely
supplied with the ordinary text books.[187]

The curriculum was often, however, a fair copy of that to
be found in the best Eastern colleges, with special stress
almost always put on the study of the classics; and a
number of the best Western institutions drew their
faculties partly or even largely from those of the East.  It
is significant, however, that the influence of Harvard, which
represented in the early nineteenth century the most
liberal thought of America, was scarcely perceptible in the
West, while the more conservative influence of Yale was
predominant, with Princeton and Hamilton Colleges also
well represented on Western faculties.  Except in Transylvania at the end of the first quarter of the nineteenth
century, where there were some signs of intellectual fer-
ment, almost the only evidence of what could be called
radical thought was the interest manifested by some faculties in the question of slavery.

---

[186] Karl Postl ("Charles Sealsfield"), *The United States of
North America as they are*, 1828, p. 105.

[187] Caswall, *op. cit.*, pp. 199-200.

Nor did the colleges reach any considerable part of the population of the new country. Though the total enrollment amounted in 1840, according to the census, to between four and five thousand, or more than one student for every thousand of the whole population, the greater part of this number were in preparatory departments engaged in the study of subjects commonly taught in the public schools or small academies. As for the number of graduates by 1840, it is extremely unlikely that it was equal to that of students enrolled in that year alone. Few of the Western colleges were at all effective until the last decade of the period. Though the number of students in 1840 — preparatory and irregular, as well as regular, college students — compared favorably with the enrollment of colleges in Eastern states as reported by the same census, it had been estimated ten years earlier that the proportion of students in college to the total population at that time was about one to twelve hundred in the Eastern states, while in the West it was only about one to six thousand.[188]

The teachers in both common schools and colleges were often ill-equipped to provide instruction. In the common schools, conditions were so primitive and chaotic that few experienced teachers of ability were tempted to remove to the West. In many communities, though not in all, persons who sought employment of this kind were, partly because of their own low level of intellectual attainment, without social standing. The difficulties which had to be met in conducting the pioneer schools, much like those of the southern Indiana later described by Edward Eggleston, served to make teaching so unattractive that in the backwoods communities this duty commonly fell to migratory adventurers with little or no fitness for the task.[189] Toward

---

[188] *The American Almanac*, for 1831, p. 169.

[189] An account of the characteristic adventures of this kind of pioneer teacher is to be found in the narrative of James Jaquith,

the end of the period, however, a distinct improvement was evident, when teachers began to regard their calling as a profession and to organize conventions and institutes for the discussion of pedagogical problems. In 1831 there met at Cincinnati the first General Convention of the Teachers of the Western Country; and from this meeting originated the Western Literary Institute and College of Professional Teachers, which was to exercise a very great influence in the evolution of the educational system of the West. The record of its proceedings affords convincing proof that a new era was at hand.[190]

In college teaching, though there must have been in the weaker institutions many men versed only in the rudiments of the subjects they professed to teach, conditions had, from the first, been much more favorable. The social standing and modest intellectual attainments of the average faculty were enough to mark them as men apart from the bulk of the pioneer people. Some able naturalists, such as Rafinesque, were drawn to the Western colleges by the

who, after working his way down the Ohio as a boat hand, turned his attention to the schools of Indiana and Kentucky. "I crossed the Ohio river," he says, "went into Indiana, and undertook a school. I had no difficulty, except being shut out at Christmas, agreeable to the custom of the country. If I had been acquainted with their customs, I should have resisted them awhile, then treated them with whiskey, and given them from Christmas to New Year's days." After teaching in two other settlements, he gained confidence in his attainments: "I did not doubt my ability to obtain a school in any part of the country. I travelled to Handing, Kentucky, about 130 miles distance. I undertook a school for three months, for $37. I agreed to take a colt in part pay." (*The History of James Jaquith*, third ed., 1830, pp. 29-30.) *Cf.* also Caroline M. Kirkland, *A New Home — who'll Follow?* 1839, pp. 94-96 and 301-305.

190 See *The Academic Pioneer*, Vol. I, *passim; The Annual Register of the Proceedings* . . . *1833*; and the six volumes of *Transactions* containing the proceedings of the Institute from the fourth to the tenth annual meeting (1834-1840), published from 1835 to 1841.

opportunity for the exploration of a new field; and men like Horace Holley, Charles Caldwell, R. H. Bishop, Charles Pettit McIlvaine, Lyman Beecher, Calvin Stowe, and Andrew Wylie were attracted by what they considered the vast opportunity for educational expansion in the West, and came with an ambition to transform the backwoods into a cultured community. Missionary zeal, sometimes sharply sectarian, sometimes entirely liberal, accounted for the presence on the frontier of such influential leaders.

## VIII

Libraries of the West before 1840 were mostly confined to the colleges. Among the finer collections of this kind was that of Transylvania, a large part of which was brought from Europe. It had grown from over two thousand volumes in 1830 to more than twice that number in 1840. Few colleges in the West, however, could boast even that number of books. Miami University had in 1840 a library about equal to that of Transylvania, while Ohio University had something over half that number, and Indiana University considerably less. Perhaps the largest library possessed by any institution of higher education in the West at the time was that of the Lane Theological Seminary, said to contain ten thousand volumes.[191] A contemporary estimate of the total number of volumes in Ohio college libraries about 1838 as thirty-four thousand was probably too large.[192]

In the older towns, subscription libraries, though founded earlier than most of the college libraries, grew very slowly. The Lexington Library, begun in 1795-1796, increased from fewer than eight hundred volumes in 1803 to

[191] For the data cited above, see *The American Almanac*, for 1831, p. 167; and for 1841, pp. 153 and 156.

[192] *Picture of Cincinnati*, for 1839, p. 66.

over six thousand in 1837.[193]  At Cincinnati attempts were
made as early as 1802 and again in 1806, in 1808, and in
1811 to organize similar associations; and in 1814 a circulating library of some three hundred volumes was opened.[194]
In later years many efforts to keep up reading rooms supplied only with periodicals failed; and, though toward 1840
there was some advanced sentiment in favor of establishing
a city library, two subscription collections, the Apprentices'
Library and the Young Men's Mercantile Library, were the
nearest approach to anything of the kind.[195]  The latter,
organized in 1835 and chartered in the following year, with
less than fifty members and about seven hundred volumes,
grew until it had in 1838 about twelve hundred volumes
and between three and four hundred members.[196]  In 1840
it had about fourteen hundred volumes, while the Apprentices' Library, many years older, had about two thousand.[197]
Such was the library equipment of the chief city in the
West.  The Louisville Public Library, the preliminary

[193] *A Catalogue of the Books, Belonging to the Lexington Library
Company; to which is Prefixed, a Concise Narrative of the Origin
and Progress of the Institution*, 1821, p. xv; and G. W. Ranck,
*History of Lexington Kentucky*, 1872, pp. 194-196.  *Cf.* also *The
Western Monthly Magazine*, II, 535 (Oct., 1834).

[194] *Liberty Hall*, Feb. 17, 1806, and July 17, 1811; *A Systematic
Catalogue of Books Belonging to the Circulating Library Society of
Cincinnati*, 1816, pp. 3-4; and Cist, *op. cit.*, p. 190.  In the meantime, libraries, usually of slight importance, were either established
or projected in many small towns of the West.  In Ohio alone 161
were incorporated before the end of 1840 (Edward A. Miller, "History of the Educational Legislation in Ohio from 1803 to 1850," in
*Ohio Archæological and Historical Publications*, XXVII, 135 [1919]).

[195] *Cinc. Daily Gaz.*, June 13, 1838.

[196] *A Catalogue of Books Belonging to the Young Mens'* [*sic*]
*Mercantile Library Association of Cincinnati*, n. d. (1838), p. 3.

[197] Cist, *op. cit.*, pp. 109-111.  *Cf.* also *Picture of Cincinnati*, for
1840, p. 63.  There is a considerable discrepancy between the two
accounts, which is perhaps due in part to the slight difference in dates.

organization of which had been effected by July, 1815, depended upon the contributions of stockholders and was for many years so feebly supported that it was scarcely able to exist.[198] St. Louis, which had a library of the sort in operation by 1824, was more successful in maintaining it. In 1825 the corporation already owned over a thousand volumes and had not far from two hundred share-holders. The collection came into being through donations of books by the share-holders; and a remarkably early municipal interest in such matters is proved by the fact that for a time at least the town authorities furnished a room for its use. By 1837 this library owned nearly four thousand volumes and seems to have had an annual income of between four and five hundred dollars.[199]

The growth of the press and of the book business in the West corresponded in general to the growth of popular education in the various states, and in less marked degree to the growth of the population. Many of the early presses printed not only newspapers, but pamphlets and books as well. Beginning with 1787, when *The Kentucke Gazette* was established at Lexington, a stream of original publications, as well as reprints, flowed from the Western press. *The Kentucke Almanack* for 1788, printed at the *Gazette* office in 1787 and published in January, 1788,[200] was one of the first publications other than a newspaper; but within slightly more than a year even a small volume of poetry seems to have been issued from this press.[201] Many pam-

---

[198] *The Western Courier*, July 13, 1815; and *Lou. Pub. Adv.*, Feb. 24, 1821, and Feb. 4, 1826.

[199] *Mo. Rep.*, Feb. 14 and 21, 1825; and Jan. 10, 1837.

[200] *The Kentucke Gazette*, Oct. 13, 1787, and Jan. 5, 1788.

[201] *Ky. Gaz.*, May 23, 1789, advertises *The Kentucky Miscellany*, by Thomas Johnson, Jun., which was probably, though not certainly, printed at the office of the *Gazette*. I have not been able to discover a copy of this edition of these poems; but, if I am right in supposing that it was printed in the West, it may possibly deserve the

phlets and a number of books of considerable bulk were to follow. From the office of *The Centinel of the North-Western Territory*, established at Cincinnati in 1793, little was to come aside from the *Laws of the Territory*, which appeared in 1798. *An Act Passed at the First Session of the Fourth Congress of the United States*, which, unless the imprint is false, was published at Detroit by John M'Call in 1796, seems to be the only evidence that a press existed in Michigan earlier than 1809; not even a successful newspaper was established there until nine years later. A printing office opened at Vincennes in 1804 produced nothing noteworthy except a remarkably long-lived newspaper. The St. Louis press, which had its beginning in the establishment, in 1808, of the *Missouri Gazette*, had, considering the importance of the town, a remarkably small share in the publishing activity of the pioneer period. The growth of the Western press in general, was, however, rapid; and as early as 1805 an association of printers and booksellers was formed, with John Bradford, of Lexington, as president.[202] Scores of presses, scattered throughout the West, printed periodicals, pamphlets, and books in considerable numbers; but the great bulk of publications of all sorts other than newspapers came from the publishing houses of Lexington and Cincinnati, and soon after 1820 the latter was beyond all comparison the greatest publishing center of the West. From the presses of this capital of the West many thousands of volumes were flowing as

honor, hitherto accorded to Adam Rankin's *A Process in the Transilvania Presbytery* (see W. H. Venable, *Beginnings of Literary Culture in the Ohio Valley*, 1891, p. 44), of being the first book both written and published in the West. In bulk, however, neither work was greatly superior to *The Kentucke Almanack*. They were in reality scarcely to be distinguished from what are usually called pamphlets.

202 *Ky. Gaz.*, Oct. 7, 1805.

early as 1831;[203] and by 1838 or 1839 probably half a million bound volumes were produced in a year, chiefly from the publishing houses of Truman and Smith, N. G. Burgess & Co., E. Morgan & Co., and U. P. James.[204] A large part of the entire output, however, consisted of schoolbooks, while the remainder were partly original works, partly reprints of standard works for Western consumption, and partly reproductions of current English publications (which were still unprotected by copyright). The quality of work done by these Western presses was, with a few exceptions, notoriously poor;[205] but the cost of importation from the East or from abroad was so great that the market was secure.

Of the 385 printing offices reported for the whole section in the census of 1840, Ohio had 159, or between a third and a half of the total, while Kentucky had fallen to fifth rank; and of fifty-seven binderies, Ohio had forty-one, or nearly four-fifths of the total, while Kentucky ranked fourth.

The whole output of the Western press, however, though perhaps surprisingly large for pioneer publishing houses, did not afford a large quota of books for a population of four millions. Even with the addition of what must have been a comparatively small amount of importations, the bulk of reading matter was not great. And as to the kind most in demand, it was clearly of controversial type, either

[203] *Niles' Weekly Register*, June 18, 1831. According to *The Cincinnati Directory, for the Year 1831*, p. 206, no less than 86,000 volumes, of which nearly a fourth were of original works, were issued from the Cincinnati press ''during the four months past.'' Within the same time, 243,200 printed sheets are said to have been issued by the periodical press.

[204] *Picture of Cincinnati*, for 1839, p. 70.

[205] For interesting comment, see *The North American Review*, XLVIII, 549-552 (Apr., 1839).

political or religious; and most of it appeared in the form of newspapers and pamphlets.[206]

## IX

While the West was painfully achieving the beginnings of culture, certain distinctly anti-cultural influences were also at work.  Of these, the most unmistakable was perhaps the activity of the great number of the lawless and vicious persons swept toward the frontier by the migratory stream.

It is true that accounts of this element in Western life were so highly colored by romancers that they grew into a kind of legend, not yet extinct.  Western writers, who protested against the unfriendly generalizations of travellers, did not hesitate to lure the reading public with stories of the prowess of backwoods outlaws.  Thus the adventures of the renegade Girtys were a favorite theme.  James Hall's *The Harpe's Head; a Legend of Kentucky* helped spread the fame of two of the most desperate of Western outlaws; and the title of the London edition, *Kentucky.  A Tale*, served to generalize this impression of Western char-

---

[206] The Westerners, according to James H. Perkins, one of the keenest observers of frontier life toward the end of the period, did not read ''as speculators and students, but as actors, as working men;  . . .  The truth is, that most persons in the West read very little upon any subject but elections; but of those who do, the majority, we believe, are readers upon religion.'' (*The Hesperian*, III, 455-456, Nov., 1839.) Timothy Flint's observations on Missouri would, in fact, apply, but with varying exactness, to the whole Middle West: '' The people here are not yet a reading people. Few good books are brought into the country. . . .  The people are too busy, too much occupied in making farms and speculations, to think of literature.'' (*Recollections of the Last Ten Years*, 1826, p. 185.)   John Bristed (*The Resources of the United States*, 1818, p. 432) thought Western reading largely confined to newspapers and political pamphlets.

acter in the public mind. Novels written by Easterners aided in popularizing similar themes. Hoffman's *Greyslaer*, for example, was partly based on the famous Beauchamp murder case in Kentucky, which was also the subject of two novels by William Gilmore Simms and even furnished some of the groundwork for Poe's "Politian"; and Bird's *Nick of the Woods* celebrated Roaring Ralph Stackpole and his race of "ring-tail roarers from Salt River."

But this emphasis on the boisterous crudity of the frontier, though too great, was not wholly unjust. Travellers who kept to the river highways became familiar with the rough, roistering boatmen and desperate adventurers who were everywhere in view. Popular legends grew up in the West around such doughty heroes as Mike Fink, king of river outlaws, whose reputation as a humorist and practical joker helped make him secure in the backwoodsman's esteem. His vivid rhetoric aroused particular admiration, and he was known for his stock challenge to a quarrel: "I can out-run, out-hop, out-jump, throw down, drag out and lick any man in the country. I'm a Salt-river roarer; I love the wimming and I'm chock full of fight." [207] The declaration of the Kentucky ruffians that they were "half horse, half alligator" early became a backwoods classic. A Western anthology of frontier sketches and anecdotes records the extraordinary ranting of one of this species who might well have been the prototype of some of Mark Twain's river men:

This is *me*, and no mistake! Billy Earthquake, Esquire, commonly called Little Billy, all the way from North Fork of Muddy Run! I'm a small specimen, as you see — a ramote circumstance, a mere yearling; but cuss me, if I ain't of the true 'imported breed,' and can whip any man in this section of country! Whoop! Won't *nobody*

[207] Ben Casseday, *Casseday's History of Louisville*, 1852, p. 81.

come out and fight me? . . . I'm the very infant that
refused its milk before its eyes were open, and called out
for a bottle of old Rye! W-h-o-o-p! I'm that little
Cupid![208]

The boatmen on the Ohio and Mississippi were, if we may
believe contemporary observers, the most riotous and lawless set of people in America.[209]   Nor did the steamboats
end the régime of the rougher boatmen of the early days.
While the new craft multiplied, flatboats on the Western
rivers remained as numerous as ever.[210]   Early travellers
also stressed the backwoodsmen's inclination for rough and
tumble fighting of a peculiarly disgusting kind — "tearing,
kicking, scratching, biting, gouging each others eyes out
by a dexterous use of a thumb and finger, and doing their
utmost to kill each other."[211]   Richard Weston's angry

[208] *The Cincinnati Miscellany*, II, 134-135 (Sept., 1845).

[209] See James Flint, *op. cit.*, p. 89; and Ferrall, *op. cit.*, p. 245.
*Cf.* also Evans, *op. cit.*, p. 156; and "R. B.," *op. cit.*, p. 128.  The
more charming side of the life of the boatmen is to be found faithfully recorded in the canvases of Caleb Bingham, an early Western
artist.   *Cf.* Fern Rusk Shapley, *George Caleb Bingham*, 1917, in
which several such pictures are reproduced.

[210] "R. B.," *op. cit.*, p. 127.   The total number of the different
kinds of boatmen increased, of course, very rapidly until after the
end of the pioneer period.   In 1838 it was estimated that there were
no less than fifty thousand boatmen on the Western waters, and they
were notorious both for their immorality and for the extent of their
influence on the population along the rivers and lakes (*Cinc. Daily
Gaz.*, Dec. 11, 1838).   In 1834 an attempt was made in the West
to establish a religious quarterly called *The Boatman's Magazine*,
and intended as an antidote to the flagrant viciousness of this class
of men.

[211] Fortescue Cuming, *Sketches of a Tour to the Western Country*,
1810, p. 118.   John Melish, who cannot be charged with malicious
overstatement, is one of the most convincing authorities on this
point (*op. cit.*, II, 180).   *Cf.* also James Flint, *op. cit.*, p. 114; John
Woods, *Two Years' Residence*, 1822, p. 132; Postl, *The Americans
as they are*, 1828, pp. 25-26; Thomas Hamilton, *Men and Manners*

characterization of Westerners as "one-eyed savages" [212] was manifestly far from the truth; and Faux's "intelligent old Kentucky planter" who informed the traveller that "the west has the scum of all the earth" and that "long ago it was said, when a man left other States, he is gone to hell, or Kentucky," [213] may well have been apocryphal. But, with due allowance for the credulity or malice of such observers, ample proof remains of the extreme crudity which was a commonplace of frontier life.

It is perhaps utterly impossible to determine what part of the religious activity of the time is to be counted on the side of anti-cultural influences. But, as for politics, it is clear that, while a remarkably widespread interest in current political issues served to sharpen the minds of the frontier partisans, the levelling influence of an almost fanatical democratic creed was everywhere felt. As a result, not only were the distinctions of social or official rank lightly held,[214] but there was little respect for cultural

in America, 1833, pp. 296-297; and The Cincinnati Miscellany, II, 135 (Sept., 1845). Additional evidence is offered by the Kentucky act of Feb. 10, 1798 (2 Litt. 10), section 10 of which provides severe penalties for those who are guilty of disabling a tongue or of slitting a nose, an ear, or a lip; or who purposely "pull or put out an eye, while fighting or otherwise" (William Littell and Jacob Swigert, A Digest of the Statute Law of Kentucky, 1822, II, 984-985). Cf. also The Revised Statutes of the State of Indiana, 1838, pp. 209-210 and 213 (sections 13 and 31, act of Feb. 10, 1831). In certain cases, at least, similar acts have remained in force to the present time, but without their original significance.

[212] Richard Weston, A Visit to the United States and Canada in 1833, 1836, p. 124.

[213] Faux, op. cit., p. 334.

[214] Ashe (op. cit., pp. 123-124) gives an amusing and characteristically overdrawn account of the democracy of the ex-army officers at Marietta in the early days of that settlement. Something of the same thing was, however, noted by numerous observers of Western life. The pride of the backwoodsmen in what they considered their

superiority.  The typical frontiersman felt a stolid pride in his disdain for intellectual attainment.  The few who possessed unusual culture were generally forced, if they wished to gain the confidence of their neighbors, to adapt themselves as rapidly as possible to the more primitive environment.  Louis Philippe, obliged to act as mediator in a backwoods tavern brawl, learned the spirit of Western democracy.[215]

Economic conditions, which also hindered the growth of culture, varied greatly in different parts of the West and changed rapidly with the passing of a few years.  Miserable villages, where large poverty-stricken families were crowded into log cabins, such as Zerah Hawley found in the Western Reserve,[216] were, however, much more characteristic of the early West than were opulent towns like Lexington; and the proportion of the population able to enjoy the comparative comfort of the large centers of culture was exceedingly small.  Conditions in the largest Western towns were indeed not widely different from those in Eastern towns;[217] but the economic as well as the social and cultural structure of the West as a whole offered a noticeable contrast.   "Life in the West," wrote a contemporary Eastern critic, "is certainly something different from any thing the world has ever seen anywhere else." [218]

---

social equality commonly displayed itself in rude familiarity which was offensive to conservative-minded travellers.  The dwellers along the waterways, for example, habitually annoyed passing boats with their impertinent questions, which often ended in rencounters of wit and blackguarding.

[215] Lewis Cass, *France, its King, Court, and Government*, 1840, p. 118.

[216] Zerah Hawley, *A Journal of a Tour*, 1822, pp. 54-59.

[217] Bristed, *op. cit.*, p. 431; and Martineau, *Society in America*, 1837, I, 139-140 and 234.

[218] *The North American Review*, XLIX, 271 (July, 1839).

## X

The reflection in literature of the vast phenomenon of the pioneer West is to be seen properly only in the great bulk of mediocre pamphleteering and journalism — and, to a much lesser extent, bookmaking — of men who wrote only incidentally to their participation in the economic, political, and religious turmoil which engaged almost their whole attention. The few self-conscious writers of the frontier, striving ineffectively for a certain artistic achievement, had their eyes fixed on an ideal rather than a reality. They yielded to the spell of a legend or looked beyond their own time to a future, in which they firmly believed, "when the mouth of the Columbia, or the head waters of the Missouri, shall be the seat of Empire and the abodes of the arts and refinement, and London and Paris may be as Nineveh and Babylon are." [219] James Hall, perhaps the most famous of contemporary writers in the West, had been lured to the new country by its suggestion of romance; and, though he came near achieving in fiction a picture of pioneer life of lasting value, he was never able to free himself from the glamour of the legend. "I shall never forget," he said,

the intense interest which I felt, while a boy, in gazing at the brawny limbs and sun-burnt features of a Kentuckian, as he passed through the streets of Philadelphia. The rough, hardy air of the stranger, the jaded paces of his nag, the blanket, bear-skin, and saddle-bags — nay, the very oil-cloth on his hat, and the dirk that peeped from among his vestments, are still in my eye; they bespoke him to be of distant regions, to have been reared among dangers, and to be familiar with fatigues. He strode among us with the step of an Achilles.[220]

Something of this same romantic haze obscured the vision

[219] Bishop, *An Introductory to a Course of Lectures on History*, 1823, p. 4.

[220] James Hall, *Letters from the West*, 1828, p. 5.

of almost every Western writer who attempted to add to his actual experience of life the element of imagination. The few who acquired a style of any charm were usually those who were thus incapable of picturing the real West.

The boldness of Western character may have been chivalrous, and the struggle of frontier life may have been, as Grund said, "the Trojan war of the Americans" with no Homer to immortalize it.[221]  As for Johnson's harsh prophecy of ages of barbarism in America, it was indeed inspired by no clear vision of what was soon to be accomplished by the advancing line of civilization along the Ohio and the Mississippi.  But the conquest of the Western wilderness was on the whole a business of prosaic economic causes exceedingly destructive and wasteful of the human material used in the process.  The price paid for the conquest was great for that generation, and it precluded for generations to come a generous devotion to cultural ideals. The achievement of this people was not at all of a stirring spiritual kind.  They had not come into a promised land flowing with milk and honey, to proclaim a new era of the human spirit.  An estimate of their achievement is after all, as Michel Chevalier said, a question of whether they did not fulfill "as perfectly as human nature is capable of doing, the mission which Providence has entrusted to them, that of acting as a nation of pioneers and subduers of the forest." [222]  The literature of the West which is most significant as a memorial of that era is the mediocre work of men whose chief usefulness was their part in that humble mission.

---

221 Francis Grund, *The Americans in their Moral, Social, and Political Relations*, 1837, I, 183.

222 Michel Chevalier, *Society, Manners and Politics in the United States*, 1839, p. 209.

# CHAPTER II

## TRAVEL AND OBSERVATION

It may, I think, be justly observed, that few books disappoint their readers more than the narrations of travellers. . . .

The greater part of travellers tell nothing, because their method of travelling supplies them with nothing to be told. He that enters a town at night, and surveys it in the morning, and then hastens away to another place, and guesses at the manners of the inhabitants by the entertainment which his inn afforded him, may please himself for a time with a hasty change of scenes, . . . but let him be contented to please himself without endeavouring to disturb others. Why should he record excursions by which nothing could be learned, or wish to make a show of knowledge, which, without some power of intuition unknown to other mortals, he never could attain? — Johnson, *The Idler*.

I read lately a small old brown French duodecimo, which I mean to send you by the first chance there is. The writer is a Capitaine Bossu; the production, a Journal of his experiences in "La Louisiane," "Oyo" (*Ohio*), and those regions, which looks very genuine, and has a strange interest to me, like some fractional Odyssey or letter. Only a hundred years ago, and the Mississippi has changed as never valley did: in 1751 older and stranger, looked at from *its* present date, than Balbec or Nineveh! — Letter from Carlyle to Emerson.

### I

The earliest literature of the West was the record left by travellers and observers who set down their impres-

sions of the new country and its people.  Among the large
number of such writers there were several important types,
which, however, were not always distinct: explorers;
adventurers among the Indians, often persons who experienced captivity; missionaries; scientists; foreign observers
of pioneer life; curious visitors from the old states to the
new; and, finally, alert observers among the Western
people themselves.

The explorers and adventurers, who were the first
Europeans to penetrate the valley of the Mississippi and of
the Great Lakes, usually followed the watercourses and
were impressed by the vastness and wildness of the country,
and the romantic spectacle of Indian life; but their records
are full too of difficulties with the savages, their own jeal-
ous rivalries, and their ambitious schemes to secure new
domains for European sovereigns and wealth for themselves.  Most of those who came during the seventeenth
century and early in the eighteenth were Frenchmen, and
some of their accounts were published only in the original
language; but usually important books were almost immediately translated into English.  Reports of the adventures
of Marquette and Joliet on the Mississippi were published
in Paris as early as 1681, but, strangely enough, seem not
to have appeared in English, except in garbled and abridged
form, until after 1840.  The various accounts of La Salle's
expeditions in the same valley during 1679-1687 were, on
the other hand, much more fortunate.  Though Hennepin's
*Description de la Louisiane*, published in Paris in 1683,
was not, apparently, reproduced in English till nearly two
hundred years later, his *Nouvelle decouverte*, which was
printed at Utrecht in 1697, appeared in London the next
year with a dedication to William III, from whom Hennepin
probably hoped for encouragement.  In this famous work,
translated into English as *A New Discovery of a Vast
Country in America*, Hennepin boldly repudiates his

earlier statement, in his *Description de la Louisiane*, that he had not been upon the lower Mississippi:

*I was then oblig'd to say nothing of the Course of the River* Meschasipi, *from the Mouth of the River of the* Illinois *down to the Sea, for fear of disobliging* M. la Salle, . . . *This Gentleman wou'd alone have the Glory of having discover'd the Course of that River: But when he heard that I had done it two Years before him, he cou'd never forgive me, tho', as I have said, I was so modest as to publish nothing of it.*[1]

He, accordingly, includes a narrative of his voyage from the mouth of the Illinois to the sea, appropriating for the purpose, as has often been pointed out, whatever he needed from a suppressed account of La Salle's journey of 1682 by Father Membré.[2] Hennepin, however, though he probably surpassed all other explorers of the West in the sheer audacity of his claims, was by no means the last of them to be convicted of falsehood. *A New Discovery* also includes not only an account of Hennepin's adventures on the upper Mississippi and of La Salle's last expedition, but an abridged version of Marquette's narrative of his Mississippi voyage of 1673, together with comments on Indian manners and customs.

In the same year with the English edition of Hennepin's book, Tonson and other London publishers brought out a translation from the French called *An Account of Monsieur de la Salle's Last Expedition and Discoveries in North America. Presented to the French King, and Published by the Chevalier Tonti, Governour of Fort St. Louis, in the Province of the Islinois.* The author, whoever he may have

---

[1] *A New Discovery*, 1698, preface.

[2] For early echoes of the debate on Hennepin's veracity, see *The North American Review*, XLVIII, 78-81 (Jan., 1839), and XLIX, 258-262 (July, 1839), in which Hennepin's account is attacked; and *The United States Magazine and Democratic Review*, V, 394-405 (Apr., 1839), where Hennepin is defended.

been — Tonti disclaimed responsibility for the work[3] — described Louisiana as a kind of paradise. Various adventures of La Salle on the Illinois and Mississippi, not simply those of his last expedition, are recorded; and the principal narrative ends with Tonti's discovery that La Salle's own men had murdered the great leader. Much the same story, given from another point of view, appeared at London in 1714 as *A Journal of the Last Voyage Perform'd by Monsr. de la Sale, . . . Written in French by Monsieur Joutel, a Commander in that Expedition; and Translated from the Edition just Publish'd at Paris*. Still another echo of the fame of La Salle's exploits is heard in the somewhat earlier *New Voyages to North-America* (1703) of Baron Lahontan, who, like Hennepin, deserves the distinction of being a kind of French Sir John Mandeville.[4] Lahontan was peculiarly fortunate in falling in with the chief actors in the La Salle story, which was already known to the public. On the Great Lakes, the author, according to his narrative, encountered some of La Salle's men, whom he suspected of concealing their commander's death; and later, in the Illinois country, he rejoined Tonti, who had accompanied him on his way to the Western country. But these are by no means the only unusual experiences Lahontan records. After much journeying about the shores of Lake Huron, he travelled, by way of the Fox and Wisconsin, to the

---

[3] Pierre Charlevoix, *Histoire et description generale de la Nouvelle France*, 1744 (Nyon Fils), II, 260.

[4] Of Lahontan's narrative, Charlevoix (*op. cit.*, I, "Liste des auteurs," p. lv) says: "En effet presque tous les noms propres y sont estropiés, la plûpart des faits y sont défigurés, & l'on y trouve des épisodes entiers, qui sont des pures fictions, tel qu'est le voyage sur *la Riviere Longue*, aussi fabuleuse que l'Isle *Barataria*, dont Sancho Pansa fut fait le gouverneur." For a biographical study of Lahontan, see J.-Edmond Roy, "Le baron de Lahontan," in *Proceedings and Transactions of the Royal Society of Canada for the Year 1894*, 1895, Vol. XII, "Mémoires Section I," pp. 63-192.

Mississippi, and thence up a great and mysterious river flowing from the west at a high latitude. Later he made explorations on the Missouri River, and a voyage to the mouth of the Ohio, finally passing up the Illinois and returning, through the Lakes, to Montreal.

The accounts of the exploits of La Salle and his contemporaries are, in their subject matter, the most fascinating of Western travel records — full of action and containing the earliest description of a great country which still had about it an air of mystery. The chief actors were engrossed in schemes of vast colonial or commercial expansion, which, in spite of their petty intrigues, should make them in the eyes of the reader men of heroic mould. La Salle, especially, whose enemies, in ridicule of his courageous attempts to find a passage to the Pacific and to China, gave the nickname of La Chine to his village on the St. Lawrence, ought to stand out as an impressive figure. It is disappointing, therefore, to find the accounts contained in the travel books of that time, not only tedious and confused, for the most part, but, for English readers, marred by the slovenly hand of translators who could hardly have been better than booksellers' hacks.

Somewhat akin to Hennepin and Lahontan, Bossu, "Captain in the French Marines," deserves fame as an entertaining teller of travel stories, which added to the already considerable sum of wonders that imaginative adventurers had discovered in the Western wilderness.[5] Carlyle's enthusiastic recommendation of Bossu's "fractional Odyssey" to Emerson testified to the French writer's love of the

[5] The pseudo-scientific interest of this school of travellers is well illustrated by Bossu in his account of the big bones discovered in the neighborhood of the Ohio. These, he conjectures, are the remains of seven elephants which perished in the swamps after making their way thus far from the mainland of Asia. Louisiana, therefore, probably adjoins that continent. (*Travels*, 1771, I, 179-180.)

picturesque and dramatic.[6]  The *Travels through that Part
of North America formerly Called Louisiana* (1771) was
intended, as the author states in the preface of the French
original, to give pleasure as well as instruction; and the
popularity of this account of his first two visits (extending
over the years 1751-1762) is indicated by the several
editions which appeared.  A separate narrative of a third
visit (in 1770-1771) followed, but was not, apparently,
translated into English.

In marked contrast with the vagaries of Hennepin,
Lahontan, and Bossu, were the accurate and thorough
accounts of Indian life contained in Charlevoix's monumental *Histoire et description generale de la Nouvelle
France, avec le journal historique d'un voyage* (1744). The
*Journal historique*, which the Dodsleys issued in two volumes as *Journal of a Voyage to North-America* (1761), is,
like the remainder of the work, largely on Canada, but contains an account of some exploration to the southward and
of a voyage down the Mississippi.  Le Page du Pratz,
whose title, *Histoire de la Louisiane* (1758), was significantly rendered by his English translators as *The History
of Louisiana, or of the Western Parts of Virginia and Carolina* (1763),[7] included in his book "a description of the
countries that lye on both sides of the River Missisipi: with
an account of the settlements, inhabitants, soil, climate,
and products"; but the most interesting part of the work
is what purports to be an account taken down verbatim by
the author from the recital of Moncacht-apé, a Yazoo
Indian, giving the story of his journey, first to the

———

6 Carlyle to Emerson, July 8, 1851 (*The Correspondence of Thomas
Carlyle and Ralph Waldo Emerson 1834-1872*, ed.  Charles Eliot Norton, 1886, II, 227-228).

7 The long preface of the English edition is largely an argument
urging the policy of immediate settlement of the Mississippi Valley
by the English.

Atlantic, by way of the Ohio River, and then to the Pacific, by way of the Missouri.[8]

British and colonial interest in exploration of the West had been forecast in such writings as *A Full and Impartial Account of the Company of Mississipi* (1720), in French and English, and Daniel Coxe's *A Description of the English Province of Carolana, by the Spaniards Call'd Florida, and by the French La Louisiane* (1722); and not quite thirty years later Christopher Gist had made his famous journey for the Ohio Company "began from Col. Cresap's, at the *old town on Potomack river, Maryland,* October 31, 1750," and "continued *down the Ohio,* within 15 *miles of the Falls,*" the account of which was published in 1776 in *A Topographical Description,* by Thomas Pownall. But with the Seven Years' War (1756-1763), which brought about the transfer of all former French territory east of the Mississippi to Great Britain, this interest began to be much more important. Robert Rogers, an American in the British service, who took over Detroit from the French in 1760, set down in *A Concise Account* his first-hand knowledge of the region of the Great Lakes; and in his *Journals* he told the story of military expeditions in the course of which he explored the shores of Erie and Huron and passed from Detroit to Pittsburg by the regular route through Ohio, visiting the Delaware Indian towns on the Muskingum. Colonel Croghan's "Journal" of a journey on the Ohio in the summer of 1765, one of the earliest accounts in English of the heart of the Western country, probably did not appear in print until 1831.[9] Philip Pittman's *The Present State of the European Settlements on the Missi-*

8 Le Page du Pratz, *The History of Louisiana,* 1763, pp. 122-129.

9 In Featherstonhaugh's *The Monthly American Journal of Geology and Natural Science,* Vol. I, No. 6 (Dec., 1831); reprinted by Mann Butler, *A History of the Commonwealth of Kentucky,* 1834, pp. 365-376.

*sippi* (1770) contained his observations on the Illinois and Missouri country, with a collection of French official documents; and about the same time the richness of the Illinois country was described in *A Voyage to North America, Perform'd by G. Taylor, of Sheffield, in the Years 1768, and 1769* (1771), which, though it devotes little space to the West, was one of the first of many writings recommending the prairies for English colonization.

A more interesting account, however, is the *Travels through the Interior Parts of North-America, in the Years 1766, 1767, and 1768*, which, though challenged by a number of early critics, generally passed, until recently, as the work of Jonathan Carver.[10] This book, which is in fact at least partly a compilation from earlier travels, purports to be a narrative of Carver's journey by way of the Fox and Wisconsin Rivers to the Mississippi and its tributaries, and his extensive explorations farther west. After the manner of Lahontan, Carver, according to the account, ascended a river emptying into the Mississippi from the west, and domiciled himself among the Indians, enjoying a residence of no less than seven months among the friendly Naudowessies. Here and elsewhere he gathered his materials for a commentary on the "Origin, Manners, Customs, Religion, and Language of the Indians," which was an

---

[10] See Edward G. Bourne, in *The American Historical Review*, XI, 287-302 (Jan., 1906). It is here pointed out that both Keating (*Narrative of an Expedition to the Source of St. Peter's*, 1824, I, 323-324) and Schoolcraft ("Journal," under date of Apr. 9, 1823) had challenged Carver's veracity, Schoolcraft even naming Charlevoix and Lahontan as the sources from which whole passages had been copied nearly verbatim. It is also suggested that the actual compiler of Carver's *Travels* in its present form may have been Dr. John Coakley Lettsom. For an attempt to show that Bourne has overstated the case against Carver, see Milo M. Quaife, "Critical Evaluation of the Sources for Western History," in *The Mississippi Valley Historical Review*, I, 167-184 (Sept., 1914).

almost indispensable part of Western travel books on the French plan. Lack of supplies for trading with the Indians having caused him to abandon more ambitious travels, the explorer made his way to the shore of Lake Superior and thence to the Falls of St. Mary, Michilimackinac, and Detroit.

After the purchase of Louisiana by the United States, in 1803, the American government turned to the exploration of the new territory, and was responsible for several expeditions, the records of which form a bulky contribution to the literature of travel, but are mainly concerned with the country on the headwaters of the Missouri and beyond the Rocky Mountains. The Lewis and Clark expedition (1804-1806), which marked the beginning of this era, and from which numerous travel accounts, many of them spurious, were to flow, was especially calculated to direct public attention to the Far West and dealt with the Middle West only incidentally. Zebulon Montgomery Pike's voyages and journeys of 1805-1807 in not quite successful quest of the sources of the Mississippi and into the Spanish Southwest, were likewise, as the author asserts, performed by order of the government; but the circumstance that General Wilkinson alone was responsible for the order, aroused suspicion that the expedition into New Spain was designed to aid the Spanish intrigues in which Wilkinson was involved.[11] *An Account of a Voyage up the Mississippi*, compiled from Pike's journal, appeared two or three years in advance of Pike's record of this and his other travels as published in *An Account of Expeditions* (1810). To the same group of travels belong Major Stephen Long's two expeditions of 1819-1820 and 1823, recorded in books by Edwin James and by William Keating. The first journey, from Pittsburg to the Rockies, afforded

---

[11] *Cf.* Theodore Roosevelt, *The Winning of the West*, 1908, VI, 178.

a mass of scientific and other data on the country along the Ohio, Mississippi, and Missouri Rivers; but was mainly concerned with the region further west and south. The Lewis and Clark explorations were the pattern of Long and his associates. "The Instructions of Mr. Jefferson to Capt. Lewis, which are printed in his travels, will," it was stated in Long's orders from the government, "afford you many valuable suggestions, of which as far as applicable, you will avail yourself." Keating's account, the *Narrative of an Expedition to the Source of St. Peter's River, Lake Winnepeek, Lake of the Woods*, compiled from the notes of Long, Say, Keating, and Colhoun, with important appendices by Say and Schweinitz, describes the country traversed — Ohio, Indiana, Illinois, Wisconsin, and the Lake region farther northwest — with much attention to geology, zoology, and botany, as well as to the customs and language of the Indians.

The characteristic stress by writers of this group on observations of scientific interest is also noticeable in several accounts of this kind by Henry Rowe Schoolcraft. His *Narrative Journal of Travels* records an expedition made in 1820, under the direction of Governor Cass, to search for the sources of the Mississippi, during which the author acted as official mineralogist. The same writer's *Travels in the Central Portions of the Mississippi Valley* was the result of a journey made the following year from Detroit to Chicago, not by one of the usual routes, but by Lake Erie, the Maumee, the Wabash, and the Ohio to Shawnee-town; thence overland to St. Louis; and finally up the Mississippi and the Illinois. Another journey which he made in 1832 for Governor Cass and for the War Department — this time to pacify and to study the Northwest Indians — is described in his *Narrative of an Expedition through the Upper Mississippi to Itasca Lake, the Actual*

*Source of this River*, in which he records what later proved to be the genuine discovery of the source of the Mississippi. The interest which American explorers such as Pike, Long, and Schoolcraft exhibited in the problem of determining the origin of that river, was emulated in the more romantic adventures of the Italian, Constantino Beltrami, whose *A Pilgrimage in Europe and America* (1828) contains a bitter attack on Major Long. Beltrami, according to his own account, fell in with Long's expedition by chance at Ft. St. Peter and accompanied it for a time, but, after harsh treatment by that officer, separated from him. Later, continuing his independent explorations, Beltrami, as he declares, had the good fortune to discover, in what he named Lake Julia, the "most northern sources of the Mississippi — sources till now unknown."

## II

Little resembling the bitter hatred of the pioneer settlers of the West for the Indians is to be found in the travel accounts of the early explorers. Often welcomed by the savages as objects of curiosity, or as purveyors of luxuries hitherto unknown to the natives, these travellers usually saw the better side of Indian character. Nor was there, on the other hand, a marked predisposition on the part of such travellers to discover in the savage an ideal. Over-wrought narrative with excursions into the purely marvelous was common, and bold generalizations on the magnificence of the vast wilderness of the West were enough to make America a legend for European readers; but descriptive detail was nearly always scanty and ineffective, and the sentimental interpretation of savage life was scarcely known until the end of the eighteenth century. It would be easy, therefore, to overemphasize the influence of such accounts on the growth of the romantic tradition of Rous-

seau[12] and Chateaubriand, which pictures the Indian as the
innocent child of the forest, living an enchanted existence
under the spell of the beauty of nature until his paradise
is violated by the white man. And, as for the influence
exerted by this romantic fiction, in its turn, it clearly was
much more potent in Europe than in America. During
a period of sentimentality in European literature, it was
no doubt responsible for the substitution of legend for
fact in the minds of many readers and even induced many
victims to emigrate to America. There were also, to be
sure, some actual travellers or even settlers who remained
for a time under the influence of this illusion. H. M.
Brackenridge's account of Dr. Saugrain and the two
French philosophers is an authentic instance: when the
three men, descending the Ohio, saw a party of warriors
approaching in a canoe, the philosophers made signs for
them to approach; whereupon the savages tomahawked the
two Frenchmen, while Saugrain, who had a better idea of
Indian character, defended himself with pistols and escaped
by swimming to the shore.[13] But usually only those
who, like Chateaubriand and Tocqueville, had scarcely
come in contact with the savages, put into their travel
accounts a picture of the sentimental charm of savage life.
As for the travels of Chateaubriand, who, in *Atala*, pictures
Chactas reciting his story to René while their peroguay
glides along the beautiful Ohio and the moon is diffus-
ing its light over the wilderness of Kentucky, it seems
unlikely that his quest of the Northwest Passage led
him farther west than Niagara; and in all probability he

[12] For a valuable study emphasizing the influence of travel literature on Rousseau, see Gilbert Chinard, *L'Amérique et la rêve
exotique dans la littérature française au XVIIe et au XVIIIe siècle*,
1913, pp. 337-362, *et passim*.

[13] H. M. Brackenridge, *Recollections of Persons and Places in the
West*, n. d. (1834), p. 44.

never beheld the Ohio — and much less the tropical jungle which he described as existing on the banks of the Mississippi.[14]

Unfortunately, however, not only Chateaubriand's sentimentality, but his eloquence as well, was lacking in the writers who, following the early explorers, created the considerable body of travel literature in which the tale of adventures, and, commonly, captivity, among the Indians is the most important matter. Usually such accounts were mere pamphlets containing little more than a bare statement of the events leading to captivity, of the route over which the captive was taken by the savages, and of the atrocities which were witnessed or experienced, with meagre remarks on Indian customs interspersed. Geographical details were naturally confused; and, except in cases where ample testimony is to be had in favor of the narrator, the authenticity of the account in general may be a matter of doubt. From the time of the French and Indian War the West began to appear commonly as the setting of such relations by American colonists, and before the end of that century the number was considerable. Among the earliest was *A Plain Narrative of the Uncommon Sufferings, and Remarkable Deliverance of Thomas Brown, of Charlestown, in New-England; who Returned to his Father's House the Beginning of Jan. 1760, after having been Absent Three Years and about Eight Months.* The journey here recorded

---

[14] The falsity of Chateaubriand's descriptions and, to some degree, the deception which he wished to practice were obvious to the more critical American readers, almost, if not quite, from the first (cf. *The American Quarterly Review*, II, 460, Dec., 1827). More recently Joseph Bédier (*Études critiques*, 1903, pp. 127-294) has shown convincingly the slender basis of fact underlying the Chateaubriand tradition. See also Chinard, "Notes sur le voyage de Chateaubriand en Amérique," *University of California Publications in Modern Philology*, IV, 269-349 (Nov. 10, 1915).

— from New England to Canada; thence to the headwaters of the Ohio; down the Ohio to the Mississippi; and, finally, back to Montreal and to New England — is not unusual in length. Of the Indian captivities which for a time increased greatly in number with the beginning of Westward emigration, a fair example is afforded by *A Narrative of the Incidents Attending the Capture, Detention, and Ransom of Charles Johnston, of Botetourt County, Virginia, who was Made Prisoner by the Indians, on the River Ohio, in the Year 1790; together with an Interesting Account of the Fate of his Companions, Five in Number, one of whom Suffered at the Stake.* According to the author of this account, not published till 1827, it contains the true version of events which Rochefoucauld had reported inaccurately in his book on America. *A Journal of the Adventures of Matthew Bunn* (1796) is a famous narrative belonging to the same period. Both the French and Indian War and the movement toward the frontier are in the background of *An Account of the Remarkable Occurrences in the Life and Travels of Col. James Smith, (now a Citizen of Bourbon County, Kentucky)*, which was printed at Lexington in 1799.

The War of 1812, in the Western campaigns of which the Indians had an important part, was the signal for a third series of narratives — recounting the experiences of soldiers, like Adam Walker, the author of *A Journal of Two Campaigns* (1816); or of frontier settlers, like Mrs. Hannah Lewis and Mrs. Eliza Swan, who were carried away into captivity. A decade and a half later public indignation was aroused against the Sac and Fox Indians, who were the last to oppose the advance of immigrants in the West, by such accounts as the *Narrative of the Capture and Providential Escape of Misses Frances and Almira Hall* (1832) and a *Narrative of the Captivity and Providential*

*Escape of Mrs. Jane Lewis* (1833), the latter a timely adaptation of the much earlier story of Mrs. Hannah Lewis.

Such were the usual narratives of Indian captivity. A few, however, stand out either as exceptionally daring fictions or as unusual attempts to supply a mass of data on Indian life. A striking example of the former type is *A Surprising Account of the Captivity and Escape of Philip M'Donald & Alexander M'Leod, of Virginia, from the Chickkemogga Indians. And of their Great Discoveries in the Western World, from June 1779, to January 1786* (1794). Their journey through the Ohio country is only the beginning of their wanderings, which take them to a marvelous island of the sea, and later to St. Petersburg, whence they return to America. Perhaps equally remarkable, however, were the experiences which Charles Dennis Rusoe d'Eres described in his *Memoirs* (1800). Falling into the hands of the "Scanyawtauragahrooote" Indians, D'Eres was carried from Quebec to Michilimackinac, then down the Red River, "which takes its rise from Lake Superior, and runs a southwesterly course very rapidly." He continued down this river, he says, forty days. During his captivity of eleven years he saw Tartarrac in New Spain; discovered monkeys; and enjoyed numerous strange adventures before his safe return to Detroit, where the inhabitants took him for an Indian. Don Alonzo Decalves' *New Travels to the Westward*, of which what purported to be a fourth edition appeared in 1796, is likewise full of remarkable occurrences. After a voyage of a month up the Mississippi from New Orleans, Decalves and his two companions set out toward the Far West, and, crossing the "Sublime Mountains," discovered a land inhabited by a nation of white Indians. In recrossing the mountains they witnessed a terrific volcanic eruption which set fire to the prairies. Returning in safety, however, to the Mississippi, they reached New Orleans after thirteen days and nights of constant rowing.

Much more plausible accounts of the Indians appeared in the comparatively voluminous narratives of John Dunn Hunter, John Tanner, and James O. Pattie. Hunter's *Manners and Customs of Several Indian Tribes Located West of the Mississippi* (1823), which was published in England the same year as *Memoirs of a Captivity among the Indians of North America, from Childhood to the Age of Nineteen*, is written, notwithstanding the author's declaration that he had been with the Indians from so early a time that he knew nothing either of his place of nativity or of his parents, in a style discovering something of the easy simplicity of Defoe. This unusually interesting account, telling of the migration of the tribe from the Illinois country beyond the Mississippi; of the eloquence of Te-cum-seh's address to the Osages, among whom Hunter was fortunate enough to be at the time; and of the author's meeting with Daniel Boone, was, however, an easily detected falsehood.[15] Although scarcely less unusual than Hunter's book, the story of John Tanner's captivity and thirty years of residence among the Indians, as recorded by Edwin James, is authentic;[16] and Tanner himself was employed by Henry Rowe Schoolcraft as a government interpreter at Sault Ste. Marie. Likewise *The Personal Narrative of James O. Pattie* (1831), filled with extra-

---

[15] An account of the unmasking of Hunter, together with a bibliography of the controversy down to 1827, is given in *The American Quarterly Review*, VIII, 113-115 (Sept., 1830). See also especially *The North American Review*, XXII, 53-119 (Jan., 1826), and the *Detroit Gaz.*, Jan. 31, 1826. Governor Cass, of Michigan, was an implacable foe of impostors and of such writers as insisted upon a sentimental view of Indian character.

[16] *The American Quarterly Review*, VIII, 108-134 (Sept., 1830). *Cf.* also James Hall, *Sketches of History, Life, and Manners, in the West*, 1835, I, 6.

ordinary adventures which occurred in the course of this
Kentucky hunter's journey of six years' duration from
St. Louis through Spanish North America, is vouched for
by its editor, Timothy Flint.

Among more sober accounts of the Indians, several, such
as Schoolcraft's, may better be regarded as scientific
studies. Of those which are unmistakably books of travel,
none is more delightful than H. M. Brackenridge's *Journal
of a Voyage up the River Missouri* (1816), the record of a
journey he made in company with Manuel Lisa, of the
Missouri Fur Company. The excitement of the race to
overtake the boats of Lisa's rival, Wilson P. Hunt; the
danger from the hostile Sioux; the violent quarrel between
Lisa and Hunt when the expeditions met far up the Missouri; and the excellent sketches of Indian life which
Brackenridge put into his book, give it unusual charm.
Valuable detailed descriptions of Indian life on the Great
Lakes some twenty years later are to be found in books by
Chandler Gilman and Thomas L. McKenney. The latter
was also the author, with James Hall, of a voluminous
pictorial *History of the Indian Tribes of North America.*

## III

Much attention was also devoted to the Indians by the
missionaries, who, from the time of the earliest explorers
and adventurers, had travelled through the new country in
an endeavor to gain converts among the savages. The last
journey of Marquette into the Illinois country was made
for the purpose of planting a mission. Hennepin was a
Récollet priest, and Charlevoix belonged to the Jesuit
order; but Hennepin was rather an adventurer than a missionary, and Charlevoix's interest was that of a historian
and observer.[17] The zeal of the missionary is much more

17 For a number of accounts by French missionaries, not trans-

---

striking in the simple narratives of the labors of John Heckewelder and of other Moravian teachers of the Delaware Indian communities on the Muskingum. Heckewelder's relation of a journey to the Wabash River, published in German as early as 1797, was not printed in English till after 1840. But the same author's history of the Indian nations of Pennsylvania and neighboring states was published in 1819; and *A Narrative of the Mission of the United Brethren among the Delaware and Mohegan Indians, from its Commencement, in the Year 1740, to the Close of the Year 1808*, also the work of Heckewelder, appeared in 1820. Heckewelder's implicit faith in the natural goodness of his Indians aroused the sharp criticism of those who, like Lewis Cass, were bent upon destroying the romantic conception of savage life; and it was asserted that the Uncas and Pawnee Hard-Heart of Cooper's novels, who had no living prototype in American forests, derived their false glamour from the accounts of the Moravian missionary,[18] who had known only a small group of Indians living under conditions which were not at all characteristic. No doubt the views of Heckewelder continued to exert a powerful influence, especially upon those who were interested in propagating the church among the Indians. The Rev. Calvin Colton, for example, attempted a "Vindication of the American Indians from the Charge of being Savages,"[19] and, like a number of other theorists

lated into English until after 1840 and therefore not included in the present study, see *The Jesuit Relations and Allied Documents*, ed. R. G. Thwaites, 1896-1901.

[18] See, in *The North American Review*, XXVI, 366 ff. (Apr., 1828), Cass's review of William Rawle's "A Vindication of the Rev. Mr. Heckewelder's History of the Indian Nations," which had appeared in the *Memoirs of the Historical Society of Pennsylvania*, I, Part ii, pp. 258-275 (1826).

[19] See *Tour of the American Lakes, and among the Indians of the North-West Territory*, 1833, I, 109-121.

of the time, was willing to believe that the Indians were descendants of the ancient Israelites.

Among other missionaries who visited the Delawares, but whose accounts, though published earlier, did not compare in influence with Heckewelder's, were Charles Beatty, David Jones, and David Maccluer. Beatty's *The Journal of a Two Months Tour; with a View of Promoting Religion* (1768) tells of his journey to the Muskingum, where he was received in audience by the King of the Delawares. Jones, the author of *A Journal of Two Visits Made to Some Nations of Indians on the West Side of the River Ohio* (1774), was a devout New Jersey minister who travelled on the Ohio in company with George Rogers Clark and Thomas Hutchins. He made a futile attempt to preach to the Shawnee tribe at Chillicothe and among the Delawares on the Muskingum, where he visited the Moravian mission. "An Abstract of the Journal of a Mission to the Delaware Indians, West of the Ohio," [20] by Maccluer, likewise records a missionary journey to the Muskingum Valley. A remarkable example of later missionary effort among the tribes which remained on reservations surrounded by white settlers, is narrated in J. B. Finley's *History of the Wyandott Mission* (1840), where the Indian, partly divested of his savagery, appears in somewhat the same guise of simplicity and helpless innocence as in Heckewelder's earlier account.

Less notable for narrative interest, but of some significance as showing the point of view of a special group of observers, are the travel accounts by preachers of various sects, arriving in the West, for the most part during the first forty years of the nineteenth century, from the East or from England, and seeking to establish their creeds, or

[20] In Eleazar Wheelock's *A Continuation of the Narrative of the Indian Charity-school, Begun in Lebanon, in Connecticut; now Incorporated with Dartmouth-College*, 1773, pp. 44-68.

to secure information on the state of the church, among
the white settlers, who had soon largely replaced the
Indians as objects of missionary zeal.  Of the early records
of this kind, perhaps the most important is *The Journal*
(1821) of Bishop Francis Asbury, who visited Kentucky
and Ohio many times from 1790 to 1815, devoting himself
to the establishment of Methodism.  Religious conditions
in the Ohio Valley of 1810 are reflected in the dreary pages
of *The Life, Experience, and Travels of John Colby,
Preacher of the Gospel* (1838) ; and the same part of the
West is described in *The Christian Traveller* (1828), a
much more valuable account, by Isaac Reed, a Presbyterian preacher, whose observations cover a period of about
nine years.  Perhaps no book of this kind contains a franker
statement of the moral and cultural conditions which were
then to be found in the smaller towns of Indiana and
Kentucky.   Other records of missionary tours by Eastern
churchmen are to be found in such books as Schermerhorn
and Mills's *A Correct View* (1814), Mills and Smith's
*Report of a Missionary Tour* (1815), and Bela Jacobs's *A
Voice from the West* (1833).   The observations of the
deputies from English churches who travelled through
both the Eastern and Western parts of the United States
were presented to American readers in *A Narrative of the
Visit to the American Churches* (1835), by Andrew Reed,
which met with the disapproval of the too sensitive Western
reviewers;[21] and in *The Baptists in America* (1836), by
F. A. Cox and J. Hoby.

## IV

The zeal of the missionary of religion was scarcely greater
than that of those travellers who, about the beginning of
the nineteenth century, began to make scientific researches

---

[21] See *The Western Monthly Magazine*, IV, 276-281 (Oct., 1835).

on the Western frontier. To the botanists, geologists, and zoologists, the new country was a land of promise offering a variety of attractions only superficially noted by early explorers. Before the end of the preceding century, the botanist André Michaux had made an extensive tour into the wilderness; and, of the accounts of scientific travellers which early appeared in English, the *Travels to the Westward of the Allegany Mountains* (1805) and *The North American Sylva* (1819), by his son, François André Michaux, are among the most important. The *Travels* is a narrative, together with much observation on Western people, of the incidents of a journey through Ohio and Kentucky in 1802, made, as the author states, for the purpose of examining forests and agriculture under the auspices of the French Minister of the Interior. The purely scientific record of his explorations is to be found in the *Sylva*. John Bradbury, the English botanist, also records in his *Travels in the Interior of America* (1817) much valuable comment on the Western country and its people; but perhaps a more attractive feature of his work is his narrative of a voyage up the Missouri in 1811, a part of which he made in company with the members of Wilson P. Hunt's overland Astorian expedition. His book, like that of H. M. Brackenridge, with whom he returned to St. Louis, has something of the atmosphere of adventure which belonged to the days of the fur traders on the Missouri. Thomas Nuttall, who had accompanied Bradbury on the Missouri River journey[22] and who had, during many years of exploration, studied the natural history of a large part of America, was the author of *A Journal of Travels into the Arkansa Territory during the Year 1819*, which included a brief account of his journey down the Ohio and thence westward. Both Alexander Wilson and John James Audu-

---

[22] *Louisiana Gazette,* Mar. 14, 1811.

bon drew a part of the materials for their monumental works from the West. Audubon, in his *Ornithological Biography* (1831-1839), showed the influence of the travel narrative of his time in the accounts of adventures and the observations on men and manners in the West which he scattered through the first three volumes.

## V

A more numerous group of travellers, with a much greater variety in point of view, were foreigners who came to observe the political, social, and economic aspects of frontier life. Some were drawn by idle curiosity, while others came to test a political or social theory or to examine the opportunities for emigration or business enterprise. A considerable number were professional authors.

National prejudice was an important influence in shaping the estimates which these writers made of the West. Volney, who, disgusted with Europe, had come to America in 1795 expecting to find an ideal democracy, was not only disillusioned by the meanness of life on the frontier, but embittered by the wave of anti-French sentiment which he encountered. He soon renounced his intention of becoming a permanent settler anywhere in the United States: "My researches," he declared, "have not led me to find in the Americans those fraternal and benevolent dispositions, with which some writers have flattered us." [23] Like suspicion of political motives was experienced at the same time by Victor Collot, whose narrative, translated into English as *A Journey in North America, Containing a Survey of the Countries Watered by the Mississippi, Ohio,*

---

[23] *View of the Climate and Soil of the United States,* 1804, p. xviii. Though the elaborate study of social and political aspects of American life which Volney had at first intended to include in the book was not written, the *View* is confined by no means to soil and climate.

*Missouri, and Other Affluing Rivers*, records the author's marked interest in military lines of defense in the West and his belief that the frontier country would eventually be politically separate from the Eastern states.[24] Although Collot had, it seems, served on the staff of Rochambeau's army during the American Revolution, he was arrested by General St. Clair at Fort Massac, on the lower Ohio; and he was equally unfortunate at New Orleans, where he fell into the hands of the Spanish governor.

Shortly after the visits of Volney and Collot, however, the enmity between France and America completely subsided; and some of the most favorable travel accounts of the West toward the end of the pioneer period were the work of their compatriots. Levasseur, who visited the West in 1825 in company with LaFayette, was a keen observer of the old decadent French communities; but the tone of his *Lafayette in America* (1829) was determined throughout by his pleasure at the remarkable reception which was everywhere accorded to the old friend of Washington. The narrative, which is enlivened with circumstantial accounts of a variety of incidents, including a shipwreck on the Ohio, in which LaFayette was in danger of losing his life, is altogether one of the most readable of the travel books of the time. Alexis de Tocqueville's impressions of some half dozen years later were expressed in his *Democracy in America* (second edition, 1836), which has long been known as one of the fairest analyses of American institutions. A supplement to this work was issued in 1840, but his much more romantic account of a visit to the Western frontier appeared only in 1861 in his *Œuvres et correspondance inédites*. Equally friendly in tone was Michel Chevalier's *Society, Manners and Politics in the*

---

[24] For a discussion of the political significance of Collot's journey, see F. J. Turner, "The Policy of France toward the Mississippi Valley," *The American Historical Review*, X, 272 (Jan., 1905).

*United States* (1839), in which is emphasized a point of view wholly absent from the estimates of most travellers who passed judgment on frontier civilization. The achievement of a pioneer people, he argues, should be judged by their success as pioneers and not by standards which can be applied justly only to the comparatively ancient civilization of Europe. The German observers Karl Postl and Bernhard, Duke of Saxe-Weimar, and Arfwedson, the Swedish traveller, were also inoffensive or even flattering in their remarks on the West.

But British travellers, who were much more numerous than others from across the Atlantic, were generally less friendly. The bitterness inspired by two wars was reflected in the flood of travel literature in which both East and West were held up to scorn, with the latter usually faring the worse. Scarcely was the Revolution at an end before this battle of the books began. The asperity of J. F. D. Smyth's *A Tour* (1784), which resulted inevitably from the persecution he had endured in America because of his loyalty to England during the Revolution, was tempered by some favorable opinions of the better qualities of frontiersmen. But among the rough Kentucky backwoodsmen, to whom he paid a visit, he seems to have been most struck by the "insolence, impertinence, and rudeness" which he discovered. And he warns Englishmen that America is unfit for any kind of emigrant, shows that the population is decreasing, and prophesies the rapid decline of the country. A much more famous onslaught, however, was Thomas Ashe's *Travels in America, Performed in 1806, for the Purpose of Exploring the Rivers Alleghany, Monongahela, Ohio, and Mississippi, and Ascertaining the Produce and Condition of their Banks and Vicinity* (1808), a confused account made up of what purport to be forty-two letters written at various places along the author's route from Pittsburg to New Orleans. After dismissing

the Eastern states in his first letter with the opinion that
they "are unworthy of your observation" he turns his
attention to the West. The lying propaganda of the early
explorers of Kentucky was of a piece with the almost
universal tendency to falsehood in America. The population of Kentucky, he thought, would soon rapidly decline.
An account of his daring descent of the Falls at Louisville
during a storm, and of his thrilling experiences while
exploring Cave-in-Rock, the headquarters of a notorious
outlaw band, are among a number of extraordinary tales
of adventure scattered through the book which make it a
strain on the reader's credulity, but not on his interest.
Even *The Quarterly Review* said that Ashe was "pretty
clearly an adventurer" and "spoiled a good book by
engrafting incredible stories on authentic facts."[25]   The
authentic facts, however, were at least partly drawn from
Zadock Cramer's *The Navigator: Containing Directions
for Navigating the Monongahela, Alleghany, Ohio, and
Mississippi Rivers; with an Ample Account of these much
Admired Waters, from the Head of the Former to the
Mouth of the Latter; and a Concise Description of their
Towns, Villages, Harbours, Settlements, &c.*, of which,
though Ashe represents it as a later book, no less than six
editions had appeared from 1801 to 1808.[26]   At Cincinnati,
to which he attributed the doubtful honor of being the best
town in the West, Ashe aroused particular hatred because
of the deception he practiced on a Dr. Goforth, from whom
he secured a valuable collection of mammoth bones.[27]

[25] I, 300, n. (May, 1809).
[26] Thomas Ashe, *Travels in America*, Newburyport, 1808, p. 78;
Zadock Cramer, *The Navigator*, sixth ed., 1808, p. 4 (the title given
above is from this edition); Christian Schultz, *Travels on an Inland
Voyage*, 1810, I, iv; and David Thomas, *Travels through the Western
Country*, 1819, p. 70.
[27] William N. Blane, *An Excursion through the United States and*

Ashe's book, insignificant as it might seem to a modern reader, became an unsavory tradition and helped keep alive the enmity which both British and Americans had inherited from the Revolution. It is perhaps true, as E. D. Mansfield asserted, that Ashe was the "first to discover that a book abusing the people of the United States would be profitable by its popularity."[28]   A more important consideration, however, is that he aroused a bitterness in America, and particularly in the West, which bred distrust of later British travellers, prepared for them an unfriendly reception certain to be reflected in their own accounts, and so prejudiced American reviewers that from this time it became a fixed principle with them to accept no travel narratives by British authors as in good faith except those which contained unequivocal praise of this country.[29]

---

*Canada*, 1824, p. 132; and Cramer, *op. cit.*, p. 69 (these authorities do not entirely agree). In his own account of some years later, Ashe does not so much as mention Goforth. Instead he takes credit to himself for his own great exertions in making the collection of bones. "I crossed the Appellactian and the Alleghany. — I descended the Ohio, the Illinois, the Wabash, the Missouri, and the Mississippi. . . . To acquire them, I spent the whole of my eleven hundred pounds, and traversed countries, and navigated waters, to the extent of ten thousand miles." (*Memoirs and Confessions of Captain Ashe*, 1815, II, 203-208.)   The collection, it seems, was placed in the Liverpool Museum (see Ashe's *Memoirs of Mammoth, and Various Other Extraordinary and Stupendous Bones*, 1806).

[28] W. H. Venable, *Beginnings of Literary Culture in the Ohio Valley*, 1891, p. 16.

[29] James Hall, perhaps the most influential critic in the West, records the extreme sensitiveness of frontier readers and a prejudice from which he himself was by no means free. "Englishmen," he says, "and indeed the gentlemen of our cities, receive rough treatment in the west, . . . They go snarling through the country, as if disdaining the soil on which they tread." (*Letters from the West*, 1828, pp. 116-117.)   See also *The Western Monthly Magazine*, I, 517 (Nov., 1833); and II, 655 ff. (Dec., 1834).

The War of 1812, a conflict more popular in the West than in the East, helped keep alive the national feeling which continued till after 1840 to be one of the most striking characteristics of the books by British travellers. In some cases even professed liberals who expected to find in the American democracy a happy contrast to conditions in Great Britain, ended by joining the ranks of this country's critics. H. B. Fearon, who came in 1817, deputed, as he declared, by "thirty-nine English families . . . to ascertain whether any, and what part of the United States would be suitable for their residence," is said to have exclaimed in a speech made shortly after his arrival in New York: "For the first time in my life, I am in a free country." [30]    And even after the disillusionment of his inland journey he refused to believe that a democratic form of government was the cause of America's ills;[31] but a visit to the West made him a defender of Ashe. It did not require a view of the interior of Kentucky to convince him that such a state was not a fit destination for English emigrants — the fact that it was a slave state was enough. In Ohio, of which he saw much more, he found, as he says, that slavery was practically existent also, though in disguise; Cincinnati was not without its attractions, but property there was already too high and many of its settlers were now moving farther West. Indiana was not to be considered. And, as for Illinois, which, he thought, Birkbeck had puffed in order to advance his own interests there, it was the habitation of only four classes of people — Indian hunters; squatters; a medley of land-jobbers, lawyers, doctors, and farmers, engaging in all kinds of speculation; and some old French settlers. Although this picture was, in fact, only slightly overdrawn, the discrepancy was

[30] *The Western Intelligencer*, Sept. 25, 1817.

[31] H. B. Fearon, *Sketches of America*, second ed., 1818, p. vi.

enough to give some plausibility to the angry denials of Westerners. Likewise his final summary of his unfavorable and favorable impressions of America, though perhaps not unfair, was calculated to give him a place beside Ashe in popular disesteem: Americans, he said, were not cleanly, not generous, not possessed of enlarged ideas, not liberal in opinions, not friendly to the advocates of liberty in Europe, and not able to comprehend true liberty or true honor; but they did enjoy some civil advantages, were not burdened with tithes or taxed without representation, had only a small debt, were free from spies and informers, had no large standing army, possessed a large territory for the expansion of population, and were rapidly advancing toward national wealth and greatness. As for English emigration to any part of America, it was a possibility to be considered by few except mechanics, small farmers with large families, and the extremely poor of all classes.

"Fearon's Falsehoods," as this book was called by Americans, who found the phrase invented by the facile William Cobbett for his own purposes[32] a convenient one, was followed shortly by a still less favorable estimate in Adlard Welby's *A Visit to North America and the English Settlements in Illinois, with a Winter Residence at Philadelphia* (1821). Welby, like Fearon, thought Kentucky out of the question for English emigrants because of its slavery, and reported a great economic decline in that state — land about Frankfort and Lexington had in three years lost five-sixths of its market value. Ohio was especially disappointing: "Instead of a garden," he says, "I found a wilderness." As for Illinois, before he arrived there he had met disappointed emigrants returning from that state to their old homes in the East; and at Birkbeck's settlement he saw a colony, the dupes of that enthusiast, who

---

[32] *A Year's Residence*, second ed., 1819, p. 598.

were still dependent on an outside supply of food. In Americans in general Welby discovered "a huge portion of blind conceit in their own superiority, and also the absence of the very essential christian principle of good-will and benevolence."

William Faux, whose *Memorable Days in America* (1823) belonged to the same group of books recording travels "principally undertaken to ascertain, by positive evidence, the condition and probable prospects of British emigrants," found life in the West not altogether unlovely. Lexington charmed him, as it did many even of the most critical-minded travellers of the time. "Who would not live," he asks, "in old Kentucky's first city?" His report on the English Prairie settlements was unusually favorable. And nothing could be more fair that the sensible conclusion of his book in which he asks British emigrants not to perpetuate home-bred prejudices, and calls for friendliness between British and Americans. But his strictures on the character of the great mass of Western people were still more prominent. "The traveller," he writes, "who must necessarily often mix with the very dregs of society in this country, should be prepared with plain clothes, or the dress of a mechanic; a gentlemanly appearance only exciting unfriendly or curious feelings, which defeat his object, and make his superiority painful." Louisville he left behind without regret — "well pleased," he says, "to turn my back on all the spitting, gouging, dirking, duelling, swearing, and staring, of old Kentucky"; but on the Indiana side of the Ohio he found himself "now quite out of society; every thing and every body, with some few exceptions, looks wild, and half savage." And the "wild bucks and bears, mixed up," which were his food, were scarcely more wild than the men with whom he barbarized, men "systematically unprincipled, and in whom the moral

sense seems to have no existence: this is the lot of all
coming here.''

Such estimates of frontier life, however fair, were certain
to arouse resentment, and helped prolong an international
debate in which most of the participants were moved by
prejudice rather than by a discriminating sense of justice.
Rich Short's *Travels in the United States*, describing three
voyages to America, includes very brief accounts of two
Westward journeys in 1828 and 1831, the only noteworthy
feature of which is the author's bitterness toward his
neighbors in Michigan, where his attempt at farming was
ended by what he says became almost open warfare against
him. The book, however, was a feeble production and
seems to have been too obscure to have much effect. The
far more important *Travels in North America, in the
Years 1827 and 1828* of Captain Basil Hall, the appearance of which, as Mrs. Trollope remarked, caused ''a
sort of moral earthquake,'' was, indeed, not wholly complimentary to American manners; and in his *Forty
Etchings* the same author revealed graphically some of
the gloomy features of frontier life. But his criticism
of neither West nor East was intemperate. He was,
however, a target for American critics, who bracketed him
along with more notorious offenders.[33]

But the most famous of such victims of American resentment was Mrs. Frances Trollope, mother of the novelist,
whose impressions of the West were gained largely from
a residence of two years in Cincinnati, during 1828-1830.
*Domestic Manners of the Americans* (1832), one of the
most widely-read books of travel in the first third of the
century,[34] was, it is true, an ill-humored and ungracious

[33] See, for example, Richard Biddle, *A Review of Captain Basil
Hall's Travels*, 1830.

[34] No less than four editions were issued before the end of 1832,

rebuke to the people among whom she had lived; but the army of critics into whose hands the work soon fell, inordinately exaggerated these faults, and there can be no doubt that Mrs. Trollope's strictures on Western life were almost entirely just. The illustrations which adorned the two despised volumes were perhaps more malicious than the rest of their contents, but the crudities of American (and especially Western) manners which they depict offered a fair mark for the author's satire. The book became, in fact, a kind of text-book of social etiquette[35] from which Americans learned some of their own short-comings while they loudly protested against the injustice which they had suffered.

No opportunity of ridicule was allowed to slip, and the baiting of the unfortunate author of *Domestic Manners* became a national pastime. Calvin Colton's *The Americans. By an American in London* (1833) was devoted largely to an ill-humored rebuttal. *The American Quarterly Review*[36] suggested that Mrs. Trollope's mistakes were not so much the result of her inclination as the fault of her education; and, from such comparatively mild revenge, some critics descended to mere blackguarding. In this art none was perhaps more offensive than F. W. Shelton, whose doggerel satire, though directed at British travellers in general, was called *The Trollopiad* (1837) and was intended especially for the author of *Domestic Manners*.

and others followed. The book also appeared in French and Spanish translations.

[35] Patrick Shirreff was pleased to find that even in New York Mrs. Trollope's admonitions had been heeded. At a theatre in that city, he says, the indelicate behavior of several in the audience was greeted with cries of "A Trollope, a Trollope," and general hissing and hooting which induced the offenders to withdraw. (*A Tour through North America*, 1835, p. 9.)

[36] XII, 109-133 (Sept., 1832).

Of the woman whose father and husband were both fellows of New College, Oxford, and whose son later became a famous English novelist,[37] Shelton writes in a note to his mock epic:

There have been divers opinions set forth with regard to the birth, parentage, and occupations of sweet Mistress Trollope. It has been to some persons a matter of doubt whether she had been a washerwoman, a seamstress, a midwife, or a chambermaid; while others declare (so eventful has her life been) that there are pretty strong reasons for believing that she has had a little experience at all.

And in couplets even more stupidly abusive he celebrates her fame:

> thy sweet name shall spread the States around,
> And, TROLLOPE, TROLLOPE, all the land resound.
> Oh! happy we! oh! thrice and four times blest,
> That thou e'er journey'd to the distant west;
> And failing there, alas! in thy "BAZAAR,"
> Hast made "DOMESTIC MANNERS" all thy care.

In a satirical play called *Tourists in America*, which was performed at Cincinnati and elsewhere, Miss Lucretia Fitzblue is the "Authoress of a book of 'Domestic Manners.' "[38] The unfortunate Bazaar, which Mrs. Trollope erected partly because of her missionary zeal for the reformation of society in Cincinnati — for the Bazaar was to be a social as well as a commercial center — and partly as an ill-judged means of establishing a son in business, received the name of "Trollope's Folly" and was pointed out to tourists. No other English writer of the century, with

---

[37] Among the large number of books by Mrs. Trollope herself, *The Life and Adventures of Jonathan Jefferson Whitlaw; or Scenes on the Mississippi* (1836) deserves some notice, which, so far as I know, it has never received, as a feeble forerunner of Mrs. Stowe's *Uncle Tom's Cabin*. The setting of the story, partly in Kentucky, is mainly, however, the lower Mississippi, and especially Natchez.

[38] *Cinc. Daily Gaz.*, July 6, 1833.

the exception of Scott and Byron, was so well known throughout the West and none so cordially hated. Even beyond the Mississippi the name soon became familiar.[39]

But, in spite of the popularity of *Domestic Manners* as proved by the numerous editions through which it passed, it is clear that a change was gradually taking place in the attitude of Englishmen toward the United States; and this change now began to be reflected in a number of British reviews, which sought to discourage wholesale disparagement of America in books of travel.[40] *The Edinburgh Review*, with "nothing more at heart than a cordial friendship between America and England," saw in the bitter attacks of English travellers (and especially of Mrs. Trollope) on America an indirect assault upon reform legislation in England; and, under the caption "The Americans and their Detractors," [41] essayed a vigorous reply. Against the author of *Domestic Manners* it was charged that her "preface of March 1832 is an express advertisement against the Reform Bill. . . . If she uncovers the nakedness of our Transatlantic children, it is out of pure alarm for the English Constitution." It was a foolish Tory conceit

---

[39] Latrobe, who travelled over the prairies in 1832, tells of a member of the party who gave the despised name to "a hound with a number of whelps" (Charles Joseph Latrobe, *The Rambler in North America*, London, 1835, I, 148); and Alphonso Wetmore, in the stories appended to his *Gazetteer of the State of Missouri*, 1837 (p. 297), thus describes the musical entertainment provided by a menagerie showing in a backwoods village: "The music, consisting of a cracked violin with three good strings, and a broken base, a clarinet, dangerously ill with influenza, and the basest of all basedrums, struck up Mrs. Trollope's march, as an accompaniment to the roar of the lion."

[40] Of the reviews of *Domestic Manners* which appeared in several English periodicals, only one of importance — that of Lockhart in the ultra-Tory *Quarterly*, XLVII, 39-80 (Mar., 1832) — was wholly favorable.

[41] *The Edinburgh Review*, LV, 479-526 (July, 1832).

that inspired what was virtually an attack on democratic institutions:

Mrs. Trollope addresses the Americans much as Touchstone addresses Corin: — 'Wast ever at court, shepherd? — No, truly. — Then thou art damned. — . . . Why, if thou never wast at court, thou never saw'st good manners; if thou never saw'st good manners, then thy manners must be wicked; and wickedness is sin, and sin is damnation: Thou art in a parlous state, shepherd.'

There was not, the critic declared, so much as one sensible observation on an important subject to be found in the two volumes; the work would not be objectionable if it were announced as a caricature, but it "is passed off as a true picture." This kind of injustice had continued too long; it was high time to put an end to the foolish quarrel between the two nations, and arrive at a just understanding:

Burlesques on one side, and mock heroics on the other, are therefore more than ever out of season. The picture is one, in judging of which it has become worth our while to make sure that we get the proper point of view; and that we are not led away by the conceit of connoisseurship to talk about what we have imperfectly seen, and have still more imperfectly understood.

Such were the effective measures taken to destroy the influence of British critics of America. The peace was to be made, however, with the Eastern states rather than with the West, which might well be conceded to deserve a doubtful reputation. One of the chief objections to Mrs. Trollope was that she had described as true for the whole of the United States what she had in fact observed only in the West. Cincinnati could, said *The Edinburgh Review*, "just as much represent the United States, as a new flourishing port in the Orkneys would represent Great Britain." And the reviewer in *Blackwood's*,[42] who had wittily ridi-

42 *Blackwood's Edinburgh Magazine*, XXXI, 829-847 (May, 1832).

culed Mrs. Trollope, granting that her book contained much truth "but truth very palpably varnished and exaggerated for the purpose of impression," wished it to be remembered that by far the greater portion of these volumes relates to the Western States, in which the standard, both of manners and morals, is decidedly lower than in those which border the Atlantic.

The attacks of the travel writers did not, in fact, cease at once; and neither East nor West was allowed to remain unchallenged. Thomas Hamilton, the British novelist, whose *Men and Manners in America* (1833) echoed Mrs. Trollope's criticism and attempted a personal defense of her, admitted that he might be guilty of national prejudice, but did not hesitate to brave criticism in an attempt to save England from imitating American institutions — a danger which seemed imminent to the conservatives during the English liberal reform movements of that time. Richard Weston's *A Visit to the United States and Canada in 1833* was marked by an unusually bitter attack on Western "savages"; and his dislike of America was general. "Throughout my wanderings in America," he says in the conclusion of his narrative, "I saw nothing to admire but the blue rolling ocean which was to waft me to my native shores."

Yet, though the books of English travellers who, like Paulding's visitor to the Birkbeck settlement in Illinois, were wont to exaggerate the shameful mistreatment which they received at the hands of Western barbarians,[43] attracted indeed greater attention than more temperate accounts, they were perhaps not more numerous. From the

---

[43] "I was four times robbed of all I had in the world," declares one of Paulding's Englishmen. "I was six times gouged, eight times dirked, and several times roasted at a log fire, before I arrived at English Prairie." (*John Bull in America; or, the New Munchausen,* 1825, p. 124.)

first there had been liberals on both sides of the Atlantic who saw the evil influence of misleading books about America and contended for better relations between Great Britain and this country;[44] and many British travellers of the early nineteenth century were either eminently fair in their estimates or willing, for the sake of good feeling, to overstate the virtues of the backwoodsmen and their country. John Melish, who came to America strongly prejudiced in favor of republican ideals, had begun his preparation for the journey by reading all books of travel on the United States that he could obtain, but found so many of them "to contain such effusions of ignorance and spleen" that he finally discarded them all. The account of his journey through the West in 1811 included in his *Travels in the United States of America* (1812) is neither flattering nor ill-tempered, but shows a remarkable accuracy, which resulted from his employment of the painstaking method of observation he had previously perfected during several years of travel in the Eastern parts of America and elsewhere. "The Journal"[45] of Thomas Hulme, a few years later, gave a very favorable account of the Western country and condemned those travellers who had maligned America. William Tell Harris's *Remarks Made during a Tour* (1821) and William Newham Blane's *An Excursion through the United States and Canada* (1824) were decidedly friendly in tone. Blane, who wrote one of the best accounts of the English Prairie settlements and of Harmonie under Rapp's régime, displayed his good sense by condemning Ashe and at the same time deploring the evil effect of the grossly exaggerated reports of British cruelty — such reports were a matter of popular belief in

---

[44] *Cf.* the English preface of 1792 to J. P. Brissot de Warville's *New Travels.*

[45] Published in Cobbett, *op. cit.*, pp. 443-519.

ost significant change, however, was in
lish travellers.

friendly spirit more evident than in
Martineau, which contained what was
mportant view of the West by an Eng-
the last years of the pioneer period.
of slavery in Kentucky and Missouri,
ich she could not heartily defend. Her
of Mrs. Trollope leads ght made her an extremely
Western people. Henry Tr rn democracy, and she
in North America (1834) little differences between
ly after Mrs. Trollope's b ati, in particular, charmed
blime tone of disdainful sup barbarize society in new
seph Latrobe, who was w gone farther west. Plain
Western tour of 1832, sough scription of the Western
uthor, to conciliate both Englis
equally the blame for the old Few things can be con-
me was becoming burdensome to is magnificent city, and
he movement for reconciliation was She is enthroned
later by Sir Charles Augustus Murray, bottoms occurring
(1839), made light of both Mrs. Trollope s notions of what
l asserted that conditions in Cincinnati ing and closing,
or four years after the author of Domestic the richest
it, were not what she had described. No by beeches
ad been a change, but the difference between and. . . .
s residence of some two years in that town Indolence, of
asty visit may account for a part of the Una trod, of
p. 300) cites as an example of such reports, a carried about
arrison telling how General Winchester was e a native artist
rs; whereas General Winchester was still ls of their houses
written. As a matter of fact, Harrison, in the country. I
d atrocity to the Indians, di ands of free-school
inst their Brit tier , "are our populace."
es an such a city.[47]

sne found other subjects for her

33
merica, 1837, I, 141 and 139-140.

discrepancy. The m
the spirit of the Eng

Nowhere was this
the books of Harriet
probably the most i
lish writer during
With the exception
she found little whi
interest in English radical thou
sympathetic observer of Weste
exhibited, in fact, a tendency to
the West and the East. Cincinn
her. "The adventurers who
places" had, she found, now
prose was inadequate for her de
capital.

Cincinnati is a glorious place.
ceived finer than the situation of th
the beauty by which she is surrounded.
upon a high platform, — one of the rich
on the Ohio, which expand the traveller'
fertility is. Behind her are hills, open
receding and advancing; here glowing wi
green pasturage, and there crested and ribbed
which seem transplanted from some giant l
These hill-sides reminded me of the Castle of
the quiet paths of Eden, of the shades that
Windsor Forest, — of all that my memory
undulating wood-lands: . . . They hav
of great genius who has adorned the wal
with, perhaps, the best pictures I saw
saw their streets filled with thous
children. "These," said a lady to me
I thought it a populace worthy of

Near the northern fron
enthusiasm:

[47] Society in

---

t
fi
wl
an
Th
con
gene
of th
extre
whose
likewi
ridicul
ority,"
Washin
like the
and Am
quarrel,
all concer
furthered
who, in his
and her bo
within thre
Manners sa
doubt there
Mrs. Trollope
and Murray's

[46] Blane (op.
letter from Gene
disemboweled by
alive when Blane
though he attribu
neglect the opportu
(see Harrison to M
William Henry Har

We passed through a wilderness of flowers; trailing roses, enormous white convolvulus, scarlet lilies, and ground-ivy, with many others, being added to those we had before seen. Milton must have travelled in Michigan before he wrote the garden parts of "Paradise Lost." [48]

Yet her partiality did not prevent much discerning criticism. The national mind of America, she declared, was of a high order if judged by its legislation; but if the nation be judged by its literature, "it may be pronounced to have no mind at all." [49] Her *Retrospect of Western Travel* (1838), like *Society in America*, clearly belongs to the literature of Anglo-American reconciliation.

Though somewhat flippant in tone, Frederick Marryat's *A Diary in America* (1839), usually regarded as unfriendly, and certainly professing no devout belief in the permanent benefits of democracy in the New World, was by no means unfair in its treatment of the West. At Cincinnati, the storm center of the old controversy, he found society as good as anywhere in the Union; and, as for Mrs. Trollope's book, it might have been much more true of Cincinnati when she wrote it, but it would have been a libel at the time of his visit. And thus the fourth decade of the nineteenth century ended with the futile debate rapidly losing its interest for both sides and with repeated overtures for reconciliation.

## VI

Narratives by travellers from the Eastern states to the West who did not identify themselves with the frontier people, are neither so numerous nor so distinct in point of view as the accounts of foreigners. They offer, however, a considerable variety. Zophar Roberts, author of one of the earliest of them, praised Ohio in *A Journal, of a Tour*

---

[48] *Ibid.*, I, 241.
[49] *Ibid.*, II, 300-301.

*from Lake-George to the North-West Territory* (1801).
Like most of the English travellers, he objected to Kentucky
on account of slavery; but the country to the north he
called "that Eden of America." Christian Schultz, whose
two volumes of *Travels on an Inland Voyage* (1810)
were remarkable as a work of some length by an early
American traveller, was a staunch defender of national
prestige against foreign attack. "The author," he said,
"will not conceal that an additional motive for consenting
to the publication of these letters, was the perusal of a
volume lately published, entitled, *'Travels in America, by
Thomas Ash, Esq.'* purporting to be a part of the same
route which he has travelled." [50]    Estwick Evans, the
author of *A Pedestrious Tour, of Four Thousand Miles,
through the Western States and Territories* (1819), who
travelled both the northern route along the shores of the
Lakes, and the older southern route down the Ohio, was
inspired in undertaking his Western journey by something
of the romantic mood of Chateaubriand. "I wished," he
says,

to acquire the simplicity, native feelings, and virtues of
savage life; to divest myself of the factitious habits, prejudices and imperfections of civilization; to become a citizen
of the world; and to find, amidst the solitude and grandeur
of the western wilds, more correct views of human nature
and of the true interests of man. [51]

And he accordingly set out on his journey dressed in buffalo skins and accompanied only by two faithful dogs. It
is not apparent, however, from his book in what way he
realized his principal purpose. At any rate a more practical result may have been to direct the attention of emigrants to Michigan, which, of all the parts of the West he
visited, was the chief object of his praise.

---

[50] Schultz, *op. cit.*, 1810, I, iv.
[51] *A Pedestrious Tour*, 1819, p. 6.

Charles Fenno Hoffman's *A Winter in the West* (1835) contained perhaps the first observation on frontier life by an Eastern author of any importance — for Irving, who had been expected to appear as a defender of the new states, had discreetly avoided the subject in *A Tour on the Prairies*.[52] Though, like Evans, possessed by a degree of romantic enthusiasm, Hoffman was no doubt influenced in his generous praise of what he saw, by a desire to retaliate against the British critics. In the larger towns of the West he found much to praise. As for life and manners in Cincinnati, the caricatures which Mrs. Trollope had drawn of it had "about as much vrai-semblance as if the beaux and belles of Kamschatka had sat for the portraits."[53] The wilderness charmed him. Whether or not it argued a want of refinement, he "would rather visit scenes where a human foot has never trod than dwell upon those gilded by the most arrogant associations of our race." He emulated Tocqueville's fervor in proclaiming the pleasures of solitude in the vast expanse of country which still remained untouched by the pioneer:

What is the echo of roofs that a few centuries since rung with barbaric revels, or of aisles that pealed the anthems of painted pomp, to the silence which has reigned in these dim groves since the first fiat of Creation was spoken![54]

Chandler Robbins Gilman's *Life on the Lakes: being Tales and Sketches Collected during a Trip to the Pictured Rocks of Lake Superior* (1836), though it contains a considerable amount of comment on both white settlers and Indians — especially the latter — and is unusual among books of Western travel for the charm of its humor and style, is chiefly remarkable for its enthusiastic descriptions of the shores of Huron and Superior. The author, who, though

---

[52] *Cf. The Western Monthly Magazine*, III, 332-333 (June, 1835).
[53] *A Winter in the West*, 1835, II, 133.
[54] *Ibid.*, I, 195-196.

a citizen of the East, was a native of Ohio, did not fail to display his loyalty to the frontier.

In sharp contrast with such panegyrics on the West were unfriendly reports like Thaddeus Harris's *The Journal of a Tour* (1805) and Zerah Hawley's *A Journal* (1822). While Harris's account of his journey to Marietta in search of a healthful climate is only mildly ill-humored, Hawley's purpose is frankly to keep misinformed people from going to such a country as Ohio. The exaggerated praises of this state which are a commonplace of traveller's narratives, have done a great deal of harm; but he is pleased to find that immigration to this part of the West has almost ceased. He is especially impressed by the misery of the inhabitants of the Western Reserve. People who must leave New England should, he advises, go no further west than New York. In New England, the endeavor to check emigration which might prove economically disastrous to the older states was also reflected in such satirical pamphleteering as " *'Tother Side of Ohio*" (1818) and Trumbull's *Western Emigration. Journal of Doctor Jeremiah Simpleton's Tour to Ohio Containing an Account of the Numerous Difficulties, Hair-breadth Escapes, Mortifications and Privations, which the Doctor and his Family Experienced on their Journey from Maine, to the 'Land of Promise,' and during a Residence of Three Years in that highly Extolled Country.* And of like purpose was the anonymous *Western Emigration. Narrative of a Tour to, and One Year's Residence in "Edensburgh," (Illinois,) by Major Walter Wilkey, an Honest Yeoman of Mooseboro' State of Maine* (1839). In this, as well as in Trumbull's pamphlet, certain "appropriate cuts" aided the ridicule heaped upon New Englanders foolish enough to think of removing to the West.

The greater number of frontier travels by Easterners

were, however, of more sober kind.  George W. Ogden's *Letters from the West* (1823), though perhaps largely a disguised compilation from other travellers,[55] contained matter-of-fact observations apparently based upon a residence of some months in Ohio and Kentucky.  In David Thomas's *Travels through the Western Country in the Summer of 1816* attention was directed to the slowly advancing line of settlement in the Wabash Valley, and a considerable bulk of statistical information was included with the author's personal narrative.  No white settlers were yet to be found north of the Terre Haute Prairie. Tilly Buttrick's *Voyages, Travels and Discoveries* (1831) contains an account, perhaps as dull as could well have been written, of several journeys that took him through a large part of the West; and Nathan Hoskins, the Vermont historian, put into his *Notes upon the Western Country* (1833) a curious hodge-podge of what he had seen and what he had not seen.  A number of narratives, such as those of Henry Ker (1816), Amos Parker (1835), Samuel Parker (1838), and J. K. Townsend (1839), record travels through the new states, but are chiefly interesting for their description of regions farther to the west or southwest.

## VII

Some of the earliest and best-known accounts by observers whose point of view was that of the pioneers themselves are difficult to classify.  John Filson, whose work called *The Discovery, Settlement and Present State of Kentucke* (1784) has gained for him a certain distinction as the earliest historian of the frontier, may equally well be classed among the explorers or adventurers.  His book was, however, the first serious attempt to describe Kentucky;

[55] For evidence tending to convict Ogden of wholesale plagiarism, see Quaife, *op. cit.*, I, 167-184 (Sept., 1914).

and his narrative of Boone, presumably taken down in the famous backwoodsman's own words, had no doubt a great influence in creating both a legend of Kentucky and a legend of Daniel Boone.[56] Gilbert Imlay, author of the equally famous work, *A Topographical Description of the Western Territory* (1792), not only asserts that he had lived for many years in the back parts of America, but would have the reader believe that his book was originally written in Kentucky as letters addressed to a friend on the other side of the Atlantic. It is almost certain, however, that Imlay, whose narrative includes events as late as the close of the year 1791, was not in Kentucky after 1785 and that the whole of his residence in that district did not amount to more than two years.[57] He had, however, trav-

[56] It seems likely that Byron's praise of Boone (*Don Juan*, VIII, lxi-lxvii), appropriately reproduced in the Brooklyn reprint of Filson (1823), was partly inspired by that author's account, the fame of which was increased by its inclusion in the later editions of Imlay's *A Topographical Description*, and its appearance in French translation (1785). It is possible also that Byron had seen Daniel Bryan's fantastic epic poem "The Adventures of Daniel Boone," published as part of *The Mountain Muse* (1813) and itself probably drawn from Filson's prose narrative.

[57] See the present writer's "The Adventures of Gilbert Imlay," in *Indiana University Studies*, Vol. X, Study 57 (Mar., 1923). An interesting proof that the shifty author of *A Topographical Description* was somewhat of a mystery to one of the earliest historians of Kentucky, is found in the fact that, though Mann Butler, author of *A History of the Commonwealth of Kentucky* (1834), had been, as he states in the preface of the latter work, an observer of Kentucky affairs since 1806 and had in his possession a body of private papers belonging to the chief actors in the history of that state, he apparently was without information on Imlay. One of fourteen questions which Butler published in Kentucky newspapers the year before his history appeared was: "Is there any knowledge of G. Imlay, who purports to have been 'a captain in the American army during the late war, (meaning the revolutionary,) and a commissioner for laying out land in the back settlements'?" (*The*

elled extensively during the time he was there; and his work as a deputy surveyor, as well as his experience as a speculator in lands, made him a keen observer. To a considerable body of information which was partly his own and partly acquired after he left the West — probably after his arrival in Europe — he added a romantic enthusiasm which impressed many transatlantic readers. The work appeared in a number of editions, all but the first of which were equipped with appendices containing accounts of the new country by Filson and other writers.

A thoroughly Western point of view is nowhere better exemplified than in the much later writings of Daniel Drake. His *Pioneer Life in Kentucky*, a series of reminiscences of his early days told in a style of great simplicity, was not yet written in 1840 and was not published until many years afterwards. His *Notices concerning Cincinnati* (1810) was directed mainly to his medical and scientific friends; but his *Natural and Statistical View, or Picture of Cincinnati and the Miami Country* (1815) contained, besides a body of geographical and other scientific data, a record of some of Cincinnati's cultural beginnings. Perhaps the best of his observations on Western life, however, are to be found in his *Discourse on the History, Character, and Prospects of the West* (1834). Originally delivered as an oration, it retained in printed form the marks of the abundant enthusiasm characteristic of frontier eloquence. It is plainly a partisan appeal, affirming faith in the literary future of the West and defending Western life and character. Except in his medical studies, Drake was, in fact, rather an inspiration to contemporary pioneer enterprise than a careful observer and recorder of what he actually saw and experienced. Caleb Atwater, whose chief interest lay in the direction of the antiquarian research

*Commonwealth*, Frankfort, Sept. 24, 1833; clipping in library of State Historical Society of Wisconsin.)

popular in his time, was, in his *Remarks Made on a Tour to Prairie du Chien; thence to Washington City, in 1829,* a true prophet of the growth of the new states. The same writer's oration on *The General Character, Present and Future Prospects of the People of Ohio* (1827) suffers from the common fault of too great sectional partiality.

A sympathetic understanding of both the Eastern and Western points of view is to be seen in Henry Marie Brackenridge's *Recollections of Persons and Places in the West* (1834). Brackenridge, son of the author of *Modern Chivalry,* was born at Ft. Pitt, and, as a child, was sent to the old French settlement of St. Genevieve, below St. Louis, that he might learn the language of the inhabitants. A year in another French village, Gallipolis, completed his first period of residence beyond the Ohio; but a dozen years after his first voyage, he began at St. Genevieve a second period of Western residence, which, although a much shorter one, afforded him opportunity to study the changes which were taking place in frontier life. His *Recollections,* like his *Journal of a Voyage up the River Missouri,* is written, not only in an entertaining style, but with an evident regard for accuracy, and deserves to be ranked as a classic of its kind. Something of the same quality is to be found in *The Far West: or, a Tour beyond the Mountains* (1838), by Edmund Flagg, whose title is to be explained by the fact that at the time his book was written he had scarcely begun his many years of residence in the West and South; for the "Far West" is, in fact, Illinois and Missouri. The book, which grew out of Flagg's "Sketches of a Traveller," a series of contributions to a Louisville newspaper, and therefore in a vein not uncomplimentary to the West, is especially valuable for its comments upon the old French towns along the Mississippi.

The storm center of a controversy over the fitness of the frontier for English emigration, Morris Birkbeck and

Richard Flower represented the point of view of the English farmer of means, well enough pleased with pioneer life to champion its advantages. Founders of the most remarkable English colony beyond the Alleghenies, these leaders actively sought to direct other emigrants from England to the rich prairie land which had hitherto been little valued. About Birkbeck's *Notes on a Journey in America* (1817) and *Letters from Illinois* (1818), both reprinted a number of times, there grew up a debate, in which it was commonly charged by his opponents — chiefly British travellers and persons who, like Cobbett, desired to draw English immigration to the Atlantic states — that he had overpraised the prairie country in order to lead others into a trap from which he himself was unable to escape.[58] Birkbeck's *An Address to the Farmers of Great Britain* (1822) and Richard Flower's *Letters from Lexington and the Illinois* (1819) and *Letters from the Illinois* (1822) were further documents for the defense in this controversy. William Bullock's *Sketch of a Journey* (1827) was an extremely favorable account of the environs of Cincinnati. There the author had purchased an estate to which he hoped to attract a colony of Englishmen.[59] A book remarkable as the work of an Englishman of some

[58] For comment reflecting the widespread distrust of Birkbeck, see letter of John Keats to Georgiana Keats, Jan. 15, 1820. Perhaps the most effective attack on Birkbeck was the caustic review of his *Notes* in *The Quarterly*, XIX, 54-78 (Apr., 1818).

[59] Here, after his return from England, Mrs. Trollope found "the well-known proprietor of the Egyptian Hall" and his family. "Certainly," she remarked, "there is more taste and art lavished on one of their beautiful saloons than all Western America can show elsewhere. It is impossible to help feeling that Mr. Bullock is rather out of his element in this remote spot, and the gems of art he has brought with him show as strangely there as would a bower of roses in Siberia, or a Cincinnati fashionable at Almack's." (Trollope, *op. cit.*, p. 60.)

cultural attainments who had become an enthusiastic
citizen of the West is Henry Caswall's *America, and the
American Church* (1839). Caswall had not only resided
on the frontier during the greater part of about ten years
spent in America, but had in the meantime revisited
England and travelled in New England, thus fitting himself peculiarly for intelligent observation. The comments
upon men and manners in Ohio, Kentucky, and Indiana
which make up no small part of his book, are thus of
unusual value.

Of all writers, however, Timothy Flint and James Hall
were generally regarded, both in their own day and later,
as the chief spokesmen for the West. Both were fair
representatives of the Eastern culture of the first decade of
the nineteenth century and both enjoyed besides something
of a cosmopolitan breadth of view. Both regarded the
West as their chief subject-matter. Both men attempted
a variety of literature — novels, tales, poetry, critical
reviews — but their most enduring contributions were
what they wrote of the frontier in a sober attempt to state
the facts as they observed them. Flint's early diary was
lost; but an attractive record of his experiences up to 1825
is to be found in his *Recollections of the Last Ten Years,
Passed in Occasional Residences and Journeyings in the
Valley of the Mississippi* (1826), which, like the best of the
later works by the same author, shows the virtues of accuracy and simplicity of style, with little added charm. In
the spring following his arrival in Cincinnati, in 1815,
where he had come in search of health, Flint set out on a
tour through southern Indiana and Kentucky which
resulted in his first rich harvest of observations on frontier
life. This journey was followed by a voyage from Cincinnati down the Ohio to the Mississippi and up that river to
St. Louis. In the Missouri country he spent nearly six
years, settling at St. Charles as a missionary. After having

removed from Missouri to New Orleans in 1822, he was compelled by sickness to return northward, revisiting Louisville and Cincinnati, and later passing Eastward to his old home in Massachusetts. A second migration to the frontier resulted in a long residence at Cincinnati; and into *A Condensed Geography and History of the Western States, or the Mississippi Valley* (1828) Flint put the remarkable fund of first-hand information and the large number of intimate observations which his wide experience had now yielded. As editor of *The Personal Narrative of James O. Pattie*, and as author of other books of a biographical or historical nature, he continued to show his interest in the new country; and in *The Western Monthly Review* (1827-1830) he became finally the open champion of the frontier and its culture.

James Hall, though his travels in the Valley of the Mississippi did not compare in extent with those of Timothy Flint, identified himself even more closely with his adopted country through long residence in Illinois and at Cincinnati. Yet he found it more difficult than did that writer to separate fact from fancy. In the short personal introduction with which he begins his *Letters from the West* (1828), Hall narrates his first voyage on the Ohio River with something more than the usual traveller's interest in wild scenery, the boat songs, and the variety of strange river craft used by immigrants; but in the remainder of the book he turns his attention to comment on geography and people and manners, illustrated in a way which became characteristic of this writer, with tales intended rather to entertain than to inform. A more serious attempt as observer and historian was shown in *Sketches of History, Life, and Manners in the West*, largely a compilation of papers which had already appeared in periodicals and other publications; and in *Statistics of the West, at the Close of the Year 1836* (enlarged and republished in 1838 as *Notes*

*on the Western States*) Hall produced something very
similar to the gazetteers and guides which at this time
composed a large part of the literature of frontier travel.

## VIII

Many books of travel and observation in which the
narrative and descriptive elements were important — such
accounts as those of Imlay, Schoolcraft, and Atwater, for
example — were heavily freighted with statistical matters;
but besides these there were numerous books, sometimes by
actual observers, sometimes by mere compilers, which were
devoted almost entirely to statistical and geographical
information.  If we leave out of account the geographies
which included brief descriptions of the West by British
writers who had not crossed the Atlantic, or by Easterners
who had not gone beyond the Alleghenies, and the universal
gazetteers, based on no greater amount of first-hand knowledge, there remain a large number of books — gazetteers,
guides, and manuals — which, though of no literary value,
must have had a great influence in directing the tide of
immigration toward the frontier.  As early as 1797 Jedidiah
Morse, the indefatigable author of such compilations,
included brief mention of the West in *The American
Gazetteer*; and from this time the attention given to the
new country by such books rapidly increased.  John Melish,
who had explored both the Eastern states and the Western
states and territories in 1811, testing the most reliable
information already in print with his own observations,
began a few years later the publication of a series of guides,
among the first of which was *The Traveller's Directory
through the United States* (1815).  Numerous guides by
other authors comprehended the whole of the United States,
with only brief accounts of the West.  Such were the statistical collections of H. S. Tanner and S. A. Mitchell

as well as numerous manuals and guides for immigrants, like Robert Holditch's *The Emigrant's Guide to the United States of America* (1818), S. H. Collins's work of the same title (1829), and Calvin Colton's *Manual for Emigrants to America* (1832).

Meantime an increasing number of works were devoted principally or wholly to the West. One of the earliest and best was *The Western Gazetteer* (1817), by Samuel R. Brown. William Amphlett, in *The Emigrant's Directory to the Western States of North America* (1819), recommended himself to English readers as "formerly of London, and late of the county of Salop, now resident on the banks of the Ohio River." *Steele's Western Guide Book, and Emigrant's Directory* enjoyed such popularity that five editions had appeared by 1836. Others of the type were J. Calvin Smith's *The Western Tourist and Emigrant's Guide* (1839); John Mason Peck's *A Guide for Emigrants* (1831), an excellent authority on Illinois and some of the neighboring states; the same author's *A New Guide* (1836); and, perhaps the best of all, "R. B.'s" *View of the Valley of the Mississippi* (1832).

Individual states and territories received special attention in such books as John Kilbourn's *The Ohio Gazetteer* (1816, with no less than ten other editions by 1833), Blunt's *Traveller's Guide to and through the State of Ohio* (1833), John Scott's *The Indiana Gazetteer* (1826), Joseph Colton's *The State of Indiana Delineated* (1838), John Mason Peck's *A Gazetteer of Illinois* (1834), the anonymous *Illinois in 1837*, Alphonso Wetmore's *Gazetteer of the State of Missouri* (1837), John T. Blois's *Gazetteer of the State of Michigan* (1838), Albert M. Lea's *Notes on Wisconsin Territory* (1836), and *Galland's Iowa Emigrant* (1840). Such works, descriptive of comparatively limited parts of the West and generally written by men familiar with their subject through careful first-hand observation, were more accurate than the greater part of the guides and manuals which attempted to treat the whole of the frontier or even the entire country.

## IX

Belonging to the West by virtue of the citizenship of their authors, but wholly distinct from other classes of travel accounts discussed above, were the extremely few books made up of the adventures and observations of Westerners in other countries. Such were J. D. Paxton's *Letters from Palestine* (1839) and Lewis Cass's *France, its King, Court, and Government* (1840). The latter, though mainly the record of Cass's impressions during several years in France, is linked more closely with the West by the fact that it contains brief reminiscences of the author's own experiences on the frontier; and perhaps the most interesting part of the whole is an account of the American travels of the exiled Louis Philippe, including a tour through Kentucky and Ohio and a voyage down the Ohio and Mississippi Rivers.[60] The events related in this narrative, says the author, are from *"one who cannot be deceived."* [61]

---

[60] Lewis Cass, *France, its King, Court, and Government*, 1840, pp. 116-118 and 134-138.

[61] *Ibid.*, p. 100.

# CHAPTER III

## NEWSPAPERS AND MAGAZINES

In truth, there are many reasons which render a very general diffusion of literature impossible in America. I can scarcely class the universal reading of newspapers as an exception to this remark; if I could, my statement would be exactly the reverse, and I should say that America beat the world in letters. The fact is, that throughout all ranks of society, from the successful merchant, which is the highest, to the domestic serving-man, which is the lowest, they are all too actively employed to read, except at such broken moments as may suffice for a peep at a newspaper. It is for this reason, I presume, that every *American newspaper* is more or less a magazine, wherein the merchant may scan, while he holds out his hand for an invoice, "Stanzas by Mrs. Hemans," or a garbled extract from "Moore's Life of Byron"; the lawyer may study his brief faithfully, and yet contrive to pick up the valuable dictum of some American critic, that "Bulwer's novels are decidedly superior to Sir Walter Scott's"; . . .

This, I presume, is what is meant by the general diffusion of knowledge, so boasted of in the United States; such as it is, the diffusion of it is general enough, certainly; but I greatly doubt its being advantageous to the population.

The only reading men I met with were those who made letters their profession; and of these, there were some who would hold a higher rank in the great republic (not of America, but of letters), did they write for persons less given to the study of magazines and newspapers. — Frances Trollope, *Domestic Manners of the Americans.*

## I

Though travellers had already created a literature of the West, newspapers, the first of which were established

in the frontier towns before the end of the eighteenth
century, were the earliest means of literary expression of
the Western people themselves.  And in quantity, as well as
in their influence on the life of the backwoods communities,
they were the most important literary product throughout
the pioneer period.  Only leaders who were adept in the
art of impassioned oratory could rival the editor of a weekly
gazette in power to shape the popular will.  The editor and
printer, by his knowledge of language and of the mysteries
of his craft, rose to the dignity of an oracle.

"Old Wisdom" was the nickname of John Bradford, who
became, in August, 1787, the founder of the first Western
newspaper, *The Kentucke Gazette*.  From his log cabin
office in Lexington, then a village only a few years old,
Bradford issued a meagre sheet which announced the news
of the world some months after it had become public knowledge in more favored communities.  But Kentucky's need
was great, and the crudity of the *Gazette* could be tolerated.
The origin of the paper was recorded by Bradford himself
some ten years later:

In the year 1786, whilst a Convention of the Citizens of
Kentucky by their Delegates, were deliberating on the propriety of separating from the State of Virginia, the want
of a proper channel through which to communicate to the
people at large,  . . .  induced them to appoint a committee of their own body, to encourage a Printer to settle
in the District.[1]

An unsuccessful attempt had been made to persuade a
printer named Miles Hunter to remove to Kentucky; but
nothing was accomplished until Bradford, who had, he says,
"not the least knowledge of the printing business," but
who did have confidence in his own mechanical talents and

---

[1] *Ky. Gaz.*, Jan. 4, 1797.  This account, which occupied two columns of the *Gazette*, was reprinted in the issues for Jan. 7, 11, 14,
18, and 21 following.

in the ability of his five sons, made an agreement with the committee which resulted in the issue ''on the 11th day of August, 1787,'' of the first number of the *Gazette*.[2] This paper, at first published by John and Fielding Bradford,[3] was, before the end of a year, in the hands of John Bradford alone;[4] and during a large part of the sixty years of its existence it was controlled by members of this family.[5]

[2] For the quotation cited above, as well as for the statement regarding Miles Hunter, see *ibid.*, Jan. 4, 1797. The spelling *Kentucke* was used until the issue of Mar. 14, 1789, when it was changed to *Kentucky*. For an account of a printer said to have left Pittsburg for Kentucky in 1784, see St. Jean de Crèvecœur, *Lettres d'un cultivateur américain*, 1787, III, 396. After mention of ''un Imprimeur établi à *Pittsbourg* il y a près de quatre ans,'' the apparently anonymous author of this curious letter dated from Louisville, Aug. 26, 1784, continues: ''son frère vient de partir avec sa presse pour *Kentuckey*, où on lui offre de l'encourager & de payer les frais de son voyage.'' Unless based on facts which I have been wholly unable to discover, this account is inaccurate in almost every detail. It is scarcely credible that such a letter was written from Louisville in 1784. It seems quite possible, however, that this part of Crèvecœur's book echoes a confused rumor concerning either the attempt to bring Hunter to Kentucky or the conveyance from Philadelphia, somewhat later, of materials for the use of *The Kentucke Gazette*. To Mr. Henri Bourdin, of Yale University, I am indebted for calling my attention to Crèvecœur's Western letter, which is not contained in the first edition of his book.

[3] *The Kentucke Gazette*, Aug. 18, 1787.

[4] *Ibid.*, June 7, 1788.

[5] On Mar. 31, 1802, John Bradford transferred the ownership of the paper to his son Daniel (*Ky. Gaz.*, Apr. 2, 1802), who owned and edited it for more than seven years, selling the property to one Thomas Smith in Sept., 1809 (*ibid.*, Sept. 26, 1809). Smith remained as proprietor and editor — except during the period of his service as a volunteer in the War of 1812, when Wm. W. Worsley acted as the manager (*ibid.*, Aug. 11 and 18, 1812) — until Sept., 1813, when John Bickley became a member of the firm and joint editor (*ibid.*, Sept. 14, 1813). In the autumn of 1814, after being out of the hands of the Bradfords for five years, the *Gazette* came

Of other early Kentucky papers, at least eight were founded before 1800, and apparently no less than thirty-two by

into the possession of Fielding Bradford, Jr. (*ibid.*, Sept. 26 and Oct. 3, 1814). Not quite three years later this proprietor took as a partner John Norvell, who was to have exclusive charge of the *Gazette*, now published under the firm name of John Norvell and Co. (*ibid.*, June 2, 1817). Early in 1819 Joshua Norvell & Co. became proprietors (*ibid.*, Mar. 5, 1819). Five months later the firm name was changed to Norvell & Cavins (*ibid.*, July 30 and Aug. 6, 1819); but in the following year, when one of the Bradfords, apparently John Bradford, was acting as editor, the Norvell interest was relinquished and I. T. Cavins was in control (*ibid.*, July 20 and 27, 1820). The history of the paper is at this point difficult to follow, but it is clear that early in 1822 Joseph Ficklin was editor (*Ky. Reporter*, Jan. 28, 1822) and that in the spring of 1825 John M. M'Calla, who had been editor and either part or whole owner, transferred his interest to John Bradford, who, as M'Calla states, ''established this paper near FORTY YEARS AGO, and until within a few years was the constant Editor'' (*Ky. Gaz.*, Apr. 28, 1825). Bradford, having retained the paper for two years more, relinquished it to Albert G. Meriwether (*ibid.*, June 29, 1827). Sometime between Aug. 22 and Oct. 10, 1828, Meriwether made way for Thomas R. Benning, whose control lasted till his death at the hands of Charles Wickliffe, a political enemy, about six months later (*ibid.*, Mar. 20, 1829). By 1830, the year of John Bradford's death, the paper was in the possession of George J. Trotter (*ibid.*, Jan. 8, 1830), but I have not made certain of the length of time during which he was in control. By the early part of 1835, Thomas J. Pew was publisher (*ibid.*, Jan. 10 ff., 1835); and on July 1 of that year Daniel Bradford, who first received the *Gazette* from his father in 1802, again became its editor and owner (*ibid.*, July 4 and 11, 1835). Somewhat more than a year later, however, failing eyesight compelled him to give over the editorial duties to Dr. Elisha Coleman (*ibid.*, Oct. 17, 1836); but he remained the proprietor, and in the following December again became editor (*ibid.*, Dec. 5, 1836). Beset by ill health as well as by financial difficulties, he retained the *Gazette* only because of family pride (*ibid.*, June 14, 1838); and early in 1840 he arranged to transfer it to J. Cunningham (*ibid.*, Mar. 12, 1840), who became editor and publisher in the April following (*ibid.*, Apr. 2, 1840). At the close of the pioneer period the *Gazette* was near the

1810,[6] when twenty or more were still being published.[7] *Stewart's Kentucky Herald*, which seems to have been the second paper in Kentucky, was founded in 1795 as a rival of *The Kentucky Gazette*, but was discontinued in Lexington after a few years, and later reestablished at the neighboring town of Paris.[8] Next to *The Kentucky Gazette*, however, the most important paper of eighteenth century Kentucky was *The Palladium*, founded by Hunter and Beaumont at Frankfort, the state capital, in 1798.

In the publication of newspapers, Ohio, which was soon to lead the West, was, from the beginning, not far behind Kentucky. Cincinnati's first paper, *The Centinel of the North-Western Territory*, founded by William Maxwell, began publication on November 9, 1793. Maxwell remained in control until the summer of 1796, when *The Centinel* became *Freeman's Journal*,[9] published, not only by the Free-

---

end of its long and useful existence. From the time when *The Kentucke Gazette* was changed to *The Kentucky Gazette*, in 1789, there was no important modification of the name, the latter form remaining always (except for the disuse of *The* a large portion of the time) the first part, or the whole, of the title.

[6] *Cf.* William Henry Perrin, *The Pioneer Press of Kentucky*, 1888, pp. 9-28 (Samuel Major's list, 1787-1811, is printed here on pp. 21-22); Isaiah Thomas, *The History of Printing in America*, 1810, second ed., 1874, II, 303 (published as Vol. VI of *Archæologia Americana*); Clarence S. Brigham, ''Bibliography of American Newspapers, 1690-1820,'' list for Kentucky, *Proceedings of the American Antiquarian Society*, N. S., XXIV, 363-403 (Oct., 1914). The numbers which I have given do not include continuations with changes only in the place of publication.

[7] See works cited in footnote 6 and *cf. The American Almanac*, for 1835, p. 282. Thomas's record of the establishment of early Western papers is almost uniformly inaccurate; but his list for 1810 is much more nearly correct. Brigham's account is the fullest and most authentic.

[8] Brigham, *op. cit.*, XXIV, 388 (Oct., 1914).

[9] For the change to *Freeman's Journal*, see Daniel Drake, *Natural and Statistical View, or Picture of Cincinnati*, 1815, p. 152. Max-

mans, but at least a part of the time by Freeman &
Carpenter.[10]   Before *Freeman's Journal* was removed from
Cincinnati, Joseph Carpenter had begun (May 28, 1799)
*The Western Spy, and Hamilton Gazette*, which was to continue for many years; and on December 4, 1804, appeared
the first number of *Liberty Hall and Cincinnati Mercury*,
destined under that name, or a shortened form of it
(beginning April 13, 1809), and later as *Liberty Hall
& Cincinnati Gazette* (from December 11, 1815) and *The
Daily Cincinnati Gazette* (from June 25, 1827, with only
a slight change in the order of the title), to become the
most important newspaper of Ohio during the pioneer
period.   Many owners and editors directed its policy during that time; but the most influential of all was Charles
Hammond, editor from 1825 until his death, in 1840.[11]

well's name as printer of the *Centinel* appears in that paper as late
as May 21, 1796.   The complete copy of the *Centinel* for May 14,
1796 (Vol. III, No. 130) and fragmentary copies for May 21 and
28 and June 4 of the same year, together with a mere shred of a
copy said to be for the following week (all in the library of the
Historical and Philosophical Society of Ohio), are the latest issues
of this paper which I have seen (*cf.* also Brigham, *op. cit.*, XXIX,
141, Apr., 1919).   According to Drake, *loc. cit.*, *Freeman's Journal*,
successor to the *Centinel*, was removed from Cincinnati to Chillicothe
early in 1800.   Edmund Freeman, however, could not have been
connected with the paper much longer, for, according to *The Western
Spy*, Nov. 5, 1800, he died on Oct. 25 of that year.

10 Brigham (*op. cit.*, XXIX, 141, Apr., 1919) gives S. Freeman,
and Son as publishers as early as Vol. I, No. 4 (July 9, 1796), with
Edmund Freeman as sole proprietor and publisher from Oct. 27,
1798, or earlier, up to the time of the last issue located, Oct. 1, 1799.
According to the issue for Oct. 27, 1798, however, the paper was at
that time "Printed and published by Freeman & Carpenter, Front
Street."

11 According to an editorial account, presumably by Charles Hammond, the paper, for which the press and types were brought from
New Jersey, was founded by the Rev. John W. Browne and a partner
named Crane, who soon withdrew.   In Apr., 1809, Browne was

On August 7, 1804, the same year in which Browne established the *Liberty Hall* at Cincinnati, there appeared at Vincennes the second number of the *Indiana Gazette*,

joined by two associates, his son, Samuel J. Browne, and James H. Looker. J. W. Browne died in Jan., 1813; and on Nov. 9 of that year S. J. Browne sold his interest to Andrew Wallace, the father of Governor Wallace of Indiana. Looker, who soon afterwards bought Wallace's interest, became associated in 1815 with Thomas Palmer and Sacket Reynolds, each of whom purchased a one-third share of the property. In December of that year the paper was rechristened *Liberty Hall & Cincinnati Gazette*. On Dec. 30, 1816, Looker & Reynolds sold their interest to Ephraim Morgan and Isaac G. Burnet; and the firm took the name of Morgan, Palmer & Co., while Burnet acted as editor. During the next decade Burnet first sold his interest to his brother-in-law, James Lodge, later purchased that of Thomas Palmer, and finally relinquished his share to Morgan & Lodge, Benjamin F. Powers being employed as editor. In 1825 Brownlow Fisher became associated with the firm; and in the same year began the long term of Charles Hammond, lawyer and journalist, as editor. It was Hammond who took charge of *The Daily Cincinnati Gazette* (later *The Cincinnati Daily Gazette*), which grew out of the old paper in June, 1827. In Aug., 1827, James Lodge sold his interest to S. S. L'Hommedieu; but in 1828 he, together with Thomas Hammond, purchased the interests of both Fisher and Morgan. In 1830 Thomas Hammond withdrew, and in 1833 R. F. L'Hommedieu was taken into partnership. When Lodge died, in Dec., 1835, the paper was in the hands of the two L'Hommedieus, who continued as sole proprietors until the death of Charles Hammond, Apr. 3, 1840. Three days later J. C. Wright became part owner and editor, and there was no further change during 1840. (The history of the paper to 1839 as here given is taken from *Cinc. Daily Gaz.*, Mar. 4, 1839. Hammond was in his time the best authority on newspaper history in Cincinnati, and he was trained to accuracy. I have been unable to discover any error in his account by comparison with data afforded by the nearly complete files of the newspapers concerned; but there is much that I have not verified, and I have made no attempt to trace the changes of ownership through the court records. For the death of Hammond and for Wright's partnership and editorship, see *ibid.*, Apr. 4, 8, and 11, 1840.)

earliest newspaper of Indiana Territory, which at that
time extended to the Mississippi on the west and to Lake
Superior on the north. Vincennes, in the path of the
Southern stream of migration, received its first important
literary impetus through Kentucky and Tennessee.[12] During
the thirty-six years of its existence prior to 1841, the *Indiana
Gazette*, which became *The Western Sun* in 1807, was carried on only in the face of great difficulties, with long
periods during which no paper was issued; but throughout
these years the founder, Elihu Stout, remained as sole or
part owner and, for practically all of the time, as editor.[13]

[12] According to Henry S. Cauthorn (*A History of the City of Vincennes*, n. d., 1902, p. 199) Stout had been employed on *The Kentucky
Gazette* at Lexington, later going to Nashville, Tenn.

[13] Stout's name alone appears on No. 2 (Aug. 7, 1804), on the
other extant issues scattered through the following year, and on the
issue for Apr. 12, 1806 (for the latter, see reproduction in *The
Western Sun*, July 4, 1904). A fire which occurred sometime in 1806
(Cauthorn, "Planting of Literary Institutions at Vincennes, Indiana," in W. H. Venable, *Beginnings of Literary Culture in the
Ohio Valley*, 1891, p. 260) seems to have put an end to the first
period of the paper's existence. On July 11, 1807, there appeared
the second number of *The Western Sun*, successor to the *Gazette*,
under the control of Elihu Stout. In the following August it was
announced that Elihu Stout & George C. Smoot would thereafter
conduct the paper (*The Western Sun*, Aug. 1, 1807); but within four
months the firm name was changed to Stout & Jennings, following
a quarrel between Stout and Smoot: the latter seems to have neglected
the paper during Stout's absence in Kentucky so that no issue had
appeared between Oct. 3 and Nov. 17 (*ibid.*, Nov. 17, 1807). At
the close of the same year the partnership of Stout & Jennings was
dissolved (*ibid.*, Dec. 23, 1807); and Stout continued alone until
nearly twelve years later, when the firm name became Stout & Osborn
(*ibid.*, Oct. 2, 1819), the name of the paper having been expanded
with the issue of Dec. 6, 1817. With Osborn's withdrawal in the
autumn of 1820 (*ibid.*, Sept. 20 and Oct. 7, 1820), Stout again
became sole owner, remaining in control until early in 1839. With
the issue of Jan. 19, 1839, the firm name became Elihu Stout and Son.

The influence of Lexington as the earliest center of journalistic activity in the West also accounted for the establishment of the *Missouri Gazette*, probably the first newspaper beyond the Mississippi, within little more than five years after the purchase of Louisiana by the United States. Joseph Charless, founder of the *Gazette*, had removed his printing office from Philadelphia to Lexington by the early part of 1803;[14] and in March of that year he, with Francis Peniston, began the publication of the *Independent Gazetteer* in opposition to the *Kentucky Gazette*.[15] Although Charless withdrew from the *Independent Gazetteer* long before it came to an end, some three years later,[16] he continued in Lexington as a printer for some time.[17] Moving farther west, he established the *Louisville Gazette, and Western Advertiser* in November, 1807, retaining some connection with it as late as April, 1809.[18] In the summer of the previous year, however, having secured the place of public printer in Louisiana Territory, he

From that time there was no change till after 1840. With the exception of the added phrase *General Advertiser* (1817), the title of the paper showed only insignificant modifications (in the use or omission of *The* and in the style *and* or *&*) from 1807 to 1841.

[14] See *Ky. Gaz.*, Jan. 11, 1803; and *The Western Spy*, Feb. 9, 1803.

[15] For preliminary announcements, see *Ky. Gaz.*, Jan. 11 and Mar. 1, 1803.

[16] *Ibid.*, Feb. 6, 1806; and Brigham, *op. cit.*, XXIV, 379 (Oct., 1914).

[17] *Cf. Charless' Kentucky, Tennessee, and Ohio Almanac for the Year 1807*, printed at Lexington, according to the title-page.

[18] See Brigham, *op. cit.*, XXIV, 392 (Oct., 1914). Charless, it seems, also conducted a general printing business in Louisville after he had begun publication of the *Missouri Gazette* (MS. Record 1781-1825 Town of Louisville, in office of the Clerks of the Boards of Aldermen and Councilmen, Louisville, p. 88, Aug. 16, 1808). In the *Mo. Gaz.*, July 19, 1809, Charless announced that he had disposed of his ''Office in Kentucky'' and had removed his family to St. Louis, ''being determined to devote my every exertion to render the Gazette a useful vehicle.''

began publication of the *Missouri Gazette* at St. Louis.[19]
This paper, under the direction of Joseph Charless for a
dozen years, and later controlled by a number of different
editors and publishers, passed through several changes of
title before the end of 1840, when it was known as the
*Daily Missouri Republican* and was owned by Chambers,
Knapp & Co.[20]  Nearly fifty years later it became *The
St. Louis Republic.*

[19] No. 3 of the first volume is for July 26, 1808. In it Charless
announces himself *"Printer to the Territory."* For Charless's
absence *"to Kentucky,"* see *ibid.*, same number, and for Nov. 16,
1808. It is not unlikely, I think, that Charless became interested
in establishing a newspaper at St. Louis through Francis Peniston,
the first of his partners in the publishing business at Lexington.
For Peniston's prospectus (1805) of a *Louisiana Herald* which was
apparently never published, see *The Farmer's Library* (Louisville),
Oct. 26, 1805.

[20] The name *Missouri Gazette* was changed on Nov. 30, 1809, to
*Louisiana Gazette*; but the title *Missouri Gazette* was resumed on
July 18, 1812, following the action of Congress in creating Missouri
Territory. Beginning with the issue for Feb. 26 or Mar. 5, 1814, the
paper was called *Missouri Gazette & Illinois Advertiser*; and on July
10, 1818, the name was changed to *Missouri Gazette & Public
Advertiser*. On Mar. 20, 1822, the style *Missouri Gazette Republican* was
adopted; and this was retained without change, even after the paper
had commenced a daily issue, until Mar. 14, 1837, when the title
*Daily Missouri Republican* was first used. The earlier caption,
*Missouri Republican*, was, however, revived on July 4, 1837; but on
Jan. 7, 1839, this form again gave place to *Daily Missouri Republi-
can*, as the paper continued to be called till after 1840. Joseph
Charless remained in control from 1808 to the autumn of 1820, when
James C. Cummins took charge (*Mo. Gaz.*, Sept. 20, 1820). In 1822,
however, the Charless family regained control in the person of
Edward Charless, with Josiah Spalding as editor (*Mo. Rep.*, Mar. 20,
1822). Edward Charless's name alone appeared as printer until
Sept. 11, 1822; but with the following issue the firm name Edward
Charless & Co. was adopted, and this was retained, except for
abbreviation of the first name, to and including Feb. 9, 1826.
Thereafter, for some two years, the style Edward Charless was again

Like both the *Indiana Gazette* and the *Missouri Gazette*,
the first paper in Illinois was in its origin a symbol of the
predominant influence of Kentucky and the migratory
stream which flowed through it and from it into the
southern sections of Indiana and Illinois and spread over
the greater part of Missouri. From Kentucky came Mathew
Duncan,[21] founder of *The Illinois Herald*, which was begun
at Kaskaskia, apparently in the spring or early summer of
1814, and certainly not later than July of that year.[22] It
was followed within about two years by *The Western
Intelligencer*, the fourth number of which appeared at
Kaskaskia May 15, 1816, printed and published by Dan'l
P. Cook & Co. On May 27, 1818, the name of *The Western
Intelligencer* was changed to *The Illinois Intelligencer*; and
under this title the paper was continued for a time at
Kaskaskia and later, for many years, at Vandalia, the new
capital of the state.

In Detroit, where the early population was made up of

---

in use. From Mar. 25, 1828, to July 3, 1837, the firm was Edw.
Charless and N. Paschall (with only minor changes in the form).
On July 1 of the latter year Chambers, Harris & Knapp came into
control of the paper (*ibid.*, July 3, 1837), and with the issue of July
4 their names replaced those of Charless & Paschall. With the issue
of Aug. 12 or 13, 1839, the name of the publishing company was
shortened to Chambers & Knapp, remaining so till Jan. 1, 1840.
Finally, from Jan. 3 till sometime after 1840 the designation used
was Chambers, Knapp & Co. In the meantime the paper had gone
through the evolutionary stages natural to its character of frontier
gazette long-lived enough to become a city daily. First a weekly
publication, it became for a time a semiweekly paper (Apr. 9, 1833-
Apr. 28, 1835), then a triweekly (Apr. 30, 1835-Sept. 17, 1836). It
was issued daily from Sept. 20, 1836.

[21] Brigham, *op. cit.*, XXIV, 397 (Oct., 1914). According to this
authority, a Matthew [*sic*] Duncan was the publisher of a newspaper
at Russellville, Ky., in 1809.

[22] See *Niles' Weekly Register*, July 23, 1814. No. 30 of Vol. I
is for Dec. 13, 1814.

the old French inhabitants with a slowly increasing admixture of New York and New England stock, an unsuccessful attempt was made in 1809 by James M. Miller of Utica, New York,[23] to establish a newspaper, which he called the *Michigan Essay; or, the Impartial Observer.* The first number appeared on August 31 of that year, but only two other issues seem to have been printed.[24] Apparently no other attempt to found a paper in Detroit was made until 1817, when Sheldon & Reed began publication of the long-lived *Detroit Gazette.* Like the *Missouri Gazette* at the old French colony of St. Louis and the *Michigan Essay* of 1809, the *Detroit Gazette* made for a time an effort to secure the patronage of both French- and English-speaking people. Its earliest issues contained considerable sections printed in the French language,[25] but this plan was abandoned before the end of the first year.[26] The *Gazette,* from its beginning

---

[23] For the statement that Miller was from Utica, see Samuel R. Brown, *Views on Lake Erie,* Troy, 1814, p. 96.

[24] So far as I know, only the first number is extant. Its continuance for two more issues may, however, be inferred from Samuel R. Brown's statement (*loc. cit.*) that Miller "did not meet with sufficient encouragement to continue it beyond the third number."

[25] The plan for this part of the paper was announced by the editors in the first issue of the *Gazette* (July 25, 1817): "Les editeurs de la GAZETTE DU DETROIT, considerant que la plus grande part des habitans du territoire du Michigan et du haut Canada sont Francaise, et pour la plupart n'entendent l'Anglois qu' imparfaitement, sachant de plus que plusieurs de leurs lecteurs Anglois, aiment avec raison la langue Francaise, annoncent a tout leurs suscripteurs, qu' ils se proposent de reserver deux ou trois colonnes pour y imprimer en Francais a chaque No. de la Gazette — un abrigé des évenemens les plus interessants qui se passent en Europe, aussi bien que les decouvertes utiles relatif a l'Agriculture et aux Arts, et une varieté d'extraits amusants et instructifs."

[26] See the *Detroit Gaz.,* Nov. 28, 1817, for announcement of a temporary abandonment of this plan, which, however, was not resumed later.

in 1817 till 1830, when, apparently, it ceased publication, underwent no change of name and few changes in management.[27]

Wisconsin and Iowa had no newspapers until the last decade before 1840. The *Green-Bay Intelligencer*, begun at Navarino (later Green Bay), Wisconsin, on December 11, 1833, was probably the first of these; and its pioneer quality was emphasized by the fact that it was designed to appear only semimonthly.[28] In Iowa no gazette seems to have been published until May 11, 1836, when John King issued the first number of the *Du Buque Visitor*.[29]

## II

In general, the newspapers of the earliest pioneer group had much the same reason for being, and similar difficulties against which to contend; and the resulting journalistic product was in most cases characterized by the same crudity in the beginning modified later by a gradual change for the better, reflecting the increasing prosperity of the frontier communities. Almost without exception, the papers whose beginnings have been chronicled were founded

[27] Sheldon & Reed retained joint control until the spring of 1825, when Ebenezer Reed withdrew, leaving John P. Sheldon in complete control (*ibid.*, May 10, 1825). During the last three months of 1825 and the first two months of 1826, however, Reed served as editor during Sheldon's absence at Washington (*ibid.*, Mar. 7, 1826). Sheldon, resuming the editorship after that time, remained in charge of the paper as late as July 3, 1828; by the 24th of the same month, however, Henry L. Ball was the publisher. Ball retained control as late as Mar., 1829; but by Dec. 10 of that year Sheldon M'Knight was publisher, and on the same date Ebenezer Reed withdrew from his duties as editor, which he had reassumed at a time I have not been able to determine.

[28] As a matter of fact, it did not appear regularly so often: No. 19 of Vol. I was issued on May 30, 1835.

[29] John Plumbe, *Sketches of Iowa and Wisconsin*, 1839, p. 64.

with either the assurance or the hope of securing government patronage; and their first concern was therefore
to publish the laws, the printing of which was their most
dependable source of revenue. But, even with this more or
less certain means of support (for many rivals were soon
in the field), their existence was at best a precarious one
until late in the pioneer period. Even the mechanical
equipment necessary for printing a paper was not easily
acquired. The types for *The Kentucke Gazette* of 1787
had to be brought from Philadelphia through a country
infested with Indians, and for many years frontier newspapers were supplied with materials only irregularly and
nearly always inadequately. By 1792 Craig, Parkers &
Co. had begun the erection of a paper mill at Georgetown,
Kentucky;[30] but often the gazettes of the most important
towns, like Cincinnati [31] and St. Louis,[32] as well as those of
less accessible places, like Kaskaskia,[33] were compelled to
reduce their issue to a fraction of its usual size or even to
suspend publication for weeks at a time on account of the
difficulty of securing paper.

Lack of financial support was not uncommonly responsible for similar interruptions. The small number of subscribers and the wide latitude allowed them in making their
payments made the maintenance of the average newspaper
an undertaking of great uncertainty.[34] A typical instance

[30] *Ky. Gaz.*, Apr. 14, 1792. *Cf.* also Mann Butler, *A History of
the Commonwealth of Kentucky*, 1834, p. 206.

[31] The editor of *Liberty Hall* (Feb. 10, 1807) offered his subscribers this apology: ''The extreme frost having closed up the Ohio,
and prevented our receiving a further supply of PAPER, we are
reluctantly obliged to furnish our readers with a small sheet.''

[32] *Mo. Gaz.*, Oct. 2, 1813-Feb. 19, 1814.

[33] See, for example, *The Western Intelligencer* through Feb., 1817,
and for May 7 of the same year.

[34] There was an almost universal complaint regarding the failure
of subscribers to meet their obligations. Unpaid subscriptions were

is afforded by *The Kentucke Gazette*, which, at or soon
after its beginning, asked eighteen shillings a year as the
price of subscription,[35] and commenced with about one
hundred and eighty subscribers.[36] Under these conditions
the paper encountered great financial difficulties, but by
1797 its success seemed assured.[37] It is impossible to say
what part of the total revenue was derived from the publication of laws and other official documents; but in 1806,
when, during the greater part of the year, the *Gazette* was
published semiweekly, at a subscription rate increased, for
this reason, from $2.00 to $3.50 (or $4.00 if paid at the end
of the year),[38] the total amount of subscriptions received
was, according to the editor, $535.50, while the cost of the
supply of printing paper alone was $916.00.[39] Toward
the end of the pioneer period, the increasing revenues
often failed to keep pace with the growing expenses, which,
by 1836, had risen to about $3600 a year for a weekly

apparently continued for long periods, though at times attempts were
made to secure delayed payments by means of notes (*cf. Ky. Gaz.,*
Feb. 6, 1806); and, later in the period, groups of newspapers serving
the same community sometimes attempted to regulate such matters
by mutual agreement (see *Detroit Journal and Michigan Advertiser,*
Nov. 27, 1833). In some cases payment in kind was allowed. The
*Indiana Gazette* (Oct. 23, 1804), for example, announced that it
would receive anyone of a number of articles in lieu of the price of
subscription: ''Beef, Pork, Bacon, Corn, Cotton, Whiskey, Wheat,
Sugar, Potatoes, Butter, Eggs, Tobacco, Salt, Tallow, Flour or Oats.''

[35] *The Kentucke Gazette*, Aug. 18, 1787.

[36] *Ky. Gaz.*, Jan. 4, 1797. The *Missouri Gazette* commenced twenty
years later with almost exactly the same number of subscribers,
increasing to nearly a thousand after eleven years (*Mo. Gaz.*, Oct.
20, 1819).

[37] *Ky. Gaz., loc. cit.*

[38] *Ibid.*, Feb. 6, 1806.

[39] *Ibid.*, Dec. 15, 1806. About four years later the total weekly
cost of publishing the *Louisiana Gazette* was said to be ''upwards of
twenty dollars'' or something more than a thousand dollars a year
(*Louisiana Gazette*, Dec. 19, 1810).

issue.[40]   In 1838, only pride in the enterprise founded by his father induced Daniel Bradford to continue the *Gazette*, though he had been able within three years to double, almost, the number of subscribers for what had been for a long time previous to 1835 "a sinking concern."[41]   The financial difficulties persisted [42] to the end of the pioneer period, and a few years later the *Gazette* was finally abandoned.   The size of the *Gazette*, and of other contemporary prints, exhibited a succession of changes reflecting not only the irregularity of the paper supply, but the difficulties of securing aid in setting type and the constantly fluctuating financial prosperity of the publisher.   Often, after reaching the normal four pages of the pioneer gazette, the paper would have to be reduced to a single sheet the size of letter paper or completely abandoned for a time.[43]   Experiments at semiweekly publication were made before the end of the eighteenth century,[44] and were repeated unsuccessfully many times for short periods.   Three issues a week were also attempted by a number of publishers before daily gazettes became firmly established in the largest towns during the last decade before 1841.

The content of most eighteenth century and early nineteenth century newspapers in the West was a compound consisting at first largely of foreign and Eastern news and

[40] *Ky. Gaz.*, Jan. 23, 1836.

[41] *Ibid.*, June 14, 1838.

[42] *Ibid.*, Jan. 3, 1839.

[43] Such occurrences were too common for citation.   One of the best examples of many long delays caused by a variety of troubles characteristic of the pioneer paper is afforded by the *Indiana Gazette* and *The Western Sun*, conducted in the remote village of Vincennes. See, for example, *The Western Sun*, Nov. 17, 1807; Feb. 9, 1808; and June 8, 1811.

[44] *Ky. Gaz.*, Jan. 4 ff., 1797.   As late as 1836 semiweekly publication was still only an occasional experiment with this paper (see *ibid.*, May 9 and Dec. 29, 1836).

government proclamations or laws, with a very limited amount of general advertising and some political controversy; but showed a gradual change toward greater attention to local concerns, especially those of a commercial or political nature. In spite of the fact that before, and for some time following, 1800, news from Europe was commonly received only after from two to three months, and dispatches from the East were often more than a month old when they reached the West,[45] such items generally made up from half to two-thirds of the Western papers of that period.[46] Publication of the laws, however, sometimes encroached upon even the foreign news, and in some cases filled nearly the whole of the available space. Commercial advertisements did not usually form an important part of the contents. The earliest gazettes often had no more than a column or two of such material, and seldom was

[45] In Nov. and Dec., 1793, for example, the important London and Paris dispatches of *The Centinel of the North-Western Territory*, at Cincinnati, were of the preceding July and August; and the same issues carried New York, Boston, and Philadelphia dispatches of October and early November. Word of the signing of the treaty of peace between Great Britain and the United States on Dec. 24, 1814, reached St. Louis in a Washington dispatch of Feb. 14, 1815, in time to be published in the *Missouri Gazette* on Mar. 11 following. More rapid transmission of news was hardly to be expected. In some cases, especially before 1800, it was much slower. A Pittsburg news item of July 21, 1787, did not appear in *The Kentucke Gazette* till Nov. 24 of that year; but the delay was not always so great.

[46] In *The Kentucke Gazette* for Nov. 24, 1787, nearly five-sixths of the total content was foreign news alone, but this was more than the average proportion of such material. More often the proportion was about that found in *Freeman's Journal* (Cincinnati) for Oct. 27, 1798, where approximately eleven of a total of sixteen columns were filled with foreign news, while two-thirds of a column was devoted to Eastern news. About half of the first issue of *The Palladium* (Frankfort), Aug. 9, 1798, was made up of foreign and Eastern news. In the *Michigan Essay* for Aug. 31, 1809, the first issue, foreign news occupied about two of the four pages.

more than one-fourth of the whole used in this way.[47]   The
revenue derived from this source must have been small.[48]
But in the chief commercial centers, toward the end of the
period, the space devoted to advertising increased even out
of proportion to the great expansion of the whole newspaper.[49]   Conventional illustrative devices were used with
increasing frequency till toward 1840, when there was a
tendency to compress all materials into smaller type with
less conspicuous headings, so that four large pages would
still contain the much greater quantity of matter.   Clever
writing was only very rarely attempted in advertisements,[50]

[47] The first number of *The Palladium* (1798) contained only one
column of advertisements; but within a few years the average amount
was perhaps something more than a page, a large part of which was,
however, filled with court notices.   The advertisements in *The Kentucky Gazette* of the eighteenth century varied from only a fraction
of a column to three-fourths of the entire paper (see, for example,
the issues for June, 1790).   *Freeman's Journal* for Oct. 27, 1798,
gave one-fourth of its columns to advertisements.

[48] In some cases, at least, the amount derived from general advertising must have been almost negligible.   The *Indiana Gazette*, Aug.
7, 1804, prints this notice: "Advertisements of no more length
than breadth, inserted three times for one dollar and fifty cents,
and twenty-five cents for each continuance."   The entire paper consisted of sixteen columns, one of which would contain six such
advertisements, thus yielding $3.00 an issue for new material or $1.50
for continuances.

[49] This was true also of the newspapers in certain comparatively
small towns which were just beginning a rapid growth and were the
centers of speculation in lands.   See, for example, the *Chicago American* for 1839, and the *Sangamo Journal* (Springfield) for 1835.

[50] Among the few examples of this kind of wit are the notices of
G. R. Lillibridge's Tontine Coffee House in the *Detroit Daily Free
Press* for 1835-1836, ending on May 13 of the latter year with his
"Valedictory," in which he announces, "with his heart upon his
hand," the unpleasant news that "he has closed his establishment
'*sine die*'" because of the unfriendly attitude of the board of "All-
dear-men of our beautiful City of the Lakes."   Among his best

and in fact no part of the average gazette of the time was characterized by the slightest departure from conventional form.

Early in the pioneer era it was usual for newspapers to declare their political independence after an assertion of fervent devotion to democratic ideals and American institutions in general. "The political complection of the paper shall be truly republican; but it never shall be prostituted to party," declared the editor of the *Indiana Gazette* in his introductory address to the public. Political neutrality was, however, difficult to realize; and even some of the oldest newspapers, like *The Kentucke Gazette*, were founded with the intention of carrying out a definite political program. And not only was the *Gazette* distinguished by its advocacy of the separation of Kentucky from Virginia, but it lent itself, as has been pointed out,[51] to the strong faction which, desiring separation from the Union, was active in its denunciation of the federal government. During the excitement accompanying the attack of England and other countries upon Revolutionary France, writers in the same newspaper called loudly for American participation on the side of France; and these attacks on American policy were echoed by the only other gazette then published on the Western frontier.[52] The early papers which disclaimed affiliation with any political party were the arenas for ponderous debates, after the fashion of the time, by contributors who appeared in

---

achievements in advertising notices with literary flavor are his offer of a prize for a New Year's address, and his ode on a cargo of oysters lost in Lake Erie.

[51] Theodore Roosevelt, *The Winning of the West*, 1908, VI, 34.

[52] See reprint, in a number of installments, of such an article in *Cent. N.-W. Ter.*, Feb. 1-15, 1794. In April of the same year the *Centinel* reprinted from the *Gazette* a "Crisis" article threatening Kentucky's withdrawal from the Union.

public masked by such appellations of classical kind as
Plebius, Manlius, and Philadelphiensis. Within less than
two decades after the beginning of the nineteenth century
it is likely that the majority of Western newspapers were
openly identified with some political party;[53] and, with the
passing of time, the political flavor of frontier journalism
became much more pronounced. To partisan editorial
propaganda of any sort, the usual preliminary was an
enthusiastic protestation of strong democratic sentiment.
"The newspaper editor," wrote a contemporary observer
of the West,

let him support whom he may for the Presidency, aims
chiefly to satisfy his neighbors that he and the party to
which he belongs are more democratic, more devoted to
the people, more favorable to entire equality, than their
opponents.[54]

Sometimes, however, bitter personal attacks characterized
the paper's participation in the campaign. From this
circumstance, editorial writing, which had earlier formed
a negligible part of Western journalism, became much
more important. What had at first been, with the exception of the new editor's introductory address to his readers,
scarcely distinguishable from simple news items, now became
distinct. At times some degree of skill was displayed
in the contests of blackguard wit in which the editors
indulged. George Dennison Prentice, who abandoned *The
New England Review* to John Greenleaf Whittier in order
to come to the West, first as the political biographer of
Henry Clay and later as the principal editor of the famous
Whig *Journal* at Louisville, was the chief teacher of this
art on the frontier. From the first his paper was a success,

---

[53] In 1834, according to a writer in *The Western Monthly Magazine* (II, 402, Aug., 1834), about ten of every thirteen periodicals
published in Ohio were supposed to be political partisans.

[54] *The Hesperian*, III, 458 (Nov., 1839).

and he was soon known throughout the country for his wit and ability as a partisan; no doubt he was the most prominent editor of the pioneer West. With uncanny skill he lashed his competitors into helpless rage. The chief butt of his ridicule was Shadrach Penn, of *The Louisville Public Advertiser*, long established as the leading paper of that part of Kentucky. Upon Prentice, in turn, Penn exhausted his powers of abuse, the nature of which is illustrated by the opening paragraph of an editorial attack headed "The Journal":

Do not be alarmed, reader. We are not about to attempt to compete with that print, in lying or blackguarding. No, No! That would be folly, were we disposed to stoop to such an undertaking. We have no idea that the whole gang of criminals in the Kentucky Penitentiary contain in their compositions as large an amount of venality and low-bred vulgarity, as is discernable in the character of the Senior Editor of the Journal, and it will be admitted that it would be madness — sheer madness — for any decent man to attempt to grapple with such a wretch, in his own way. We shall do no such thing. If we occasionally remind the public, that he is one of the dirtiest villains, the most reckless liars, and ineffable paltrons, that ever walked, it is only done to prevent forgetful individuals from losing sight of his true character.[55]

Quarrels of the kind, on a smaller scale, had become common before 1840. In Detroit the long feud between the *Detroit Journal and Michigan Advertiser* and a prominent contemporary is reflected in a lengthy editorial printed in the former, which begins in this characteristically belligerent tone:

The Free Press, a paper whose stupid inanity is only equalled by its licentiousness, has had the insolence, without any new or special provocation, to arraign the conduct and character of this journal.[56]

---

[55] *Lou. Pub. Adv.*, Nov. 13, 1835.

[56] *Detroit Journal and Michigan Advertiser*, Apr. 2, 1834.

It was not unusual for editorial utterances, or even editorial prejudice as exhibited in the publication of partisan
communications, to arouse harsh feeling which resulted in
personal assault. In 1807 the editor of *Liberty Hall* was
beaten with a club by a prominent citizen of Cincinnati
because the former, according to his own account, refused
to divulge the name of the author of an offensive article.[57]
The withdrawal of Joseph Charless from the *Missouri
Gazette* in 1820 was apparently occasioned by the violent
opposition of rival editors. More than a year before the
paper was sold, a certain D. Kimball requested ''the
incendiaries of St. Louis to defer burning Mr. Charless'
establishment, until his removal, which will be on the 20th
April next'';[58] and a few months later Charless wrote:

The history of our establishment for the past 11 years
would present an interesting and singular detail. It would
exhibit violence, persecution, arrogance and unprincipled
ambition; in many instances connected with power, all
arrayed against us. We have been attacked repeatedly,
abused and slandered, both by men in power and men out
of power.[59]

In the spring of the following year events rapidly drew
to a climax: according to ''*A Spectator*,'' whose narrative
appeared at length in the *Gazette*, Charless was assaulted
by one of the editors of the rival *St. Louis Enquirer.*[60]
Within a few months the *Gazette* was in the hands of a new
owner. The most conspicuous example of violence in
answer to editorial policy was, however, the persecution of
Elijah P. Lovejoy. Driven from St. Louis because of the
antislavery propaganda in his *Observer*, he attempted to

---

[57] *Liberty Hall*, Nov. 3, 1807. A similar quarrel, more than twenty
years later, resulted in the death of an editor of the *Kentucky Gazette*
(see above, footnote 5 of the present chapter).

[58] *Mo. Gaz.*, Jan. 1, 1819.

[59] *Ibid.*, Oct. 20, 1819.

[60] *Ibid.*, May 17, 1820.

reestablish the paper at Alton, Illinois. The state of public feeling was such, however, that there was only the slightest prospect of success. Four printing presses were destroyed in succession, and finally Lovejoy himself was murdered by a mob.[61]

In a comparatively few instances before 1840 editorial writing showed a noticeable development distinct from open partisan propaganda. In this kind of journalism, perhaps no writer was more successful than Charles Hammond, editor for many years of *The Daily Cincinnati Gazette*.

Matters of local interest other than political or personal quarrels occupied an extremely limited portion of the pioneer newspapers. A frontier flavor was given to *The Kentucky Gazette* for a number of years by its laconic narratives of Indian atrocities in various quarters of Kentucky. Valuable sketches of pioneer history were contained in the "Notes on Kentucky," which John Bradford published in the *Gazette* nearly forty years after the beginning of his first term as its editor.[62] Other papers, especially those on the extreme frontier, contained some description of the new country intended to attract immigration. Such was the acknowledged purpose of the first newspaper published in Wisconsin, the *Green-Bay Intelligencer*, whose editor, though he professed a desire to write "on the character, manners &c. of the Aborigines," asserted that his principal object was "*the advancement of the country west of Lake Michigan*" and called upon his subscribers for aid in "transmitting the blooming beauties of Wisconsin, to our friends on the Atlantic." [63]

---

[61] See Edward Beecher, *Narrative of Riots at Alton: in Connection with the Death of Rev. Elijah P. Lovejoy*, 1838, pp. 5-108.

[62] Section XXXVII, ending with the events of 1791, appeared on June 1, 1827. The "Notes" were partly reprinted in G. W. Stipp's *The Western Miscellany*, 1827, pp. 9-131, where they constitute a history of Kentucky to 1788.

[63] *Green-Bay Intelligencer*, Dec. 11, 1833.

Few pioneer papers failed to make some effort to furnish their readers with what was considered matter of purely literary interest. Practically every gazette, however drab its dress, displayed more or less regularly a corner devoted to verse, usually of the nondescript kind bandied about among obscure periodicals everywhere, but often made up of a few stanzas from some famous poet. This small section of the average frontier paper, constituting its chief claim to cultural dignity, appeared variously as "Seat of the Muses," "Parnassiad," "Poetical Asylum," "Poet's Corner," "Sacred to the Muses," "The Muses," "Selected Poetry." Bits of original verse were also published; and the carrier's annual New Year's address, sometimes a prize production, was often displayed prominently in the paper or printed on a separate sheet.[64]   A prose "Miscellany," likewise a purveyor of literary mediocrity, but at times containing excerpts from writers of note, was common in two types of papers — early gazettes, especially those published in places difficult of access, and periodicals with some pretentions to magazine quality and usually exhibiting something above the ordinary literary taste. A single volume such as Goldsmith's essays might furnish a considerable portion of many issues of a newly established paper. Occasionally the miscellany assumed the proportions of a serial novel, sometimes even an original one.[65]

[64] Perhaps the most popular poem which appeared as a New Year's address was John Finley's "The Hoosier's Nest," a humorous description of a backwoods cabin "written in 1830, for the *Indianapolis Journal.*" For this well known frontier classic and for some account of its author, see William T. Coggeshall, *The Poets and Poetry of the West*, 1860, pp. 83-85.

[65] An early example is "Edwin and Edelia, a Novel, in a Series of Letters," in *Liberty Hall*, Jan. 27-May 26, 1806.

## III

In Cincinnati, and in the other large towns, the leading papers, however crude mechanically as compared with the journalistic product of a later day, showed, by 1840, the results of a remarkable process of evolution. They were much more complex than they had been at the beginning of the century, and their mechanical execution was equally improved. Meantime the most important of them had been successful in establishing "daily" editions which, in reality, never appeared more than six times a week. By January, 1826, the *Commercial Register*, of Cincinnati, "designed to be altogether commercial," had begun to appear daily.[66] *The Daily Cincinnati Gazette* followed in June of the next year. *The Commercial Daily Advertiser*, also at Cincinnati, dated from 1829.[67] From this time the number of such papers rapidly increased. *The Louisville Public Advertiser*, founded by Penn in 1818 as the *Public Advertiser*, began a daily issue on January 1, 1830, and was called the *Daily Louisville Public Advertiser* (but with changes at intervals) from June 14 of that year. The wide geographical distribution of these publications during the last decade before 1841 was illustrated by the transformation of the *Missouri Republican* and the appearance of such papers as the *Detroit Daily Free Press* and the *Daily Cleveland Herald*. At the end of this period there were, according to the census of 1840, twenty-nine daily papers in the West, of which number Ohio had nine, Missouri and Michigan six each, Kentucky five, and Illinois three. The circulation of the dailies was, however, surprisingly small. In 1841 the combined issue of the seven published in Cincinnati, the largest

---

[66] See *Detroit Gaz.*, Jan. 31, 1826.

[67] E. S. Thomas, *Reminiscences*, 1840, II, 96.

town, was estimated at 5612, or an average of eight hundred.[68]

Since the founding of *The Kentucke Gazette*, in 1787, the total number of newspapers in the West had increased, except during one decade, much more rapidly than the population. In 1790 there was 1 newspaper to about 75,000 people; in 1800 there were perhaps 8 [69] to a population of 271,195, or 1 for every 34,000 people; in 1810 there were about 40 [70] to a population of approximately 700,000, or 1 for every 17,000 persons; in 1820 there were at least 79 [71] to a population of 1,423,622, or 1 for every 18,000 persons; in 1834 there were, according to the best information available, 227 [72] to a population of perhaps 3,000,000, or 1 for every 13,000 persons; in 1840 the census reported 354 newspapers[73] to a population of 4,131,310, or more than 1 for every 12,000 persons. At the same time Western newspapers, which had comprised less than a tenth of the total number of such publications in the United States in 1810, were more than a fourth of the 1404 now published. Ohio, which had gained the lead over Kentucky shortly after

[68] Charles Cist, *Cincinnati in 1841*, 1841, p. 93. At the same time four triweekly editions of Cincinnati newspapers were supposed to have a total issue of 1100, while six weekly editions of the same type of periodical totaled 8050 (*ibid.*, pp. 93-94).

[69] *Cf.* Brigham, *op. cit.*, XXIV, 363-403 (Oct., 1914), and XXIX, 129-180 (Apr., 1919); and authorities cited in footnotes 6 and 9.

[70] *The American Almanac*, for 1835, p. 282, gives the number as thirty-three; but *cf.* Brigham, *loc. cit.*, and *ibid.*, XXIII, 398-403 (Oct., 1913), and XXVI, 93-95 (Apr., 1916).

[71] *Cf.* Brigham, *loc. cit.*; and *ibid.*, XXIII, 395-397 (Oct., 1913), and XXVI, 82 (Apr., 1916).

[72] *The American Almanac*, for 1835, p. 282.

[73] This and all data on newspapers in 1840 which follow are derived from the *Compendium of the Enumeration of the Inhabitants and Statistics of the United States, as Obtained at the Department of State, from the Returns of the Sixth Census, . . . Prepared at the Department of State*, 1841.

1810, had, at the end of the period, over one-third of all
the newspapers in the West, while Indiana was second with
more than one-fifth, followed by Illinois with somewhat
more than half as many. Kentucky, Missouri, and
Michigan, ranking in the order named, had together fewer
than Ohio. Wisconsin had six and Iowa, four. The great
majority of Western newspapers at the time were weekly,
those issued semiweekly and triweekly not quite equaling
the total of daily papers.

## IV

A considerable number of weekly papers[74] showed, but
in varying degrees, a radical divergence in aim and method
from the bulk of periodicals which might more properly
be called newspapers. They were, in fact, a distinct
product, and often, in mechanical form as well as in
content, weekly journals devoted to such ends as religious,
political, or social propaganda, or to general literature,
with only slight attention to news and commercial advertising.

Among the comparatively numerous papers of this kind[75]
which sought to advance the interests of particular religious
sects or, less commonly, of orthodox Christian teachings
with no marked sectarian bias, one of the earliest was *The
Philanthropist*, edited and published by Elisha Bates, the

[74] All weekly periodicals are apparently included in the census
numbers and other estimates cited above showing the growth of newspapers; and it does not seem possible to determine the proportion
of the total which belongs to the group discussed in the present
section.

[75] According to Cist (*op. cit.*, pp. 93-94) seven of the thirteen
weekly periodicals published in Cincinnati in 1841 were religious.
The popularity of the religious papers of that town is reflected in
their total estimated weekly issue at that time of 22,900 as compared
with an estimated total of only 8050 for non-sectarian weekly
publications.

leader of the orthodox Friends in the West, which appeared for the first time at Mountpleasant, Ohio, in December, 1818, and continued until 1822. The sixteen pages of each issue comprised a weekly journal of essays, moral, religious, domestic, agricultural, and mechanical, together with brief notices of current events; but the predominant doctrinal purpose was revealed in the added declaration of the title-page that the public sentiment should be improved and refined, till man, in every situation, should become the friend of man. A long-lived interdenominational journal was *The Western Luminary*, begun in 1824, and printed at Lexington by Thomas Skillman, a prominent publisher and editor of religious periodicals and pamphlets. On October 21, 1835, the *Luminary* finally ceased publication, at least in Lexington, and its whole establishment was transferred to Eli Taylor, of the Cincinnati *Journal*.[76] *The Gambier Observer*, begun in 1830, was for a long time the official gazette of the Protestant Episcopal Church in Ohio; and Universalist doctrine was disseminated for a number of years by *The Sentinel, and Star in the West* (1829), which was published at various places. *The Catholic Telegraph*, begun at Cincinnati in 1831, was inspired by the polemical spirit of the time. The editor did not wish, he declared in his first issue, to provoke controversy, but he would never shrink from it. The *Western Christian Advocate* (1834), destined to a long life following the pioneer period, was a symbol of the rapidly growing power of the Methodist Church. By the end of the period it was probably the most widely circulated periodical in the West.[77]

Journals of purely political interest were ephemeral, appearing and disappearing with the rising and ebbing of

---

[76] See *Ky. Gaz.*, Oct. 24, 1835.

[77] According to Cist (*op. cit.*, p. 94), the weekly issue in 1841 was 14,000, far greater than that of any other Cincinnati periodical of the time.

the tide of public interest in successive crises. Such were *The Patriot* and *The Spirit of '76*, founded almost simultaneously at Frankfort in 1826 to debate the vexed question of the abolition of the Court of Appeals. The Presidential election of 1840, which, with its log cabin and hard cider parades, stirred the enthusiasm of the West as nothing before had done, was the inspiration of such partisans as *The Campaign*, which appeared at Frankfort in April of that year, issuing twenty-five numbers before November, and a final one much later.

Among the few weekly publications devoted to social theory without respect to political parties or religious sects, the most remarkable was *The New-Harmony Gazette* (1825-1828), which began by announcing its program as the purveyor of Robert Owen's teachings:

In our Gazette we purpose developing more fully the principles of the SOCIAL SYSTEM; that the world, with ourselves, may, by contrast, be convinced — that INDIVIDUALITY DETRACTS LARGELY FROM THE SUM OF HUMAN HAPPINESS. . . .
As the writings of Mr. Owen will necessarily occupy a considerable portion of our columns, it is deemed proper, that the publication should commence with a biographical notice of this gentleman.[78]

During the greater part of the journal's existence, two of the famous theorist's sons, William and Robert Dale Owen, acted as editors, a part of the time jointly, and at other times independently or in cooperation with other persons.[79]

[78] *The New-Harmony Gazette*, Oct. 1, 1825.

[79] See *ibid.*, Mar. 19, 1828, for an account of the editorial management of this journal from the beginning (Oct. 1, 1825) to that time. Others who had a hand in the editorial conduct of the *Gazette* during the same period were Robert L. Jennings, William Pelham, and Thomas Palmer. From Mar. 19 to Oct. 22, 1828, the date of the last number issued, the editors were first William and Robert Dale Owen, then Frances Wright and William Owen, and finally Frances Wright and Robert Dale Owen. The ideals of the *Gazette* were

Unusual interest attaches to this publication because of the
record which it contains of the controversies and numerous
constitutional changes incident to the rise and decline of a
remarkable communistic society. A new scheme of government is framed and adopted for "a Community, to be
entitled 'THE NEW-HARMONY COMMUNITY OF
EQUALITY.'"[80]   The "Superintendents of Departments" under the new order are announced: Dr. Wm.
Price for Agriculture; J. K. Coolidge for Manufactures
and Mechanics; Thomas Say for Literature, Science, and
Education; Richesson Whitby for Domestic Economy;
Stedman Whitwell for General Economy; William Owen
for Commerce.[81]   A few weeks later, signs of disintegration
appear with the emergence of "Principles and Articles
of Association of a Cooperative Community," to be established on the New Harmony estate, under the name of
Macluria.[82]   Enthusiasts were ready with numberless recom-
mendations for the good of the experiment, such as C. S.
Rafinesque's "Outlines of a Plan for Cooperative Associations and Mutual Societies. Addressed to Wm. Maclure."[83]   Further progress in the evolution of the communistic scheme is reflected in such articles as "Robert
Owen to the Ten Social Colonies of Equality and Common
Property, Forming on the New-Harmony Estate, on his
Leaving them in the Spring of 1827"[84] and his address to
the people of New Harmony of the following year intended

perpetuated in *The New-Harmony and Nashoba Gazette, or the Free
Enquirer* (Oct. 29, 1828-Feb. 25, 1829) and in *The Free Enquirer*
(New York), which followed the New Harmony paper without delay,
its first number appearing on Mar. 4, 1829.

80 *The New-Harmony Gazette*, Feb. 8, 1826.
81 *Ibid.*, Feb. 22, 1826.
82 *Ibid.*, Mar. 29, 1826.
83 *Ibid.*, May 17, 1826.
84 *Ibid.*, May 30, 1827.

to "explain his views of what has passed during his late absence in Europe."[85]

Such a periodical on the Western frontier was unique, and it is likely that even faint echoes of its radical policy were few. Something of the kind, however, was to be found in Samuel Underhill's *Cleveland Liberalist* (1836), a journal of opinion, directed especially against fanaticism. But within a little more than two years this venture ended in financial failure. A very different sort of social propaganda was developed in the numerous weekly publications which, toward the end of the period, were devoted to a constantly strengthening campaign against the notorious intemperance of the pioneer people. And another variety of reform agitation was represented by Elijah P. Lovejoy's *Observer*, a medley of social, political, and religious interests, but of most importance as an early partisan of the abolitionist movement in the West.

A type of journalism bordering upon the purely literary, but chiefly interesting because of its abusive satirical quality, is illustrated by *The Gridiron*, founded at Dayton in 1822, and significantly captioned by the couplet —

> "burn, roast meat burn.
> Boil o'er ye pots, ye spits forget to turn."

Another of the kind, perhaps more adept at witty blackguarding, was T. H. Roberts's *The Microscope*, begun at Louisville in April, 1824, but removed to New Albany in the following September, after a mob had raided the publisher's establishment on the Kentucky side of the Ohio.[86] A certain dignity of moral purpose was claimed by the editor in his frank determination

> To lash the rascals naked through the world.

---

[85] *Ibid.*, Apr. 2 and 23, 1828.
[86] See *The Microscope*, Sept. 22, 1824.

In the Bible, *Tristram Shandy*, and, curiously enough, *The Spectator*, he attempted to find justification for his indulgence in obscenity. And in the latter he found a suggestion of the better features of his own style. *The Microscope*, like *The Spectator*, had its fictitious characters with names slightly reminiscent of the flavor of the eighteenth century essays: Timothy Tightlace, Margaret Telltruth, Julia Wellbred, Tommy Roaster, Nettleton Touchy, Simon Snuffle, Titus Tadpole, and Nelly Nettletongue people its pages; but they are themselves the contributors and are by no means content with genteel satire. Something of Goldsmith's influence is perhaps discernible in the considerable number of issues which contain articles called "The Chinese Philosopher. From Li-en-chi-al-tang, a Traveller now in Louisville, to Fum-ho-am, First President of the Ceremonial Assemblies at Pekin in China" and others of similar title. Verse of a racy kind occupies a prominent place. The charge of lewdness brought against *The Microscope* was, it is plain, not without foundation; but its wit and keen satire were an asset such as few backwoods periodicals could claim.

Among weekly publications of more serious literary purpose *The Cincinnati Literary Gazette* (1824-1825)[87] was perhaps the earliest to enjoy any degree of success, and even this paper was continued beyond its first year only in the face of financial disaster.[88] The *Gazette* had a number of Western contributors of some importance; but its attention was largely occupied by Eastern and European literature, and it was the declared purpose of the editor "to select from worthy sources, such sentiments as may accord with our own, particularly when the thoughts hap-

---

[87] Begun Jan. 1, 1824, and continued as late as Oct. 29, 1825.

[88] See editorial in *The Cincinnati Literary Gazette*, Dec. 25, 1824; and "To the Literary Gazette, on its Proposed Discontinuance," *ibid.*, Jan. 1, 1825.

pen to be expressed in better language than our compositions may at all times exhibit.'' [89]    A like policy was practised by other Western periodicals of the same kind.  *The
Literary Register* (1828), a short-lived publication edited
by the faculty of Miami University, contained a negligible
amount of original material.  A better edited weekly literary journal was *The Cincinnati Mirror, and Western Gazette of Literature and Science*, which grew out of *The Cincinnati Mirror and Ladies' Parterre* in 1833, and was continued (with an intermission of three months in 1835-1836,
when it was superseded by *The Buckeye and Cincinnati
Mirror*) as late as September, 1836.  The *Missouri Saturday News*, begun at St. Louis by Alphonso Wetmore and
Charles Keemle early in 1838, consisted of such materials
as chapters from *The Phantom Ship* of Captain Marryat,[90]
who had recently visited St. Louis, ''Selected Tales,'' and
an extensive magazine miscellany, together with a few
''Original Essays'' and editorials.    Even the *Louisville
Literary News-letter*, perhaps the best of this kind, drew
largely upon English and Eastern sources for its lengthy
book reviews and for its matter of general literary interest.
It contained, however, many valuable original articles on
the Western country by its first editor, Edmund Flagg, as
well as by such authoritative contributors as J. M. Peck;
some tales, also by Flagg; and a considerable amount of
verse by George D. Prentice, one of the publishers.    Even
a department of ''Fine Arts'' was attempted.  When this
unusually ambitious journal was begun, at the close of
1838, there were prospects of success.    It was at that time
thought to be ''the only literary periodical of the kind published west of Cincinnati or north of Natchez in the West-

---

[89] *Ibid.*, Jan. 10, 1824.

[90] This serial was commenced in the first number, Jan. 6, 1838,
while the novel does not seem to have appeared in book form until
at least a year later.

ern valley,'' and it began with more than a thousand sub-scribers.[91]   But it was abandoned at the end of two years.[92]

## V

Among the scores of monthly periodicals and the lesser number which appeared semimonthly, perhaps a dozen are of considerable literary importance; and of these the earli-est was *The Medley, or Monthly Miscellany*, the twelve numbers of which were printed by Daniel Bradford and issued during the year 1803 from the office of the *Kentucky Gazette* in Lexington.   Advertised to appear on January 4 of that year,[93] the first issue was postponed till the end of the month;[94] but it is unlikely that there was any marked irregularity during the rest of the year, and the final number was ready on December 27.[95]   The contents of the diminutive backwoods magazine were a fair imitation, on a less pretentious scale, of what *The Columbian Maga-zine, or Monthly Miscellany*, of Philadelphia, had published sixteen years earlier.   The Western magazine was a med-ley, as its title-page declared, of ''essays, on a variety of subjects, sketches of public characters, moral tales, poetry, &c., &c., intended to combine amusement with useful in-formation.''   A reflection of the old radical sympathies of Bradford's *Gazette* of a few years earlier may, perhaps, be seen in the choice of such subjects as Helvétius, Charles James Fox, and Jefferson.   Some articles of this kind, especially A. B. Magruder's characterization of Jefferson,[96]

---

91 *Louisville Literary News-letter*, Dec. 1, 1838.

92 *Ibid.*, Nov. 28, 1840.

93 *Ky. Gaz.*, Oct. 1, 1802.

94 *Ibid.*, Jan. 4, 1803.

95 *Ibid.*, Jan. 3, 1804.

96 It was apparently this essay, together with one on John Adams by the same author, which was later reprinted in *The Political Char-acters of John Adams and Thomas Jefferson* (see *The Lamp*, of Lincoln County, Ky., Jan. 12, 1808).

displayed a degree of excellence; but, for the most part, the contents of *The Medley* were of no more literary distinction than might be found in the miscellany of an ordinary frontier newspaper. The amount of original material printed in the monthly issues varied from practically nothing to four-fifths of the whole; but by far the greater part of the contents would have had exactly the same appeal had its publication been delayed half a dozen years. The remarkable fact is, however, that *The Medley* existed at all in 1803. It was offered for a year at seventy-five cents, in advance, or a dollar if payment was delayed; and the publisher, who hoped to find readers not only in Kentucky, but in other parts of the West,[97] was, according to his own statement, not disappointed in the number of his subscribers.[98] Yet for at least a year after the magazine had ceased publication he was still attempting to dispose of copies which remained unsold.[99] The name of the editor of *The Medley* was not revealed. Apparently some of the contributors believed that Daniel Bradford, the publisher, was also responsible for its editorial management;[100] but there is, on the other hand, some reason for supposing that the work was under the supervision of Allan B. Magruder, whose name appears as a contributor.[101]

For some years, although there were periodicals of slight literary interest, there was in the West no worthy successor to even so feeble a pioneer as *The Medley*. When, in August, 1819, there appeared at Lexington the first number of *The Western Review and Miscellaneous Magazine, a*

[97] Cf. *The Western Spy*, Oct. 20, 1802.

[98] *Ky. Gaz.*, Jan. 4, 1803.

[99] *Ibid.*, Dec. 25, 1804. It is, however, barely possible that the copies here advertised were reprints.

[100] *The Medley*, p. 181 (Oct., 1803).

[101] A copy of *The Medley* in the possession of the State Historical Society of Wisconsin contains manuscript notes by an unknown hand stating that Magruder was the editor.

*Monthly Publication, Devoted to Literature and Science,*
its predecessor had long been forgotten. The new magazine was, wrote Caleb Atwater, the Ohio antiquarian, the
"first attempt to publish a work of the kind in the
west." [102]

William Gibbes Hunt, the founder of the *Review*, was a
man whose cultural attainments were equal to the task he
undertook; and he rallied to his support a corps of contributors who, if not versed in practical journalism, displayed unusual erudition. The influence of Transylvania
University, then entering upon its first period of prosperity,
is reflected in the publication of numerous poems in foreign
languages as well as translations and imitations of foreign
literature. This pedantry, though in keeping with the
affected taste for the pseudo-classic and the exotic which
found expression in more than one way in the early West,[103]

[102] Letter of Sept. 13, 1819, published in *The Western Review and
Miscellaneous Magazine,* I, 177 (Oct., 1819).

[103] Cincinnati, first christened with the pedantic appellation of
Losantiville, a cryptic blend of English, Latin, Greek, and French
intended to suggest the location of the town opposite the mouth of
the Licking, was renamed for a society of retired army officers who
had chosen the title of Cincinnati for its classical significance. Marietta, the first permanent settlement in the North-West Territory,
was named for Queen Marie Antoinette, and it contained a square
called the *Capitolium,* a street called the *Sacra Via,* and a *Campus
Martius* for the military establishment. In Detroit, where the influence of Marietta was strongly felt, there was also a *Campus Martius.*
Louisville was named by American settlers for Louis XVI; but the
naming of this and certain other towns in the same part of the
West was probably to some extent a reflection of a genuine admiration for France on the part of many prominent Kentuckians. Perhaps the most thoroughgoing example of pedantry, however, is to
be found in the abortive scheme for the "Catholepistemiad, or University of Michigania" (see above, Chapter I). The naming of college literary societies throughout the West, as in other parts of the
country at that time, afforded likewise an opportunity for the display
of a curious erudition.

can hardly have made the magazine widely popular.  Constantine Rafinesque, a professor in the University, was especially prominent among contributors of this kind of verse.  A curious spectacle was afforded by this cosmopolitan pedant's publication, in a monthly designed to serve the needs of an almost primitive Western community, of original French verse, with the accompanying direction that "the reader must supply the accents."  He seems also to have been the author of certain idylls in Greek style, written for the *Review*.  Poems in Latin and Italian were admitted to the columns of this periodical, while German verse was published in translation.  A proof that the editor was aware of literary currents in contemporary England was afforded by a number of very enthusiastic reviews of the Scotch novels of "the Great Unknown" and of the poems of Byron — reviews sometimes a score of pages or more in length, which appeared remarkably soon after the original publications.  But, with all its pedantry and its genuine interest in current English literature, the magazine did not wholly neglect the West.  A defense of the study of Greek was followed hard upon by "Adventures with the Indians," a topic several times repeated; and such current writings of, or about, the West as the editor could meet with were noticed in his reviews.  The magazine had, at all events, marked a great advance in frontier journalism; and the editor was justified in the feeling of pride in the difficult accomplishment expressed in his valedictory address, along with his acknowledgement of failure to arouse sufficient interest among Western readers to make possible continuation of the enterprise.  The last number was issued in July, 1821.

The failure of the *Review* may have been due in part to the unfriendly activities of Rafinesque, for some time one of its prominent contributors.  In October, 1820, he had begun a campaign for the establishment of a rival journal to be called the *Western Minerva, or American Annals of Knowledge and Literature,* designed as a quarterly;[104] and in the following January one number was actually printed, and at least a few copies were distributed. The contents, consisting of a study in ichthyology by Rafinesque, the editor; the same writer's unfriendly review of Caleb Atwater's essay on the antiquities of the West; "Letters on Cincinnati," described as "a miserable attempt at wit"; and "fifteen or twenty pages" of "sing-song and rhyme" — the whole recommended "to all lovers of the *bathos,* as the finest medley of *scraps* that we have ever seen," seem not to have pleased the public.[105] The new quarterly was, in fact, immediately discontinued, ostensibly because of the lack of subscribers,[106] though the editor charged that it had been maliciously suppressed by the publisher under the influence of its secret foes.[107]

After the passing of the first two important Western magazines at Lexington, a third and more ambitious monthly was established in Cincinnati, which had by this time become the capital of the frontier. There, in May, 1827, appeared the initial number of Timothy Flint's *The Western Magazine and Review,* which presently became *The Western Monthly Review.* Already known as the author of a valuable record of observations on the Western states, Flint had also published an anonymous novel and was to produce three or four more works of the latter kind before his *Monthly Review* ceased publication, in June, 1830. He

---

[104] *Ky. Reporter,* Oct. 23 and later, 1820. Each quarterly number was to contain eighty pages, and the subscription price was to be two dollars. Thomas Smith, of the *Reporter,* was to be the publisher.

[105] The description here given of the contents of the *Western Minerva* is taken entirely from *Liberty Hall,* Feb. 7, 1821. I have been unable to discover a copy of this magazine.

[106] *Ky. Reporter,* Jan. 29, 1821.

[107] C. S. Rafinesque, *A Life of Travels and Researches in North America and South Europe,* 1836, p. 66.

had, moreover, a serious appreciation of the importance for Western literature of the issues of this ambitious magazine. "We can easily enjoy in anticipation," he wrote in the advertisement to the collected edition of Volume I, "the eagerness, with which the future historian will repair to them, as a synopsis, of most of what has been said, and written, in the Western country, touching its own natural, moral, and civil history." As editor and chief contributor, he sought to attain a new standard of originality and literary quality. "The public has judged, and correctly," he wrote in the same advertisement,

that most of the articles in this work, have been from one hand. A few contributors are now pledged for the coming year, . . . We feel sure of our mark, so far as our judgment can reach, that mere ordinary and common place writing, shall find no admittance into our pages. . . .

The poetry, except two articles, has been altogether original, and of domestic fabric. . . .

Most of the tales, moral essays, and articles of natural history, have been copied into the papers; and in many instances have been seen wandering over the country, without 'a local habitation and a name.'

Much of the *Monthly Review* is, in fact, taken up with synopses and critiques of current literature, with special emphasis on whatever was written in the West. In the first number Flint explained his ideals as a critic in what he called an "Editor's Address":

Our view of the proper object of such a work is to foster literature. . . . We see no possible harm, that can result from encouraging authorship, especially in a new country, to the utmost extent. . . . Instead of wishing there were fewer books published, than there are, we wish, there were five times as many. . . . Dull books are necessary for dull readers. . . . But do we mean to praise every book? Not at all. We mean to bestow as much honest and discriminating praise, as we can.

The editor was, however, often uncritical in his praise of

whatever sprang from the frontier, a circumstance of considerable importance to his monthly, which was from the
first intended primarily as a review, though a variety of
material was admitted, including extracts from his own
fiction.[108]

An intermission of two months between Volumes I and
II, and again between II and III, was suggestive of the
difficulties which had to be met. Volume III was the end,[109]
in spite of the fact that Flint, at the risk of financial disaster, had determined to continue the work as a quarterly
after an intermission of three months.[110] The amount of
labor expended on this periodical seems remarkable in view
of the fact that, during the three years of its existence,
the editor brought out at least three novels. Besides a
large number of reviews, which he seems to have based
upon a conscientious perusal of the books concerned, he
put into his pages, from time to time, substantial articles
on Western literature. Later, however, the quality of the
magazine depreciated greatly. The early standard of originality was discarded in practise, and other periodicals
were generously copied. Probably before the end came
Flint had grown weary of his task as critic and had
exhausted his original vein.

The West, in fact, was not ready for a literary review.
Such literature of the kind as was demanded by the small
reading public of the frontier was actually supplied by
Eastern editors or in reprints of British magazines. Yet
there was little intermission in the attempts to establish
such a periodical in the West. Scarcely had *The Western
Monthly Review* ceased publication before the *Illinois*

---

[108] Extracts from *The Shoshonee Valley* appeared in Vols. II and
III.

[109] See *Niles' Weekly Register*, Oct. 30, 1830; and *Western Literary Journal and Monthly Review*, I, 3 (Nov., 1844).

[110] *The Western Monthly Review*, III, 668 (June, 1830).

*Monthly Magazine,* by James Hall, made its appearance in the backwoods town of Vandalia. Hall, like Flint, had already gained some fame as the author of books reflecting Western life and manners; and his predilection for elegant and sentimental literature helped gain him the reputation of a *"censor morum* and *arbiter elegantiarum."* [111] It was his plan that the periodical should be

Devoted chiefly to criticisms on new books, descriptions of scenery, statistics of Illinois, essays on rural economy, scientific papers, periodical essays, biography, tales, literary intelligence, fugitive poetry.

"Notices of the fine and useful arts" were to be included, and borrowed materials of various kinds were to be used for variety.

Under the difficult circumstances of journalism in the Illinois of 1830-1832, a complete realization of this program was impossible. The editor, by his own exertions, supplied about two-thirds of the magazine throughout its two years of existence,[112] even drawing upon material he had already published in book form;[113] and he received some aid from other Western contributors. But, from the first, the proportion of borrowed matter was large; and the inclusion of lengthy extracts from the files of a Vandalia newspaper and a fourteen-page review of a government report on the culture of silk, proved a dearth of material. From time to time the monthly published formidable quantities of "Notes on Illinois," showing an interest in statistical description of the West which was later to find expression in further books by the editor. A dozen or more tales, mostly by Hall himself and on Western life, were used in the two volumes. It was in its department of liter-

---

[111] See E. S. Abdy, *Journal of a Residence and Tour in the United States,* 1835, II, 401.

[112] See *The Western Monthly Magazine,* III, 93 (Feb., 1835).

[113] *Cf. The Western Souvenir,* n. d. (1829).

ary criticism that the *Illinois Monthly Magazine* fell farthest short of its mark.  Soon after the beginning the editor
realized the serious difficulties surrounding such a task in
a backwoods town, and frankly confessed his inability to
furnish any considerable amount of the promised literary
intelligence.[114]  The second volume fell below even the
standard set by the first.  Book reviews formed an almost
negligible portion of its contents.  The "Notes on Illinois"
were continued, and data on such Western subjects as
Mississippi floods were relieved by a few tales and a slight
amount of poetry.  But it was plain that the *Monthly* was
doomed to early decay, and the financial loss to Hall was
considerable.[115]

The whole of the first volume seems to have been printed
by Blackwell and published by Blackwell & Hall at Vandalia; but long before the end of the magazine, in September, 1832, with the completion of the second volume, Vandalia had been to some degree, if not entirely, abandoned
as the place of publication.  At least one number was
brought out in St. Louis, where Charles Keemle was printer
and publisher.[116]  To Cincinnati, which had for many years
afforded the best opportunities in the West for such a publication, Hall removed his magazine; and there, after an
intermission of three months, it reappeared in January,
1833, as *The Western Monthly Magazine, a Continuation
of the Illinois Monthly Magazine.*

The periodical thus metamorphosed became one of the
most important of the pioneer period.  It was "devoted
chiefly to elegant literature" and was the only one of its

---

114 *Illinois Monthly Magazine*, I, 142 (Dec., 1830).

115 See *The Western Monthly Magazine*, III, 93 (Feb., 1835).

116 See cover of No. xix (Apr., 1832).  The second volume, in its
complete form, was issued by Corey and Fairbank, at Cincinnati,
1832.

kind beyond the Mountains.[117]   The editor, with the wider
influence made possible by a removal to the largest town on
the frontier, regarded his work as a kind of official gazette
of literary culture.   "The literature of the West," he
wrote, "is still in its infancy, and we trust that we are
not unconscious of the responsibility which rests on those
who attempt to direct it."[118]   As in the *Illinois Monthly
Magazine*, the purpose was not so much to introduce the
East to the West as to make the West conscious of itself.
Western character was distinguished from Eastern,[119] and
was defended against detractors both in the East and in
England.[120]   Western drama and other literary productions
were reviewed somewhat more critically than had been
done by Flint,[121] tales with frontier flavor were included,[122]
and poetry descriptive of pioneer life was given a place.[123]
Prizes for original compositions were offered,[124] one of
which was awarded to Harriet E. Beecher,[125] later the
author of *Uncle Tom's Cabin*.   The second volume alone
contained articles by thirty-seven different writers (not
counting anonymous ones); and of this number thirty
were residents of the West.[126]   Western travel sketches
appeared in many issues.[127]   Pioneer biography was given

[117] *The Western Monthly Magazine*, I, 1 and 4 (Jan., 1833).

[118] *Ibid.*, I, 1 (Jan., 1833).

[119] *Ibid.*, I, 49-55 (Feb., 1833).

[120] See especially the satirical rejoinder, *ibid.*, II, 655-660 (Dec.,
1834).

[121] *Ibid.*, I, 59-66 (Feb., 1833); 262-273 (June, 1833); *et passim.*

[122] *Ibid.*, I, 385-391 (Sept., 1833); 458-466 (Oct., 1833); etc.

[123] *Ibid.*, I, 174-176 (Apr., 1833).

[124] *Ibid.*, I, 429 (Sept., 1833) and 574-588 (Dec., 1833); III, 95
(Feb., 1835).

[125] *Ibid.*, II, 169-192 (Apr., 1834).

[126] See *ibid.*, III, 94 (Feb., 1835).

[127] *Ibid.*, II, 486-492 (Sept., 1834), 528-539 (Oct., 1834), 589-596

some attention.[128] There were also narratives of early
frontier history[129] and statistical accounts of the new
states.[130] Thus, although Eastern and English literature
were, indeed, by no means neglected, it was the policy of
*The Western Monthly Magazine* to be as nearly Western in
character as was possible; and this program was more successfully carried out than similar aims had been by earlier
periodicals.

In the length of time during which it continued, Hall's
experiment in frontier journalism was also an advance over
what had been done before. The *Illinois Monthly Magazine* and *The Western Monthly Magazine* together covered
a span of six years. After the removal to Cincinnati, the
enterprise even attained a degree of financial prosperity:
beginning there with less than five hundred subscribers,
Hall had secured nearly three thousand before the end of
the first year, "a support greater than has ever been given
to any western periodical, and which few of those of the
eastern cities have attained."[131] There was, however, so
much difficulty in collecting debts owed by subscribers,
amounting to thousands of dollars,[132] that the income during the first two years did not exceed disbursements.[133]
Later, public disapproval of the editor's defense of the
Catholics against their critics, and his attack on abolition-

(Nov., 1834), 637-646 (Dec., 1834); III, 29-40 (Jan., 1835); IV,
85-90 (Aug., 1835).

[128] *Ibid.*, III, 82-90 (Feb., 1835), 113-128 (Mar., 1835), 222-231
(Apr., 1835); V, 398-402 (July, 1836), 462-470 (Aug., 1836), and
516-523 (Sept., 1836).

[129] *Ibid.*, I, 73 ff. (Feb., 1833); 205-214 (May, 1833); 253-262
(June, 1833); and 309-321 (July, 1833).

[130] *Ibid.*, I, 193-200 (May, 1833); and V, 26-31 (Jan., 1836).

[131] *Ibid.*, I, 428 (Sept., 1833).

[132] *Ibid.*, II, 388 (July, 1834).

[133] *Ibid.*, III, 93 (Feb., 1835).

ists, caused disaster.[134]   The feeling against Hall became
very bitter; it was even hinted that a mob might seek to
punish him.[135]  And, though he for some time maintained
his position in defiance of the rising tide of protest, he
finally announced, in June, 1836, that other engagements
necessitated his withdrawal as editor.  Joseph Reese Fry
succeeded him in the conduct of the magazine,[136] which,
after continuing for six months longer, ceased its independent existence, being presently merged, with *The Western Literary Journal, and Monthly Review*, in *The Western
Monthly Magazine, and Literary Journal*, which was destined to but a short and feeble life.

[134] *Ibid.*, IV, 131 (Aug., 1835); V, 1-10 (Jan., 1836), and 239
(Apr., 1836).  Hall later declared that the magazine had been a
financial success; but in this statement he was contradicted by his
publisher, and Hall himself stated that there were unpaid subscriptions to the amount of from seven to ten thousand dollars.  See *ibid.*,
V, 8 (Jan., 1836); and 371 (June, 1836).

[135] *Ibid.*, V, 5 (Jan., 1836).

[136] *Ibid.*, V, 371 (June, 1836).  Even during Hall's editorship
the direction of *The Western Monthly Magazine* had been in a number of cases delegated to other persons.  Its first three numbers,
as well as the last two of the *Illinois Monthly Magazine*, were prepared under the supervision of a group of Hall's friends (see *ibid.*,
I, 4 and 5, Jan., 1833; and 189 and 190, Apr., 1833).  The issue
for Aug., 1835, was to be ''under the superintendence of a friend''
(*ibid.*, IV, 58, July, 1835).  Fry was also an inconstant editor,
intrusting the management of the issues for Oct. and Nov., 1836, to
other hands (*ibid.*, V, 693, Nov., 1836).  The publication of the magazine was at first undertaken by Corey & Fairbank (see title-page,
Vol. I), who transferred their interest to Eli Taylor after not quite
a year and a half (see *ibid.*, II, 280, May, 1834).  In July of the
same year it was announced (*ibid.*, II, 388) that Joshua L. Tracy had
become associated with Taylor as publisher.  A quarrel between
Taylor and Hall resulted, in Jan., 1836, in the transfer of the magazine (*ibid.*, V, 1-10, Jan., 1836) to Flash, Ryder & Co., who were the
publishers at the end of the last year, 1836 (see title-page, Vol. V).

William Davis Gallagher, after Flint and Hall, one of
the best-known of Western writers, was the editor of *The
Western Literary Journal, and Monthly Review*, the first
number of which was issued at Cincinnati in June, 1836.
Just five other numbers followed, the last one being for
November of that year.  Gallagher, as in every periodical
which he edited, labored loyally to promote Western literature: "One object of this magazine, as set forth in our
Introductory, is to represent to ourselves and our neighbors, correctly and thoroughly, the literary character of the
Great West." The *Literary Journal*, in fact, printed a
great many contributions by frontier writers, as well as
critical comments by the editor on Western literature.
Something like equal attention was paid to each of seven
departments — "Tales," "Sketches," "Essays," "Miscellaneous," "Poetry," "Reviews, and Literary Notices," and
the "Editor's Budget," while another department, "Biographical Sketches," contained comparatively few articles.
Somewhat less than a third of the signed contributions were
by Gallagher; and he was probably the author of most, or
all, of the eighteen anonymous reviews and literary notices,
as well as the like number of articles in the "Editor's
Budget." Little, if any, borrowed material was used.  In its
original form, the *Literary Journal* ceased publication in
November, 1836; but shortly afterwards it was united with
*The Western Monthly Magazine* to form *The Western
Monthly Magazine, and Literary Journal. New Series*,
which began publication at Louisville in February, 1837,
under the joint supervision of Gallagher and James B.
Marshall. But the *New Series* was destined to a brief
career — the last number appeared in June, four months
later.

After the financial failure[137] of *The Western Monthly*

------

[137] The amount received since the magazine had been under their
direction, the editors declared, had not been sufficient to defray the

*Magazine, and Literary Journal,* in 1837, Gallagher resolved to make one more effort to establish a magazine of
merit that should succeed financially. The result was the
elaborate medley which, in his unflagging sectional loyalty,
he called *The Hesperian; or, Western Monthly Magazine.*
This periodical, later known as *The Hesperian; a Monthly
Miscellany of General Literature, Original and Select,*
began publication at Columbus in May, 1838. Otway Curry
bore a part of the responsibility until October of that
year;[138] but thereafter Gallagher, who from the first had
been the moving spirit of the enterprise, was sole editor.
No attempt was made to keep the bulky numbers, usually
containing between eighty and ninety pages, up to the
standard of originality set in the *Literary Journal.* The
first issue announced the editors' plan not only to seek the
aid of the ablest writers of the frontier, but to lay
tribute upon the best of both foreign and American publications of all kinds. In fact, about one-third of each number was generally occupied by the "Select Miscellany."
Yet the character of the remainder justified the magazine
in its claim to speak for the West. Only the dearth of
Western literature of value prevented the book reviews in
*The Hesperian* from attaining excellence in a field where
they were authoritative. Unimportant addresses in pamphlet form were the staple literary output available and
had to be noticed at undue length. The critic deserted
his Western field at times to evaluate such contemporary
Eastern works as Hawthorne's *Twice-told Tales* and Longfellow's *Hyperion* and such English authors as Lamb,
Shelley, Carlyle, and Wordsworth. Columbus, however,
though not so remote as Vandalia, where Hall had begun
his attempts as a reviewer, proved to be an unfortunate

expenses of its cover (*The Western Monthly Magazine, and Literary
Journal,* I, 362, June, 1837).

[138] *The Hesperian,* II, iv (Nov., 1838).

location; and the editor, before the end of the first year, realized the necessity of removal:

> Owing to the small number of new books that reach this market, and the long intervals at which those that do come here are received, we have not been able to give that spirit and variety to our critical department, which we originally designed.[139]

Upon the completion of Volume II, in April, 1839, *The Hesperian* was removed to Cincinnati, the first number of the third and last volume making its appearance there in the following June. A fourth volume was announced, to begin in January, 1840;[140] but the issue for November, 1839, was, in fact, the last.[141] The project had been another financial failure.[142]

Perhaps the highest point in the literary achievement of early Western magazines was reached by a publication whose professed purpose was religious. Before *The Western Monthly Magazine* had ended its unusually long career and before either *The Western Literary Journal* or *The Hesperian* had been commenced, *The Western Messenger; Devoted to Religion and Literature* began its remarkable career. The first number appeared at Cincinnati in June, 1835; and the magazine was to continue publication, with slight interruptions, either at Louisville or at Cincinnati[143] until after 1840. The chief purpose of the *Messenger* was to spread Unitarianism in the West: "This periodical," wrote one of its editors, "is devoted to the spread of a

---

139 *Ibid.*, II, 412 (Mar., 1839).

140 *Ibid.*, III, 500 (Nov., 1839).

141 See *Western Literary Journal and Monthly Review*, I, 5 (Nov., 1844). Gallagher's account which is here given (I, 1-9) contains valuable information on Western magazines in general, but especially on those with which the writer was himself connected.

142 For some account of the financial distress experienced by the indefatigable editor, see Venable, *op. cit.*, p. 450.

143 See below, footnote 162.

rational and liberal religion";[144] but it was the determination of the founders to make it "the leading Western periodical,"[145] and a large portion of the matter actually published was of greater literary importance than the contents of most Western magazines which professed to be entirely literary. For a time this critical interest was directed toward the West. Comment on frontier verse was introduced with the declaration that

It ought to be one object of a western journal to encourage western literature. . . . This, in our limited sphere, and in subordination to the main object of our work, we mean to do.[146]

For several issues this policy was continued. Western authors were criticized with sympathy but discrimination. Frederick W. Thomas's novel *Clinton Bradshaw*, for example, was given some praise; but, said the reviewer, "The style is negligent and defective." Gallagher and Hall were given favorable notice, and poems by Charles D. Drake and Thomas Shreve were published. Critical articles by Mann Butler appeared in quantity. An extract from the verse contained in R. J. Meigs's Fourth of July oration delivered at Marietta in 1789 is introduced as the first poem written in the West. But, with the fifth issue, the department of "Western Poetry" came to an end; and thenceforth little space was given to Western writings of any sort. Some three years later the *Messenger* published a comment on the frontier culture which makes clear the reason for the change:

Our people, perhaps, have as yet no literature because they

---

[144] See *The Western Messenger*, I, viii, "General Preface to Vol. I. and Prospectus of Vol. II."

[145] Clarke to "G. T. D.," Feb. 20, 1835, in *James Freeman Clarke Autobiography, Diary and Correspondence*, ed. Edward Everett Hale, 1891, p. 108.

[146] *The Western Messenger*, I, 60 (June, 1835).

have nothing to say. They are busy living, doing, growing. The age of reflection and imaginative reproduction has not yet arrived.[147]

The *Messenger's* interest in literature had soon turned permanently in another direction — almost from the first, in fact, it pointed toward England and New England. The British writers who were the subject of most comment were Coleridge, Wordsworth, Shelley, Keats, Carlyle, and Tennyson. It is significant that to Wordsworth, still comparatively little known in America, the *Messenger* gave the highest praise, proclaiming him, in 1836, as a rival of Milton.[148]   Such criticism, however, was largely influenced by Wordsworth's later religious teachings:

We love and revere Wordsworth, however, not so much because a great poet, as because a great Christian Philosopher. His words to us compare with those of Milton and Southey, as the deep, human poetry of the Gospels does, with the super-human verse of Job and the Prophets.

But the tolerance of the sectarian reviewers in the *Messenger* was proved by their attitude toward Shelley: "Even what is called his atheism is better than the theism of some of his bigoted condemners."[149]

The English poet who, however, received the greatest attention was Keats. The circumstance of George Keats's residence in Louisville at that time accounts for the publication of both poetry and prose that entitle *The Western Messenger* to fame. Although editors of Keats have failed to give the *Messenger* credit, it was in the columns of this frontier periodical that one of his poems, as well as parts of his correspondence, first appeared in print. In June, 1836, the *Messenger* contained the "Ode to Apollo. By John Keats," which was "for the first time published from

---

[147] *Ibid.*, V, 71 (Apr., 1838).
[148] *Ibid.*, I, 460-465 (Jan., 1836).
[149] *Ibid.*, III, 475 (Feb., 1837).

the original manuscript, presented to the Editor by the Poet's brother.'' [150] ''Winander Lake and Mountains, and Ambleside Fall,'' [151] which, until recently, was unknown ,to students of Keats, and ''Icolmkill, Staffa, and Fingal's Cave'' [152] were drawn from the same source.

Something of the same distinction belongs to the *Messenger* for its early attention to New England authors.

[150] *The Western Messenger*, I, 763. The ''Ode to Apollo'' here given was the poem later called ''Hymn to Apollo,'' beginning ''God of the golden bow.'' In spite of the fact that this early publication was long ago pointed out (see Venable, *op. cit.*, pp. 74-75), editors of Keats have apparently remained unaware of the existence of *The Western Messenger*. It has been generally taken for granted that the poem in question first appeared in Lord Houghton's *Life, Letters, and Literary Remains, of John Keats*, 1848.

[151] *Ibid.*, I, 772-777 (June, 1836). This journal-letter, addressed to Tom Keats, was begun at End Moor on June 25, 1818, continued at Bowness on the 26th, and concluded at Ambleside on the 27th. Strangely enough, it has escaped all of the poet's editors and biographers, remaining buried in the *Messenger* for nearly ninety years. Almost, if not quite, the finest example of Keats's descriptive prose, it is remarkable, not only for its unusual history, but for its not very reverent comments on Wordsworth, for its detailed and enthusiastic description, and for its relation to the ''Bright Star'' sonnet and, perhaps, to other important poems by Keats. For a reprint of this newly recovered journal, see the present writer's ''Keats in the Wordsworth Country,'' in *The North American Review*, CCXIX, 392-397 (Mar., 1924).

[152] *Ibid.*, I, 820-823 (July, 1836). The matter here printed was drawn from the letter to Tom Keats of July 23 and 26, 1818, and is not the version sent to George and Georgiana Keats at Louisville in the long letter of Sept. 17-27, 1819. The extract begins ''*My Dear Tom,—*'' and ends ''You can go but a small distance any where from salt water in the Highlands.'' It is almost, but not quite, identical with what is to be found in *Letters of John Keats*, ed. Sidney Colvin, 1891, pp. 147-152. The editor of *The Western Messenger* thought Keats's prose still better than his poetry. ''We feel a little proud,'' he wrote, ''that we, in this western valley, are the first to publish specimens of these writings.''

Bronson Alcott and Oliver Wendell Holmes were reviewed.
Articles by Margaret Fuller and by Elizabeth Peabody
were printed.  Eighteen sonnets were contributed for a
single issue, and others for another number,[153] by Jones
Very, who wrote to the editor:

I was moved to send you the above sonnets; that they may
help those in affliction for Christ's name is ever the prayer
of me his disciple, called to be a witness of his sufferings
and an expectant of his glory.[154]

Holmes also sent a poem for the fortunate periodical.[155]
But the chief claim of the magazine to distinction in its
service to New England literature was its defense of Emerson against his critics and its publication of "almost the
first poetical specimens of his writing which have appeared
in print." [156]  Several, later famous, but until then unpublished, poems were sent by Emerson to James Freeman
Clarke, at that time editor of *The Western Messenger*.
"Each and All" appeared with a slightly different title.[157]
"To the Humble-bee," as the poem was then called, was
printed in a form somewhat different from that into which
it grew under later revision, beginning in the *Messenger*
with the couplet:

>Fine humble-bee! fine humble-bee!
>Where thou art is clime for me [158]

and exhibiting several other minor differences.   These

153 *Ibid.*, VI, 308-314 (Mar., 1839); and 366-373 (Apr., 1839).

154 *Ibid.*, VI, 308 (Mar., 1839).

155 *Ibid.*, V, 78-80 (May, 1838).  The poem here printed is not
marked as an original contribution.  But see Clarke to Venable,
Feb. 19, 1886, in Venable, *op. cit.*, p. 74.

156 *Ibid.*, VI, 229 (Feb., 1839).

157 As published in the *Messenger*, VI, 229-230 (Feb., 1839), the
poem was entitled "Each in All."  Two lines printed in the *Messenger* were later dropped from the poem, and other very slight
changes were made.

158 *Ibid.*, VI, 239-241 (Feb., 1839).  Of Emerson's poems pub-

poems were followed by "Good-bye, Proud World!" [159] and "The Rhodora." [160]  *The Western Messenger* was, in fact, the work of a group of New England men — a part of the intellectual coterie who afterwards founded *The Dial* —[161] who sought during their sojourn in the West to plant there an offshoot of the new liberal theology and the high cultural ideals which characterized the chief teachers of that doctrine. There were a succession of editors, all imbued with these purposes — Ephraim Peabody, James Freeman Clarke, W. H. Channing, and James H. Perkins.[162]

lished in the *Messenger* this one was later to undergo the most important revision.

[159] *Ibid.*, VI, 402 (Apr., 1839). Emerson made only very minor changes in later years.

[160] *Ibid.*, VII, 166 (July, 1839). With the exception of two lines, which were later entirely recast, the version here given is almost the same as the form in which Emerson finally left the poem.

[161] See *ibid.*, VIII, 301-303 (Nov., 1840), for a defense of *The Dial*, of which the number for Oct., 1840, is noticed.

[162] *The Western Messenger* was established at Cincinnati by a group of friends — James Freeman Clarke, William G. Eliot, and Ephraim Peabody (see *James Freeman Clarke Autobiography, Diary and Correspondence*, 1891, p. 251). In Feb., 1836, Peabody, who seems to have acted as editor from the first, but with much help from James H. Perkins and a certain Howe, resigned control and was replaced by Clarke, under whose care the magazine was conducted at Louisville (*The Western Messenger*, I, 588, Feb., 1836, 658, Apr., 1836, and 731, May, 1836; and *The Western Monthly Magazine, and Literary Journal*, I, 280, May, 1837). Beginning with the number for May, 1839, the *Messenger* was again published in Cincinnati, with W. H. Channing acting as joint editor with Clarke and Perkins (see *Lou. Pub. Adv.*, May 7, 1839). The October issue was the last for 1839 (*The Western Messenger*, VII, 436, Oct., 1839); and publication was not resumed until the following May, when W. H. Channing seems to have been sole editor (*ibid.*, VIII, No. 1, May, 1840; *cf.* also *James Freeman Clarke*, 1891, p. 223). A year later the magazine came to an end. I have been unable to determine all the details of publication and printing. Vols. I-III, according to the title-pages, were issued in complete form in 1836 and 1837, from

Handicapped by the unpopularity of its religious creed, *The Western Messenger* must have had, however, slight influence on the West. "There was our poor little 'Western Messenger,'" wrote Clarke many years later —

When it was printed in Louisville, I had to be publisher, editor, contributor, proof-reader, and boy to pack up the copies and carry them to the post office.[163]

For a time, it is true, the support of the magazine increased. The original subscription list was doubled before the second volume had been completed;[164] but it could never have been large. There were at one time a hundred subscribers in Cincinnati; yet before the end of 1838 the number there had decreased to sixty, while at Louisville there were slightly more, and at St. Louis about half that number.[165] In 1839 there might have been only a small profit if the readers of the magazine had paid for it — as they did not do.[166] It was only after a long cessation — not the first

Louisville, with the Western Unitarian Association as publishers and Morton & Smith as printers. A large part of the first volume, however — probably all which appeared at Cincinnati — seems to have been published by Gallagher and Shreve (*The Western Messenger*, I, 731, May, 1836). The title-page of the collected edition of Vols. IV and V shows that this double volume was issued at Louisville in 1838 with Morton & Griswold as printers. R. P. Brooks, of Cincinnati, was the printer from May to Sept., and probably in Oct., 1839 (*Lou. Pub. Adv.*, May 7, 1839; and *The Western Messenger*, cover for Sept., 1839). The cover for Sept., 1840, shows that the publisher was then John B. Russell and the printers were Shepard and Stearns. The title-page of the collected edition of Vol. VIII shows that it was published in 1841 at Cincinnati by John B. Russell.

163 Clarke to J. H. Allen, Feb. 17, 1885, in *James Freeman Clarke*, 1891, p. 380.

164 *The Western Messenger*, II, 431 (Jan., 1837).

165 *Ibid.*, VI, 67 (Nov., 1838).

166 *Ibid.*, VII, 436 (Oct., 1839). In 1841, according to Cist (*op. cit.*, p. 95), the *Messenger* issued a thousand copies a month. Cist's

irregularity in its publication — that the *Messenger* reappeared in May, 1840; and it was finally discontinued with the number for April, 1841.[167]

Far more popular,[168] but comparatively insignificant in the annals of Western literature, was *The Family Magazine; or, Monthly Abstract of General Knowledge*, which first appeared at Cincinnati — an edition was also published, at least for a time, in the East — in January, 1836, within a few months after the *Messenger* had been commenced in the same place, and also continued till 1841. The general character of *The Family Magazine* is aptly described by the prospectus for one of its volumes:

IN the fifth volume of the Family Magazine, we shall pursue the general plan of its predecessors; . . . We do not pretend to send forth a work replete with originality of ideas or style, or as a vehicle for conveying to the people the rich and beautiful specimens, in detail, of modern belles-lettres; but our prime object is, to disseminate useful information, . . . In it, the choicest contents of books are presented in a condensed yet perspicuous form, illustrative of HISTORY, GEOGRAPHY, the FINE ARTS, NATURAL HISTORY, AGRICULTURE and RURAL ECONOMY, USEFUL ARTS, the NATURAL SCIENCES, BIOGRAPHY, TRAVELS, BOTANY, &c., &c., agreeably spiced with POETRY and MISCELLANEOUS READING.[169]

A number of brief literary notices appeared from time to time, but not many had to do with the West or contained

figures, however, are plainly rough estimates and are probably too high.

[167] *Cf. The Western Messenger*, VIII, 572 (Apr., 1841); and *Western Literary Journal and Monthly Review*, I, 5 (Nov., 1844).

[168] During the first year *The Family Magazine* (see I, preface dated Dec., 1836) claimed "an increase of five thousand subscribers." Cist (*op. cit.*, p. 95) estimated its monthly issue in 1841 as three thousand.

[169] *Ibid.*, IV, iii, advertisement, dated Dec., 1839.

anything of importance. The regular business of the magazine was to retail second-hand materials of a popular scientific sort. A notable feature was the generous use of illustrations, heretofore practically unknown in Western monthly periodicals.

*The Monthly Chronicle of Interesting and Useful Knowledge*, established in December, 1838, was a somewhat more dignified miscellany of borrowings, in which the illustrations are now of unusual value as picturing the most important public buildings of contemporary Cincinnati, the place of its publication. Its editor, Edward D. Mansfield, was already known as a writer on political and economic subjects. A less pretentious periodical of the same sort was the *Western People's Magazine*, an illustrated popular miscellany at Cincinnati, commencing in March, 1834, and attaining before the end of that year a circulation of four thousand.[170] Perhaps, however, the lowest point in journalistic mediocrity was reached by *The Rose of the Valley*, begun at Cincinnati, probably in January, 1839. Its weak sentimentality was scarcely relieved by anything of literary value, and its apparent popularity is a significant comment upon the state of culture in the West at the time. *The Rose* does not seem, however, to have continued beyond 1840.[171]

A curious monthly publication, strangely in contrast with such popular entertainers as *The Family Magazine* and *The Monthly Chronicle*, and affording an eloquent example of the whole-hearted attempts of isolated college communities to urge their cultural ideals upon the backwoodsmen about

---

[170] *Western People's Magazine*, I, 176 (Dec. 19, 1834).

[171] The twelfth number of Vol. I (published by G. G. Moore and stereotyped by J. A. James, 1839) ended with the declaration that the subscription list now contained "several *thousands*" of names "and is yet rapidly filling up from every state in the Union." There is, however, no mention of this periodical in Cist's list for 1841 (Cist, *op. cit.*, pp. 93-95). The individual numbers are not dated.

them, was *The Extra Equator*, the first number of which appeared at Bloomington, Indiana, in November, 1840. Heavily freighted with original translations from the works of Plato and reviews of college addresses, with comparatively slight space reserved for almost equally pedantic sketches of travel and scenery, this magazine was little calculated to reach a large reading public, and seems, in fact, to have owed its existence entirely to its character as an "extra" number of a weekly paper. Something of the same kind, but much more feeble, was to be found in such earlier monthlies as *The Literary Focus* and *The Transylvanian or Lexington Literary Journal*, both of which were the products of college communities. The *Focus*, founded at Miami University in 1827, was conducted by the members of two literary societies of that institution and was issued from their press. Juvenile essays on trite subjects betrayed the real purpose of the magazine, which was "not to make an exhibition of ripened talent, but by practice to endeavor to improve."[172] The experiment failed, and the publication ended with the completion of the first volume, in May, 1828, making way for a short-lived weekly edited by the faculty. *The Transylvanian*, which was begun in the following January at Lexington, seems to have ended with the ninth number, in September. "Miscellaneous Selections" were allowed a large portion of its columns, while the "Original Communications" which made up the remainder could scarcely have been popular. There were many articles on scientific subjects; and even the fiction — as in "Letters from Theodoric to Aspasia" — was distinguished by a pedantic flavor.

## VI

Among periodicals of some importance which approximated the form of the literary newspaper, were such semi-

[172] *The Literary Focus*, I, 92 (Nov., 1827).

monthly publications as *The Cincinnati Mirror and Ladies'
Parterre*, which appeared at Cincinnati in October, 1831.
W. D. Gallagher, the editor, attempted, as he was later
to do in his monthly magazines, to make the *Mirror* distinctly Western, and included reviews of Western publications; many of his own poems, as well as some by other
pioneer writers; and a number of original stories with frontier setting. After the completion of the second volume
(September, 1833) the *Mirror* passed under the joint control of Gallagher and Thomas H. Shreve. They enlarged
it, rechristening it *The Cincinnati Mirror, and Western
Gazette of Literature and Science*, under which name it
continued, as a weekly, for some years.

Much resembling the *Mirror*, but later in date and
decidedly inferior in value, was the *Western Mirror, and
Ladies' Literary Gazette*, begun at St. Louis in January,
1837. It first appeared monthly, but was changed in July
to a semimonthly. The editor, Mrs. H. A. Ruggles, was
possibly the first woman in the West to undertake this
kind of journalism. The *Western Mirror*, however, was
little more than a literary newspaper from the first; and
some nine months after its founding it was announced that
lack of support made it necessary to change the character
of the periodical, so that it must have become, if indeed
it did survive, simply a semiweekly newspaper.[173]

## VII

Quarterly, monthly, and semimonthly publications designed, not to entertain, but rather, simply to spread purely
technical scientific knowledge or to further religious, political, or social propaganda, were numerous. Of these, religious periodicals made up the greater number. They
began almost with the nineteenth century. By May, 1804,
shortly after the great Kentucky Revival, which brought

---

[173] *Western Mirror, and Ladies' Literary Gazette*, Oct. 11, 1837.

violent sectarian disputes in its train, the first number of the *Alethian Critic; or Error Exposed* had appeared, and was *"to be continued quarterly,"* apparently by Abel M. Sarjent, in Lexington. Its controversial quality is clear from the fact that the initial number contained "The Doctrine of Endless Miseries Investigated; or the Sinews of Antichristian Religion Exploded." [174]

*The Evangelical Record, and Western Review,* founded at Lexington in January, 1812, may have been the first of the series of religious magazines issued by Thomas T. Skillman in that place. In *The Evangelical Record* the polemical character almost universal in the pioneer religious publications, was prominent. Calvinism was a favorite theme, while Methodism was sharply attacked. Doctrinal books were reviewed at great length. At least twelve monthly issues were completed and probably more; but it was very likely at an end, however, before April, 1814, when Skillman began a short-lived bimonthly journal called *The Almoner. The Christian Register,* also published by Skillman at Lexington, but edited by James Blythe, followed in June, 1822. The purpose of the *Register* was entirely serious; and the editor, in his introductory remarks, made no attempt to court popularity:

It is proposed, in a few of the first numbers, to place before the public, as distinctly as we can, a view of what has been done in the church, for the promotion of christianity, during the last thirty years. This will comprise a condensed view of the operations of Bible Societies, and Missionary Societies, and the various auxiliary institutions in the form of Sabbath-day Schools, Tract Societies, &c. &c. [175]

"Religious papers," he declared, "ought to be, as far as possible, exclusively so." If political intelligence were included, it would tempt young people to violate the Sab-

---

[174] See *Ky. Gaz.*, May 1, 1804.

[175] *The Christian Register*, I, 2 (June, 1822). The quotations which follow in this paragraph are from the same volume, pp. 3 and 5.

bath, as it would be difficult to prevail on them to halt their Sunday reading after finishing the religious portion of the periodical.  He was determined "to enrich his Magazine with choice dissertations and arguments in support of the grand doctrines of our holy religion" and sought aid for this project "from the pens of such men as Magee on the Atonement, Horsley's Tracts, Stewart, &c. &c."  Of the importance of his mission to the West he felt sure, for, said he,

It is well known, that in no part of America, except in the neighborhood of Boston, are the soul-destroying errors of Socinus, and Arius, so industriously circulated as in Kentucky, and the adjacent states.

The *Register* was exactly what it was advertised as being. It was well stocked with accounts of the state of religion, with verbatim reports of sermons, and with the proceedings of religious societies.  But it was not a financial success. At the close of the first year it was announced that the subscriptions had not covered expenses, and that the work would be suspended for two or three months, and permanently, unless more favorable circumstances should offer.[176] Such was the pioneer religious magazine in its most rigid doctrinal form.

Many others differed from the *Register* only in their varying degrees of intentness on religious teaching and of enthusiasm for sectarian aims; but in general such publications were more successful financially than those devoted to literature.  Denominational loyalty was often a solid support.  Elisha Bates, leader of the orthodox Friends in Ohio, was editor and publisher, at Mountpleasant, Ohio, of *The Moral Advocate, a Monthly Publication, on War, Duelling, Capital Punishments, and Prison Discipline*, begun in March, 1821, and continued through at least three volumes; and of *The Miscellaneous Repository*, of which the first

---

176 *Ibid.*, I, 764 (May, 1823).

number of Volume II appeared, also at Mountpleasant, in January, 1829. The *Repository*, which was, in spite of its title, very largely doctrinal, and especially directed against the errors of the Hicksites, was continued, very irregularly, as late as December, 1836. Suspending publication while Bates was passing from Ohio to England, it was revived by him at Kendal, England, where some of the earlier numbers of the fifth volume were reprinted from the American edition, and succeeding numbers were added to be reprinted at St. Clairsville, Ohio.[177]

*The Western Religious Magazine*, edited by a committee of Baptists, was begun at Cincinnati (1826), but was soon suspended. It was later revived at Zanesville, where George Sedwick, the publisher, was pastor of the Baptist church. In 1829 this was succeeded by Sedwick's new monthly, *The Western Miscellany*, which became, in August, 1830, *The Regular Baptist Miscellany*, finally ceasing publication in June, 1831. *The Baptist Advocate* (Cincinnati, 1835) and *The Regular Baptist* (Indianapolis, 1839) were among other monthlies of the same sectarian purpose.

*The Religious Examiner*, published in the interest of the Associate Reformed Church, first at Cadiz and later at Washington and at St. Clairsville, Ohio, extended over the remarkably long period of seven years, beginning in September, 1827, and ending in December, 1834, when the twelfth number of Volume VII was issued. Still more successful was *The Christian Intelligencer* (later *The Christian Intelligencer, and Evangelical Guardian*), a propagandist of the same sect and of antislavery doctrine. It was begun in January, 1829; temporarily abandoned during 1832; revived in March, 1833; and continued, with only slight interruption, until long after 1840.

Among other religious bodies, the Disciples were espe-

---

[177] *The Miscellaneous Repository*, V (Kendal), No. 23 (5th Month, 16, 1836).

cially active in propagating their doctrines through monthly periodicals. One of the earliest and longest-lived of these must have been *The Christian Messenger*, by Barton W. Stone, of which the first number appeared at Georgetown, Kentucky, in November, 1826. Some eight years later it was removed by Stone to Jacksonville, Illinois, where it seems to have continued, with some interruptions, until 1847.[178] *The Evangelist*, edited and published for many years by Walter Scott, was begun at Cincinnati in January, 1832;[179] *The Christian Panoplist*, of Versailles, Kentucky, under the direction, at first, of B. F. Hall and W. Hunter, and, later, of Hunter alone, completed twelve monthly issues during 1837. Early in the same year Arthur Crihfield began *The Northern Reformer, Heretic Detector, and Evangelical Review* as a quarterly at Middleburg, Ohio, afterwards changing it to monthly form and to the name of *The Heretic Detector*, and continuing it till the end of 1840, or later.

Methodism was represented by such monthlies as *The Gospel Herald*, begun in August, 1829, at Lexington, and edited by O. B. Ross. The doctrine of the New Jerusalem Church was taught in *The Precursor* (Cincinnati, 1836) and *The Errand Boy* (Chillicothe, 1839).

Unusual historical interest attaches to the journalistic activity of the Mormons during the 'thirties, when their most important centers were in Ohio, Missouri, and Illinois. Though all four of the periodicals to be considered here were published in a form resembling more a newspaper

---

178 For the history of this magazine subsequent to 1840, see N. S. Haynes, *History of the Disciples of Christ in Illinois*, n. d. (1915), p. 663.

179 There seems to have been at least one long intermission before 1841; but in that year, according to Cist (*op. cit.*, p. 95), *The Evangelist* was still in course of publication, printing, as he estimated, a thousand copies of each issue.

than an ordinary magazine, they were all issued monthly, and paid little attention to general news topics. The *Evening and Morning Star* was printed at Independence, Missouri, from June, 1832, to July, 1833, when it was removed to Kirtland, Ohio, resuming publication there in the following December.[180] The contents were largely doctrinal, with scant space devoted to other subjects sometimes classed as "Worldly Matters." Of the same kind was the *Latter Day Saints' Messenger and Advocate*, which, as the successor to the *Star*, was published at Kirtland, beginning in October, 1834, a month after the earlier journal had come to an end.[181] In September, 1837, the *Messenger* was discontinued, and was succeeded, in October, by the *Elders' Journal of the Church of Latter Day Saints* (the title varies), while Oliver Cowdery was replaced as editor by Joseph Smith, Jr.[182] After two monthly issues, however, the new official gazette was suspended on account of the Mormon troubles in Ohio — Smith left the state in the following January — being revived in July, 1838, at Far West, Missouri. With the religious feud rapidly drawing to a climax at Far West, it is unlikely that publication was long continued.[183] The *Elders' Journal* was almost wholly devoted to Mormon propaganda and the reports of official

[180] See *Evening and Morning Star*, II, 225-231, *et passim* (Dec., 1833) for an explanation of the delay and an account of the change. Matters are somewhat complicated by the fact that the whole of the two volumes of this monthly were reprinted, from Jan., 1835, to Oct., 1836, at Kirtland, Ohio, for its successor, *Latter Day Saints' Messenger and Advocate*.

[181] For an announcement of the intended change, see *Evening and Morning Star*, II, 369 (Sept., 1834).

[182] See *Latter Day Saints' Messenger and Advocate*, III, 545 (Aug., 1837), for an announcement of this change.

[183] No. 3, for July, 1838, in the Shroeder Collection, State Historical Society of Wisconsin, is the latest copy I have seen. Probably it was the last published.

meetings of the church. A fourth monthly of the customary sixteen-page size was *Times and Seasons*, which was begun in November, 1839, at Commerce (later Nauvoo), Illinois, where large numbers of the Missouri Mormon colonists had by that time taken refuge. In November of the following year, it became a semimonthly, continuing until after 1840.

## VIII

Political journalism was largely confined to the newspapers, but there were a few exceptions. Slavery was early an important issue — there were groups of men who sought to make it clearly an issue to be decided by political action. By 1821 the antislavery doctrine of the Friends had found expression in the *Genius of Universal Emancipation*, edited by Benjamin Lundy and first issued at Mountpleasant, Ohio, in July of that year, and continued there until the spring of 1822, when it was removed to Greenville, Tennessee.[184] Following closely upon the *Genius of Universal Emancipation*, there appeared in Kentucky a magazine partly devoted to this program and partly to religious propaganda — the *Abolition Intelligencer, and Missionary Magazine*, which was begun at Shelbyville in May, 1822, edited and published by John Finley Crow. It was divided into two distinct sections, the first and major portion dealing with the subject of abolition, and containing, in particular, the proceedings of the Kentucky Abolition Society, under whose auspices the work was apparently issued. Abolition was, however, not yet a popular doctrine; and the *Intelligencer* must have come to an end at the close of the first volume or, perhaps, a month earlier.[185]

---

[184] Nos. 1 and 3-8 bear the imprint "Mount Pleasant, Jefferson County, Ohio." No. 9 (3d Month, 1822) shows no imprint, while Nos. 10 and 11 (4th and 5th Months, 1822) clearly belong to Greenville.

[185] See *Abolition Intelligencer*, I, 161 (Mar., 1823).

Among publications of more decided partisan political complexion, but of a purely ephemeral nature,[186] was *Truth's Advocate and Monthly Anti-Jackson Expositor*, which was printed as a campaign document at Cincinnati from January to October, 1828. The temper of the political controversialists of the time was reflected in a lengthy "View of Gen. Jackson's Domestic Relations, in Reference to his Fitness for the Presidency," which appeared in the first number. Another monthly propagandist of the same kind was the *Investigator and Expositor*, published at Troy, Ohio, for some time prior to, and during, the campaign of 1840.

## IX

A number of technical periodicals, usually quarterly or monthly, were produced by, and for, members of the medical profession. Of these the earliest [187] was *The Western Quarterly Reporter of Medical, Surgical, and Natural Science*, edited by John D. Godman, and published at Cincinnati. Begun early in 1822, it appeared regularly for six issues, being discontinued in the following year, after Godman had returned to Philadelphia.[188] Before the end of 1823 it was arranged that the *Reporter* should be revived at Lexington, where it was to be edited by Daniel Drake and other members of the faculty of the Medical School of Transylvania;[189] but the plan does not seem to have been carried into effect.

---

[186] *Truth's Advocate*, for example, was designed from the beginning to continue for only ten months (see *Daily Cin. Gaz.*, Nov. 7, 1827).

[187] See *The Western Journal of the Medical and Physical Sciences*, IV, 605 (Jan., Feb., Mar., 1831).

[188] *Ibid.*

[189] See *The Cincinnati Literary Gazette*, Jan. 1, 1824. I have found no trace of this continuation. It is hardly possible that Drake, at any rate, edited a medical journal during 1824-1826.

Within three years, however, there followed a semi-monthly journal, founded by Guy W. Wright and James M. Mason, and first called *The Ohio Medical Repository*, but becoming, upon the completion of the first volume, *The Western Medical and Physical Journal*, with Daniel Drake in Mason's place.[190] Under the latter title, practically a new enterprise, it began publication as a monthly, at Cincinnati in April, 1827. After the twelfth number, however, the name was changed to *The Western Journal of the Medical and Physical Sciences*, with Drake as proprietor and sole editor. With the beginning of the third volume, in 1829, the publication became quarterly. In the following year Drake was aided by James C. Finley and later by other associate editors; but during the whole life of this remarkable journal, which continued into its twelfth volume,[191] Drake was in control. Upon the dissolution, in 1839, of the medical school of Cincinnati College,[192] with which he had been connected since its founding in 1835, Drake transferred *The Western Journal* from Cincinnati to Louisville, where he was now a member of the faculty in the recently established Medical Institute. Here, as successor to the *Louisville Journal of Medicine and Surgery*, which had been begun in 1838 by Professors Miller and Yandell and Dr. Thomas H. Bell, but suspended after the second issue, this extraordinary periodical was revived in January, 1840, under the title of *The Western Journal of Medicine and Surgery*.[193] Drake and Lunsford P. Yandell

190 See Daniel Drake, *Second Discourse before the Medical Library Association of Cincinnati*, pp. 77-78, as reprinted in E. D. Mansfield, *Memoirs of the Life and Services of Daniel Drake*, 1855, p. 185.

191 See *The Western Journal of Medicine and Surgery*, I, publishers' notice (Jan., 1840).

192 Daniel Drake, *loc. cit.*

193 *Ibid.*, and *The Western Journal of Medicine and Surgery*, I, *loc. cit.*

were the first editors of the monthly, which was destined
to continue for many years.

Of all other medical publications, perhaps the most important was *The Transylvania Journal of Medicine and the
Associate Sciences*, founded at Lexington early in 1828
under the direction of John Esten Cooke and Charles W.
Short. Twelve volumes had appeared before the end of
1839, making *The Transylvania Journal* one of the longest-
lived of all quarterly and monthly periodicals in the early
West. Among its editors there were, besides Cooke and
Short, Lunsford P. Yandell and Robert Peter. All were
members of the medical faculty at Transylvania University. The journal was fortunate in the personnel of editors
and contributors alike until 1838, when it fell into new
hands after the withdrawal of a part of the medical faculty
to Louisville.

John Eberle was the central figure in the changing editorial board of *The Western Medical Gazette*, which was
begun at Cincinnati in December, 1832, "the firm advocate
of the Medical College of Ohio,"[194] under whose auspices
it was conducted.[195] The failure of the original proprietor caused a suspension from September, 1833, to February, 1834, after which date the *Gazette* appeared at
monthly intervals as late as February, 1835. Eberle was
also senior editor of a much more pretentious publication,
*The Western Quarterly Journal of Practical Medicine*, the
first number of which was issued at Cincinnati in June,
1837. Eberle's assistants in both the *Gazette* and the
*Quarterly Journal* were numerous: in the former he was
aided by Doctors Mitchell, Staughton, Bailey, Smith, and
Gross; and in the latter by Doctors Smith, Moorhead,
Locke, Cobb, and Shotwell. A less important but remark-

---

194 *The Western Medical Gazette*, I, 1 (Dec. 15, 1832).

195 See *The Western Monthly Magazine*, II, 445 (Aug., 1834).

able collegiate product was *The Western Medical Reformer*, a monthly, published by the medical faculty of Worthington College at Worthington, Ohio, where Volume II was completed in December, 1837.[196] Late in the following year, however, this journal, unable to continue in so small a town,[197] was suspended, not to be revived until 1844, after removal to Cincinnati.

Besides the medical repositories conducted by such prominent men as Godman, Drake, Eberle, and John Esten Cooke, and closely related, almost invariably, to some school of recognized standing, there were a number of less valuable journals representing independent enterprise, like Anthony Hunn's semimonthly and monthly *Medical Friend of the People* (Harrodsburg, 1829-1830); or, as in the case of the numerous Thomsonian periodicals, advocating an unorthodox system of medicine. Perhaps the most prosperous publication of the sort was *The Thomsonian Recorder, or Impartial Advocate of Botanic Medicine*, which was begun at Columbus in September, 1832, under the editorship of Thomas Hersey, as agent for Samuel Thomson, founder of the botanical system. It continued under the original title, with much irregularity — sometimes it appeared weekly and sometimes trimonthly, but was for the most part semimonthly — until the close of the fifth volume, in 1837, when it became *The Botanico-medical Recorder*. The ninth volume was completed in 1841. Hersey, the first editor of the *Recorder*, withdrew soon after the commencement of the third volume[198] and established, also at Columbus, in May, 1835, a rival publication, *The Independent Botanic Register*, which, however, continued

---

[196] *Cf.* proposals for publication of a *Western Medical Reformer* at Richmond, Ky., to begin in May, 1836 (*Ky. Gaz.*, Feb. 20, 1836).

[197] See *The Western Medical Reformer*, IV, 1 (June, 1844).

[198] *The Thomsonian Recorder*, III, No. 23 (Aug. 15, 1835).

only to the end of the first year.[199]   To the same group of partisans belonged the monthly *Botanical Luminary*, which had begun to appear at the village of Saline, Michigan, by July, 1836.[200]   An early example of medical journalism reduced to mere commercialism was *Jewett's Advertiser*, begun at Columbus in January, 1835.

X

During the last decade before 1840, a number of periodicals devoted to the improvement of education in the West began to make their appearance.   The General Convention of the Teachers of the Western Country, which met in Cincinnati in June, 1831, published its proceedings in No. 1 of *The Academic Pioneer, and Guardian of Education*,[201] the second number of which did not appear till December, 1832.   Less than two years later, a semimonthly called *The Schoolmaster, and Academic Journal*, "devoted exclusively to the subject of education," was begun at Oxford, Ohio, apparently under the auspices of Miami University.[202] Within a short time similar publications were becoming comparatively numerous, proving the rapidly increasing public interest in schools and the awakening of the professional spirit in the teachers of the West.   In the year 1837 alone no less than four such journals were commenced. The *Common School Advocate*, founded at Madison, Indiana, in January of that year, was continued as late as July, 1840, when the forty-third monthly number was issued in Cincinnati.   By March, 1837, a miniature monthly called the *Universal Educator* had made its first appearance in

---

[199] *The Independent Botanic Register*, I, 191 (Apr., 1836).

[200] See *Detroit Daily Advertiser*, July 30, 1836.

[201] See *Transactions of the Fourth Annual Meeting of the Western Literary Institute*, 1835, preface.

[202] See *The Western Monthly Magazine*, II, 334 (June, 1834).

Cincinnati;[203] and in the same month John W. Picket began *The Western Academician and Journal of Education and Science*, perhaps the best of its kind in the frontier country. Among its contributors were such leaders in the Cincinnati cultural group as William Holmes M'Guffey and Alexander Kinmont. A proof that this sort of educational propaganda was, however, not confined to the larger towns was the founding, probably shortly after Picket's *Academician*, of *The Common School Advocate, and Journal of Education* at Jacksonville, Illinois.[204] A little later a monthly periodical called *The Common School Journal* (1838) and published at Cincinnati, is said to have been distributed free to teachers throughout the West.[205]

## XI

A group of magazines marking the beginning of a new practical and scientific interest in matters which occupied the almost constant attention of the great mass of people in the West, were those devoted to agriculture. The monthly *Farmer's Reporter, and United States Agriculturalist*, "containing original and selected essays on agriculture, horticulture, culinary art, farriery, live stock, valuable receipts, and every branch of husbandry" and "illustrated with engravings," began its New Series at Cincinnati in October, 1831. It was followed in September, 1839, by *The Western Farmer* (later *The Western Farmer and Gardener*), also published at Cincinnati.

## XII

Besides the considerable variety of literary, religious, political, medical, educational, and agricultural periodicals,

---

[203] See *The Western Monthly Magazine, and Literary Journal*, I, 143 (Mar., 1837).

[204] See *The Western Emigrants' Magazine*, I, 15 (May, 1837).

[205] See *The Western Messenger*, VI, 212 (Jan., 1839).

there were a number of others more difficult to classify.
The growing power of secret orders was reflected in such
publications as *The Masonic Miscellany and Ladies' Literary Magazine*, of which the second and last volume began
in July, 1822, at Lexington, with William Gibbes Hunt as
editor.[206] Literary sections, inferior, however, to the matter which Hunt had earlier published in *The Western
Review*, were interlarded among Masonic orations and articles of like kind. The bitter opposition to Masonry, widespread at the time, is voiced in Dyer Burgess's semimonthly,
*The Anti-conspirator, or, Infidelity Unmasked* (1831).
Among periodicals of special interest to youth, though
exhibiting a variety of aims, were *The Herald of Literature
and Science* (1831), continued for a few months by the
Detroit Debating Society; *The Juvenile Museum* (1822),
conducted by Horton J. Howard at Mountpleasant, Ohio,
first as a semimonthly and later, in 1823, as a monthly;
*The Disseminator of Useful Knowledge* (1828), also semimonthly, published, for not quite two years and a half, by
the pupils of the School of Industry at New Harmony; the
*Youth's Magazine*, an illustrated periodical issued from
Cincinnati at like intervals, probably beginning in October,
1834;[207] and *The College Mirror* (Cincinnati, 1839), which,
in spite of its name and its declared devotion "exclusively
to literature and literary criticisms," was, in fact, a thoroughly juvenile performance. Other publications of slight
importance, but remarkable for their frontier flavor, were
the *Ohio and Michigan Register, and Emigrants Guide*, of
Florence, Ohio, which seems to have been founded as early

---

[206] I have seen no copies of the first volume; but Nos. 7 and 8
were, it seems, for Jan. and Feb., 1822 (see *The North American Review*, XIV, 460, Apr., 1822). If Hunt was the editor from the
beginning, he must have commenced *The Masonic Miscellany* immediately upon giving up *The Western Review*, of which the last
issue appeared in July, 1821.

[207] No. 27, the last issue in Vol. I, is for Sept. 29, 1835.

as January, 1832;[208] Galland's *Chronicles of the North American Savages*, which first appeared, at Carthage, Illinois, in May, 1835;[209] and *The Western Emigrants' Magazine, and Historian of Times in the West*, begun in May, 1837, at the same place.

It is impossible to estimate with any degree of accuracy the total volume of semimonthly, monthly, and quarterly periodicals in the early West.[210] The most numerous, and often the most successful, were those devoted to religious concerns, constituting, if the proportion of the kind among the total which have been examined may be taken as proof, slightly more than one-third of the whole. Literary magazines, by the same computation, were about one-fourth the total; and medical journals, perhaps most remarkable for their long life, were next in number, amounting to nearly one-sixth of all publications.

The life of the average enterprise of the kind, whether religious, literary, technical, or of other aims, was unprosperous and short; but the number increased with considerable rapidity in spite of the difficulties that beset both publisher and editor — the lack of qualified contributors, the scarcity of books and literary intelligence, the poverty of educated persons in backwoods communities and the small proportion of the population which they formed, and the preference of many persons of taste for periodicals from the East and from England. In 1840 there were, according to the census, forty-one current Western periodicals, exclusive of all newspapers and weekly journals. Twenty of them were published in Ohio alone, nine in Illinois, eight in Kentucky, three in Indiana, and one in Michigan.

---

[208] No. 12 of Vol. I is for Dec., 1832.

[209] See *The Western Monthly Magazine*, IV, 64-65 (July, 1835).

[210] The approximately one hundred such publications listed below (see the bibliography for Chapter III) doubtless include the most important, and possibly the majority, of the whole.

Though more remarkable for mere number than for literary or other excellence of achievement, they were, nevertheless, evidence of a cultural growth of great historical importance.

# CHAPTER IV

## CONTROVERSIAL WRITINGS

Le catholicisme, avec son immobilité formidable, ses dogmes absolus, ses terribles anathèmes et ses immenses récompenses; la réformation, avec son mouvement incessant et ses variations continues; l'antique paganisme, trouvent ici leurs représentants. On y adore déjà en six manières différentes l'Être unique et éternel qui a créé tous les hommes à son image. On s'y dispute avec ardeur le ciel que chacun prétend exclusivement son héritage. Bien plus, au milieu des misères de la solitude et des maux du présent, l'imagination humaine s'y épuise encore à enfanter pour l'avenir d'inexprimables douleurs. Le luthérien condamne au feu éternel le calviniste, le calviniste l'unitaire, et le catholique les enveloppe tous dans une réprobation commune.

Plus tolérant dans sa foi grossière, l'Indien se borne à exiler son frère d'Europe des campagnes heureuses qu'il se réserve pour lui. Fidèle aux traditions confuses que lui ont léguées ses pères, il se console aisément des maux de la vie, et meurt tranquille en rêvant aux forêts toujours vertes que n'ébranlera jamais la hache du pionnier, et où le daim et le castor viendront s'offrir à ses coups durant les jours sans nombre de l'éternité. — Alexis de Tocqueville, "Quinze jours au désert."

### I

Controversial books and pamphlets, which constituted a large part of the total bulk of early Western literature, were partly an overflow from the periodical press. But often they were an independent means of giving some degree of permanency to oratory, which was a much more important influence in that day than later. Such writings, chiefly religious and political, but inspired by a wide variety of aims, bore in common the mark of an oratorical style than which, perhaps, nothing in the West was more Western. In them were exhibited the freedom of the Western orator to say what he thought on any subject, either within or without the province of his knowledge, and to defy all critical dicta. Unrestrained superlatives and extravagantly florid diction were set down to the credit of the frontier propagandist as proofs that he might worthily represent a race of vigorous men who were the possessors of a new and vast country destined to become the commercial, political, and cultural center of the world.

And yet this oratorical style, with its roots in the widely different racial characteristics of the Northern and Southern communities of the Atlantic coast, was not homogeneous. Timothy Flint, whose wide experience as a traveller made him an observer of unusual merit, recognized not only the New England and Southern types of eloquence, but a "mixed" style, originating in the Middle Atlantic states. Through the West in general, however, he found the Southern influence on speech predominant.[1] The New England style, chiefly influenced, as Flint thought, by common school training, and marked by a resultant susceptibility to ridicule and a tendency toward self-criticism, was characterized by much repression of "the strong movements of the heart" and "a more severe manner, more chastened regard to the rules of criticism, a more shrinking dread of exaggeration, mock grandeur, and false sublime." The Southern style was, on the other hand, according to the same observer, self-confident, demonstrative, florid. John Newland Maffitt, a Methodist pulpit orator widely known in Kentucky at the end of the pioneer period, clearly re-

---

[1] For this and the references to Flint immediately following, see "Thoughts on the Style and Eloquence of the Pulpit, the Bar, and the Press, in the Three Great Divisions of the United States," in *The Western Monthly Review*, III, 639-647 (June, 1830).

garded what Flint describes as the Southern influence the essential characteristic of true Western eloquence, while the New England type stood, in his eyes, for the whole of the East: "The eloquence of the East," he wrote, "is sober, passionless, condensed, metaphysical; that of the West is free, lofty, agitating, grand, impassioned. . . . the West defies and transcends criticism."[2]

Even the discipline of schooling and of scientific research did not avail to destroy the enthusiasm for florid oratory all but universal in the Ohio Valley communities which determined the complexion of Western culture before 1840. Charles Caldwell, a noted scientist, and for years a professor in Transylvania, thus eulogized the attainments of Horace Holley, who had served as president of that university:

> Although not himself a frequent or successful suitor in the bowers of the Muses — for he rarely attempted the witcheries of song, and never touched, with deep effect, 'the minstrel's bold and high-strung lyre' — he, notwithstanding, looked on creation with the frenzied eye, and felt her charms with all the thrilling ecstasy of the poet.[3]

"What orator," asked Mann Butler, a Kentucky teacher and historian, "can deign to restrain his imagination within a vulgar and sterile state of facts?"[4] Daniel Drake, "the Franklin of Cincinnati," a university professor and

[2] "Eloquence of the West," in *The Rose of the Valley*, I, 170 (Aug.? 1839). For a significant characterization of Maffitt's own style of eloquence, see *Ky. Gaz.*, Nov. 30, 1837. Two volumes of verse, *Ireland* and *Poems*, and a series of sermons, *Pulpit Sketches*, all published at Louisville in 1839, offer further proof of the extravagance of Maffitt's manner. These three books are, however, omitted from the present study as scarcely belonging to the Middle West as here defined.

[3] Charles Caldwell, *A Discourse on the Genius and Character of the Rev. Horace Holley*, 1828, p. 88.

[4] Mann Butler, *A History of the Commonwealth of Kentucky*, 1834, p. 149.

the most famous medical authority in the West, not only understood the peculiar quality of frontier eloquence but heartily defended it:

The literature of a young and free people, will of course be declamatory, and such, so far as it is yet developed, is the character of our own. Deeper learning will, no doubt, abate its verbosity and intumescence; but our natural scenery, and our liberal political and social institutions, must long continue to maintain its character of floridness. And what is there in this that should excite regret in ourselves, or raise derision in others? Ought not the literature of a free people to be declamatory? . . . Whenever the literature of a new country loses its metaphorical and declamatory character, the institutions which depend on public sentiment will languish and decline; . . . For a long time the oration, in various forms, will constitute a large portion of our literature. A people who have fresh and lively feelings, will always relish oratory.[5]

And that Drake could, on his own account, make use of the accepted principles of Western eloquence is proved by the final paragraph of the same address:

Then, in the hour of death, when your hearts shall pour out the parting benediction, and your eyes are soon to close, eternally, on the scene of your labors, you will enjoy the conscious satisfaction, of having contributed to rear in your native Valley, a lovely sisterhood of states, varying from each other, as the flowers of its numerous climates differ in beauty and fragrance; but animated with the same spirit of patriotism, instinct with one sentiment of rising glory, and forever united by our Great River, as the Milky-way, whose image dances on its rippling waters, combines the stars of the sky into one broad and sparkling firmament.

With due allowance for the excess of enthusiasm in the oratory of all sections of the United States at the end of the eighteenth, and until late in the nineteenth, century, it can

[5] For this and the following quotation from Drake, see *Discourse on the History, Character, and Prospects of the West*, 1834, pp. 32-33 and 45.

scarcely be doubted that pioneer life and, to some extent, the vastness of the physical features of the new country, greatly emphasized that quality in the characteristic expression of Western people.  The emotional fervor of the revival camp meeting and the sectarian bitterness of a period remarkable for the appearance of a bewildering number of new creeds, characterized the eloquence of the frontier preacher even in the larger towns;[6] and the shrill, declamatory vainglory of the Fourth of July address was echoed by the political orators of the time.  The folly of the endless sectarian controversies which occupied a large part of the attention of nearly all religionists was, it is true, denounced by a. few moderates like Andrew Wylie;[7] and the inordinate patriotic boastfulness especially marked in Western orators was rebuked by such liberal-minded men as John C. Young, the president of a Kentucky college. "This perpetual self-laudation," he declared,

is sickening and disgusting — and we are in danger of fostering a national vanity, that will make us ridiculous for our self-sufficiency, our pretensions, and our sensitiveness — that will effectually arrest our improvement, rivet our prejudices, perpetuate our immoralities.[8]

The strongly marked sentimentality which remained, until long after the end of the pioneer period, an almost inevitable quality of Western oratory, flourished from the time of the earliest settlement.  Here, for example, is the peroration of an address by the citizens of Marietta in welcoming the first governor of the North-West Territory:

---

[6] *Cf.* "This is what they Call Eloquence," in *The Western Messenger*, I, 860-863 (July, 1836).  The account here given of the oratory of a popular preacher, though perhaps partly inspired by sectarian enmity, affords a true characterization of the usual pulpit manner in the West at that time.

[7] For example, in *Sectarianism is Heresy*, 1840.

[8] John C. Young, *An Address Delivered before the Union Literary Society of Miami University*, 1838, pp. 26-27.

GREAT Sir, . . . may the cold hand of death never arrest you, until you shall have accomplished all the objects, which a great and a good man can embrace! and then, when life shall lose her charms! when nature shall begin to sink beneath the weight of mortality; and when the mind, impatient to be free, shall burst the brittle shell which holds it here, may you rise triumphant, on cherub's wings, to enjoy your GOD, in realms of endless felicity! [9]

There was, on the other hand, among Western orators of a less dignified kind, a marked tendency toward a vulgarity of style calculated to win the approval of the great number of people who had a contempt for cultural attainments. Often there were men of some literary taste who sought consciously to imitate the crudities of popular speech that they might not be suspected of undemocratic feeling. Such was the Illinois governor described by Gustave Koerner.[10] Thomas Hart Benton and Henry Clay, the most distinguished orators in the West, were, to be sure, men of a finer type; but it is clear that the great majority of frontier politicians and lawyers, as well as a large number of the preachers, helped impress upon the minds of the people whom they influenced, a disrespect for correct speech-habit and for accurate thinking. "A love of literature," declared one of the best contemporary observers, is, indeed, against a lawyer, and even to speak thoroughly good English is at some points disreputable. At Cincinnati and Louisville — at both of which places many highly educated men are practicing — it is rare to hear a speech of any length that is not ornamented by various gross inaccuracies, such as "my client, gentlemen, *done* all he could,"

---

[9] *An Oration, Delivered at Marietta, July 4, 1788, by the Hon. James M. Varnum, Esq. one of the Judges of the Western Territory; the Speech of his Excellency Arthur St. Clair, Esquire, upon the Proclamation of the Commission Appointing him Governor of Said Territory; and the Proceedings of the Inhabitants of the City of Marietta*, 1788, p. 12.

[10] Gustave Koerner, *Memoirs*, 1909, I, 335.

or "he had not went" . . . In the pulpit, before a jury, on the stump, and in the senate, the western orator is wordy, theatrical, and confused.[11]

## II

Little distinguished for their quality, the writings of the controversialists constitute, nevertheless, a valuable record of the reaction to both political and religious issues of the time on the frontier. Even if one leaves out of account the considerable bulk of literature resulting from Western participation in the debates on national policy in the Congress at Washington[12] — literature which scarcely needs comment — there remains much which is significant in the history of the West and, to a lesser extent, the history of the nation.

[11] *The Hesperian*, III, 461 (Nov., 1839). *Cf.* also an English observer's criticism of oratory as practised at Cincinnati, in Harriet Martineau, *Retrospect of Western Travel*, 1838, II, 52-53.

[12] Besides receiving attention in the official reports of proceedings in Congress, speeches by almost all senators and representatives of any prominence were, of course, published in pamphlet form. I have gathered as many of these separate publications as I could find into the bibliography for the present chapter. Clay, who was by far the most famous of Western orators, gained, partly through partisan political interest, no doubt, the distinction of appearing in at least two collected editions before 1840. *The Speeches of Henry Clay, Delivered in the Congress of the United States* (published in 1827) seems to have been "the first volume of speeches of one individual" to be published in the United States (*The North American Review*, XXV, 425-451, Oct., 1827). "We are quite sure," wrote the reviewer of these speeches in the magazine referred to, "that not one of them was written before it was delivered, and we perceive in the greater part of them no marks of subsequent revision.

"It is a necessary consequence of this, that they contain few single passages likely to be quoted as prominent specimens of oratorical declamation." In 1839, however, there was published at New York a book of selections called *The Beauties of the Hon. Henry Clay.*

Kentucky, until late in the pioneer period, was of the first importance in political as well as religious agitation. For a short time — at the end of the eighteenth century and the beginning of the nineteenth — this state became the political storm center of the whole country. The earliest intrigues of the faction which sought to separate Kentucky, not only from Virginia, but from the Union, were not, for a number of years, reflected in a war of books and pamphlets. But the new state, after passing through the struggle for independence from Virginia, entered into national politics with a zest which inspired a great amount of pamphleteering. The whole of the new West displayed at that time a militantly radical temperament. The Terror did not destroy sympathy for France. The Fourth of July, 1795, was celebrated at Cincinnati with a toast to "The French nation, and confusion to all despots" and a salute of thirteen guns.[13] In Kentucky, the passage of the Alien and Sedition Laws of 1798 caused high excitement and produced the famous Kentucky Resolutions, which, though in their original form the work of Thomas Jefferson, were a true index of the ultrademocratic sentiment of the majority of frontiersmen. This excitement also inspired one of the first and one of the most eloquent Western political pamphlets, *A Letter from George Nicholas, of Kentucky, to his Friend, in Virginia. Justifying the Conduct of the Citizens of Kentucky.* Like other supporters of the Kentucky Resolutions, Nicholas denied that the state thought of rebellion against national authority. It was the federal government, he insisted, that was violating the constitution, by suppressing liberty of speech. In defense of this liberty, he spoke courageously:

So far from it's being right to abridge the freedom of speech or of the press, when it is exercised to censure the

[13] See *Cent. N.-W. Ter.*, July 11, 1795.

measures of government; it is the only time, when it is necessary to protect either of them. . . . I have lived too long as a freeman ever to act *well* the part of a slave.

This remarkable letter, which was printed at Lexington in 1798, was answered in the following February by ''an Inhabitant of the North-Western Territory'' in *Observations, on a Letter from George Nicholas*, which appeared at Cincinnati. Later in the same year a pamphlet called *Correspondence between George Nicholas, of Kentucky, and Robert G. Harper, Member of Congress, from the District of 96, South-Carolina*[14] showed the continued public interest in the controversy.

Almost from the first, Kentucky's relations with New Orleans and the territory west of the Mississippi had been close. The accession of Louisiana by the United States in 1803 was a matter of deep interest to the whole Western people. Their feeling of satisfaction at the end of the Spanish and French intrigues and at the prospect of American development further west is manifested in Allan B. Magruder's *Political, Commercial and Moral Reflections, on the Late Cession of Louisiana, to the United States*, published in the year of the purchase. This work, dedicated to President Jefferson, showed the relation of the cession of Louisiana to European politics, set forth the economic resources of the new country, and gauged its possible effect on slavery. Louisiana, declared the author, was a charter of the economic independence of the United States; and it offered an opportunity for Americans to abolish slavery by colonizing their negroes in the newly acquired territory.

From a time shortly after Kentucky's admission as a state, the question of the navigation of the Mississippi had given rise to Spanish intrigues which continued after formal settlement of the Mississippi question had been agreed upon and which involved, to some extent, a number

---

14 Advertised in *Ky. Gaz.*, Sept. 26, 1799.

of Kentuckians; but little was definitely known of these proceedings until the history of General James Wilkinson was given some publicity during the trial of Aaron Burr. At that time appeared a pamphlet by "a Kentuckian" entitled *A Plain Tale, Supported by Authentic Documents, Justifying the Character of General Wilkinson*. Already, however, there had been published at Frankfort (1806) *The Report of the Select Committee*, an account of government proceedings proving the guilt of Judge Sebastian of the Kentucky Court of Appeals, who had long received a pension from the Spanish government. The Burr conspiracy itself was a matter of intense interest in Kentucky, which Burr had personally canvassed for aid in his Southwestern enterprise. When Joseph Hamilton Daveiss, United States attorney in Kentucky, having detected Burr's movements, was dismissed by President Jefferson, he appealed to the public in *A View of the President's Conduct, concerning the Conspiracy of 1806*. Embittered by the action of the President in removing him from office, Daveiss vigorously attacked Jefferson and his "*snoring* administration." "If I had possessed sufficient power," he wrote, "I should have taken the start of mr. Jefferson by removing him from office." This pamphlet included a lengthy "Sketch of the Political Profile of our Three Presidents," in which the same writer made the most of the opportunity to attack Jefferson for what was characterized as his overweening ambition and long scheming for the Presidency. Daveiss was also the author of *An Essay on Federalism*, favoring centralization and containing an exceptionally able attack on the principles espoused by Jefferson's party.

An early political writer of less bitterness was William Littell, a Kentucky lawyer. In 1806 he published his *Political Transactions in and concerning Kentucky, from the First Settlement thereof, until it Became an Independent*

*State, in June, 1792.* "In the heart of Kentucky," said the author,

a faction has lately been organized for the determinate purpose of consigning to infamy every citizen on whose talents and integrity the people have habitually reposed confidence. . . . To refute as far as an accusation of this kind can from the nature of things be refuted, is the object of the writer in the following pages.

Littell confessed that "In executing this work, the author is not to be considered as an historian"; he was, in fact, participating in a political debate. This pamphlet concludes with a collection of documents extracted from the journals of the convention held at Danville in 1785 and from several later sources. Another work shows Littell in much lighter vein: *An Epistle from William, Surnamed Littell, to the People of the Realm of Kentucky*, which appeared at Frankfort in the same year with the *Political Transactions*, is written in Biblical style, with a display of humor that makes the author's partisan observations on the questions of the day more palatable. Topics of contemporary interest are referred to only periphrastically, except in the chapter headings. As to the practical result of the pamphlet on Kentucky politics, the author asserted in 1814 that by that time many of the reforms advocated in *An Epistle* had been written upon the statute books.[15] Littell early gained notoriety through his publication of the "book of the law" to which he refers in his *Epistle*.

The relief and anti-relief agitation of 1820-1826, following the failure of many Kentucky state banks, was the cause of much bitter controversy; and from 1824 this contest was centered in the attempt of the legislature to reorganize the Court of Appeals, which had nullified a bill intended for the relief of debtors. Among the speeches against this bill that appeared in pamphlet form were

15 See William Littell, *Festoons of Fancy*, 1814, pp. 21-22.

those of Benjamin Hardin, George Robertson, and Philip Triplett. The court's defense of itself was addressed to the public in *The Response of the Judges of the Court of Appeals*.

Shortly after the end of the relief and anti-relief discussion, the struggle between Jackson and Clay began to engross the attention of Kentucky and the West. One echo of this long controversy was the *Letters of Gen. Adair & Gen. Jackson, Relative to the Charge of Cowardice, Made by the Latter against the Kentucky Troops at New Orleans*, which appeared at Lexington in 1827 as a reprint from the files of the *Kentucky Reporter*. Many speeches made by Clay and others during the campaigns waged between him and Jackson were spread broadcast in pamphlet form.

Antislavery agitation, though it did not gain much momentum until near the end of the period, began on the frontier at the end of the eighteenth century. Perhaps the earliest pamphlet on this subject by a Western writer was David Rice's *Slavery Inconsistent with Justice and Good Policy*, which was printed at Philadelphia in 1792.[16] Besides being morally wrong, slavery, he argues, is a bad national policy — slavery would furnish recruits to an enemy in time of war; and its very inconsistency with democratic principles must be a source of weakness to a republic. Moreover, it tends to make industry a disgrace. "Holding men in slavery," concludes Rice's appeal,

is the national vice of Virginia; and, while a part of that state, we were partakers of the guilt. As a separate state, we are just now come to the birth; and it depends upon our free choice, whether we shall be born in this sin, or

[16] The title here given is from R. H. Bishop, *An Outline of the History of the Church in the State of Kentucky*, 1824, p. 385, where the speech is reprinted. There are many reprints extant; but I have found no copy of the original edition. The quotation given below is from *Slavery Inconsistent with Justice and Good Policy*, London, 1793, p. 24.

innocent of it. We now have it in our power to adopt it as our national crime; or to bear a national testimony against it. I hope the latter will be our choice; that we shall wash our hands of this guilt, and not leave it in the power of a future legislature, ever more to stain our reputation or our conscience with it.

From about 1820 until long after 1840, antislavery propaganda rapidly increased; and the excitement caused by the great debate was reflected both in certain periodicals already discussed and in an ever increasing volume of pamphlets.

In Illinois, an important controversy was aroused when the attempt was made in 1823 to call a constitutional convention in order to legalize slavery. One of the most notable opponents of this program was the English immigrant Morris Birkbeck, already known in both Europe and America for his books recommending the Illinois country to English farmers. A relic of the pamphlet and newspaper war in which Birkbeck was a leading figure is *An Appeal to the People of Illinois on the Question of a Convention*, which he published at Shawneetown in 1823. The author, after attempting to show that the action of the legislature in approving a call for a convention was dishonestly secured, launched a whole-hearted invective against slavery. The question was decided favorably to Birkbeck's party at the election held shortly afterwards.

In the year following the publication of Birkbeck's pamphlet, there was printed at Vevay, Indiana, James Duncan's remarkable work, *A Treatise on Slavery; in which is Shewn forth the Evil of Slave Holding, both from the Light of Nature and Divine Revelation*. In 1826 John Rankin, "Pastor of the Presbyterian Churches of Ripley and Strait-creek, Brown County, Ohio," published his *Letters on Slavery, Addressed to Mr. Thomas Rankin, Merchant at Middlebrook, Augusta County, Virginia*, in

CONTROVERSIAL WRITINGS 217

which he pleaded with his brother to liberate the slaves he
had purchased. Other churchmen in Ohio were presently
engaged in forwarding the antislavery agitation. The
Synod of Cincinnati, in 1830, appointed a committee which
published at Georgetown, Ohio, in the following year, *An
Address to the Churches on the Subject of Slavery*. Two
years later, Samuel Crothers, who had served as a member
of this committee, wrote his *Strictures on African Slavery*,
which was published by the Abolition Society of Paint
Valley, at Rossville, Ohio. African slavery, he maintained,
was introduced into the Christian church by the Pope; it
was against all reasonable interpretations of the Scripture;
it had polluted the churches; all arguments in its support
were absurd. In a later pamphlet, *The Gospel of the Jubilee*, he sought to reinforce his assertion that there were no
valid Scriptural arguments for slavery.

During the remaining years of the last decade of the
pioneer period Western writers participated in the slavery
controversy in much greater numbers. The most important
organizations which moulded public opinion in this crisis
were the churches — still far, however, from unanimity —
and the great number of abolition and colonization societies which had by this time sprung up, especially in Ohio.
*Letters on Slavery* (1833), by J. D. Paxton, a Kentucky
Presbyterian preacher, was addressed to his former parish-
ioners in Virginia. In the following year, James G. Birney, one of the most noteworthy of Western agitators, published, among other propagandist pamphlets, a *Letter on
Colonization*, to the secretary of the Kentucky Colonization
Society, and, a little later, *Mr. Birney's Second Letter.
To the Ministers and Elders of the Presbyterian Church
in Kentucky*. Other works by the same author followed,
until so conspicuous a mark had Birney become for the
friends of slavery that in 1836 a Cincinnati mob, cheered
on by several thousands of sympathizers, destroyed the

printing press from which his abolitionist paper was published, and sought, unsuccessfully, to capture Birney himself.[17]  Somewhat later, Birney was active in the legal defense of a former slave, in the famous dispute which occasioned the publication of the *Speech of Salmon P. Chase, in the Case of the Colored Woman, Matilda* (1837).

In 1837, Alton, Illinois, became the center of interest in the antislavery movement, when Elijah P. Lovejoy, editor of the *Observer*, was killed by a mob, shortly after the meeting of the Illinois Anti-slavery Convention at Upper Alton, for which Lovejoy had issued the original call.[18]  A valuable record by a sympathizer with the reformer is Edward Beecher's *Narrative of Riots at Alton: in Connection with the Death of Rev. Elijah P. Lovejoy*, which was published at Alton in 1838.  This story of the tragedy is based on the author's personal acquaintance with Lovejoy (who had converted him to the idea of immediate emancipation) and on careful inquiry from eyewitnesses.  The second part of the book is purely argumentative; and the whole constitutes a fervent plea for free speech — a less sublime *Areopagitica*, tinged with religious feeling:

> The exigency calls for no unholy spirit of defiance, no resentment for injuries and wrongs, and no spirit of revenge over the grave of the dead. . . .  But let the strength of holy purpose become daily more intense for God and for the right to know, to proclaim, and to do his will: — for this to live, and for this, if need be, to die.

[17] *Detroit Daily Advertiser*, Aug. 19, 1836.  For a more moderate and more circumstantial account, with excerpts from the Cincinnati press, see *James G. Birney and his Times* (1890, pp. 240-255), by Birney's son, William Birney, who was an eyewitness of a part of the proceedings.  *Cf.* also the contemporary pamphlet called *Narrative of the Late Riotous Proceedings against the Liberty of the Press, in Cincinnati*, 1836.

[18] For this convention and for Lovejoy's call for its meeting, see *Proceedings of the Ill. Anti-slavery Convention.  Held at Upper Alton*, 1838.

## III

No sooner had religious organizations taken root in the West than sectarian controversy began. David Rice, who, soon after his arrival in Kentucky in 1783, became a general counselor and guardian of Presbyterian congregations, published at Baltimore in 1789 one of the first pamphlets written in Kentucky — *An Essay on Baptism*. This he followed with a number of other religious publications, among them being *A Lecture on the Divine Decrees* (1791) ; *A Sermon at the Opening of the Synod of Kentucky, 1803* ; and *An Epistle to the Citizens of Kentucky, Professing Christianity; especially to those that are, or have been, Denominated Presbyterians* (1805). The latter exemplifies "Father" Rice's solicitude for the welfare of the church of which he was guardian. He points out how departure from Calvin leads step by step through Arminianism, Universalism, Pelagianism, Semi-pelagianism, Arianism, Socinianism, and deism, to atheism. In 1808 appeared *A Second Epistle*, directed to the same readers, in which he confesses his distress at the state of religion in the land and attacks the religious errors that he sees practiced about him, but in measured terms, without the personal abuse common in the pamphlet wars carried on by a number of his contemporaries.

Almost at the same time with David Rice, there came to Kentucky from Virginia a preacher destined to a career of bitter controversy. Adam Rankin, who settled at Lexington in 1784 or 1785, succeeded in a short time in arousing the enmity of his colleagues, and in 1789 was brought before the Presbytery on a charge of slandering his brother ministers.[19] This charge, after a long delay, was sustained ;

[19] For these facts, see Bishop, *op. cit.*, pp. 140-143. The titles cited above of Rice's publications for 1791-1803 are from this work, pp. 113-114. For reprints of *An Epistle* and *A Second Epistle*, see *ibid.*, pp. 321-384. I have not found a copy of either original.

and Rankin, in defiant mood, fired a literary broadside which has been called — wrongly, I think[20] — the first book both written and published in the West. This book, or rather, pamphlet, *A Process in the Transilvania Presbytery*, was published at Lexington, where it was "Printed by Maxwell & Cooch. At the Sign of the Buffalo. Main-Street." The dedicatory note signed by Rankin is dated January 1, 1793; and it is clear that *A Process* had issued from the press by the middle of March.[21] For the contents of this celebrated book, the author himself apologized, and not entirely without reason: "CANDID READER," — he thus began his introduction — "It grieves me not a little, that my first address should present you with a trite subject of debate." Of the several charges made against Rankin the essential matter, according to his own account, was his opposition to the use of Watts's version of the Psalms as being a modern composition marred by doctrinal errors and wholly without the divine sanction enjoyed by the original Psalms. Perhaps the most curious accusation is the fifth in Rankin's list: "I do charge Mr. Rankin, with pretending to an immediate revelation from heaven in a dream which determined him, not to use Doctor Watts' psalms and hymns"; but this Rankin denied, though only half-heartedly: "The defendant solemnly declares, he opposed human psalmody from ever he entered the ministry, publicly and privately, for many months before ever he dreamed about the subject." On March 11, 1793, Rankin was to appear for another trial.[22]

The Presbytery published its own view of the case in *A Narrative of Mr. Adam Rankin's Trial*;[23] and to this the

---

20 See above, Chapter I, footnote 201.
21 See *Ky. Gaz.*, Mar. 16, 1793.
22 *Ibid.*, Feb. 9, 1793.
23 I have found no copy of this work. The title is from Rankin's

now well-seasoned controversialist answered in *A Reply to A Narrative of Mr. Adam Rankin's Trial &c. lately Published by Order of the Transylvania Presbytery* (1794). The author's apology for putting his case once more before the public will suffice as an example of the characteristic manner of many controversialists who were to follow in his steps. "IN Justice to my own feelings," he says,

I must inform my reader, that it is with the utmost reluctance I enter into Religious disputation. Nothing but a Supreme love to truth, an exoneration of my conscience, and an awful regard to the Divine injunction "*To contend earnestly for the faith once delivered to the Saints,*" could engage me in a business which has a tendency in some instances to disturb the equable flow of the milk of human kindness.

In spite of the Presbytery's assertion that not the matter of psalmody, but Rankin's slander of his fellow ministers, was the principal charge against him, he overwhelms them with proofs of their own error in " 'refusing the waters of Shiloah that go softly,' " and rejoicing "in the muddy and bubbling streams of the imitations of Watts, and the crude effusions of other scribbling poetasters." He closes his book with two lengthy quotations from Milton's *Paradise Regained*,[24] a part of which he aptly entitles "Upon Scripture Psalmody." Such was the stuff of religious controversy in the early West. From the time of Rice's and Rankin's eighteenth century tracts, the stream of such literature continued to flow through the first four decades of the nineteenth century.

Rankin's later history was as stormy as his first years in Kentucky had been. In May, 1793, shortly after the pub-

rejoinder, which also purports to give the main contentions of *A Narrative*.

[24] III, 105-133; and IV, 321-350. The passages quoted above from *A Reply* are on pp. 3 and 16 of that work (1794).

lication of *A Process*, he and his followers, of whom many remained faithful to him, were received into the Associate Reformed Church; but eleven years later he was again cited before his Presbytery for slander, and also for having imposed upon the Associate Reformed Church when he and his followers were admitted into that body. On the first charge Rankin was compelled to undergo a trial finally resulting in a decision, by a commission of the General Synod of the Associate Reformed Church, that the defendant was "a scandalous person, and ought not to continue in the exercise of the christian ministry."[25] This decision, however, served only to inspire a rejoinder called *Rankin's Second Process. To All the Faithful in Christ Jesus* (1818). And this same pioneer controversialist, who had long since issued *A Review of the Noted Revival* (1802), published at least one more work, this time a book of some length called *Dialogues, Pleasant and Interesting, upon the All-important Question in Church Government* (1819), perhaps the most incoherent of all Rankin's writings.

The excitement of the great revival of 1800 and the following years brought into the Presbyterian Church in Kentucky much more serious dissention than was caused by the debate on psalmody. When disciplinary measures were applied to disaffected members at a meeting of the Synod in 1803, Barton W. Stone, Richard McNemar, John Dunlavy, and others withdrew, formed what they called the Springfield Presbytery, and issued *An Apology* (1804), which discarded characteristic Calvinistic beliefs, and rejected all creeds, acknowledging only the authority of the Bible. During the year 1804, however, in order to avoid more effectively all restriction of authority, they dissolved their independent organization, the end of which was announced to the public in *The Last Will and Testament*.[26]

25 Bishop, *op. cit.*, pp. 142-143.
26 See *Observations on Church Government, by the Presbytery of*

The pamphlet war which began in 1803 continued unabated during the following years between the church and those who withdrew, and later among the seceders themselves. McNemar and Dunlavy were converted to Shakerism. Stone continued for a time an independent course, calling his followers simply "Christians," but later joined forces with Alexander Campbell to form the church of the Disciples of Christ, to which Stone's name of "Christians" still continued often to be applied. *An Apology for Calvinism* was published by R. H. Bishop, of the Associate Reformed Church, in 1804. Stone's *Letters* on the atonement appeared in 1805. John P. Campbell, of Danville, who entered the lists for the Presbyterians, followed his *Strictures on Two Letters* (1805) with a lengthy pamphlet called *Vindex: or the Doctrines of the Strictures Vindicated, against the Reply of Mr. Stone* (1806). The quarrel by this time was partly personal, though John P. Campbell, after expressing indignation at Stone's methods, promised to "proceed without railing or recrimination" to his arguments. In 1809 appeared T. B. Craighead's *A Sermon on Regeneration, with an Apology and an Address to the Synod of Kentucky*; and in the following year John P. Campbell answered this on behalf of the orthodox Presbyterians in *Several Letters, Addressed to the Rev. T. B. Craighead*, and a year later reinforced his own *Letters* with *The Pelagian Detected; or, a Review of Mr. Craighead's Letters, Addressed to the Public and the Author*. Stone's pamphlet *An Address to the Christian Churches in Kentucky, Tennessee & Ohio* (1814) was answered, the following year, in Cleland's *The Socini-Arian Detected: a Series of Letters to Barton W. Stone*. Half a dozen years later Stone published an enlarged edition of *An Address*, where-

Springfield. *To which is Added, The Last Will and Testament of that Reverend Body*, 1807. For some of the facts cited above, see Bishop, *op. cit.*, pp. 130-135.

upon Cleland renewed the discussion in *Letters to Barton W. Stone* (1822). His opponent, in 1824, defended himself once more in *Letters to James Blythe, D.D. Designed as a Reply to the Arguments of Thomas Cleland, D.D. against my Address.*

Alexander Campbell, of Virginia, with whom Stone later joined, was the object of many attacks by such writers as Milton Jamieson, Joseph Sleigh, John Walker, and William Phillips; and was the central figure in a long debate on the subject of baptism.

In 1814 there was issued at Lexington *The Body of Christ: a Series of Essays on the Scriptural Doctrine of Federal Representation,* which had already appeared in briefer form in a religious periodical. The author, James M'Chord, a minister of the Associate Reformed Church, had been a student at Transylvania University and had studied law with Henry Clay before his conversion and his consequent preparation for the ministry at a New York theological seminary. *The Body of Christ* was censured by his Presbytery; and M'Chord, suspended in 1815, was convicted before the Synod two years later. Received, however, by the Presbytery of West Lexington, he continued to preach. In 1817 he published his defense before the Synod, and in 1818, *A Last Appeal.* No writings of the West, it was said by a contemporary, met with such an extensive and respectable patronage as his.[27]

Of later Western Presbyterian controversial literature, a large body of which is extant, the most notable examples are, perhaps, the *Trial of the Rev. Lyman Beecher, D.D. before the Presbytery of Cincinnati, on the Charge of Heresy* (1835); and *Views in Theology* (1836), which Beecher published at the request of the Synod of Cincin-

---

[27] For this estimate and for some of the facts of M'Chord's life as given here, see Bishop, *op. cit.,* pp. 171-179.

nati. The charge against Beecher, as stated by himself, was that he held and taught Pelagian and Arminian doctrines, in respect to the subject of free agency and accountability, original sin, total depravity, regeneration, and Christian character.

Among the minor sects which afforded occasion for numerous polemical writings were the Shakers, whose missionaries entered the West just in time to benefit by the extraordinary religious agitation that swept Ohio and Kentucky at the dawn of the nineteenth century. Among the converts gained by the new faith from the broken ranks of the Presbyterians were Richard McNemar, who became its most prominent defender, and John Dunlavy. The first important plea for Shakerism was contained in McNemar's book *The Kentucky Revival, or, a Short History of the Late Extraordinary Out-pouring of the Spirit of God, in the Western States of America, agreeably to Scripture-promises, and Prophecies concerning the Latter Day: with a Brief Account of the Entrance and Progress of what the World Call Shakerism, among the Subjects of the Late Revival in Ohio and Kentucky.* This was printed at Cincinnati in 1807, and in 1808 McNemar published an annotated edition of *Observations on Church Government.* In the latter year appeared an officially indorsed summary of Shaker theology in *The Testimony of Christ's Second Appearing,* attributed to Benjamin Youngs. Shortly afterwards, when the excitement over Shakerism in Kentucky had begun to take on political significance, an attack on the new sect was made by John Bailey in a pamphlet called *Fanaticism Exposed: or the Scheme of Shakerism Compared with Scripture, Reason and Religion, and Found to be Contrary to them All.* James Smith's strictures on the Shakers, issued about the same time, were answered in McNemar's *Shakerism Detected . . . Examined* (1811).

By 1818 John Dunlavy, too, was active in the defense of the Shakers. In that year there appeared at Pleasant Hill, Kentucky, his work called *The Manifesto, or a Declaration of the Doctrines and Practice of the Church of Christ*, a book of considerable bulk. The author dismissed as of no importance the attacks of Smith and Bailey, as well as Christopher Clark's work, *A Shock to Shakerism*, which had been published in 1816. Besides chapters on theological questions, there is a series of letters addressed to Barton W. Stone, who, before he became the leader of the "Christians," was a friend and associate of Dunlavy. Among later publications of the Shakers were many by McNemar — his pamphlets, or those in which he had a part, probably numbered a score in all.[28] *The Other Side of the Question* (1819), which was an answer to *An Account of the Conduct of the Shakers* (1818), by Abram Van Vleet, was probably partly McNemar's work; and such anonymous publications as *A Concise Answer to the General Inquiry, Who, or what are the Shakers* (1823) and the *Investigator; or a Defence of the Order, Government & Economy of the United Society Called Shakers* (1828) have been attributed to him.

The Methodists, who made remarkable headway because of their adaptability to pioneer conditions, had a smaller share in controversial writings than did a number of less flourishing sects. Lorenzo Dow, perhaps the best-known of their itinerant preachers before the time of Cartwright, was, as he himself said, a "Cosmopolite"; and few, if any, of his numerous writings can be claimed as Western literature. His *History of Cosmopolite; or the Four Volumes of Lorenzo's Journal* (1814) contains, however, something of his experience in the West. His pamphlet called *A Cry from the Wilderness!* (1830), which is filled with curious

---

[28] See J. P. MacLean, *A Sketch of the Life and Labors of Richard McNemar*, 1905, pp. 64-67.

prophetic interpretations of the Bible and of history, was probably published at Cincinnati.[29] More authentic expressions of Methodist doctrines had, however, already appeared in the West. According to Peter Cartwright,[30] the beginning of controversial writings by members of his sect was occasioned by the appearance of *A Familiar Dialogue between Calvinus and Arminius* (1805),[31] by Thomas Cleland; and another attack on Methodists issued about the same time. Two satirical pamphlets by Methodists were written in reply — *A Useful Discovery; or, I never Saw the Like before* (1806? republished 1811?)[32] and *The Dagon of Calvinism, or the Moloch of Decrees; a Poem, in Three Cantos. To which is Annexed a Song of Reason* (reprint? 1811).[33] Both were reprinted by Cartwright and spread broadcast over Kentucky; and his enemies, supposing him to be the author, wrote him a complimentary letter in the name of the Devil, which Cartwright published in a pamphlet with his "Reply to the Letter. To the Right

[29] The advertisement which it contains of Lorenzo Dow's Family Medicine, which was to be had at the postoffice in Cincinnati, also suggests that this famous religious enthusiast was a purveyor of other wares than religion.

[30] Peter Cartwright, *Fifty Years as a Presiding Elder*, 1871, p. 92. Cartwright gives the title as *A Dialogue between Calvinists and Arminians*, evidently from memory, as he is uncertain of the date.

[31] Thomas Cleland, *Memoirs of the Rev. Thomas Cleland*, ed. E. P. Humphrey and T. H. Cleland, 1859, p. 131.

[32] The title is from Cartwright, *loc. cit.* As for the dates, I am uncertain whether I am right in identifying this pamphlet with the one called *Useful Discovery, in a Letter Addressed to the Rev. Mr. C—— and Mr. M——*, which is said to have been published in 1806 and reprinted in 1811 (*The Evangelical Record, and Western Review*, I, 49, Feb., 1812).

[33] This pamphlet is not dated; but, according to J. L. Wilson (*Episcopal Methodism; or Dagonism Exhibited*, 1811, pp. 13-14), it was issued in Cincinnati in Oct., 1811.

Honorable, the Devil."[34] The satire of *The Dagon of Calvinism* brought a reply by Joshua Lacy Wilson, who was convinced after a correspondence with John W. Browne & Company, the publishers of that work, that it was written by the Methodists. Wilson's rejoinder, called *Episcopal Methodism; or Dagonism Exhibited* (1811), was the signal for the appearance in the following spring of a lengthy pamphlet by William Burke called *The Methodist Episcopal Church, their Doctrines and Discipline, together with the Characters of Certain Individuals, Vindicated from the Unjust Representations of Joshua L. Wilson* (1812). The importance in the eyes of contemporary partisans of the bitter controversy waged in this manner is reflected in the many monthly installments of reviews devoted to Burke by a religious magazine of the time.[35]

Later attacks upon Methodism, both from within and from the outside, marked the phenomenal growth of this church in the West. In *An Appeal to the Public*, the quarterly meeting of the Associate Methodist Church held in Zanesville, in April, 1829, stated the "causes of their late secession from the M. E. Church." In 1832 appeared Cornelius Springer's *A Review of the Late Decision of the Supreme Court of Ohio*, an attack upon "the principles of the government of the M. E. Church — shewing that the creation of such a corporation, holding a vast amount of property, is a dangerous engine in a free government." The author was a Methodist preacher who had withdrawn from the church to espouse the cause of the Methodist Protestant Church. The early interest of the Methodists in the sectarian debates of the time is further proved by

---

[34] Cartwright, *op. cit.*, pp. 92-193. Both the letter and the reply are here reprinted.

[35] See *The Evangelical Record, and Western Review*, I, 204-338 (July-Dec., 1812), *passim*.

the fact that the first original work[36] published by the Western Methodist Book Concern was William Phillips's *Campbellism Exposed* (1837).

The Protestant Episcopal Church in the West, though it had no prominent part in the doctrinal warfare which arrayed other sects against each other, passed through a period of internal dissention occasioned by the attacks upon Bishop Chase, of Ohio. In his *Defence of Kenyon College* (1831), Chase answered "the slanders of the Rev. G. M. West," who had acted as his chaplain. Among other pamphlets brought forth by this quarrel were Samuel Chase's *Remarks upon Recent Publications against the Rt. Rev. Philander Chase* (1832); William Sparrow's *A Reply to the Charges and Accusations of the Rt. Rev. Philander Chase*, published the same year; and *Bishop Chase's Defence of himself, against the Late Conspiracy at Gambier, Ohio.*

Other Protestant sects were likewise scarcely heard above the din caused by the bitter disputes among the larger religious organizations, and especially among the Calvinists and the groups who had seceded after the great revival. Augustine Eastin's *Letters on the Divine Unity. Addressed to Mr. David Barrow, in Answer to his Letter to a Friend* was among the earliest controversial pamphlets in the West, appearing at Lexington in 1804. J. Kidwell's *A Series of Strictures on the Subject of Future and Endless Punishment* (1830), containing "the substance of the arguments used in a public debate held at Indianapolis," was the work of one of the most active Universalist propagandists of the time. Elisha Bates's *Extracts from the Writings of the Early Members of the Society of Friends* (1825), to which he added original observations; William

[36] J. B. Finley, *Sketches of Western Methodism*, 1856, pp. 302 and 488.

M'Kimmey's *The Plea of the Innocent, or Hicksiteism: a New Name for Quakerism* (1834) ; and Charles Fisher's *A Serious Expostulation with the Followers of Elias Hicks* (1829) dealt with the controversial issues that engaged the attention of the communities of Friends in Ohio and Indiana.

Towards 1840, while the quarrels among the Protestant sects were still continued, though with waning interest, religious controversy was quickened by a widespread hostility to Catholicism. *The Real Principles of Roman Catholics* (new edition, 1805), an anonymous work by Stephen Theodore Badin,[37] a priest, was one of the earliest defenses of that church to be published on the frontier. *Remarks on the Catholic and Protestant Religions*, apparently intended as an attack on Catholicism with personal charges against a Kentucky priest, was written by Bertrand Guerin, a professor in Transylvania University. It is just possible, however, that this early controversial work was, after all, not published.[38] It was not until some years later that feeling against the Roman church became bitter. Bardstown, the oldest Catholic settlement in Kentucky, was for a time the center of the dispute. Nathan L. Rice, a Presbyterian minister of that town, and one of the most active opponents of the Catholics, was the author of *Infallibility of the Church, Tested by Scripture* (1834) and *An Account of the Law-suit Instituted by Rev. G. A. M. Elder, President of St. Joseph's College, against Rev. N. L. Rice* (1837).

An answer to Rice's contentions was contained in *A Few Chapters to Brother Jonathan, concerning "Infallibility, &c." or, Strictures on Nathan L. Rice's "Defence of Protestantism," &c. &c. &c.* (1835), purporting to be a collection

[37] For the attribution to Badin, see *The Western Sun*, July 25, 1807.

[38] For the prospectus, see *Liberty Hall*, Oct. 30, 1811.

of letters from Philemon Scank to Jonathan his brother, and published by the latter against the advice of their author. The author, though the champion of the Catholic cause, seems to disclaim any partisan interest; and his controversial purpose is made still less offensive by his familiar and almost humorous style. The pamphlet includes a poem called "The Ursuline Convent," dedicated to J. Q. Adams, and intended to illustrate the cruelty practised upon Catholics as a result of agitation.

In Cincinnati, the climax of the excitement came with the forensic battle recorded in *A Debate on the Roman Catholic Religion: Held in the Sycamore-Street Meeting House, Cincinnati, from the 13th to the 21st of January, 1837. Between Alexander Campbell, of Bethany, Virginia, and the Rt. Rev. John B. Purcell, Bishop of Cincinnati*. The widespread interest in this kind of polemics at the time was proved by the rapid sale of the book, of which more than fourteen thousand copies are said to have been sold within less than three years.[39]

The most bitter religious controversy in the West, however, was caused by the Mormons, who did not make their appearance until the last decade of the pioneer period. The early opposition encountered by the colony at Kirtland, Ohio, was reflected in such works as E. D. Howe's *Mormonism Unveiled* (1834; some copies were issued in 1840 under the title of *History of Mormonism*),[40] which, with much detailed narrative of Mormon origins, denounced the creed

---

[39] *The Hesperian*, III, 455 (Nov., 1839). For detailed contemporary comment on the progress of this debate, see *Cinc. Daily Gaz.*, Jan. 13-23, 1837. The editorial comment here given is unfavorable to Campbell.

[40] The *History of Mormonism* of 1840 differed from *Mormonism Unveiled* only in its title-page, and was actually made up of sheets printed in 1834. For the genesis of the edition of 1840, see MS. note by O. D. Howe, son of the author, in the copy of the *History* in the library of the Western Reserve Historical Society.

and its propagators and gave currency to the theory concerning the *Book of Mormon* that "the historical part of said Bible was written by one Solomon Spalding, more than twenty years ago, and by him intended to have been published as a romance." Joseph Smith, Jr., Oliver Cowdery, Sidney Rigdon, and F. G. Williams were the joint authors of *Doctrine and Covenants of the Church of the Latter Day Saints: carefully Selected from the Revelations of God* (1835), containing a series of lectures which had been delivered before a theological class at Kirtland, together with a set of regulations said to have been derived from revelation and intended for the government of the church. Parley P. Pratt, one of the boldest of the Mormon missionaries in the West, published, in 1837, *A Voice of Warning, and Instruction to All People, or an Introduction to the Faith and Doctrine of the Church of Jesus Christ, of Latter Day Saints.* The same author issued, in the following year, a vindication of this sect in *Mormonism Unveiled: Zion's Watchman Unmasked.*

In the closing years of the period, intense partisan interest was aroused by the persecution which the Mormons experienced in Missouri. John P. Greene, acting as "an authorized representative" of the new church, published, at Cincinnati, his *Facts Relative to the Expulsion of the Mormons or Latter Day Saints, from the State of Missouri, under the "Exterminating Order."* Meetings had recently been held in the same town to express sympathy for the persecuted sect. In 1839, the year of Greene's pamphlet, appeared *A Brief History of the Church of Christ of Latter Day Saints, . . . with the Reasons of the Author for Leaving the Church. By John Corrill, a Member of the Legislature of Missouri.* A history of Mormonism, which was, in fact, a special plea in its defense, was supplied in 1840 by Parley P. Pratt's book *Late Persecution of the Church of Jesus Christ, of Latter Day Saints.* Ten

*Thousand American Citizens Robbed, Plundered, and Banished; Others Imprisoned, and Others Martyred for their Religion. With a Sketch of their Rise, Progress and Doctrine.* In the same year, Pratt published *The Millenium, and Other Poems: to which is Annexed, a Treatise on the Regeneration and Eternal Duration of Matter.* The *Treatise,* like some of the poems, was written in the "lonely dungeons of Missouri where the author was confined upwards of eight months during the late persecution." William Swartzell, "sometime a Deacon in the Church of 'Latter-Day-Saints,' " was the author (1840) of *Mormonism Exposed, being a Journal of a Residence in Missouri from the 28th of May to the 20th of August, 1838.*

In spite of the vast amount of hopelessly confused and prejudiced debate among the many religious organizations which sought the support of the pioneer settlers, some signs of moderation, rare enough in the earlier years of the nineteenth century, were to be seen before the end of the period. Nothing of the kind was more remarkable than Andrew Wylie's *Sectarianism is Heresy* (1840), with its promise of a new era.

The general principles of religion without regard to purely sectarian views, formed the subject of one of the most notable contributions in the whole course of Western religious controversy, the *Debate on the Evidences of Christianity; Containing an Examination of "The Social System," and of all the Systems of Scepticism of Ancient and Modern Times,* a record of the public discussion between Robert Owen and Alexander Campbell at Cincinnati in 1829. This debate, like the one held eight years later between Campbell and Purcell, lasted more than a week and created great excitement. In the same year there appeared a separate account, *Robert Owen's Opening Speech, and his Reply to the Rev. Alex. Campbell, in the Recent Public Discussion in Cincinnati, to Prove that the*

*Principles of All Religions are Erroneous, and that their
Practice is Injurious to the Human Race.* Owen's earlier
work, the *Oration, Containing a Declaration of Mental
Independence, Delivered in the Public Hall, at New-
Harmony* (1826) and a portion of William Maclure's
*Opinions on Various Subjects,* published at New Harmony,
1831-1838, are also to be accounted a part of the literature
of controversy in the early West, though some of the essays
included in the latter book were written at Paris, many
years earlier, for the *Revue encyclopédique.*[41]

## IV

Aside from politics and religion, a wide variety of subjects appeared in the controversial works of pioneer
authors; but the total amount of such literature was small
in comparison with that of the partisan and sectarian books
and pamphlets already discussed. Early evidences of a
reform movement which was destined to a more or less
steady growth for many decades to come were Daniel
Drake's *A Discourse on Intemperance* (1828) and Samuel
Crothers's *The Use of Strong Drink, Contrary to the
Scriptures,* published by the Greenfield Temperance Society, at Chillicothe, in 1829. Discussions of this kind
became numerous before 1840, and many societies were
formed to forward the new propaganda. So open-minded
were the persons who initiated this agitation and those
who listened to their arguments that, according to trust-
worthy evidence, the temporary adjournment of a temperance meeting so that those in attendance might indulge in
refreshments at a neighboring bar, was not an unheard-of
event.[42]    The principles of a secret society which aroused

---

[41] Prefatory notice in the first volume of *Opinions,* 1831.

[42] For an account of such proceedings, see E. D. Mansfield, *Memoirs of the Life and Services of Daniel Drake,* 1855, pp. 189-190.

much discussion among religionists and politicians of the time, were defended by Philander Chase, a member of the order, in his *Christianity and Masonry Reconciled* (1818) and attacked in such works as Dyer Burgess's *Solomon's Temple Haunted, or Free Masonry, the Man of Sin, in the Temple of God* (1830). A number of pamphlets containing constitutions and other Masonic literature were published by grand lodges, especially in Kentucky. Perhaps the most notable of the purely academic controversies not uncommon in the early West, was that which concerned the conduct of the Medical College of Ohio. Among the writers on this subject were Daniel Drake and John F. Henry.

# CHAPTER V

## SCHOLARLY WRITINGS AND SCHOOLBOOKS

What a rich harvest of fame awaits the early authors of
Ohio? The scholar and the man of science may proceed
with alacrity in their peaceful, useful career, . . . because millions on millions shall yet read their writings with
filial reverence and affection, fully appreciating the difficulties, their authors had to encounter, and the obstacles
which they had to surmount, without learned men to con-
verse with, or libraries to consult. — Caleb Atwater, *The
General Character, Present and Future Prospects of the
People of Ohio.*

### I

Participation, on a small scale, in historical and scientific
investigation was fostered in the early West by the colleges,
whose growth has already been noted; and by societies
much less limited in membership, but more local in interest, which were formed in various communities. One of
the earliest organizations of the latter kind was, no doubt,
the Vincennes Historical and Antiquarian Society, established in 1808.[1] The long annals of the old French settlement and the important part played by the town in the
Revolution and during the Indian troubles, as well as its
prominence as the early capital of Indiana, inspired some
interest in activities of a sort hardly known in other parts
of the West till some twenty years later; but its first publication outside the columns of *The Western Sun* may have
been Judge Law's *Address Delivered before the Vincennes*

---

[1] Henry S. Cauthorn, "Planting of Literary Institutions at Vincennes, Indiana," in W. H. Venable, *Beginnings of Literary Culture
in the Ohio Valley,* 1891, p. 262.

*Historical and Antiquarian Society, February 22, 1839,*
printed at Louisville the same year.

The earliest of the Western state societies of this kind
seems to have been the Antiquarian and Historical Society
of Illinois, founded at Vandalia in 1827, with James Hall
as one of its organizers.[2] *An Address Delivered before the
Antiquarian and Historical Society of Illinois, at its Second Annual Meeting, in December, 1828, by James Hall,
President of the Society* was published the following year,
and perhaps other pamphlets followed.[3] An active interest
in this field in early Michigan, then still a territory, was
shown by the formation of the Historical Society of Michigan, incorporated in 1828, with Governor Cass as the
president [4] and long one of its most active members. Six
years later there appeared at Detroit a volume called *Historical and Scientific Sketches of Michigan. Comprising a
Series of Discourses Delivered before the Historical Society of Michigan, and Other Interesting Papers Relative
to the Territory*, containing monographs by Cass, Schoolcraft, Henry Whiting, and John Biddle, a number of which
had already appeared in pamphlet form. In December,
1830, the Historical Society of Indiana was organized at
Indianapolis;[5] and shortly afterwards Benjamin Parke
was chosen president.[6] Perhaps the most active of all
such associations for research was the Historical and Phil-

[2] See *The Western Monthly Review*, I, 563 (Jan., 1828).

[3] Edmund Flagg (*The Far West*, 1838, I, 228) mentions the "published proceedings" of this society as evincing "much research and
information."

[4] See *Constitution and By-laws of the Historical Society of Michigan, Incorporated June 23d, 1828*, 1829, p. 2. For the later history
of this society, see *Supplement to Library Service*, published by the
Public Library, Detroit, Vol. IV, No. 11 (Jan. 15, 1921).

[5] See MS. book containing minutes of the first meeting (Dec. 11,
1830) and the constitution, in Indiana State Library.

[6] *Detroit Journal and Michigan Advertiser*, Feb. 9, 1831.

osophical Society of Ohio, at Columbus, incorporated in
1831.[7]  In *A Discourse Delivered before the Historical
& Philosophical Society of Ohio, at the Annual Meeting of
Said Society, in Columbus, December 22, 1832*, Benjamin
Tappan, the president, included "a rude and hasty outline" of what might be done: his plan embraced not only
the investigation of the ancient monuments of Ohio and of
the history of its early white settlements, but the study of
the geology and botany of that state.  In 1838 and 1839 the
Society published Volume I, Parts I and II, of its *Transactions*.  Dr. S. P. Hildreth, James McBride, James H.
Perkins, Jacob Burnet, and William Henry Harrison were
among the contributors.  The Kentucky Historical Society
was founded at Louisville in 1838.[8]  The activity of the
latter organization resulted, within six months after its
establishment, in the collecting of nearly a thousand pamphlets and about two hundred volumes, besides maps, newspapers, and manuscripts.[9]  Its prosperity was, however,
destined to be brief.[10]

Among less important organizations somewhat similar in
purpose were the Western Methodist Historical Society, at

[7] See *Journal of the Historical and Philosophical Society of Ohio*,
1838, p. iii.

[8] See *Act of Incorporation, and Constitution and By-laws of
the Kentucky Historical Society, Organized March, 1838, at Louisville, Kentucky*, 1838.

[9] *The Western Messenger*, VI, 61 (Nov., 1838).

[10] From 1841, when the legislature passed an act for the benefit
of this society, until 1878, when "reorganization" occurred, the
history of the corporation is obscure.  For at least twenty years it
must have been practically nonexistent.  The society of 1878, in
reality an entirely new enterprise, was also unfortunate.  Its charter, granted by the legislature of 1879-1880, was, however, still in
force when a revival of interest occurred in 1896.  Ten years later
the present name, the Kentucky State Historical Society, was adopted.
To the officers of this society I am indebted for the facts here cited
regarding the period 1840-1923.

Cincinnati (1839) ;[11] the Historical and Philosophical Society of Ashtabula County, at Jefferson, Ohio (1838) ;[12] and the Western Academy of Natural Sciences, at Cincinnati (1835).[13]

A learned organization not interested in historical or scientific research in the ordinary sense, but perhaps exerting a greater influence upon later scholarly writings than any of the societies mentioned above, was the Western Literary Institute and College of Professional Teachers, beginning in the General Convention of the Teachers of the Western Country, which met at Cincinnati in 1831 under the auspices of the Academic Institute. The early records of these meetings printed in *The Academic Pioneer* and *The Annual Register of the Proceedings* of the society were followed by those of the seven annual meetings for 1834-1840, which were published in six volumes of *Transactions* from 1835 to 1841. Albert Picket, Sr., the president of the society during all these years, Daniel Drake, Edward D. Mansfield, Alexander Kinmont, Calvin Stowe, Joshua L. Wilson, William Holmes M'Guffey, Bishop Purcell, Robert Hamilton Bishop, and Andrew Wylie were among the prominent Western men whose studies of educational problems are printed in these remarkable volumes.

## II

To the early settlers of the West, few of whom were in the slightest degree equipped for the study of ethnological problems, the remains of an aboriginal people and the presence of the Indian tribes, opened a field for antiquarian speculation and study that was by no means neglected.

---

[11] See *Proceedings of the Board of Managers of the Western Methodist Historical Society*, 1839.

[12] See W. D. Gallagher, *Facts and Conditions of Progress in the North-West*, 1850, p. 77.

[13] Charles Cist, *Cincinnati in 1841*, 1841, p. 109.

Daniel Drake included in his *Natural and Statistical View, or Picture of Cincinnati and the Miami Country* (1815) a description of the mounds near Cincinnati, together with theories of their origin. But perhaps the best-known research of this kind was done by Caleb Atwater, whose name became identified with the subject of mounds and aboriginal relics. "He is," said the Duke of Saxe-Weimar in his account of a visit to Atwater at Circleville, "a great antiquarian, and exists more in the antiquities of Ohio, than in the present world."[14] Atwater's "A Description of the Antiquities Discovered in the Western Country," included in his collected *Writings* (1833), was originally contributed to *Archæologia Americana*, the publication of the American Antiquarian Society.[15] Western antiquities, according to Atwater's conclusions, were of three kinds — those belonging to the Indians, those belonging to people of European origin, and those belonging to the race who erected the ancient forts and tumuli. Although mainly concerned with minute descriptive detail, the author made some attempt to outline the character and customs of the builders of ancient works, whom he regarded as allied to the Aztecs and Incas, other members of the racial group who were the architects of the great chain of such works extending from Ohio into Mexico.

Henry Rowe Schoolcraft, in his books primarily devoted to travel, seldom failed to include important digressions on antiquarian subjects. In *A View of the Lead Mines of Missouri* (1819), he had dealt at length with archæological problems, but had clearly recognized the inadequacy of the data at hand for any important conclusion; and as author of *Travels in the Central Portions of the Mississippi Val-*

---

[14] Bernhard, Duke of Saxe-Weimar, *Travels through North America*, 1828, II, 148.

[15] *Archæologia Americana. Transactions and Collections of the American Antiquarian Society*, I, 105-267 (1820).

*ley* (1825), he kept the same point of view. To the *Historical and Scientific Sketches of Michigan*, already noticed, Schoolcraft contributed a discourse containing "remarks upon the origin and character of the North American Indians"; and in his two volumes of *Algic Researches* (1839), a collection of Indian folk-lore tales, he furnished much of the raw material from which Longfellow made *Hiawatha.* Here appeared such characters as Paup-Puk-Keewiss; Shawondasee; the strong man Kwasind; and Pauguk, the lord of death. And, though certain errors of Schoolcraft's were responsible for inaccuracies in what Longfellow, except for the romantic love story, came near making a true picture of Indian customs and folk-lore,[16] much credit is due to this Western ethnologist for opening up a new source of material for American poetry. Although incredulous in his attitude toward the work of contemporary antiquarians, Schoolcraft nevertheless advanced theories of his own regarding the prehistoric Indians. "Algic" he derived from "Alleghany" and "Atlantic" as descriptive of a race that had originally belonged to that area but had, at the end of the fifteenth century, extended themselves far toward the northwest. He was attacked as the henchman of Governor Cass, and his books were ridiculed as the "Fruits of Executive Patronage"; but it is certain that his equipment as a student, though not of the conventional sort, and his opportunities as an observer, of Indian customs and folk-lore, were such as few writers on these subjects could boast. Lewis Cass, who, as Governor of Michigan, employed Schoolcraft in exploration and in the conduct of Indian affairs, and who,

---

[16] For a summary of recent scholarship dealing with the genesis of Longfellow's poem, and for some valuable conclusions, see Stith Thompson, "The Indian Legend of Hiawatha," in *Publications of the Modern Language Association of America*, XXXVII, 128-140 (Mar., 1922).

as a critic for *The North American Review,* defended him and assailed many other writers on the Indians, was the author of an address on the early condition of the North American Indians. This study is to be found in the *Historical and Scientific Sketches,* sponsored by the society of which Cass was the chief founder.

An ambitious contribution to antiquarian research was *An Inquiry into the Origin of the Antiquities of America* (1839), by John Delafield, with an appended ethnological study by James Lakey, and a preface by Bishop McIlvaine. William Henry Harrison's *A Discourse on the Aborigines of the Valley of the Ohio,* published both as a part of the proceedings of the Historical and Philosophical Society of Ohio and in pamphlet form, was reprinted in 1840 to further Harrison's political fortunes. "At a moment," says the advertisement,

when thousands are looking at the venerable author of this Essay with the deepest interest, perhaps the larger part of the community regard him chiefly as a successful warrior and veteran statesman, and are not aware that he has also been distinguished through life by his devotion to the pursuits of literature.

III

*The Discovery, Settlement and Present State of Kentucke,* which appeared in 1784, only a few years after the permanent settlement of that district began, secured for John Filson, the schoolmaster who was its author, the name of being the first historian of the West. He earned, however, a much less questionable right to be regarded as one of the earliest writers of travel and observation in the new country, his place among whom has already been noticed. A period of twenty-eight years — unless Imlay's *A Topographical Description* is also to be ranked as a historical study — separated Filson's work from the next important attempt of this kind, Humphrey Marshall's *The History of Kentucky*, which appeared at Frankfort in 1812. This book, which was only the first of the two volumes promised by its title-page, brought the narrative down to 1791, but seven years later than the date reached by Filson's account. Not until 1824 was the author able to complete the work. It now included, however, both a revised and expanded version of the volume of 1812 and the projected second volume; and an account of the antiquities of Kentucky by Constantine Rafinesque first appeared in this edition. The sources, though partly conversations with early settlers and partly Filson's report of Boone's narrative, M'Afee's *History of the Late War*, and various public documents, were in considerable measure the observations and experiences of the author,[17] who had been too bitter a partisan in the political affairs he recorded to succeed in writing an unbiased history.

From Marshall, Mann Butler drew a large part of the materials for *A History of the Commonwealth of Kentucky* (1834); but the later work shows many important differences in the complexion of events and the character of the actors. Butler severely criticizes his predecessor for misrepresenting those who came into collision with him or his friends, and offers a very different estimate. Marshall's judgment concerning the guilt of General Wilkinson is reversed by the later historian, who finds satisfactory proof of "the honor and fidelity" of that officer.[18] Butler is also an earnest apologist for the conduct of other important Kentuckians during the excitement of the separatist movement:

To try the conduct of Kentucky statesmen in 1788, under a confederation in ruins and in factions, by the same principles, which should now direct the mind, under an efficient

[17] Humphrey Marshall, *The History of Kentucky*, 1824, I, v.

[18] Mann Butler, *A History of the Commonwealth of Kentucky*, 1834, p. 162.

and beneficent government; would be absurd and unjust.
The peculiar circumstances of the times must be adverted
to, in order to arrive at any just estimate of the measure,
or of its authors. What, then, were these circumstances?
They are eloquently and no less truly narrated by General
Wilkinson.[19]

The bitter debate concerning Wilkinson and the separatist agitators was, in fact, the most significant topic of
the Kentucky historians after Filson. Butler, although he
makes much of Marshall's personal interest in the political struggles which he narrates, was himself perhaps not
wholly free from prejudice. For Marshall's account, other
early works, and "a body of private papers belonging to
some of the principal actors in Kentucky history"[20] were
not the only sources upon which he drew. He had, he
explains, been an observer of Kentucky affairs since 1806.
In spite of his evident feeling of loyalty to his state, however, Butler deserves credit for a faithful picture of men
and manners during the earliest pioneer times. His account of the Indian troubles is especially interesting; and
the value of his book is further enhanced by his reprint
(from *The Monthly American Journal of Geology and
Natural Science*) of the "Journal" of Col. Croghan, who
visited Kentucky and other parts of the West in 1765.

Excepting Kentucky, whose long and eventful history
was the first to attract attention, Ohio and Michigan were
the only Middle Western states whose history was written
with any degree of thoroughness before 1840.[21] A preliminary attempt at Ohio history was made in 1833 by

19 *Ibid.*, p. 173.

20 *Ibid.*, p. vii.

21 In that year John Mason Peck, author of important guides to
Illinois and the West, was said to be engaged in the preparation of
a history of Illinois, at the request of members of the legislature of
that state (*Lou. Pub. Adv.*, Sept. 7, 1840). This work seems, however, never to have been printed.

Salmon P. Chase in *A Sketch of the History of Ohio*, which, though intended to serve as an introduction to the same author's compilation of laws, was also issued separately in pamphlet form. But a much more extensive treatment was contained in Caleb Atwater's *A History of the State of Ohio, Natural and Civil* (1838), whose author, disregarding Chase's modest attempt, called his own work "this first HISTORY OF OHIO."[22] Atwater, who exhibited an unmistakable desire to treat his subject thoroughly, wished his readers to regard his earlier writings on ancient works and on the Indians as a part of the history. He included lengthy sections on geology, zoology, botany, and climate, together with the much longer civil and political history of Ohio to the year 1837; yet his original plan, published, he says, twenty years earlier, still required a future volume to complete it, and particular accounts of the legal and medical professions were left unattempted, as subjects belonging properly to Charles Hammond and Daniel Drake.[23] Only a few months behind this ambitious account of Ohio, James H. Lanman's *History of Michigan, Civil and Topographical* (1839), a work of substantial value, exemplified the remarkably rapid growth of cultural interest which characterized this state, only about two years before admitted into the Union. Less varied in its subject-matter than Atwater's work, Lanman's history was more largely

[22] John H. James's *A Statistical, Topographical, and Political History of Ohio, with Sketches of its Distinguished Pioneers, and Notes on the State of Society and Manners* — a work which might have been of much greater importance than Chase's sketch — seems also to have been written before Atwater's book appeared. For an announcement of it as "forthcoming," see *The Western Monthly Magazine*, I, 239 (May, 1833). James's history, however, probably remained unpublished.

[23] For the account here given of the plan of this work, see Caleb Atwater, *A History of the State of Ohio*, n. d. (1838), pp. 5-6, *et passim*.

political, but gave some attention to the social aspects of frontier life.

Meantime there had been attempts, less adequate, to study the history of the West as a whole. Timothy Flint's *A Condensed Geography and History of the Western States* (1828) was, though a formidable undertaking, little more than an exceptionally voluminous and authentic guidebook, with little unity of purpose. His main concern was with the geography of both Middle West and Southwest; and in the enlarged edition of this work, first published in 1832, he greatly reduced the already comparatively small space allotted to history, though he at the same time added short accounts of the Eastern states, of Mexico, and of South America. James Hall's historical writings, appropriately entitled *Sketches of History, Life, and Manners in the West* (1834), are largely a compilation of articles he had already printed in magazines, and deal principally with Kentucky. Missouri and Michigan are scarcely mentioned except in connection with the early French settlements; and Ohio, Indiana, and Illinois are given but scant attention. The appearance of this book, devoted mainly to Kentucky history, shortly after the publication of Mann Butler's work upon that subject, brought from the latter historian some sharp criticism with a hint of plagiarism.[24] Hall attempted to answer this attack in his preface to *Statistics of the West, at the Close of the Year 1836*, ridiculing Butler for appropriating as his own property the facts of Kentucky history. Butler continued the controversy in *An Appeal from the Misrepresentations of James Hall, respecting the History of Kentucky and the West* (1837), while his opponent issued, in 1838, a *Reply to Strictures on Sketches of the West*.[25]

---

[24] *The Western Messenger*, I, 675-687 (May, 1836).

[25] This pamphlet was in reality a reprint of Hall's preface to *Statistics of the West, at the Close of the Year 1836*, and appeared

An anthology of historical relations illustrative of life on the frontier during the second half of the eighteenth century, and recording, in particular, the long series of minor conflicts between the white settlers and the Indians, was supplied by Samuel L. Metcalf in *A Collection of Some of the most Interesting Narratives of Indian Warfare in the West* (1821) and by John A. M'Clung in his *Sketches of Western Adventure* (1832). Some thirty stories, or groups of stories, fill the latter volume. These "true accounts" were drawn largely from documentary sources, mostly already in print.

Border warfare of a more regular sort afforded subject-matter for Robert B. M'Afee's *History of the Late War in the Western Country* (1816) and John A. Wakefield's *History of the War between the United States and the Sac and Fox Nations of Indians* (1834). M'Afee's narrative is practically limited to the events of the War of 1812 which took place west of the Alleghenies; and two Western commanders, General Harrison and Governor Shelby, supplied valuable materials for the book. The author shows a regard for historical accuracy and fairness, so far as compatible with patriotism, in his desire to make his sources available to critics.[26] A strong anti-British prejudice, which it would hardly have been possible for a Kentuckian wholly to escape in 1816, is shown in his wholesale condemnation of the official reports published by the British as "so notoriously false, that no reliance can be placed upon

at the same time with the enlarged edition of this work, called *Notes on the Western States* (1838), in which the same material was again used as a preface.

[26] Robert B. M'Afee, *History of the Late War*, 1816, p. v. "Most of these papers," says the author concerning his source materials, "will remain in the possession of colonel C. S. Todd, subject to be examined by any person, who may wish to see the authorities on which any statement in this history is founded."

them"; but he acknowledges, nevertheless, a possibility of unfairness in his own book:

> In justice to our late enemies, as well as to myself, it may be proper to add, that my information with respect to them has unavoidably been very imperfect; and hence I may have made erroneous statements respecting them in many instances.[27]

Wakefield, as the author of an account of the last Indian war east of the Mississippi, combined the advantage of some first-hand knowledge with the serious disadvantage of prejudice; for he had himself served against Black Hawk.

Among ecclesiastical records, the one Western contribution of marked importance was *An Outline of the History of the Church in the State of Kentucky* (1824), by Robert Hamilton Bishop, a professor in Transylvania and later president of Miami University. This work, containing a store of valuable information about the rise of the various sects which were prominent during the early years of Kentucky, and especially concerning the schisms in the Presbyterian Church following the revival of 1800, includes also valuable memoirs of early leaders like David Rice, Adam Rankin, and Barton W. Stone. For minor biographical sketches, the author relied upon the aid of such men as John M'Farland and James Blythe, who had served in the ministry as colleagues of the persons whose lives they narrated. The appendix is remarkable for containing reprints of some of the earliest pamphlets written in the West. Other religious historical works, which displayed, however, almost no originality, were published by Martin Ruter and B. F. Ells. Ruter's *The Martyrs, or a History of Persecution, from the Commencement of Christianity to the Present Time* (1830) was "compiled from the works of Fox and others"; and the same author's *A Concise History of the Christian Church* (1834) was drawn

---

[27] *Ibid.*, p. vi.

from "Dr. G. Gregory, with numerous additions and improvements." Ells's *A History of the Romish Inquisition* (1835) acknowledged indebtedness of the same kind to various authors.

## IV

Of biographical and autobiographical writings, the greater part were of a noticeably pioneer type; and, without attaining excellence in any other way, were none the less valuable portraits of the life of the time. Characteristically Western in flavor were such accounts of Indian heroes as the *Life of Ma-Ka-Tai-Me-She-Kia-Kiak or Black Hawk* (1834). The autobiography of the great Indian chief, though necessarily influenced by the translator, Antoine Leclair, and doubtless made to differ still more from the original by the work of the editor, J. B. Patterson, remains very simple in style — a continuous succession of incidents in the traditional Indian manner. It constitutes a partisan plea for Black Hawk's people against the whites.[28] A book about the same chief, written from the point of view of the white man but expressing sympathy for the lost cause of the Indians, was *The Life and Adventures of Black Hawk: with Sketches of Keokuk, the Sac and Fox Indians, and the Late Black Hawk War* (1838), by Benjamin Drake. Half the volume is devoted to the life of Black Hawk; and the remainder, besides its narrative of Keokuk and its account of the Sac and Fox nation, includes sketches of the Sioux and a discussion of various phases of the Indian question. Perhaps no more popular biographical work, with the exception of campaign pamphlets, appeared in the early West.[29] The author acknowl-

[28] For general comment upon the book, see the introduction by Milo Quaife in his reprint edited for the Lakeside Press, Chicago, 1916.

[29] Thirteen editions had appeared within a few months (see *Cinc. Daily Gaz.*, July 20, 1839).

edged the assistance of James Hall, who, in collaboration
with Thomas L. McKenney, had already prepared a part
of the voluminous *History of the Indian Tribes of North
America, with Biographical Sketches and Anecdotes of the
Principal Chiefs* (1836-1844). McKenney, formerly a
member of the Indian Department at Washington, made
use of the national gallery of portraits of the Indian chiefs
who had visited the capital during some ten years. For
the *History of the Indian Tribes*, these paintings were
copied in engravings, and an attempt was made to supply
the original colors. Whatever the artistic success of the
venture, it is clear that it was of considerable historical
importance. A separate edition, from entirely new plates,
was published in London for the British public.[30]

The pioneer settlers of the West, like the Indians, had
already become curious subjects of biographical inquiry
before 1840. Accounts of the kind, confined, for the most
part, to articles in periodicals, at times rose to the dignity
of independent publications, usually including a series of
sketches, rather than a single well-rounded biography.
The authors were usually men whose chief equipment for
the task was their first-hand knowledge of frontier men
and conditions. John McDonald, of Ohio, who wrote *Biographical Sketches of General Nathaniel Massie, General
Duncan McArthur, Captain William Wells, and General
Simon Kenton* (1838), was, he confessed, "without any of
the advantages of education, having but little leisure."[31]
But better qualified biographers were not forthcoming,
and there were materials to be preserved which, without
the work of such men as McDonald, might have been lost.
"It must be remembered," he said,

that the period is almost at hand, when to speak of the
enterprising men who first settled on the banks of the

---

30 *The North American Review*, XLVII, 134-148 (July, 1838).
31 John McDonald, *Biographical Sketches*, 1838, p. iii.

beautiful river Ohio, from personal knowledge, will be closed forever.[32]

His narratives, moreover, are not without a certain charm because of their simplicity. And something of the same virtue is to be found in *Biographical Sketches; with Other Literary Remains of the Late John W. Campbell, Judge of the United States Court for the District of Ohio*, which appeared in the year of McDonald's *Biographical Sketches*. The major portion of this book is, however, occupied by Campbell's own essays, speeches, and correspondence, together with some attempts at verse. The famous eighteenth century relation of Daniel Boone contained in Filson's *The Discovery, Settlement and Present State of Kentucke* has already been noticed for its value as an account of the frontier by an early observer. A popular treatment of the same theme was contained in Timothy Flint's much longer *Biographical Memoir of Daniel Boone, the First Settler of Kentucky* (1833).

An autobiography and commonplace book are combined in the two volumes of Ebenezer Smith Thomas's *Reminiscences of the Last Sixty-five Years* (1840). The author, who had immigrated to Cincinnati at the end of 1828, was for many years a journalist; and into his *Reminiscences* he gathered much that had earlier appeared in the two papers which he had edited since his arrival in the West. Purely autobiographical details are interspersed with political articles, as well as discussions of commercial concerns and even lengthy narratives of travel in America and Europe. Some attention is given to the progress of the fine arts on the frontier; but insistent emphasis on such subjects as future railway connections is more characteristic of the book. Thomas's work, as contrasted with the autobiographical writings already mentioned, is modern in tone. It looks less backward, to the early pioneer days, than

---

[32] *Ibid.*, p. v.

forward, to the rapidly approaching time of a new economic and political empire.

A group of biographies exhibiting many of the characteristics of the controversial pamphleteering of the time, were inspired by Henry Clay and William Henry Harrison, the chief political figures of the Middle West. When Clay came into prominence as a leader likely to be the National Republican candidate for the Presidency in 1832, the party managers dispatched George D. Prentice from New England to Kentucky to write a campaign life. The result was a volume called the *Biography of Henry Clay*, which appeared in 1831. Prentice was in close touch with Clay, as well as with the party organization, and could hardly deny the bias of his narrative. "I have," he said, already been freely charged with undertaking the Biography of Henry Clay, with a view to influence an approaching political election. That I have formed my opinions on the subject of that election is certainly true.

The book, though showing some of the keen partisan ability of Prentice, is tiresomely eulogistic and exhibits the exuberant figures of speech characteristic of his writings. Prentice found Clay everywhere the hero: "Publick feeling flowed after him as the tides of ocean follow the moving moon."

The popularity of Clay throughout the West, however, was not to be compared with that of William Henry Harrison, whose campaign of 1840 stirred the sectional loyalty of the frontier more than any other political interest had done. For years he had been regarded by his friends as a great man, the eclipse of whose fame was unjust and must not be allowed to be final. As early as 1824, Moses Dawson, a Cincinnati editor, had issued his ponderous, ill-organized, and ill-written eulogium called *A Historical Narrative of the Civil and Military Services of Major-General William H. Harrison, and a Vindication of his Character*

*and Conduct as a Statesman, a Citizen, and a Soldier.*[33]
Although maintaining that an impartial history could be
written in the lifetime of the chief persons concerned in
it, Dawson did not conceal the fact that the purpose of his
book was to refute the "foul and unjust aspersions"
which had served to keep the famous warrior in political
obscurity; and that, to this end, he had received the aid of
General Harrison himself. The narrative extends to the
year 1819. Many documents and speeches were included
as proof of the partisan contention which gave the book its
reason for being. James Hall's *A Memoir of the Public
Services of William Henry Harrison* (1836) shared with
Dawson's *A Historical Narrative* the criticism of Richard
Hildreth, who found the arrangement very defective and
the main narrative so obscured by unimportant details that
it failed to leave a clear impression on the reader's mind.[34]

In 1840, with the height of Harrison's popularity and
political importance, came numerous campaign biographies,
of which Western writers furnished a part. Charles S.
Todd and Benjamin Drake were joint authors of *Sketches
of the Civil and Military Services of William Henry Harrison*, a narrative which comes down to the time of Harrison's nomination for the Presidency. And an anonymous
author, probably Moses B. Corwin, issued at Columbus a
pamphlet called *A Sketch of the Life and Public Services
of William Henry Harrison*, which also appeared the same
year as *Eine Skizze des Lebens und der öffentlichen Dienste
von William H. Harrison*. Several other trifles of like
kind appeared in all sections of the country during the

[33] Even Timothy Flint, in his comment on the book, found its
style inelegant, though he admitted the value of the materials used
(*The Western Monthly Review*, I, 542-553, Jan., 1828).

[34] Richard Hildreth, *The People's Presidential Candidate*, Boston,
1840, pp. 3-4. Hildreth, however, drew his own materials largely
from Dawson and Hall.

campaign.  A considerable work intended to further the
fortunes of the candidate opposing Harrison was *Sketches
of the Life of Martin Van Buren* (1840), written, curiously
enough, by Moses Dawson, author of the much earlier
life of Harrison.  Dawson's account of Van Buren was
particularly intended as an answer to a biography of that
candidate which contained serious "falsehoods and misrepresentations" fostered by partisan enemies.[35]

Of biographical writings of miscellaneous kinds, Charles
Caldwell's *A Discourse on the Genius and Character of the
Rev. Horace Holley* (1828) is remarkable for its controversial quality, as well as for its oratorical style.  *The Life
of Bonaparte, Late Emperor of the French, &c. &c. &c.
from his Birth until his Departure to the Island of St.
Helena*, which was printed at Salem, Indiana, in 1818, may
have been the work of a Western writer.[36]  Another curiosity of biographical literature was Francis Glass's *Georgii
Washingtonii, Americæ Septentrionalis Civitatum Foederatarum Præsidis primi, vita* (1835).  The author, a poverty-
stricken Ohio school teacher, who did not live to see his
book in print,[37] was taken to task by his reviewers for his
inaccurate Latin.[38]  The work was intended for use in
schools.

---

[35] Moses Dawson, *Sketches*, 1840, p. 3.

[36] For a discussion of the conjecture that this book was written
by the son of Marshal Ney, who, according to tradition, joined the
small French colony near New Albany, Indiana; and for the alter-
native theory that it was the work of a priest, formerly a soldier
under Napoleon, but, at the time this biography was written, a
member of the same French colony, see *The Indiana Catholic*, Jan.
1, 1915, p. 1, col. 7.

[37] Francis Glass, *Georgii Washingtonii, Americæ Septentrionalis
Civitatum Foederatarum Præsidis primi, vita*, 1835, editor's preface,
signed "J. N. R." (J. N. Reynolds).

[38] *The North American Review*, XLIII, 37-43 (July, 1836).

## V

The early West had peculiar attractions for the scientist in search of new data for the study of medicine, botany, zoology, geology, or geography. Of medical studies, by far the most important appeared in technical journals. Independently of these channels, even Daniel Drake, not only a professor in the most important medical schools, but famous as the ablest practitioner in the West, published no substantial work until after 1840. But his many years of service were marked by numerous minor publications. As early as 1810, he had issued a pamphlet partly devoted to a discussion of the climate and diseases of Cincinnati; and in 1815 he included a section on "Medical Topography" in his *Natural and Statistical View*. Introductory and inaugural discourses, printed in pamphlet form, marked the progress of his career as a pioneer teacher of medical science. *A Practical Treatise on the History, Prevention, and Treatment of Epidemic Cholera* appeared during the serious epidemic of 1832.

An even more prolific maker of addresses and pamphlets was Dr. Charles Caldwell, for many years a professor at Transylvania University. His "Thoughts," on various subjects, prove the catholicity of his interests and his zest for controversy; but his chief concern was with medical problems. His *Medical and Physical Memoirs* (1826) was continued in a lesser publication the following year. These "Memoirs" ranged, however, from a "Defense of the Medical Profession against the Charge of Irreligion and Infidelity" (which had already appeared independently) to "Thoughts on Optimism." In 1831 he published a volume of *Essays on Malaria, and Temperament*; and in 1834 he issued *Thoughts on Quarantine and Other Sanitary Systems*, a prize essay of the Boylston Medical Committee of Harvard University. The next year there appeared at

Lexington his *Phrenology Vindicated,* one of his several
papers on the same theme. Throughout his career in the
West he continued to publish pamphlets and books, mostly
on professional matters. He had, he conjectured in later
life, written to a greater extent and on a greater variety
of subjects "than any other medical author in America." [39]

Among other medical writers of some prominence were
John Esten Cooke, of Transylvania University; John
Eberle, of the Medical College of Ohio; and John P.
Harrison, of Cincinnati College. Two of the three pro-
jected volumes of Cooke's *A Treatise of Pathology and
Therapeutics* were published in 1828. Eberle's voluminous
work called *A Treatise on the Practice of Medicine* ap-
peared in a second edition in 1831; and the same author's
*A Treatise on the Diseases and Physical Education of
Children* followed two years later. Harrison's *Essays and
Lectures on Medical Subjects* (1835) was partly made up
of addresses originally delivered at Louisville, of which
town the author was for many years a citizen.

Biological research, which had made great headway
in early years through the efforts of such travellers as the
Michaux, Bradbury, and Wilson, owed much in the latter
part of the period to a number of Western scientists. Of
these the most spectacular, as well as the most prolific, was
Constantine Rafinesque. In spite of his extraordinary
genius, his pompous pedantry made him many bitter
enemies and brought down upon him the ridicule of such
wits as Thomas Peirce, in whose verse the scientist appears
as Professor Muscleshellorum and is characterized in lines
drawn from Peirce's Latin namesake as

> Bolanus, happy in a skull
> Of proof, impenetrably dull.

---

[39] Charles Caldwell, *Autobiography,* ed. Harriot W. Warner, 1855,
p. 417.

On the title-page of a book by Rafinesque, says Peirce, the real name of the author "bears the proportion to his scientific titles, as a paper-kite to the length of its tail." [40] Many of Rafinesque's works appeared after his angry leave-taking of Lexington and Transylvania University and his return to the East; but the later books showed more and more the effect of the mental ailment that had an important part in the misfortunes of the scientist's last years. His best books are those that belong to his seven years spent in research and lectures at Transylvania. Among these works, the most widely known is his *Ichthyologia Ohiensis, or Natural History of the Fishes Inhabiting the River Ohio and its Tributary Streams, Preceded by a Physical Description of the Ohio and its Branches* (1820). An interesting passage in Rafinesque's life at Lexington is reflected in his *First Catalogues and Circulars of the Botanical Garden of Transylvania University at Lexington in Kentucky, for the Year 1824*, written in English and French, and containing an appeal for aid in carrying on his pioneer project. *A Monograph of the Fluviatile Bivalve Shells of the River Ohio* (1832) had originally appeared in French at Brussels.[41]

Thomas Say, "the father of American zoology," was a contributor to Western scientific literature during his residence in the Owenite community at New Harmony. One of the most notable books published on the frontier was his *American Conchology, or Descriptions of the Shells of North America. Illustrated by Coloured Figures from Original Drawings Executed from Nature*, which was

[40] Thomas Peirce, *The Odes of Horace in Cincinnati*, 1822, pp. 22-24 and 102.

[41] According to C. A. Poulson, who translated the work into English, the original was published in *Annales générales des sciences physiques*, for Sept., 1820 (see *A Monograph of the Fluviatile Bivalve Shells*, 1832, introductory letter).

printed at New Harmony in 1830. The illustrations, a generous number of which were included, were not the least remarkable part of the work. Ten years later his *Descriptions of Some New Terrestrial and Fluviatile Shells of North America* was published, also at the village of New Harmony. John L. Riddell, for a time a lecturer on botany and chemistry in the Cincinnati Medical College, was the author of *A Synopsis of the Flora of the Western States* (1835) and *A Supplementary Catalogue of Ohio Plants* (1836). I. A. Lapham described the plants and shells found near Milwaukee; he issued two brief pamphlets on these subjects, in 1836 and 1838. C. W. Short attempted *A Sketch of the Progress of Botany, in Western America* (1836).

Among the first important results of geological study were the reports of state and federal surveys (1838-1840) conducted in Kentucky and in Ohio by W. W. Mather and his associates; in Indiana and, to some extent, in Illinois, Iowa, and Wisconsin by David Dale Owen and others; and in Michigan by Douglas Houghton and his assistants. Owen also published a *Catalogue of Mineralogical and Geological Specimens, at New-Harmony, Indiana*, describing collections made by William Maclure. An *Essay on the Formation of Rocks*, published at New Harmony in 1832, was from the pen of Maclure himself.

The most widely known contribution of the early West to geographical study was Captain John Cleves Symmes's theory of concentric spheres, which brought its author to the attention of the world and drew upon him the ridicule of the reviewers and the wits of burlesque writers. Convinced of the truth of his revolutionary hypothesis, Symmes endeavored for years to secure financial aid and companions who would volunteer to accompany him on an exploring expedition to prove his theory. In April, 1818, he issued at St. Louis a proclamation "TO ALL THE WORLD," which was published broadcast:

I declare the earth is hollow, and habitable within; containing a number of solid concentrick spheres, one within the other, and that it is open at the poles 12 or 16 degrees; I pledge my life in support of this truth, and am ready to explore the hollow, if the world will support and aid me in the undertaking. . . .

I ask one hundred brave companions, well equipped, to start from Siberia in the fall season with Reindeer and sleighs . . . I engage we find warm and rich land . . . on reaching one degree northward of latitude 82; we will return the succeeding spring.[42]

Symmes's efforts in journalism were, however, ineffectual. On April 17, 1821, he sent out from Newport, Kentucky, an address *"To the Maritime and other civilized Powers of the World,"* pledging himself to the first country which would accept his services and declaring his determination to devote his life if necessary "to the utmost practicable examination of the NEW WORLD" which he had announced.[43] Petitions addressed to Congress in 1822 and 1823, and to the General Assembly of Ohio in 1824, were of no avail.[44] And neither the interest aroused by courses of lectures which Symmes gave,[45] nor the financial aid

[42] *Ky. Reporter*, June 10, 1818, *"From the Missouri Gazette, May 22."* The proclamation also appeared in the form of a broadside dated "St. Louis, (Missouri Territory,) North America, April 10, A.D. 1818," a copy of which is in the possession of the St. Louis Mercantile Library. According to *Symmes's Theory of Concentric Spheres*, 1826, p. 160, a copy of this circular was addressed "to every learned institution, and to every considerable town and village, as well as distinguished individuals, . . . throughout the United States, and to several learned societies in Europe."

[43] *Mo. Gaz.*, June 6, 1821.

[44] *Symmes's Theory of Concentric Spheres*, 1826, p. 165.

[45] See, for example, *Ky. Reporter*, Feb. 26, 1821; and *cf. Symmes's Theory of Concentric Spheres*, 1826, p. 163.

secured through theatrical benefit performances,[46] served to make it possible for the theorist to undertake his proposed expedition.

Perhaps the only serious work of importance that resulted from the teachings of Symmes was a book called *Symmes's Theory of Concentric Spheres* (1826), a defense of the theory by a writer "said to be a resident of the Miami country,"[47] probably James McBride. Satirical echoes of the eccentric theorist's vagaries were, however, numerous, both in the West and in the East. An extravaganza by "Captain Adam Seaborn," called *Symzonia; a Voyage of Discovery*, appeared at New York in 1820. The adventures of Captain Seaborn in the South Seas and, later, among the inhabitants of the interior of the earth, as narrated in that work, were paralleled in the much later Gulliverian romance, purporting to be by Montgomery Letcher, called *Wonderful Discovery! Being an Account of a Recent Exploration of the Celebrated Mammoth Cave, in Edmonson County, Kentucky, by Dr. Rowan, Professor Simmons and Others, of Louisville, to its Termination in an Inhabited Region, in the Interior of the Earth!* (1839). The careful journal kept by Letcher's explorers records such events as the discovery of the gigantic birds called the "Om-mos," upon which the subterranean dwellers ride, and the visit to the village of Tan-tu; and it contains detailed descriptions of the customs of the inhabitants of Captain Symmes's country. An account of a "visit to the great city of 'Ku-ku,' the residence of the king, and the

---

[46] For announcements of plays to be given at the Cincinnati Theatre by the Thespian Society of Newport for "the benefit of Col. Symmes's Polar Expedition," see *Liberty Hall*, Mar. 23 and 26, 1824.

[47] *Symmes's Theory of Concentric Spheres*, 1826, advertisement. For mention of McBride as the probable author, see *The Western Monthly Review*, II, 17 (June, 1828).

mighty wonders seen there'' was reserved for a later narrative. Symmes was long a favorite subject of humorous allusion,[48] and the most successful Western writer of satirical verse devoted an ''ode'' to his memory.[49]

Timothy Flint, author of *A Condensed Geography and History of the Western States*, mentioned above, also published *Lectures upon Natural History, Geology, Chemistry, the Application of Steam, and Interesting Discoveries in the Arts* (1833), a popular miscellany of materials borrowed largely from Aimé Martin's *Lettres à Sophie*, itself a compilation from various sources.[50] A much more ambitious work, equally broad in its scope, was Augustus B. Woodward's *A System of Universal Science* (1816), containing ''Considerations on the divisions of human knowledge; and on the classification, and nomenclature, of the sciences.'' This book, which attempted, among other things, a kind of history of universal science, was designed to be even more comprehensive, but was cut short by the author's duties as a justice of the Supreme Court of the Territory of Michigan.[51]

## VI

Few writers of the period attempted scholarly discussion of philosophical questions. Joseph Buchanan, who was disappointed in his early plan for establishing a medi-

[48] See, for example, Calvin Colton, *Tour of the American Lakes*, 1833, I, 55-56; James Hall, *The Soldier's Bride and Other Tales*, 1833, pp. 97-98 and 218; and Timothy Flint, *The Life and Adventures of Arthur Clenning*, 1828, II, 163.

[49] Peirce, *op. cit.*, pp. 28-32.

[50] Flint, *Lectures*, 1833, p. v.

[51] Augustus B. Woodward, *A System of Universal Science*, 1816, p. 371. For MS. letters dealing with this and other literary work by Woodward, see the Woodward papers, 1808-1821, in the Burton Historical Collection, Public Library, Detroit. See also *Detroit Gaz.*, Nov. 21, 1817.

cal school in connection with Transylvania, prepared a
series of lectures on philosophy which he thought ought to
precede a course in medicine.   In 1812 he published these
lectures in a book called *The Philosophy of Human Nature*,
in which, without much claim to originality, he discussed
such subjects as the kinds of excitement and their laws,
sentiments, temperament, and volition.   According to his
own statement, he borrowed most from Locke, Hartley,
Hume, and Darwin.   In 1837-1838 Alexander Kinmont, a
teacher at Cincinnati, delivered there a series of lectures
of a general philosophical nature, which met with so much
popular applause that they were published, soon after his
death, as *Twelve Lectures on the Natural History of Man,
and the Rise and Progress of Philosophy*.   W. C. Bell, of
Lexington, was the author of an *Analysis of Pope's Essay
on Man: to which are Added an Essay on Practical Education, and a Theory of Matter, Motion and Life* (1836).

Among works dealing more particularly with the theory
of education were Calvin E. Stowe's important study *The
Prussian System of Public Instruction, and its Applica-
bility to the United States* (1836) and his *Report on Elementary Public Instruction in Europe, Made to the Thirty-
sixth General Assembly of the State of Ohio* (1837).   Perhaps the most voluminous work on educational problems
was *Lectures on Education* (1833), by George Brewster,
Principal of Cleveland Academy.

## VII

Both in number and in widespread influence, schoolbooks surpassed all other Western publications except
newspapers, and, indeed, all other books whatsoever except
the Bible, which was itself often used as a kind of schoolbook.   At first, it is true, the supply was largely of Eastern
origin; and a large part of it continued to come from that

quarter throughout the period. Among such Eastern schoolbooks was Jedidiah Morse's *Geography Made Easy* (New Haven, 1784), which, in the course of many transformations of title and contents, became the national dispenser of geographic knowledge. The influence of books of this sort penetrated far beyond the classroom. In Michigan, for instance, the sluggish current of immigration in the early part of the nineteenth century is probably to be attributed partly to the adverse influence of Morse's *Geography*, the contemporary editions of which described Michigan as a land of swamps.[52]   The great popularity of the works of this author is shown by the fact that *A New System of Geography, Ancient and Modern, for the Use of Schools*, which appeared in 1826, was announced as the twenty-fifth edition. Kirkham's and Lindley Murray's grammars were other examples of imported texts which attained a wide popularity.

The West, however, soon found means of supplying a large part of its own schoolbooks. Spellers and primers were issued in considerable number from the time of the first settlements; and grammars were scarcely less common. As early as 1796, Samuel Wilson, of Kentucky, announced his intention of publishing an English grammar;[53] and in 1802 the same author was able to advertise a new issue of "the KENTUCKY ENGLISH GRAMMAR."[54] Four years later a third edition was printed, in 1810 a fourth, and in 1812 a fifth.[55]   Toward the end of the pioneer period, Western schoolbooks of this kind were more numerous. In 1826 Joseph Buchanan's *A Practical Gram-*

---

[52] G. N. Fuller, *Economic and Social Beginnings of Michigan*, 1916, pp. 51 and 56.

[53] *Ky. Gaz.*, Oct. 1, 1796. Within less than two years this work was for sale in Lexington (*ibid.*, Aug. 8, 1798).

[54] *Ibid.*, Oct. 26, 1802.

[55] *Ibid.*, Apr. 26, 1806; Jan. 30, 1810; and Sept. 1, 1812.

*mar of the English Language* appeared,[56] and it was followed the next year by John Locke's *An English Grammar
for Children.* H. T. M. Benedict, a Kentucky teacher,
revised and adapted *Murray's English Grammar* (1832);
and Robert S. Holloway was the author of *An Easy and
Lucid Guide to a Knowledge of English Grammar* (1833).
*The Dialogue Grammar,* by B. F. Ells, which was first
printed in 1834,[57] reappeared in revised form the following
year. Leonard Bliss, of Louisville, won the praise of even
the Eastern reviewers[58] with *A Comprehensive Grammar
of the English Language* (1839).

School readers, which, of all the elementary literature of
learning, must have had the greatest general cultural influence, were early produced in the West, and in some cases
were notable for their emphasis on Western ideas and
ideals. As early as 1803, Samuel Wilson, author of *The
Kentucky English Grammar,* issued his prospectus of
*The Polyanthos; or Kentucky Elegant Selections,* intended
for schools,[59] which, although it possibly never appeared
in print,[60] is worthy of note as exemplifying the ideals
which inspired many frontier compilers of such texts.
Drawn "from the most celebrated authors," the contents
of the book, like those of the most successful readers later
produced in the West, were especially recommended for
"inculcating the purest principles of morality."[61] The
same solicitude for moral instruction, with an evident at-

---

[56] For significant praise of this work, see Leonard Bliss, *A Comprehensive Grammar,* 1839, preface.

[57] For a review of the first edition, see *The Western Monthly
Magazine,* III, 253-255 (Apr., 1835).

[58] *Cf. The North American Review,* L, 291 (Jan., 1840).

[59] *Ky. Gaz.,* Nov. 29, 1803.

[60] At any rate the book is mentioned in none of the several lengthy
advertisements of Wilson's grammar after 1803. *Cf.* above, footnote 55.

[61] *Ky. Gaz.,* Nov. 29, 1803.

tempt to make the application unmistakable, characterized
Rufus W. Adams's reader called *Young Gentleman and
Lady's Explanatory Monitor*, the fifth edition of which
appeared at Columbus in 1818. "The pieces chosen for
this collection," wrote the author,

> are such as paint virtue and magnanimity in the most con-
> spicuous manner, and by frequent perusal, are calculated
> to instil those principles into the minds of youth; at the
> same time they display an abhorrence and detestation of
> vice.[62]

The social and religious conservatism which lay at the root
of Middle Western civilization in a later period were, by
such books as this, instilled into the minds of the pioneer
generations. Conspicuous among Adams's themes were
"Distribution of Happiness, more Equal than commonly
Supposed"; "The Mortifications of Vice Greater than
those of Virtue"; "On Contentment"; "Rank and Riches
Afford no Ground for Envy"; "Patience under Provoca-
tions our Interest as well as Duty"; and "On the Immor-
tality of the Soul." The sentimentality of the age found
expression in selections like "Pathetic Piece. The Close
of Life"; and the national vanity which passed for patriotism is reflected in an extract from a Fourth of July oration
and in kindred pieces. Religious, moral, and patriotic
teachings all but fill the volume.[63]

Western sectional feeling, scarcely to be found in
Adams's book, and not strongly marked in later successful
schoolbooks written by frontier authors, characterized
James Hall's *The Western Reader*, which was published at
Cincinnati in 1833. "Most of the selections," said Hall,

[62] Rufus W. Adams, *Young Gentleman and Lady's Explanatory
Monitor*, fifth ed., 1818, p. 8.

[63] Of the seventy selections or original pieces in this book, no less
than fifty-six are clearly to be classed under these heads. Still others
may not unreasonably be regarded as of the same purpose.

are such as have never appeared before in any similar compilation; . . . It is a work of Western origin and manufacture; having been prepared in this city expressly for the use of our own schools, and published here by means of our own workmanship and materials.[64]

"Scenery of the Ohio," "Reminiscence of the Scioto Valley," "A Remarkable Escape" (from M'Clung's *Sketches of Western Adventure*), and "The Emigrant's Abode in Ohio" (from Timothy Flint) dealt with peculiarly Western themes. From Western writers, too, were borrowed such sentimental pieces as Benjamin Drake's "The Morning of Life," H. D. Little's "The Infant's Grave," and Otway Curry's "The Stranger's Grave." Both Henry Clay and his biographer, George D. Prentice, are represented in this singularly sectional anthology. Nor was the compiler unmindful of the importance of a proper moral and religious tone. "No sentiment has been admitted," he declared,

which could be pernicious to the young mind, nor any in which serious things are treated with unbecoming levity. A considerable portion of the lessons are of a moral, and some of a decidedly religious character.[65]

Other frontier readers merged sectional pride in national feeling with special intent to avoid the teaching of British authors. Such was the *Federurbian, or United States Lessons; Intended to Promote Learning and a Knowledge of Republican Principles, in the Minds of our Youth* (1839), by Henry Houseworth, an Indiana schoolmaster. "Most of our school books," he complained,

have not been adapted to our National Literature, . . . In this work fewer extracts from British authors will be

---

[64] Hall, *The Western Reader*, 1833, pp. v-vi.

[65] *Ibid.*, p. v. Of the 106 lessons included in the book, forty are moral or religious; twenty-six are Western either in subject-matter or in authorship, or both (this number includes four already counted as moral or religious); and sixteen of the remainder are patriotic.

inserted than is usual in our school books, because it is considered they are not suited to our republican institutions.[66]
The reading lessons which make up the *Federurbian* are selected in accordance with this doctrine. Bridge's *The New American Speaker* (1837), though it put decided stress upon authors like Webster, Halleck, and Percival, was well stocked with poetry from recent English writers. In *The New American Reader, No. 3* (1839), by the same author, not far from half of the selections were designed to teach morality, religion, or patriotism, while a few others were on Western subjects. Catharine Beecher's advanced reader, called *The Moral Instructor* (1838), was, as its title suggests, entirely made up of pieces clearly intended to convey either moral or religious doctrine.

Truman and Smith's Eclectic Series, of which Miss Beecher's book was a part, was destined to a rapid rise to fame as the most successful series of schoolbooks written in the West, a distinction which it owed to the group of readers contributed to it by William Holmes M'Guffey, then a professor in Miami University. The contract between M'Guffey and his publishers, made on April 28, 1836,[67] marked the beginning of an epoch in the cultural growth of the West. Within less than a year, the firm of Truman and Smith, of Cincinnati, later to become the American Book Company, announced a sale of 20,000 copies of the Eclectic Series;[68] and within half a dozen years the sales of these books seem to have mounted to 700,000.[69] Upon

---

[66] Henry Houseworth, *Federurbian*, 1839, p. iii.

[67] For the history of the publisher's part in the development of the M'Guffey readers, and for comment on the *First Reader*, which I have not examined, see Henry Hobart Vail, *A History of the McGuffey Readers*, new ed., 1911, p. 33, *et passim*.

[68] William Holmes M'Guffey, *The Eclectic Third Reader*, 1837, advertisement following p. 165. *Cf.* also preface of the same edition.

[69] Vail, *op. cit.*, p. 47.

the generation immediately succeeding the pioneer period, the influence of M'Guffey may well have been greater than that of any other writer or statesman in the West. His name became a tradition, not yet extinct.

The slight revisions necessary in 1838 because of the charges of plagiarism brought against the first editions of the readers by Eastern publishers who were, as the author thought, prompted partly by sectional jealousy,[70] scarcely changed the character of these classics. In *The Eclectic First Reader* and *The Eclectic Second Reader*, both first published in 1836, the characteristic style and tone of the series was already determined. In the *Second Reader*, for example, no less than fifty-three of the eighty-six lessons were unequivocally moral or religious in purpose, while the others were almost uniformly intended to teach useful information. In the revised edition of the same reader, there is simply a more emphatic stress on the moral and religious purpose of education: of the whole number of lessons there given, which remained eighty-six, there were now sixty-two devoted to that end. "The Little Idle Boy," "The Idle Boy Reformed," "The Greedy Girl," "The Kind Little Girl," "The Passionate Boy," and "The Lord's Prayer" are characteristic titles which appear in both editions. *The Eclectic Third Reader* and *The Eclectic Fourth Reader*, both of which appeared in 1837, were designed to continue the same kind of instruction. "The Compiler," wrote M'Guffey,

begs leave to state, that he has aimed to combine *simplicity* with *sense; elegance* with *simplicity*, and PIETY, with both.[71]

In the first edition of the *Third Reader* more than forty of

---

[70] See, for example, M'Guffey, *Revised and Improved Edition of the Eclectic Second Reader*, n. d. (1838), p. 1.

[71] M'Guffey, *The Eclectic Third Reader*, 1837, preface, dated Feb., 1837.

the sixty-six selections were religious or moral, dealing with such themes as "Effects of Rashness," "The Consequences of Idleness," "Importance of well Spent Youth," "The Bible," "Sermon on the Mount," "The Goodness of God," and "Gospel Invitation." Though both the *Third Reader* and the *Fourth Reader* showed an increased interest in poetry, and the latter a greater variety of subjects, their character, for the most part, differed but slightly from that of the earlier books in the series. Emphatic in the glorification of moral, religious, and purely practical concerns, and aiding thus on one side of cultural growth, they failed almost completely to stir the imagination, and they scarcely suggested the possibility of enjoyment in music and the fine arts or in literature freed of too immediate didactic purpose. Thus, while these vastly influential educational classics helped destroy much of the crudity of the older frontier civilization, they may also be held largely responsible for withholding from later generations of Westerners an appreciation of some of the finer elements of culture.

Of other readers, none compared in importance with the M'Guffey series, and few were remarkable for any unusual qualities. Illustrative cuts, but sparingly used in other schoolbooks of the time, were made a prominent and attractive feature of *The Picture Reader* (1833), an early publication of Truman and Smith (then known as Truman, Smith & Co.). Albert and J. W. Picket's readers, though important among Western publications of the kind, belonged originally to the East.

School texts in other subjects than reading were surprisingly numerous, though far less significant for their influence on the future ideals of the Western people. Perhaps the most popular arithmetics were those of Joseph Ray, published by Truman and Smith, and of Martin Ruter.

As early as 1806 a geography by Du Fresnoy, "greatly augmented and improved by a teacher of Kentucky," had been printed in Lexington.[72]  John Kilbourn, of Ohio, was the author of the *Columbian Geography* (1815) and of an *Introduction to Geography and Astronomy* (sixth edition, 1826).  Among other books of this kind was a *Primary Geography for Children* (1833?), written by Harriet Beecher, later the author of *Uncle Tom's Cabin*, in collaboration with her sister Catharine Beecher.[73]  A work remarkable for its time was an astronomical text called *Picture of the Heavens* (1840), by Samuel D. M'Cullough. Scientific texts of other kinds included *Elements of Geology*, by W. W. Mather, of which a second edition appeared in 1838, in the same year with the author's reports of geological surveys in Ohio.   Thomas D. Mitchell, of the Medical College of Ohio, wrote *Elements of Chemical Philosophy* (1832) ; and John Locke was the author of *Outlines of Botany*.[74]

A *Manual of Logic* (1831) and *Elements of Logic*, a revision (1833), were by Robert Hamilton Bishop, the president of Miami University.  The same writer published in 1839 his *Elements of the Science of Government*; but a much more popular work on this subject was Edward Deering Mansfield's *The Political Grammar of the United States* (1834), which passed through many editions.[75] Texts on law included John M. Goodenow's *Historical Sketches of the Principles and Maxims of American Jurisprudence* (1819) and Timothy Walker's *Introduction to American Law* (1837).

Even text-books in the ancient languages by frontier

---

[72] *Ky. Gaz.*, Apr. 16, 1806.

[73] *The Western Monthly Magazine*, I, 287 (June, 1833).

[74] *The Western Monthly Review*, I, 101 (June, 1827).

[75] The sixteenth edition appeared in 1849, and other editions followed.

scholars were not wholly unknown.   For students of Latin, there were M. A. H. Niles's *Elements of Latin Grammar* (1834), which, however, professed to be nothing more than a compilation; a *Græca Minora*, with English notes (1823?),[76] possibly by William Gibbes Hunt; and Ormsby M. Mitchell's edition of *The Works of Quinctilian* (1833?).[77] William Nast, of Kenyon College, published there, in 1835, his text called *The Greek Verb*.   Martin Ruter was the author of a Hebrew grammar which appeared in 1824.[78]

Books worthy of mention merely as literary curiosities are David Zeisberger's *Essay of a Delaware-Indian and English Spelling-book, for the Use of the Schools of the Christian Indians on Muskingum River* (1776) and James Ruggles's *A Universal Language, Formed on Philosophical and Analogical Principles* (1829).   Zeisberger's Indian speller, if actually written on the Muskingum (as it almost certainly was), must have been one of the earliest books by a resident of what is now the state of Ohio.[79]

---

[76] *The Cincinnati Literary Gazette*, Jan. 1, 1824.

[77] *The Western Monthly Magazine*, I, 286 (June, 1833).

[78] *Liberty Hall*, Mar. 16, 1824.

[79] There is, so far as I am aware, no reason for supposing that the book was not produced on the Muskingum.   For an account of Zeisberger's arrival on that river in May, 1772, and of his activities in the West from that date till 1776, see John Heckewelder, *A Narrative of the Mission of the United Brethren among the Delaware and Mohegan Indians*, 1820, pp. 117-144.   The speller was used in the schools for Indian children at all three settlements on the Muskingum (*ibid.*, p. 144).   Zeisberger became the patriarch of the Christian colony.   He died at Goshen, on the Muskingum, in 1808 (*ibid.*, p. 418).

# CHAPTER VI

## FICTION

The failure of Mr. Cooper in his Prairie, and Mr. Paulding in his Westward Ho, is conclusive evidence, that in delineating the West, no power of genius, can supply the want of opportunities for personal observation on our natural and social aspects. No western man can read those works with interest; because of their want of conformity to the circumstances and character of the country, in which the scenes are laid. — Daniel Drake, *Discourse on the History, Character, and Prospects of the West.*

The best productions of American literature are, in my opinion, the tales and sketches in which the habits and manners of the people of the country are delineated, with exactness, with impartiality of temper, and without much regard to the picturesque. Such are the tales of Judge Hall of Cincinnati. — Harriet Martineau, *Society in America.*

### I

When an Easterner wrote, he was conscious of the fact that he was an American; but, when a Westerner attempted authorship, he was troubled by the consciousness of the fact that he was not only an American but a Westerner. Unfortunately, though the Western writer could speak his frontier convictions courageously so long as he had to do with what seemed to him matters of fact, once upon the borderland between fact and imagination, he too often sought either to idealize the life with which he was actually acquainted or else to disguise his identity as a frontiersman by copying conventional themes in no way connected with the West. Lacking unusual power of artistic achievement,

he thus often failed to put into his tales and novels the
one thing which might have made them of great value —
a faithful delineation of pioneer life.

It was, indeed, a common complaint among Western
critics that Eastern and English writers of fiction had
failed lamentably in attempting to picture the life of the
frontier people. There was, besides, quite enough theoriz-
ing on the unusual opportunities offered for both fiction
and poetry about the backwoods by writers who knew the
country at first hand. Editors of such magazines as *The
Western Monthly Review, The Western Monthly Magazine*,
and *The Hesperian* made it a fixed policy to encourage
sectional loyalty in literary matters.[1] Such, too, was the
all but universally declared sentiment among thoroughgoing
Western writers. "It is also our humble hope," wrote
the author of a prize essay on fiction, in 1833,

that views may be presented, which will induce the writers
of western fiction to confine their range more within western boundaries, and to feel, that while the body of western
literature is fashioned from native materials, its spirit
should be an inspiration of western genius.[2]

It was remarked that "in this wilderness of the west, human nature has been manifested under original and striking aspects."[3] The situation of the first immigrants was
unique. "Considerations like these," declared the author
of the essay,

have induced us to believe, that in the modes of thought,
feeling and utterance; in the habits, adventures, and striking character of the Pioneers, are most appropriate and
original subjects for the pen of fiction.[4]

---

[1] See above, Chapter III, *passim.*

[2] Isaac Appleton Jewett, "Themes for Western Fiction," in *The
Western Monthly Magazine*, I, 576 (Dec., 1833).

[3] *Ibid.*, pp. 575-576.

[4] *Ibid.*, p. 578.

Yet it is clear that the writer of this manifesto of the militant Western spirit in literature was thinking, after all, not so much of a faithful likeness of the rude frontiersmen as of a romantic glorification of them. The likeness of the hunter of the wilderness which he paints in attractive colors as a model for writers of fiction, is, he declares, ''a portrait from real life, tinged though it be with the softest hues of poetry and romance.'' [5] The rough backwoodsmen were, we are told, men who ''abandoned the refinements of cultivated society, for the wild charms of a Huntsman's life''; and Daniel Boone is offered as the most illustrious example of these cultured lovers of nature.[6]

Moreover, though he disclaims belief in the sentimental view of savage life, this critic's notion of the Indian as a figure in fiction is no less romantic than is his conception of the backwoodsman. For is not the red man ''one of those mysterious beings whom the Genius of Romance may justly regard as created for her own especial use''? [7]

Whether dashing through solitudes in pursuit of game, or sporting in his light canoe upon the bosom of his native lakes, or casting his proudest trophies at the feet of her in whom are garnered up his gentle affections, or silently worshipping the Great Spirit amidst lightnings and storms, he is always romantic, always poetical.[8]

Such were the critical doctrines given special recognition by the most important magazine on the frontier, a magazine edited by James Hall, himself the most distinguished writer of Western fiction.

## II

Among writers of short narratives, the most characteristically Western fiction of the time, James Hall was

[5] *Ibid.*, p. 579.
[6] *Loc. cit.*
[7] *Ibid.*, p. 584.
[8] *Loc. cit.*

clearly preeminent; and he became the central figure in a
kind of school of experimenters in the materials of frontier
life.  Already known as the author of *Letters from the
West*, which revealed his bias for picturesque detail and
romantic incident, as well as for sentimental moods, he
appeared a few years later as the editor and chief author
of an anthology of tales and verse intended to represent the
West among the annuals and gift books then fashionable
in the East and abroad.  *The Western Souvenir, a Christmas and New Year's Gift for 1829* was the first important
challenge of this kind.  "We have endeavoured," said the
editor,

to give it an original character, by devoting its pages exclusively to our domestick literature.  It is written and published in the Western country, by Western men, and is
chiefly confined to subjects connected with the history and
character of the country which gives it birth.[9]

Among the writers of the somewhat more than fifty pieces
of prose and verse in the *Souvenir* were Otway Curry,
Nathan Guilford, Morgan Neville, John M. Harney, John
B. Dillon, Benjamin Drake, and Timothy Flint.  Hall himself furnished more than a fourth of the whole number.
The theme varied from the frontier interest of Nathan Guilford's "Ohio," Hall's "The French Village," and, perhaps best of all, Morgan Neville's "The Last of the Boatmen"[10] to such sentimental trifles as were almost everywhere characteristic of the annuals of the second quarter
of the nineteenth century.  Timothy Flint's "Oolemba in
Cincinnati" reflected the pride of the pioneer in the progress of civilization in the backwoods.  Hall's contributions

---

[9] *The Western Souvenir*, ed. James Hall, n. d. (1829), p. iii.

[10] This narrative, which preserves the fame of Mike Fink, the
Western boatman and king of rowdies, was given greater vogue by
its inclusion in Miss Mitford's *Lights and Shadows of American
Life* (1832).

illustrated both the new interest in frontier materials and the conventional preference for sentimental fustian. Among the purely Western stories which he included were some, like "The Indian Hater" and "Pete Featherton," which appeared in later collections entirely by him.

The separate volumes of Hall's tales began to appear in 1832, with the first issue of *Legends of the West*. In the following year, when the success of *Legends* was proved by the announcement of a second edition, the author published a new collection called *The Soldier's Bride and Other Tales*. In 1835, a third volume of the kind was offered to the public under the title of *Tales of the Border*.

The romanticism of Byron's and Scott's verse tales and of the latter's novels had taken deep hold upon Hall,[11] and in Cooper he found an example of the romantic method making use of a frontier setting peopled by backwoodsmen and Indians far removed from reality. He must have had, on the other hand, some acquaintance with Hugh Henry Brackenridge's more satirical pictures of earlier Pennsylvania frontier types;[12] and he had, of course, his own intimate knowledge of persons and places in the West, especially in Illinois. The result, in Hall's tales, is a mixture of the realistic and the romantic which falls only little short of achieving a true portrait of pioneer life.

Raw immigrants matching their courage against the practised shrewdness of the Indians; the lover bent on the rescue of his lady, who is a captive of the savages; the

[11] See below, Chapter IX.

[12] For a bibliography showing several early editions of this work, see *The Cambridge History of American Literature*, 1917, I, 526. Hall, in all probability, was acquainted with *Modern Chivalry* before he came to the West; but the fame of that novel had also penetrated to the most remote settlements. For an incident illustrating this fact, see H. M. Brackenridge, *Recollections of Persons and Places in the West*, n. d. (1834), p. 227.

marvellously clever white hunter, wise in the lore of the forest, who sets matters right, outwitting the redskins and reuniting the lovers — these are the somewhat conventionally romantic figures introduced to the reader in "The Backwoodsman," the first story in *Legends of the West*. The setting of this story, too, is a high-colored one. "The beautiful forests of Kentucky, when first visited by the adventurous footsteps of the pioneers" and the vast valley of which Kentucky was a part are depicted at length.

The scale of greatness pervaded all the works of nature. The noble rivers, all tending towards one great estuary, swept through an almost boundless extent of country, and seemed to be as infinite in number as they were grand in size. The wild animals were innumerable.[13]

The narrative begins, to be sure, with an account of a revival camp meeting, an occasion not peculiarly Western, but characteristically so. Yet there is scarcely a suggestion here of the crudity and emotional excess of the religious celebrations of this sort described in many accounts by eyewitnesses who attempted to state facts without fiction.[14] The singing of the women about the camp fires in the morning was a charming pastoral, unspoiled by ugliness:

It was thus our first parents worshipped their Creator in Paradise, thus the early Christians assembled in groves and secluded places; and so close is the union between good taste and religious feeling, that while civilized nations have set apart the most splendid edifices for worship, ruder communities, in a similar spirit, assemble for the same purpose at the most genial hour, and the most picturesque spot. The heart powerfully excited by generous feelings always becomes romantic; the mind elevated by the noble pursuit of a high object becomes enlarged and refined.[15]

[13] James Hall, *Legends of the West*, second ed., 1833, pp. 1-2.
[14] *Cf.* the account given above, Chapter I.
[15] Hall, *op. cit.*, p. 10.

Nor is there anything here to betray the fanatical uproar of the midnight exhortations; instead, the beauty of the forest setting is enthusiastically painted:

But nothing could exceed the solemn and beautiful effect of the meeting at night. The huts were all illuminated, and lights were fastened to the trunks of the trees, throwing a glare upon the overhanging canopy of leaves, now beginning to be tinged with the rich hues of autumn, which gave it the appearance of a splendid arch finely carved and exquisitely shaded. All around was the dark gloom of the forest, deepened to intense blackness by its contrast with the brilliant light of the camp.[16]

Even the old hunter, who presently appears as the hero of the Indian adventure to which the account of the camp meeting is only an introduction, utters a panegyric on unspoiled nature,[17] as if he were speaking out of a stanza in Byron's idyllic characterization of the Kentucky backwoodsman. Hall's old hunter is, in fact, Daniel Boone himself, but with little except a very slender stock of Kentucky dialect to make him authentic. He would "fix" the Indians in a way that "would be curious," and he found the behaviour of the savages *"ridic'lous;"* [18] but under stress of great excitement he forgets all dialectical peculiarities and speaks the purest English of a rather stilted kind:

Let us creep to yon log, and rest our guns on it when we fire. I will shoot at that large warrior who is standing alone — you will aim at one of those who are sitting; the moment we have fired we will load again, without moving, shouting all the while, and making as much noise as possible; — be cool — my dear young friend — be cool.[19]

Only by means of a few excerpts from the speech of a second hunter, who lacks Boone's historical dignity, does

---

16 *Ibid.*, p. 11.
17 *Ibid.*, p. 28.
18 *Ibid.*, p. 25.
19 *Ibid.*, p. 34.

Hall make some amends for the feebleness of his attempt at realism. The second hunter, who came too late to participate in what he calls a "pretty chunk of a fight," explains that he "couldn't get here no sooner, no how;" describes the camping ground as "emptied *spontenaciously*;" comments upon the heroine's injuries as "a mere *sarcumstance*;" and wishes the Indians "*tee-totally obflisticated* off of the face of the whole *yearth*." [20]

Such were the not wholly successful efforts of a pioneer writer to inaugurate a school of fiction which should be peculiarly Western and peculiarly — as he conceived of such a thing — realistic. He had introduced his narratives with this explanation:

The sole intention of the tales comprised in the following pages is to convey accurate descriptions of the scenery and population of the country in which the author resides. The only merit he claims for them is fidelity. [21]

In greater or less degree, the same half realization of the same purpose is the significant fact in most of Hall's stories. Among others contained in *Legends*, several are of some value as records of pioneer life. The old settler's faith in the efficacy of the divining rod; the trickery of the quack doctors, who found a haven in the newly settled country; the battle of the missionary against disease and poverty and the loneliness of the backwoods; and the simplicity of the French villagers of Illinois, are themes which Hall treats humorously or sentimentally. The tale called "The Emigrants" possibly reflects the early southern Illinois prejudice against prairie lands and against the English of the Birkbeck colony. Its hero, a young American who embodies the virtues of both East and West, fails to turn his fellow travellers, an English family, from their

[20] *Ibid.*, pp. 37-38.
[21] *Ibid.*, preface.

mistaken purpose of investing in such lands, but later appears at their settlement in time to save them from the ravages of sickness and the danger of prairie fire. The Englishman's daughter is his reward. "The Indian Hater" no doubt contains a true picture of the bitterness of the earliest pioneers toward the savages; but the romantic vein of "The Indian Wife's Lament" and "The Isle of Yellow Sands," both of which pretend to be Indian legends, justifies the author's transition from prose to verse in relating them.

In his next volume, *The Soldier's Bride and Other Tales* (1833), Hall failed to maintain the Western quality which the public now expected of him. Though his fiction was still "strictly American," [22] only one story in this collection of thirteen was entirely Western, and not more than two others had anything to do with the West. [23] The hero of "Pete Featherton," however, is a more convincing portrait of the Kentucky hunter than is to be found in the earlier story of "The Backwoodsman." Whiskey, the favorite drink of the frontier, acts as an evil charm against Featherton's uncanny skill with the rifle. In "The Useful Man," another of the pieces in this second volume, there is expressed characteristic Western disdain for the Eastern dandy who sought to overawe the Illinois settlers with his display of wealth.

*Tales of the Border* (1835), the third volume made up entirely of the same author's stories, was, like the first, almost wholly Western. Again Hall protests his devotion to realism as the guiding principle of his fiction; [24] and, as before, this declared purpose is partly realized. The

[22] Hall, *The Soldier's Bride and Other Tales*, 1833, preface.

[23] "The Philadelphia Dun" is left out of this account because it has its setting in Tennessee, though it might as well have been in any other part of the frontier.

[24] Hall, *Tales of the Border*, 1835, pp. 9-10.

collection contains six stories and a poem; but almost a third of the whole is occupied by "The Pioneer," which, like "The Indian Hater" of *Legends*, gives a true impression of the frontiersman's attitude toward the savages — generally one of bitter hatred, which Hall's own experiences had afforded him no occasion to feel. The pioneer of the tale is an itinerant preacher, back of whose religious mission lies the long history of his career as an Indian fighter. The setting is not without realistic touches. The pioneers of Illinois are described as "a rude but a kind people" who live in "wretched hovels, built of rough logs." [25] The Methodist circuit rider who is the narrator of the principal part of the tale, was "the most accomplished woodsman" but "seemed to have no acquaintance with books." [26] There is, however, very little attempt to reproduce the Kentucky-Illinois dialect, which the prototype of the circuit rider spoke in real life.

"The Silver Mine," another of the *Tales of the Border*, is a somewhat satirical portrait of the professional emigrant who belonged to the great caravan of ne'er-do-wells who made their way through Tennessee, Kentucky, and southern Indiana and Illinois, and into Missouri, during the early decades of the last century. "The Dark Maid of Illinois" and "The New Moon, a Tradition of the Omawhaws" exploit again the romantic possibilities of the Indian as described in Jewett's essay on Western themes for fiction. "The Dark Maid," which is a fantastic tale from the days of the first explorers in the West, narrating the brief honeymoon of Pierre, a French barber, and the daughter of an Indian chieftain, contains an admixture of humor. "The New Moon," however, is entirely tragic, and exhibits Hall's sympathy with the savages as against

---

[25] *Ibid.*, p. 15.

[26] *Ibid.*, pp. 30-31.

the unscrupulous white adventurers who sought to rob them.

Mild as Hall's realism was, it was enough to stir the resentment of some contemporary critics in both West and East, persons who were too seriously engaged in defending the culture of the West, or of America as a whole, against the sneers of foreign writers, to relish the slightest reminder of the less charming side of frontier life. A Cincinnati editor who expressed a deep admiration for Mrs. Hentz's extravagantly romantic Indian play *Lamorah, or the Western Wild*, reprimanded Hall for tiring the reader with vulgar backwoods expressions in *Legends of the West*.[27] It was apparently felt that a writer who could coolly display to the world, even in fiction, the shortcomings of Western civilization was no true son of the border. "Mr. Hall," according to an estimate published in another periodical and by a critic who could himself frankly admit the crudities of the West,

is less western in his writings than Mr. Flint; he writes more as an on-looker — less as an actor; more as one who by a long residence has acquired a knowledge of the land, than as one who has been changed by the spirit of that land into something new.[28]

In the meantime, the chief Eastern review had given currency to a similar appraisal of Hall:

He professes to be a western man; the scene of his stories is generally in the west; his incidents are taken from western life; but of the western character he knows little, and of the western spirit he possesses nothing. He wants the intellectual *openness*, which would enable him to catch the spirit of society. His mind is shut up in its own ways of thinking and feeling, and his writings, in consequence, give no true reflection of western character.[29]

27 *The Cincinnati Mirror and Ladies' Parterre*, Sept. 15, 1832.
28 *The Hesperian*, III, 463 (Nov., 1839).
29 *The North American Review*, XLIII, 2 (July, 1836).

## III

The day of realism in Western fiction was not fully come until Eggleston appeared as the portrayer of southern Indiana life. But there were some minor writers of tales during the pioneer period who achieved much the same results that Hall had shown possible. Some Western dialect sketches of unusual value are to be found in Alphonso Wetmore's *Gazetteer of the State of Missouri* (1837) ; and all but one of the half dozen tales of this obscure collection are definitely Western in setting. The first of these, called "The Dead Husband," depicts the hardships and miseries of a family belonging to the less respectable class of Southern immigrants to the Ozark region of Missouri. At the death of her husband, the wife goes a long journey to find a neighbor who can help bury the dead. A sketch called "Annals of the Shop," describing the characters of a Western village as they appear at "the shop" which serves as post office, notary's office, and doctor's office, is remarkable for its realistic turn. All but one of the tales buried in this volume show a humor and lightness of tone unusual in early Western writers.

Benjamin Drake's *Tales and Sketches, from the Queen City* (1838) was also an attempt to reproduce various phases of frontier life. The rapid growth of the important towns is illustrated in the first sketch, called "The Queen City," much as in Flint's "Oolemba in Cincinnati." The two incidents of the tale are separated by an interval of fifty-five years. A hunter who, in early days, kills an Indian on the banks of the Ohio, returns to the same spot fifty-five years later to find it occupied by a city. "The Novice of Cahokia" is a love story connecting the horrors of the French Revolution with peaceful scenes in the American Bottom. Other stories depict, with fidelity perhaps superior to Hall's, the life on the river steamers, the re-

ligious fanaticism of early Kentucky, and the crudity of
early Western colleges.

For realistic treatment of pioneer communities, however, perhaps the most notable work of fiction to appear
before 1841 was Caroline M. Kirkland's account of society
in the upstart villages of the Michigan wilderness, in the
writing of which she was inspired by Mary Russell Mitford's sketches of life in the small English town.[30]  The
author's notions of life on the frontier before her removal
there, had been colored by Chateaubriand's romantic descriptions, with the result, she says, that her

floating visions of a home in the woods were full of important omissions, and always in a Floridian clime, where
fruits serve for *vivers*.[31]

But actual residence in the new country made her a realist
with a bent for satire; and into *A New Home — who'll
Follow? or, Glimpses of Western Life* (1839), a work which
may be described almost equally well as a journal of observations, a novel, or a series of connected sketches and
tales, she put such frank and intimate comments on the
domestic manners of the backwoods as are not to be met
with in any contemporary.

Other writers, like Hall, had scarcely been able to con-
ceive of Western fiction without adventure as the central
point of interest.   More, indeed, was hardly to be expected
of a generation of authors fathered by James Fenimore
Cooper.   But Mrs. Kirkland dispensed with the theatrical.
The rise of Montacute and Tinkerville, the two rival villages in the woods which supply the setting for the incidents narrated, exhibited nothing of the heroic.   It is
especially noteworthy that the women of the settlements
were now given employment other than either as heroines

---

[30] Caroline M. Kirkland, *A New Home*, 1839, p. vi.

[31] *Ibid.*, p. 83.

of love tales or as victims of Indian captivity. The daily
round of annoyances experienced by the cultured newcomers among the rude frontier people was recorded in detail.
The servant girls, bred to backwoods independence, were,
like Mrs. Trollope's domestic aids, a constant irritation.
One of them, the author complains, ''would put her head
in at a door, with — '*Miss* Clavers, did you holler? I
thought I *heered* a yell.' ''[32]  The democratic equality of
the community is illustrated by the appearance of the
schoolmistress, who offered her services as a domestic, but
was refused on the ground that her habit of smoking a pipe
would make the house uncomfortable.[33]  The schoolmaster
who succeeded her was a second Ichabod Crane with none
of Ichabod's charm. His uncouth speech accorded well
with his childish curiosity regarding such strange symbols
of civilization as a piano, or even a carpet or an inkstand.[34]
The social jealousies from which even the backwoods villages were not free are shown in the conduct of the Montacute Female Beneficent Society,

the prime dissipation of our village, the magic circle within
which lies all our cherished exclusiveness, the strong hold
of *caste*, the test of gentility, the temple of emulation, the
hive of industry, the mart of fashion, and I must add,
though reluctantly, the fountain of village scandal, the
hot-bed from which springs every root of bitterness among
the petticoated denizens of Montacute.[35]

The book was, the author declared, very nearly ''a veri-
table history; an unimpeachable transcript of reality'' and
even ''a sort of 'Emigrant's Guide.' '' There were, she
admitted, ''glosses, and colourings, and lights, if not
shadows,'' yet it was ''only in the most commonplace''

[32] *Ibid.*, p. 68.
[33] *Ibid.*, p. 96.
[34] *Ibid.*, pp. 302-303.
[35] *Ibid.*, p. 224.

things that she had departed from plain fact; [36] and ten
years after she first published the work she declared that "if
the picture lack verity in any particular, it is not through
exaggeration, but the opposite." [37]   The realistic and satirical method which she employed served effectively to destroy the romantic conception of frontier life.   The serious
attempt at the reproduction of dialect which is noticeable
throughout the book adds to its force as a realistic document.   In fact, the author had, in all that concerns sheer
realism, gone farther in 1839 than Eggleston was to go
many years later.   It was only a certain imaginative, artistic quality that was lacking in *A New Home.*

Among other volumes of narratives which must be mentioned is *Tales of the North West, or Sketches of Indian
Life and Character, by a Resident beyond the Frontier*
(1830).   It is possible, however, that the author may not
have been a resident of the Middle West when he wrote
down these records of his observation.   The characters
who appear in the book are "the Indians, the half-breeds,
and the American and English hunters, that roam through
the vast solitudes of the Missouri territory."   The representation of savage customs here given was "somewhat less
poetical, but probably more true than that of Cooper." [38]
"Indian tales" which were "taken down from the mouths
of the natives" were a part of the contents — "all of home
origin" — of a book called *Souvenir of the Lakes,* which
appeared at Detroit in 1831 and was apparently intended

---

36 *Ibid.,* pp. v-vi.

37 *Ibid.,* "Preface to the Fourth Edition," 1850, p. 5. For a recent
study of Mrs. Kirkland, including comment upon *A New Home* and
upon later works by the same author, see Edna M. Twamley, "The
Western Sketches of Caroline Mathilda (Stansbury) Kirkland," in
*Michigan Historical Collections,* XXXIX, 89-124 (1915).

38 *The North American Review,* XXXI, 200 (July, 1830). I have
seen no copy of this book. Both the title and all of the comment
here given are from the review cited.

as a gift book or annual,[39] possibly in emulation of *The Western Souvenir*, issued by Hall at Cincinnati in 1829.

Among the numerous authors who wrote stories for Western periodicals, a few were to attain more or less distinction after 1840. Of these the most important was Harriet E. Beecher, later known as Mrs. Stowe. Her ''A New England Sketch'' was printed in 1834 as a prize tale in a magazine published in Cincinnati,[40] where the author lived for many years.

## IV

The greater part of Western fiction which had an existence independent of magazines appeared in the form of novels. Like the writers of tales and miscellaneous fiction already noticed, the novelists flourished during the last fifteen years of the pioneer period.[41] The earliest of them was Timothy Flint, whose reputation as one of the most important writers of the West was assured both by his contributions to the literature of travel and observation and by his work as the editor of a review. Possessed by an insatiable love of change and by the hope of finding a climate favorable to his health, Flint was a citizen of every section of the country.[42] His residence in the West, beginning in 1815 and ending in 1833 or 1834, was inter-

[39] For the title as well as for the description here quoted in part, see the *Detroit Journal and Michigan Advertiser*, Jan. 5, 1831. I have not seen a copy of the *Souvenir*.

[40] *The Western Monthly Magazine*, II, 169-192 (Apr., 1834).

[41] Gilbert Imlay, whose three-volume novel called *The Emigrants* (1793) was based, to a certain extent, on observations made by the author during his residence in Kentucky, is here omitted on the ground that it was in all probability written long after the author had removed from the West and very likely after his arrival in Europe. For a reference to a study of the biographical problems involved, see above, Chapter II, footnote 56.

[42] For a valuable biographical study of Flint, see John Ervin Kirkpatrick, *Timothy Flint*, 1911.

rupted by long periods of travel, and even of residence, in
the Southwest and the East, so that it is impossible to regard the writings of these years as wholly belonging to the
Middle West. But Cincinnati was, more than any other
place, the center of his literary work, especially during
the period of his activity as a novelist.

The first of his novels, *Francis Berrian, or the Mexican
Patriot* (1826) owed, however, its existence to Flint's
travels and residence in the Southwest. It is significant
that the scene of action is beyond the farthest frontier
which Flint saw, and that the materials, derived, as we are
told, largely from a narrative of fact,[43] are clearly transformed by the author's romantic imagination. Though
the hero, Francis Berrian, is represented as drawn to the
frontier by a desire to realize Chateaubriand's descriptions
of scenery,[44] the narrative which is put into his mouth
shows not disillusionment, as in the case of Mrs. Kirkland,
but a realization of romantic possibilities scarcely imagined
even by Chateaubriand. The young enthusiast's observations on nature were interrupted, not by disenchantment
caused by unlovely realities, but by a series of thrilling
adventures in love and in war. His good fortune in saving
the life of Doña Martha, daughter of the Spanish governor
of Durango, introduces him into her home as a guest. In
his love for this lady, he has, however, a formidable rival
in the villanous Don Pedro, whose hatred he incurs. A
timely Mexican revolution gives Berrian his opportunity.
Because of his merits as a leader, as well as his devotion to
liberal principles, he becomes chief of the rebel forces and
conducts a successful campaign against the loyalists under
Don Pedro. After more than once saving the life of his
rival, the American adventurer is rewarded for his generosity by a stroke of fate which takes off Don Pedro, leav-

---

[43] Timothy Flint, *Francis Berrian*, 1826, I, iii.
[44] *Ibid.*, I, 133.

ing the hero not only victor in battle, but in undisputed possession of Doña Martha.

Of like romantic stuff were the characters, the incidents, and the setting which Flint employed in his later novels. Not only was he devoted, as he declared, to "the contemplation, and the study of nature," [45] but he indulged freely in the most extravagant invention. Both sentimental nature description and romantic action were given striking emphasis in his second novel, *The Life and Adventures of Arthur Clenning* (1828). To a plot copied from Defoe's sober journal of Crusoe's shipwreck on a strange island, Flint adds the glowing colors of much more romantic incident and descriptive detail which make the book an excellent document illustrative of the change in the spirit of English and American literature within the century following Defoe. The charm of the Defoe legend made Flint a slavish imitator, even to the point of introducing a cannibal feast on the island, together with the rescue, by the exiled white man, of one of the intended victims, who then becomes a domestic servant after the manner of Friday. But Bernardin de Saint-Pierre is called upon to supplement Defoe with "his unrivalled powers of singing the rural life of love in the shades of such a retirement;" [46] and Flint's hero is provided not only with a savage for serving-man, but with a more congenial companion in a beautiful woman, the only other survivor of the wreck, who is eventually united to Clenning as partner in the idyllic pleasures of his island. In *Francis Berrian*, the author, as if to give his novel an authentic Middle Western character, had imagined the story told to him by a fellow passenger on an Ohio River steamer (had not Chateaubriand's *Atala*, though too early for the steamboat, suggested

---

[45] *The Western Monthly Review*, I, 18 (May, 1827).

[46] Flint, *The Life and Adventures of Arthur Clenning*, 1828, II, 5.

the propriety of such a device?) ; in *The Life and Adventures of Arthur Clenning*, a curious Western touch is given to the narrative by the immigration of Clenning and his bride, after their return to a civilized country, to the Birkbeck settlement in Illinois.

*George Mason, the Young Backwoodsman; or 'Don't Give up the Ship,'* which Flint published in 1829, is, as the title-page describes it, "a story of the Mississippi" and has its setting entirely on the frontier, though principally in the Southwest rather than the Middle West. The situation of the family whose fortunes are followed by the author was not unlike that of Flint and his own family during a part of their wanderings on the lower Mississippi. Though for once perfectly familiar with the setting as well as the types of characters and kind of action introduced into his fiction, the author used them as awkwardly as he could well have done. Written in his weakest and most sentimental style, the novel succeeds in nothing but a wearisome enforcement of the moral that "we ought never to despond;" yet it gained the honor of reproduction in one of Miss Mitford's anthologies of fiction about American life.[47]

Another novel, called *The Lost Child* and published probably in 1830 (certainly not later), must remain, for the present, a matter of mere conjecture, though one may suspect from the evidence offered by the title that this work was of somewhat the same sentimental and moral kind as *George Mason*.[48]

Whatever the quality of *The Lost Child*, another of

---

[47] Mary Russell Mitford, *op. cit.*, II, 1-196. There was also a London reprint of *George Mason* under the title *Don't Give up the Ship* (1833). For the latter, see Kirkpatrick, *op. cit.*, p. 308.

[48] I have been unable to discover a copy of this book. Kirkpatrick (*op. cit.*, p. 310) suggests that if the work was a novel it may have been an expansion of a short narrative introduced into the first volume of Flint's periodical, *The Western Monthly Review* (in

Flint's fictions which appeared in 1830, and was probably the last of his original novels, achieved something in many ways better, and in some ways certainly worse, than the author had done in earlier books. Into *The Shoshonee Valley; a Romance*, a story of the Far West beyond the mountains antedating Irving's *Astoria* and *Captain Bonneville* by half a dozen years, Flint put materials which, he says, he derived from travellers to the Pacific regions, among whom was one M. Mackay, commandant, under the Spanish régime, of the district of Carondelet.[49] The adventures of these men he had heard at first hand, possibly during his residence in Missouri, on the main route to the Far West.

Upon these relations Flint exercised his imagination with but little restraint from his judgment. The resulting novel, though distinguished by some passages of greater charm, perhaps, than Flint had ever written before, is marred by the most complex and impossible of all his plots. He gathers his characters from the four ends of the earth and puts them down among the Shoshonee Indians near the banks of the Oregon. For the heroine, the daughter of a European father and a Chinese mother, he

pp. 20-23, May, 1827). In the light of what we know of *George Mason*, there seems, however, to be no reason for doubting that the classification of the book as a novel by *The North American Review*, XXX, 564 (Apr., 1830), was correct. It may be added that the work is also mentioned among the publications of E. H. Flint, the author's son, as advertised in the *Cinc. Daily Gaz.*, Jan. 31, 1834. Here it is immediately preceded by *George Mason*, each of them being described as "by T. Flint" and as published in "1 vol. 12mo." The inference to be drawn from this advertisement that the book was actually published by E. H. Flint and therefore probably a different edition from the one described by *The North American Review* as published at Boston by Putnam & Hunt in "18mo." is not, I think, to be taken very seriously, although E. H. Flint did publish some of his father's books.

[49] Timothy Flint, *The Shoshonee Valley; a Romance*, 1830, I, iv.

provides no less than four suitors. One of them is the son of the Shoshonee chief and a Spanish lady carried captive from California; another, the leader of the subject Shienne, who hate their Shoshonee masters. The remaining two are white adventurers. Of the white suitors, one is bent on seducing Jessy; the other, on marrying her. The series of melodramatic situations resulting from all these complications is more than adequate for the novelist's purpose. Before she can be united to her deserving American suitor, the heroine is compelled to suffer many ills, mainly through the machinations of Landino, her villanous white lover. She is abducted and imprisoned in a secret valley, but is rescued. Her parents are murdered. In attempting to escape from the country, she is kidnapped and carried away to a harem on the island of Ostroklotz. Another rescue is achieved; and her tormentor, fallen into the hands of the justly enraged Shoshonee, suffers at the stake. It is only after a variety of other adventures that the much-enduring heroine sails away for China with her faithful lover; and even then the tragic account is not complete. Before they reach the shores of Asia, she takes her own life to escape the torment of haunting visions of the scenes of horror she has witnessed; and on his return voyage to America her lover himself is lost at sea.

Aside from the immoderately melodramatic plot, the book is remarkable for its expression of strong feeling for nature; lengthy passages are devoted to description of the grand scenery of mountains and rivers. "I earnestly desire," said Flint,

that no one will intermeddle in this work, in the way of criticism, who has neither eyes to see, imagination to admire, or heart to feel simple nature, as I have communed with her in scenes, the memory of which is attempted to be transferred to these pages.[50]

---

[50] *Ibid.*, I, iii.

Much attention is also given to Indian customs; and the account of the salmon festival of the Shoshonee and Shienne [Cheyenne] tribes is of unusual interest. The subject race of Shiennes is pictured as restless and vengeful, but usually Flint's Indians are the noble savages of the legend. It is the white intruders who spoil the paradise of the Indians. But even the white men might have lived among these tribes in happiness. Contact with nature and with her children, the savages, by no means destroys the finer enjoyments of the cultured. The heroine possesses a well-equipped studio where she can reproduce on her canvas the grand scenery of the valley; and the hero finds time at odd hours for both painting and botanizing, even when the tribe is moving over the plains on the annual buffalo hunt. The Indians themselves are wont to 'imitate the conventional speech of educated Americans.

The translation of a French novel, which possibly belongs to the Cincinnati period, was still to follow; but, with *The Shoshonee Valley*, Flint's original work as a novelist came to an end. He had heeded the admonitions of his critics. "I mean never again," he wrote, "to perpetrate offences of romance on a large scale." [51] Mrs. Trollope, it is true, praised *Francis Berrian*. She declared its vigor and freshness were "exactly in accordance with what one looks for, in the literature of a new country" and "exactly what is most wanting in that of America." [52] James Hall preferred *The Life and Adventures of Arthur Clenning* to the earlier romance.[53] It is clear, however, that, though some of Flint's novels were printed several times, none of them could compare in value with the sober account of Western life which he had put into his *Recollec-*

---

[51] *Ibid.*

[52] Frances Trollope, *Domestic Manners of the Americans*, New York, 1832, p. 251.

[53] *Illinois Monthly Magazine*, I, 142-143 (Dec., 1830).

*tions* and *Geography.* Less than ten years after the appearance of *The Shoshonee Valley,* all of the novels were, according to a contemporary critic, "now almost forgotten." [54]

Other novelists of the West, who followed Flint, exploited a variety of themes. John M'Clung, later the compiler of *Sketches of Western Adventure,*[55] published in 1830 his only novel, *Camden; a Tale of the South,* with incidents of the American Revolution as its historic framework. The story opens on August 12, 1780, four days before the American defeat at Camden. The actual events of this exciting campaign are woven, not without some skill, into a story of love and intrigue touched here and there with a realism almost unknown to the romances of Timothy Flint. The early chapters are especially convincing, particularly the account of the entry of an English subaltern and his mounted men into the little Southern town, where they are greeted by the taunts of the villagers, dramatically interpreted by a local wit named Dusky. The first fighting takes place when the group of British cavalrymen overtake Templeton, the young American who is from that time at the center of the narrative. Templeton's escape to the home of the old patriot General Simon Lethbridge affords an opportunity to introduce Caroline Lethbridge as heroine of a love story. At the same time the author adds one of the most realistic characters in the book, the old general himself, whose delight in expounding the campaigns of Frederick the Great makes him blind to the love affair going on before his eyes. From this point the action moves rapidly on through the incidents of the campaign of 1780 and 1781, with such complications as the capture of Templeton and his friends in the battle of Camden; their release; Templeton's disgrace, brought about by the treach-

---

[54] *The Hesperian,* III, 463 (Nov., 1839).

[55] See above, Chapter V.

ery of an unscrupulous suitor for the hand of Miss Lethbridge; a brutal attack on Templeton by ruffians in the pay
of his rival; Templeton's vindication by the new commander, General Greene; the young hero's rise to fame in
a victorious battle against the British; and, a little later,
his marriage to Miss Lethbridge.

The influence of a number of authors is justly acknowledged by M'Clung; [56] but Cooper's successful use in his
early novels of the incidents of the American Revolution
was, doubtless, the chief influence on the author of *Camden*. In spite of its superiority over Flint's romances,
however, M'Clung's book remained unknown. According
to the author, it had been almost entirely forgotten within
a year or two after publication.[57]

James Hall, although the most prolific of Western
writers of short fiction, produced only one narrative long
enough to be regarded as a novel. This appeared first in
1833 under the title of *The Harpe's Head; a Legend of
Kentucky*; and was republished, in London, the following
year, as *Kentucky. A Tale*. *The Harpe's Head*, like most
of Hall's shorter narratives, was distinctly Western. Again,
however, the full measure of the realism for which his
subject-matter gave ample opportunity was avoided by
the romancer. The Harpe brothers were, in fact, famous
in the early days of Kentucky as the most desperate and
cruel of border outlaws. But Hall, though he desired to
make the most of the spirit of daring adventure associated
with their names, had no intention of allowing himself to
be restrained by facts. ''The real incidents of the lives of
those persons,'' he admits,

have been very sparingly alluded to, as most of them were
of a character too atrocious for recital in a work of this
description, . . . The individuals alluded to, have

---

[56] John M'Clung, *Camden; a Tale of the South*, 1830, I, x.
[57] M'Clung, *Sketches of Western Adventure*, 1832, preface.

therefore been merely introduced into a tale wholly fictitious.[58]

Nor did the author have any serious intention of setting down a faithful account of the society on the fringe of which these sinister characters were at home. Instead, he is mainly concerned with the fortunes of a group of aristocratic Virginian emigrants. Both in Virginia and in Kentucky, Miss Pendleton and her friends are persecuted by the Harpes. And in the frontier country they are also attacked by the Indians. The safety of the girl is, however, watched over successfully by a daring youth, whose wife she finally becomes. Most of the actors are little more than puppets — especially the hero and heroine, who are of the most conventional sort. But Hark Short, the snake-killer, whose manner of life and connection with the Harpes surround him with mystery, is a character strikingly individual. Nor is narrative interest lacking in the book, though the succession of desperate adventures, occurring with little intermission, gives the novel a melodramatic air.

The latest of the important novelists of the period, and perhaps the only writer of fiction whose achievement bears comparison with that of Hall and of Flint, was Frederick William Thomas, who began his literary career a few years after his immigration to Cincinnati, in 1831.[59]

---

[58] Hall, *The Harpe's Head*, 1833, pp. vii-viii.

[59] The statements of various authorities regarding the date of Thomas's removal to the West afford an example of the inaccuracies characteristic of nearly all biographical accounts of Western writers. Evert A. and George L. Duyckinck (*Cyclopædia of American Literature*, 1856, II, 548) give the date as 1830. William T. Coggeshall (*The Poets and Poetry of the West*, 1860, p. 184) is not explicit, but implies that the year was 1830. S. Austin Allibone (*A Critical Dictionary*, 1871, III, 2386) says Thomas commenced the practice of law in Cincinnati in the year 1830. W. H. Venable (*Beginnings of Literary Culture in the Ohio Valley*, 1891, p. 290) asserts that the novel-

The first [60] and probably the best-known of Thomas's novels was *Clinton Bradshaw; or, the Adventures of a Lawyer* (1835). The setting is entirely Eastern; [61] and ist came to Cincinnati with his father's family in 1829. Thomas himself wrote, apparently in Apr., 1833 (*The Emigrant, or Reflections while Descending the Ohio*, 1833, preface), that he had arrived in the West "three years since," thus leaving the matter not quite definite. If the author himself may be taken as authority, the question may, however, be set at rest; for he states definitely in his MS. Recollections of E. A. Poe that he emigrated to Cincinnati in 1831. For this passage in his manuscript, see J. H. Whitty's "Memoir" of Poe in *The Complete Poems of Edgar Allan Poe*, 1911, p. xxxiii. Though Thomas spent much of his time between 1831 and 1841 in travel through the Mississippi Valley and in the East (see *ibid.*, pp. xxxiii-xxxiv; and Frederick William Thomas, *Howard Pinckney*, 1840, II, 216), it is clear that during his period of novel writing from 1835 to 1840 he was regarded as a citizen of Cincinnati. See, for example, *The Western Monthly Magazine*, IV, 351 (Nov., 1835), and V, 756 (Dec., 1836); and *Cinc. Daily Gaz.*, Nov. 30, 1836, and Apr. 28, 1840.

[60] The attribution to Thomas of *The Polish Chiefs: an Historical Romance. By the Author of Sketches of Character, &c. &c. &c.* (see Library of Congress card catalogue and MS. note on title-page of this work in the same library) is almost certainly an error. The mistake is possibly due to the fact that, according to Allibone (*loc. cit.*), Thomas was the author of a work entitled *Sketches of Character*, published in 1849. *The Polish Chiefs*, however, had appeared in 1832; and its preface was dated "New-York, December, 1831," when Thomas was almost certainly in the West. It may be added that, according to the *Cinc. Daily Gaz.* (Nov. 30, 1836), where *East and West* is reviewed at length, the latter was Thomas's second novel, a statement which would allow for no earlier work of the sort except *Clinton Bradshaw*. This review was probably by the editor of the *Gazette*, Charles Hammond, to whom the novelist had dedicated his poem *The Emigrant* some three years before. See also the preface to *East and West* (1836), where Thomas alludes to *Clinton Bradshaw* as his first attempt at novel writing, and calls *East and West* his second.

[61] Thomas, *Clinton Bradshaw*, 1835, I, 13 and 26, *et passim*.

the only Western touch in the story is the introduction of a Kentuckian, enthusiastically loyal to the frontier. The story of the rise of a young law student to success in politics and in love is peculiarly American in quality and, in many of its details, is even suggestive of the actual experiences of the author. Much of the interest in both plot and character depends, however, on the adventures of the hero in the underworld of a large city, among whose denizens he moves like a charmed being, bearing judgment to the wicked and help to the oppressed. In spite of the pedantic weakness for quotations from Byron, Scott, and other English authors, the book was, to some extent, suggestive of what Dickens was a little later to do in works like *Oliver Twist* and *Our Mutual Friend*.[62]

In *East and West* (1836), Thomas again sought to use commonplace materials. He wished, he declared, ''to portray such scenes, characters, and incidents as may fall under the observation of the generality of readers.'' [63] The story, the early setting of which is an Eastern city, follows the fortunes of two young men who are drawn together by their blood relationship, but are later carried farther and farther apart by opposite tendencies in character. Ralph Beckford, who began in poverty, wins fortune and happiness, while Henry Beckford, who began in prosperity, ends in disgrace and suicide. The broad divergence between these two characters results, however, in a somewhat conventional hero and villain. The business of the latter is to slander the virtuous hero, and to endeavor to separate him from his equally virtuous lady. The moral perfection of the hero is shared by his uncle, the father of Henry Beckford, whose generosity is as unbounded as his son's villainy. But some individuality of character is

---

[62] *Cf.* especially *ibid.*, I, 158-246; and II, 5-131.

[63] Thomas, *East and West*, 1836, I, preface.

achieved in a number of the people introduced, and especially in the rough but honest Hearty Coil, who escapes
from a life of poverty in the East to comparative affluence
as keeper of the Boon House in a Kentucky settlement.
And something of the same excellence is to be found in
the roistering Western river man, Blazeaway, who exhibits
an entertaining facility for persecuting Eastern dandies.
An element of humor is present in the grotesque episode
of the loves of the foolish old bachelor, Dr. Julius Cake, and
Miss Judson, an elderly maiden who, through the roguery
of a practical joker, receives the fervent address which
the Doctor intended for a younger and fairer woman. East
and West are linked together in the story by the emigration of the important characters from the Eastern city to a
Kentucky town, and finally to a Southern plantation on
the Mississippi. The long narrative of a disastrous race
between two steamers on the Ohio, and the story of the
festival celebrating the installation of the landlord at the
Boon House, are valuable passages of intimate observation
on Western life.

In 1840 Thomas published his last important fiction,
*Howard Pinckney*, the action of which is confined almost
entirely to an indefinite setting, apparently in the East.
The story, though principally about a love affair involving
the members of certain cultured and well-to-do families,
derives its real interest from the desperate intrigues of a
band of counterfeiters and from the complicated love
affairs of several of the humble country folk who are
neighbors of the aristocratic Fitzhursts. Howard Pinckney and the Fitzhursts, left to themselves, talk conventional
love and indulge in long and insipid dissertations on
Byron's poetry; but are happily transformed when drawn
into the affairs of their neighbors, which are fraught with
the tragic interest of love rivalry, revenge, and murder.

A considerable portion of the second volume amounts to a detective story, well stocked with thrilling adventure.

It is, however, only because of the comparative excellence of his work and because of his residence in the West that Thomas stands beside the chief writers of Western fiction. In spite of the realistic sketches of frontier life which he achieved in *East and West*, it is clear that he had no such serious interest in the rise of Western literature as inspired Hall and Flint. He did not set out, as did Hall, to write the character of the West in fiction. Nor did his imagination turn naturally to far frontiers, as did Flint's in *Francis Berrian, The Life and Adventures of Arthur Clenning*, and *The Shoshonee Valley*. Life in the city or on the country estates of wealthy families, under conditions often at the farthest possible remove from those characteristic of the new country, supplied most of the material which Thomas used in fiction. That he appears as an important figure in the literature of the Western frontier is, his reader feels, a matter purely accidental and not of great significance.

Among pioneer novelists of much less importance was Caroline Lee Hentz, destined in later years to enjoy for a time an unusual success as a writer of popular fiction.[64] Her novel called *Lovell's Folly* (1833), though apparently written during her residence on the Ohio,[65] has its setting entirely in the East. The story, marred by the pedantry of foreign phrases and forced literary allusions, and not remarkable for character portrayal, is sufficiently supplied with incident and melodramatic complication. The arrival of a Southern beauty, Lorelly Sutherland, sets going, in a New England village, a train of love intrigue in which she is pitted against the unlovely but wealthy Penitence Marri-

---

[64] According to Allibone's account (*op. cit.*, 1874, I, 827) no less than 93,000 volumes of her works were sold within three years.

[65] *Cf. The Western Monthly Magazine*, I, 424-427 (Sept., 1833).

wood in a contest for the affections of the hero, Rovington. The imminence of financial ruin causes Rovington to accept the aid of the Marriwoods, which is offered on condition that he receive Penitence as his wife. Once the financial difficulty has been solved, however, the death of Penitence, whose life is lost in the burning of her father's mansion, leaves Rovington free. Some further suspense is caused by the chance arrival of Lorelly's long delinquent father, who, not realizing her identity, makes love to his own daughter. The story ends, however, with the latter's marriage to Rovington and the reunion of her parents.

Thomas H. Shreve, a Cincinnati writer who gained some local celebrity by his contributions to periodicals, wrote a novel called *Betterton*, which, however (unless it was indeed the book issued as *Drayton* many years later), probably remained unpublished, in spite of a preliminary announcement in 1837.[66] Robert Burt,[67] a young Cincinnati writer,[68] was the author of a romance called *The Scourge of the Ocean* (1837), said to be a sea tale of the American Revolution in Cooper's style, and so successful that the publishers began preparation of a second edition within a few months after it first appeared.[69] Nathaniel Beverley

---

[66] For some notice of *Betterton: a Novel* and for the announcement that it was expected to be "brought out during the approaching summer," see *The Western Monthly Magazine, and Literary Journal*, I, 214 (Apr., 1837). William Davis Gallagher, one of the editors of this magazine and a former business associate of Shreve's, did not, however, make any mention of *Betterton* in his biographical sketch of its author printed in Coggeshall, *op. cit.*, pp. 174-176.

[67] The name of the author is given thus in *A Catalogue of Books Belonging to the Young Mens' [sic] Mercantile Library Association of Cincinnati*, n. d. (probably 1838), No. 1131, where the book is listed as a romance in two volumes, published in Philadelphia in 1837. I have been unable to discover a copy of this novel.

[68] *The Western Monthly Magazine, and Literary Journal*, I, 215 (Apr., 1837).

[69] *Mo. Rep.*, Oct. 20, 1837.

Tucker, author of *George Balcombe* (1836), a romance of Virginia and of Missouri, and of *The Partisan Leader* (1836), a prophecy of the Civil War, cannot, perhaps, without very doubtful justice, be regarded as belonging to the West.[70] *The Partisan Leader* especially marked Tucker as belonging to another section. "This," said a contemporary reviewer, "is a Virginian story, affording strong internal evidence that it is written by a Virginian."[71]

---

[70] For the tradition that Tucker wrote *George Balcombe* and *The Partisan Leader* while he was still a resident of Missouri, see John Thomas Scharf, *History of Saint Louis City and County*, 1883, II, 1589; and Alexander Nicolas De Menil, *The Literature of the Louisiana Territory*, 1904, p. 71.   Dr. De Menil, to whom I am grateful for his generous interest in the present work, informs me that during the 'seventies and 'eighties he often heard old members of the bar state that Tucker wrote both the novels in St. Louis County, Missouri, and that some of these lawyers claimed to have heard parts of the MSS. read by the author. It is clear, however, that Tucker had removed to Virginia by the autumn of 1833 (see *Mo. Rep.*, Nov. 15, 1833), while the novels were not published till 1836. It seems likely that there is some significance in the circumstance that *George Balcombe* has not only its beginning but its end in Virginia. The fact that the postscript (II, 319), which is a part of the novel, is dated Feb. 13, 1836, seems to show that, at any rate, so much of the narrative was written more than two years after the author had returned to Virginia. Mr. Charles W. Coleman, of Washington, D.C., the grandson of Beverley Tucker, has kindly permitted me to add that in his opinion the view here presented is correct.

[71] *The Southern Literary Messenger*, III, 73 (Jan., 1837).

# CHAPTER VII

## POETRY

Those Americans are great, but they are not sublime Man — the humanity of the United States can never reach the sublime. Birkbeck's mind is too much in the American style — you must endeavour to infuse a little Spirit of another sort into the settlement, always with great caution, for thereby you may do your descendants more good than you may imagine. If I had a prayer to make for any great good, next to Tom's recovery, it should be that one of your Children should be the first American Poet. I have a great mind to make a prophecy, . . .

> It dares what no one dares
> It lifts its little hand into the flame
> Unharm'd, and on the strings
> Paddles a little tune and sings
> With dumb endeavour sweetly!
> Bard art thou completely!
> Little child
> O' the western wild,
> Bard art thou completely!

— Letter from John Keats to George and Georgiana Keats, at Louisville.

## I

It is a natural consequence of the rapid changes which have taken place in Western life that there remains in our day little trace of the popular balladry which constituted, perhaps, the better part of the poetry belonging to the pioneer period. There are no living heirs to the lore of the *coureurs de bois*, of the hunters and trappers, of the boatmen, or of the emigrants of a century ago; and records

303

of any sort are scanty. Travellers, who might have been expected to notice such songs, seldom made any mention of them and were never interested in collecting them. As the fruit of their observations of the Canadian voyageurs during a long journey up the Missouri in 1811, neither H. M. Brackenridge nor John Bradbury had anything better to show than some snatches from a boat song called "Les trois canards," which seems to have been sung by the men under Wilson P. Hunt as well as those belonging to the independent expedition under Manuel Lisa.[1] The latter commander, we are told, used the song to hearten the men at the oars.[2] An early popular historian of the frontier recorded two French songs used by the same type of adventurers. One is a love song concluding with this stanza:

> Tout les amants
> Changent de maîtresses;
> Qu'ils changent qui voudront,
> Pour moi je garde la mienne,
> Le bon vin ni endort;
> L'amour me réveille.[3]

The other begins:

> Dans mon chemin j'ai rencontré
> Trois cavaliers bien montés,
> Lon lon laridon daine,
> Lon lon laridon dai.[4]

And from the songs of the English-speaking boatmen of the Ohio we have only similar fragments. James Hall,

---

[1] H. M. Brackenridge, *Journal of a Voyage up the River Missouri,* second ed., 1815, p. 58; John Bradbury, *Travels in the Interior of America,* 1817, pp. 12-13. This catch was, says Bradbury, "one of their most favourite songs."

[2] Brackenridge, *loc. cit.*

[3] Henry Howe, *Historical Collections of the Great West,* 1853, I, 86-87.

[4] *Ibid.,* p. 87.

amused at the spectacle of "poetry dressed in rags and limping upon crutches"[5] presented in the journal of his first voyage on that river some verse of this kind "*verbatim,* as it flowed from the lips of an Ohio boatman":

> It's oh! as I was wal-king out,
>     One morning in July,
> I met a maid, who ax'd my trade —
>     Says I, I'll tell you presently,
>     Miss, I'll tell you presently.

> And it's oh! she was so neat a maid,
>     That her stockings and her shoes
> She *toted* in her lilly white hands,
>     For to keep them from the dews.[6]

Among others he got from the same source were two which seem to be without any peculiarities marking their origin among those who sang them:

> Here's to those that has old clothes,
>     And never a wife to mend 'em;
> A plague on those that has halfjoes,
>     And has'n't a heart to spend 'em!

and

> Oh! its love was the 'casion of my downfall,
> I wish I had'n't never lov'd none at all!
> Oh! its love was the 'casion of my miser*ee*;
> Now I am bound, but once I was free!

But to these fragments, Hall, fortunately, adds one refrain which could have originated only on the Ohio. The men kept time with their oars to this song:

> Some rows up, but we rows down,
>     All the way to Shawnee town,
>         Pull away — pull away![7]

---

[5] James Hall, *Letters from the West*, 1828, p. 90.

[6] *Ibid.*, p. 91.

[7] For the last three songs quoted, see *ibid.*, pp. 92-94.

Doubtless such chanteys as the last had numerous variants, the invention of which gave opportunity for a contest of wits among the boatmen. To the ruffian Mike Fink and his fellows, another writer attributes this somewhat similar catch:

> Hard upon the beech oar! —
> She moves too slow! —
> All the way to Shawneetown,
> Long while ago.[8]

The "boat horn," itself celebrated in a popular poem of the time, is said to have given a wholly original quality, marked by wildness and pathos, to the music of Western boatmen. "The Mississippi and Ohio, after the St. Lawrence," said a contemporary journalist,

are perhaps the only part of our country which can boast of its own native musick. . . . There is no cord which will vibrate sooner to the heart of a Kentuckian or Tennessean, when in a distant land, than the reminiscence of these native but rude ballads, to which his ear had been familiar from infancy, and which he associates with all the grandeur and beauty of the scenery of his home.[9]

The columns of immigrants moving Westward decade after decade must have made songs celebrating their adventures on the long journey. They must have had songs of leave-taking for their old homes in the East. They had, certainly, songs celebrating the new country to which they were going. Perhaps there were many, now lost, which had some such charm as the "New-England ballad," a quatrain of which appears in a British periodical of that time:

> 'Tis I can delve and plough, love,
> And you can spin and sew;

---

[8] Morgan Neville, "The Last of the Boatmen," in *The Western Souvenir*, n. d. (1829), p. 114.

[9] *The Family Magazine; or, Monthly Abstract of General Knowledge*, I, 238 (June, 1836).

> And we'll settle on the banks
> Of the pleasant Ohio.[10]

There were also commonplace verses sung in praise of particular states or territories, recommending them to home-seekers. One such rime, "The Michigan Emigrant's Song," of which there were twelve stanzas, to the tune of "John Anderson my Jo," invited farmers to come to Michigan from various New England states.[11] A similar piece, said to have been popular in 1833 and during the following years, when the tide of immigration through Detroit was at its height, begins in this manner:

> My eastern friends who wish to find
> A country that will suit your mind,
> Where comforts all are near at hand,
> Had better come to Michigan.[12]

Doubtless many ballads were improvised in the Western country about contemporary events of local or historic importance. A famous example from the days of the Spanish régime on the Mississippi is Jean Baptiste Trudeau's "Chanson de l'année du coup," a dramatic ballad celebrating the surprise attack on St. Louis by Indians and Canadians in 1780. This remarkable bit of verse, composed, it is said, at the time of the event which inspired it, was for many years popular among the citizens of that town.[13] Many English-speaking frontiersmen must have

[10] *The Edinburgh Review*, LV, 480 (July, 1832).

[11] Printed in the *Detroit Gaz.*, Apr. 2, 1819. It is, I think, a reasonable supposition that this song was in actual use among immigrants and settlers; but the evidence is not conclusive.

[12] "A Michigan Emigrant Song," said to have been contributed to the *Detroit Post and Tribune*, Feb. 13, 1881, by "a correspondent at Unadilla;" copied in *Pioneer Collections. Report of the Pioneer Society of the State of Michigan* (reprinted, 1903), III, 265.

[13] For the ballad and comments upon its history, see Wilson Primm's "History of the 'Chanson de l'année du coup,'" reprinted from *The Weekly Reveille*, Feb. 17, 1845, and edited by William Clark

been familiar with such echoes of the days of Indian fighting in Ohio as are contained in Matthew Bunn's song of "St. Clair's Defeat," which begins with these lines, not without a certain genuine ballad quality:

NOVEMBER the fourth, in the year ninety-one,
We had a sore engagement near to Fort Jefferson;
St. Clair was our commander, which may remembered be,
Since we have lost nine hundred men in the western territory.[14]

"The Battle of Point Pleasant,"[15] though it celebrated a fight which occurred on the Virginia shore of the Ohio, must also have been well known in early Kentucky and Ohio, which were first opened to immigrants by the victory of General Lewis's men over the Shawnee Indians in 1774.

A number of purely American or imported songs of miscellaneous kinds which have been recorded by recent ballad collectors were almost certainly sung in the West before 1841. The sources and history of these pieces cannot usually, perhaps, be traced; but cases in which some light is to be had on such matters are numerous enough to show a wide variety of origin. For example, the song called "Wood's Execution," the complaint of a soldier condemned by court martial, is clearly an American composition and is, in fact, based upon an incident of Andrew Jackson's campaign against the Creek Indians in 1814:

I enlisted to fight with the brave
And to march to that Southron land;

---

Breckenridge, *Missouri Historical Society Collections*, IV, 295-302 (No. 3, 1914).

[14] Matthew Bunn, *Narrative of the Life and Adventures of Matthew Bunn*, seventh ed., 1828, p. 57.

[15] For this ballad, see Kate Aplington, *Pilgrims of the Plains*, 1913, p. 209. In the same work are to be found several other songs and ballads still known in the West.

Our country from slaughter to save
Was Jackson who bore the command.
To fight the red savages bold
We marched without any delay
Through wet, and through hunger and cold
  We bore great fatigue by the way.

English antecedents, it is equally certain, must account for
the song of "The Jollie Thresherman," a colloquy between
a lowly laborer, who is content with his lot, and a lord, who
is so much impressed by the poor man's honesty and courage that he bestows upon him the life tenancy of a small
farm with the provision that, if the land is well cared for,
it shall become the possession of the thresherman's heirs.
The song, which consists of six stanzas, begins thus:

I met a jollie thresherman all on the highway,
His flail was on his shoulder . . .
  . . . his jug was full of beer,
And as happy as a lord with ten thousand a year.

When asked by what means he maintains his family, the
thresherman replies:

Why, sometimes I reap and sometimes I mow;
A-hedging and a-ditching ofttimes I go.
There's nothing comes amiss, I can wagon, reap and plow,
And I earn all my living by the sweat of my brow.

"The Squaw Song," another set of verses which, like the
two just quoted, is said to have been sung by emigrants
from Ohio to Iowa at the end of the pioneer period,[16]

[16] For the stanzas here quoted from "Wood's Execution" and
"The Jollie Thresherman," as well as for excerpts from "The
Squaw Song," I am indebted to Professor E. F. Piper, of the State
University of Iowa. On the authority of Mrs. Lydia Hinshaw, of
Richland, Iowa, Professor Piper has set down these pieces and several
others in his unpublished collection as sung by emigrants from Ohio
to Iowa in 1840. The origin of "Wood's Execution" is, I think, to
be found in the execution, by order of General Jackson, of John
Woods (not Wood), a private in the Twenty-eighth Regiment of

affords an interesting example of the purely literary composition on its way toward becoming a traditional ballad. This piece was, in fact, drawn, with only the slightest changes, from James Hall's "The Indian Wife's Lament," a poem which was printed in at least two different works by Hall long before 1840.[17]

Of the old English and Scottish pieces which belong to the recognized body of what we may call standard popular ballads, many, in a variety of forms, are sung in isolated communities in the West at the present day. Variants of such favorites as "Lady Isabel and the Elf Knight," "Young Beichan," "Fair Margaret and Sweet William," "Little Musgrave and Lady Barnard," and "Barbara Allen" may still be heard in the mountains of Kentucky;[18]

West Tennessee Light Infantry, on Mar. 14, 1814. For a detailed account of this affair, see James Parton, *Life of Andrew Jackson*, n. d. (1859), I, 504-512. According to the same authority (p. 509), the condemned man "wrote a letter of farewell to his parents in rhyme;" and this letter, one may reasonably conjecture, may have been the actual source of the piece quoted above. Woods's death was, at all events, a notorious episode in Jackson's military career, and was often recalled, in later years, by the general's political enemies. A curious feature of one of the stanzas of the ballad as now known is the mention of Fort Sumpter, which may have displaced Fort Strother, the correct name, sometime after the beginning of the Civil War. The probability of an English origin for "The Jollie Thresherman" was, it should be said, first remarked by Professor Piper himself. For other traditional verses known in the West before 1841, see, for example, "James Bird," "Young Charlotte," "Calomel," and "Pastoral Elegy" (the latter two drawn from Professor Piper's collection), in Louise Pound, *American Ballads and Songs*, n. d. (1922), Nos. 41, 44, 54, and 95.

[17] For the original, see *Illinois Monthly Magazine*, I, 17-19 (Oct., 1830); and Hall, *Legends of the West*, second ed., 1833, pp. 105-108. The principal difference between Professor Piper's version and the original as I have found it in Hall is in length: the former contains thirteen stanzas; the latter, eighteen.

[18] The ballads here named are represented by versions heard in

and, though there are, so far as has been determined, no contemporary records, it seems almost certain that these songs were brought to the West by the Southern current of immigration at the end of the eighteenth, and beginning of the nineteenth, century. The same may, with equal reason, be said of many variants recently reported from other Middle Western states.[19]

The airs of the popular ballads, with new words fitted to them, were also made to serve a religious purpose.[20] The camp meeting, where religious excitement reached its highest pitch, was a prolific source of "spiritual songs," or hymns. Perhaps few occasions anywhere ever afforded a closer approximation to the conditions of the mythical

Kentucky by Mrs. Campbell and recorded, with the airs, in Olive Dame Campbell and Cecil J. Sharp, *English Folk Songs from the Southern Appalachians*, 1917, Nos. 2C, 12B, 17B, 20D and G, and 21F. The existence of all of these ballads and of fourteen other parallels to pieces in Child's collection had previously been noticed by Hubert G. Shearin in "British Ballads in the Cumberland Mountains," *The Sewanee Review*, XIX, 313-327 (July, 1911). In the same study, Professor Shearin mentions many additional songs and ballads which he believes were brought to Kentucky from the British Isles by the pioneers, making a total (including all songs and ballads, whether parallels to Child or not) of thirty-seven independent pieces or fifty-six variants. *Cf.* also the same author's "History in Kentucky Folk Song," in *Seventh Annual Report of the Ohio Valley Historical Association*, n. d. (1913), pp. 52 ff., where a parallel to Child's "King John and the Bishop" is noticed; and G. L. Kittredge, "Ballads and Rhymes from Kentucky," *The Journal of American Folk-lore*, XX, 251-277 (Oct.-Dec., 1907).

[19] See, for example, Louise Pound, "Oral Literature," in *The Cambridge History of American Literature*, 1921, IV, 507; H. M. Belden, "Old-Country Ballads in Missouri," *The Journal of American Folk-lore*, XIX, 231-240 (July-Sept., 1906), 281-299 (Oct.-Dec., 1906), and XX, 319-320 (Oct.-Dec., 1907); and Phillips Barry, "Native Balladry in America," *ibid.*, XXII, 365-373 (Oct.-Dec., 1909).

[20] Hall, *Legends of the West*, second ed., 1833, p. 10.

choral throng of the folk-lorists than did such meetings, in which emotions were so deeply stirred that conventional restraint was forgotten. Songs to suit the need of the moment were often improvised in the preaching stand, and never had existence except in oral form, or, at best, in manuscripts which soon perished.[21] But, though some of the songs which survive from this period bear evidence of the influence of camp meeting traditions, they are clearly the work of individual authors.

One of the earliest collections of the kind must have been *The Pilgrim's Songster*, which first appeared in 1804, as the work of John A. Granade,[22] a Methodist itinerant preacher on the Tennessee-Kentucky border;[23] but was later enlarged under the editorship of Thomas S. Hinde, a Kentucky preacher of the same denomination.[24] Some light is thrown upon the psychology of such songs as this volume contains by an account of Granade's own transition from religious melancholia, resulting from a conviction of guilt, to the ecstasy of conversion:

[21] B. St. James Fry, "The Early Camp-meeting Song Writers," in *Methodist Quarterly Review*, XLI, 407 (July, 1859).

[22] For an advance advertisement of this work, which is described as "by *JOHN A. GRANADE*, Minister of the Gospel, M. E. C." and as "*A new Composition, never before published,*" see *Ky. Gaz.*, Jan. 10, 1804; and, for a notice of its publication, see *ibid.*, May 8, 1804. Fry (*op. cit.*, pp. 401-413, *passim*) is thus wrong in stating that the first edition of this remarkable songbook was published in 1810 and in implying that, though Granade and Caleb Jarvis Taylor had contributed a large part of the volume, Thomas S. Hinde, editor of "a new edition," was the original compiler. I am indebted to Professor W. W. Sweet for calling my attention to Fry's account, with the valuable songs, some of which Professor Sweet has quoted in *The Rise of Methodism in the West*.

[23] Fry, *op. cit.*, p. 402.

[24] For an account of Hinde and for hymns in addition to those noticed below, see *ibid.*, pp. 401-413, *passim*. I have not found a copy of this songbook.

Almost maddened by this conviction, the society of men became a burden to him, and he fled to the mountains, his despairing soul giving vent to his agony in mournful songs. Most of his friends concluded that he was hopelessly insane. But in the midst of it all his soul sought after God, . . . Alone, upon the mountain side, as he lay upon the damp ground, insensible to all earthly impressions, faith grew strong, . . . Now the light was as brilliant as the darkness had been dense, the joy as rapturous as the despair had been distressing, and henceforth he sang of love, joy, and hope.[25]

Caleb Jarvis Taylor, the Kentucky revivalist, many of whose songs eventually found a place in the same collection with Granade's compositions, shared the latter's emotionalism, and put into his exuberant figures something of the dramatic tenseness that pervaded the camp meeting when great throngs became frantic under the spell of the exhorters:

> Hark! the victor's singing loud,
>   Emanuel's chariot wheels are rumbling;
> Mourners weeping through the crowd,
>   And Satan's kingdom down is tumbling.[26]

The sudden mystical change from melancholy brooding on the terrors of hell, a theme dwelt upon with almost brutal insistence by the backwoods preachers, to an opposite state, is described in another song, also attributed to Taylor:

> Sinners through the camp are falling;
>   Deep distress their souls pervade,
> Wond'ring why they are not rolling
>   In the dark, infernal shade.
> Grace and mercy, long neglected,
>   Now they ardently implore;
> In an hour when least expected
>   Jesus bids them weep no more.[27]

---

25 *Ibid.*, p. 403.

26 *Ibid.*, p. 409.

27 *Ibid.*, p. 413.

*A New Kentucky Composition of Hymns and Spiritual Songs; together with a Few Odes, Poems, Elegies, &c.* (1816) was, with the exception of a negligible number of lines, entirely the work of William Downs, of Hardin County, Kentucky.[28]   Among the more than two hundred rude songs of Downs's book are included many which seem to reflect with peculiar fidelity the Kentucky frontier of his time.   The contemporary revivalist's lurid descriptions of eternal punishment are embodied in such verses as these:

> The rocks shall melt with fervent heat,
> And worlds pass off with noise so great,
> In flames they and their works shall burn,
> While sinners down to hell shall turn.
>
> Sinners enwrapt in flames shall mourn,
> With devils howl! with devils burn;
> But saints shall mount beyond the void,
> Leave flames behind and dwell with God.[29]

And something of the same kind is to be found in another song of warning, scarcely less extravagant:

> Sinners shall howl, damnation roll
>   Throughout this thwarted globe;
> In blood the moon, sackcloth the sun,
>   Shall speak the wrath of God!
> The stars shall fall, the nation's all
>   Shall hasten to the bar,
> To hear their doom they all shall come,
>   For judgment then prepare!
>
> . . . . . . .
>
> The earth in flames, sinners with screams,
>   Your fate shall awful be,
> For God doth say he'll in that day,
>   Cast off eternally![30]

[28] William Downs, *A New Kentucky Composition of Hymns and Spiritual Songs*, 1816, pp. v-vi.
[29] *Ibid.*, p. 25.
[30] *Ibid.*, pp. 242-243.

But, while the writer celebrates the might of the church
as displayed in the great revival at the beginning of the
nineteenth century,[31] he records also the miseries which
have fallen upon her through the admission of a throng of
hypocrites at that time and through the schisms which
arose during the intense religious excitement.[32] Yet, notwithstanding the lament for church divisions, such doctrinal matters as baptism by immersion are made into
songs of sectarian zeal.[33] Nor is partisan patriotic feeling
wholly absent from these compositions for the use of
churches. The anti-British sentiment rampant in the West
during the period of the War of 1812, finds expression in at
least one set of verses composed for a special occasion:

> Lord, since we are compell'd to take,
> The implements of death, to check
> The savage rage of British charms,
> May we successful prove in arms! [34]

Into some of the author's songs of personal religious experiences, there enters, on the other hand, a certain simple
ballad quality that is not unpleasant, as in these verses:

> OH! come my Father's children,
> Attention give to me,
> And I'll inform you candid,
> Of my puerility.
> I'll tell you how I've wander'd
> And from the pathway stroll'd,
> Have harken'd to intruders,
> Departed from the fold.

And much the same tone is noticeable in another piece,
which begins thus:

---

[31] *Ibid.*, pp. 248-250.

[32] *Ibid.*, pp. 250-257.

[33] E. g., *ibid.*, pp. 272-275, ''The Criticism of Pedobaptists, Refuted.''

[34] *Ibid.*, pp. 13-14.

> My friends and acquaintance to you I'll relate,
> My trials and troubles, likewise my hard fate.[35]

A number of other collections of religious songs, usually characterized by some special Western quality, appeared before 1841. *A New Collection of Hymns and Spiritual Songs, by David Wells of Kentucky* had been published as early as 1811.[36] *The Columbian Harmonist*, which was brought out at Cincinnati in September, 1816, was announced as containing pieces "particularly adapted to the different Churches in the Western Country;" and the project, according to the same advertisement, was inspired by sectional loyalty.[37] The compiler is said to have been Timothy Flint.[38] *The Missouri Harmony* (1820), which Flagg found in use as the repository of musical lore in a southern Illinois village,[39] was "a choice collection of Psalm and hymn tunes and anthems, selected from the most eminent authors" and containing "an introduction to grounds of music."[40] The popularity of the book was attested by various editions, during the course of which the original work was revised and a supplement was added "by an amateur."[41] The title of this frontier classic may well have been suggested by Samuel L. Metcalf's *The Kentucky*

[35] For this and the preceding passage, see *ibid.*, pp. 196 and 200-201.

[36] As advertised in *Ky. Gaz.*, Nov. 5, 1811. I have found no copy of these songs.

[37] *Liberty Hall*, Sept. 2, 1816.

[38] Charles Theodore Greve, *Centennial History of Cincinnati*, 1904, I, 471-472. I have been unable to discover a copy of the *Harmonist*. *Cf.* also John Ervan Kirkpatrick, *Timothy Flint*, 1911, p. 306, where it is stated that "A Collection of Hymns from European Books" was printed for Flint in 1815 or 1816. The work is, according to this account, mentioned in Flint's reports.

[39] Edmund Flagg, *The Far West*, 1838, II, 116.

[40] Allen D. Carden, *The Missouri Harmony*, revised ed., 1832, title-page.

[41] *Ibid.*, 1839, title-page.

*Harmonist*, a second edition of which was printed in 1820.
H. Miller, of Ohio, was the compiler of *A New Selection of
Psalms, Hymns and Spiritual Songs* (1826?), the ninth
edition of which appeared at Cincinnati in 1831. It was
apparently in the latter year that another anthology of
sacred music, *The Western Lyre*, by W. B. Snyder and W.
L. Chappell, was published at the same place. A Shaker
songbook called *A Selection of Hymns and Poems; for the
Use of Believers*, issued at Watervliet, Ohio, in 1833, under
the pen name of Philos Harmoniæ, has been attributed to
Richard McNemar.[42] James Gallaher, the compiler of
*New Select Hymns* (1835), was a Presbyterian preacher of
Cincinnati. *The Juvenile Harmony* (1825?), another collection of sacred music, was by W. C. Knight, of the same
state. In 1831 it reached a fifth edition.

Of much less enduring popularity, but remarkably influential in their day, were the political songbooks which were
published in considerable numbers during the "log cabin
and hard cider" campaigns of 1840. Though confined to
no section of the country, the songs which appeared in this
way may be regarded as owing their existence, in large
measure, to the enthusiasm of the West for its own Presidential candidate. *The Tippecanoe Song Book*, published
at Cincinnati by U. P. James in May, 1840, must have been
characteristic of this type. "It embodies, therefore," says
an advertisement,

portions of the songs which have, within the three or four
months last past, burst spontaneously from the depths of
the popular heart, throughout the entire Union.[43]

With due allowance for the exaggerations of political partisans, we may regard such pieces as a kind of property, if

[42] J. P. MacLean, *A Sketch of the Life and Labors of Richard
McNemar*, 1905, p. 65.

[43] *Cinc. Daily Gaz.*, May 30, 1840. See also *The Daily Chronicle*,
June 1, 1840.

not product, of the masses of the people who had been
stirred to enthusiasm by the spectacle of log cabins hauled
in noisy parades, perhaps too by overindulgence in the
hard cider which was symbolic of Western hardihood, and
certainly by oratorical glorification of the Battle of Tippecanoe, by means of which a frontier Indian skirmish was
made to appear in the eyes of the people as one of the
decisive battles of the world.

Other Western collections inspired in like manner were
*Harrison Songs*, advertised in 1840,[44] and *The Harrison
and Log Cabin Song Book*, published by I. N. Whiting at
Columbus the same year. Almost all of the sixty-nine
songs contained in the latter campaign document celebrate
Harrison's picturesque personality.

Songbooks primarily neither religious nor political seem
not to have been numerous. A. P. Heinrich, who was, at
least for a time, an actor in Kentucky theatres, projected an
original collection to be called *The Dawning of Music, in
Kentucky, or, the Pleasures of Harmony, in the Solitudes
of Nature*.[45] It is not clear, however, that this work ever
appeared in print. *The Eolian Songster* (1832?), a very
popular work published by U. P. James, of Cincinnati, and
said to have been compiled by him,[46] contained "sentimental, patriotic, naval, and comic songs."[47] The same
publisher issued *The American Minstrel*[48] and *The United
States Songster*.[49] The latter included many songs sung

---

[44] *The Daily Chronicle*, June 2, 1840. It is just possible, however,
that the songs here advertised were published separately and not
in the form of a collection.

[45] See advertisements in the *Lou. Pub. Adv.*, Jan. 26 to Sept. 16,
1820.

[46] See MS. note on flyleaf of an undated copy in the Cincinnati
Public Library.

[47] *Ibid.*, title-page.

[48] *The Daily Chronicle*, June 1, 1840.

[49] This book was entered by J. A. James & Co. in 1836; but the

in the theatres, which, like the churches, afforded a great
impetus to popular interest in singing. Of the thousands
of dramatic performances noted in a later chapter,[50]
scarcely one was complete without songs by the favorite
actors.

## II

Sharply in contrast with the fervid enthusiasm of political and religious songs and with the serious tone pervading
much of the other rude poetry which often attained an
existence independent of the printed page, was a body of
satirical verse, the work of some of the earliest writers who
gained celebrity as laureates of the backwoods. The satirical mood, hostile to the romantic legend of the West, cannot be too much insisted upon by one who would under-
stand not only the charm but the ugliness of the pioneer
period. It is, we may be sure, by no means a fantastic
picture of the men and manners of the time which appears
through this medium; and, whatever its shortcomings, due
in a few cases to an excess of bitterness or to downright
lewdness, it is a much more faithful record than can be
found in the abortive epics or in the flood of conventional
sentimental poetry which came from the press before 1841.

It is a remarkable fact that satirical verse was, on the
whole, the earliest of these three kinds. *The Kentucky
Miscellany*, which may well have been the first independent
publication of the sort, was advertised for sale in Lexing-

title and other information here given is taken from an undated
copy, probably much later.

[50] See Chapter VIII. Among the songs heard in the theatres,
perhaps none on a Western theme was better known than Woodworth's "The Hunters of Kentucky," celebrating the valor of the
Kentucky troops at the Battle of New Orleans. Negro melodies
were also very popular. For an account of the shower of silver
which often greeted the actor when such songs were sung, see Joseph
Cowell, *Thirty Years Passed among the Players in England and
America*, 1844, p. 87.

ton and Danville by May, 1789.[51]  The date of composition
may have extended over some years, but at least one of the
poems in a later edition goes to prove that Johnson was in
Kentucky by 1787.[52]  Though there are many newspaper
notices of earlier issues,[53] the fourth edition, dated 1821,
seems to be the only one extant.[54]

Johnson's satire is many-edged.  He hated the miserable

[51] The *Ky. Gaz.*, for May 23, 1789, has the following advertisement: "THE KENTUCKY MISCELLANY, BY THOMAS JOHN-
SON, *Jun* May be had at Mr. Benjamin Beall's in Lexington, and at
Gillespie Birney and company, and Gen. Wilkinson's stores in Danville." The year 1796, given by J. W. Townsend (*Kentuckians in
History and Literature*, 1907, p. 91; and *Kentucky in American
Letters*, 1913, I, 19) as the date of the first appearance of this
work, is therefore more than six years too late. It should be added,
however, that to this historian of Kentucky literature must be
credited the rediscovery of Johnson, who, before Mr. Townsend made
him known to present-day readers, had long been forgotten.

[52] Thomas Johnson, *The Kentucky Miscellany*, fourth ed., 1821,
p. 13, "The Mercer Election, for the Year 1787." According to
Townsend (*Kentuckians in History and Literature*, 1907, p. 90),
Johnson was born in Virginia about 1760 and emigrated to Kentucky when he was twenty-five. The same authority, however, seems
to have found no trace of Johnson in Kentucky earlier than 1793,
for which year an advertised letter is cited.

[53] See, for example, *Ky. Gaz.*, *loc. cit.*; Jan. 16 and Mar. 19,
1796; Sept. 13, 20, and later, 1803; July 3, 1804 (there is a bare
possibility that this advertisement refers to Samuel Johnson's
poems); Apr. 30, 1806; and Feb. 13 and 27, 1815 (where the
*Miscellany* is advertised as "just published"—evidently a new
edition).

[54] The only copy of this edition which I have found is in the
Durrett Collection, University of Chicago. It is a miniature pamphlet, 5 and 13/16 inches by 3 and 3/8 inches, containing thirty-six
pages. An upper corner of every leaf is torn off, leaving usually
from about three to six lines imperfect. The title-page, in its
present mutilated condition, reads as follows: "-iscellany. By
Thomas Johnson, Jun. Fourth edition. Lexington: Printed at the
Advertiser Office. 1821."

frontier town in which he lived, and had no such interest in its future greatness as Mrs. Kirkland's people of Montacute and Tinkerville had in that of their rising settlements. To him the place seemed wholly bad:

> ACCURSED *Danville*, vile, detested spot,
> Where knaves inhabit, and where fools resort.[55]

Nor did he feel any loyalty for the state which in pioneer days was known by the proud appellation of "Old Kentucky." Byron's romantic conception of "this unsighing people of the woods" is strangely in contrast with the likeness drawn by the backwoods satirist:

> I HATE Kentucky, curse the place,
> And all her vile and miscreant race!
> Who make religion's sacred tie,
> A mask thro' which they cheat and lie;
> Proteus could not change his shape,
> Nor Jupiter commit a rape,
> With half the ease those villains can,
> Send prayers to God and cheat their man.[56]

Among the most successful of his poems are the satiric thrusts directed at individuals whose eccentric behaviour attracted his attention. An "Epigram on William Hudson who Murdered his Wife" consists of this quatrain:

> STRANGE things of Orpheus poets tell,
> How for a wife he went to Hell;
> Hudson, a wiser man no doubt,
> Would go to Hell to be without.[57]

And the verses "On Maurice Nagle, Esq." begin thus:

> LET not Maurice be forgotten
> Tho' he lies here dead and rotten;

---

[55] Johnson, *op. cit.*, p. 12.

[56] *Ibid.*, p. 21.

[57] *Ibid.*, p. 24. In the original the third line ends with a period.

> But to his mem'ry be it said,
> Here lies the man that never paid
> A debt but this, which we all must;
> Nor would he this if death would trust.[58]

In "A Grace Extempore, at Gill's Tavern," the stinginess of the old landlord offers a broad target for Johnson's epigrammatic wit:

> O THOU, who bless'd the loaves and fishes:
> Look down upon these empty dishes!
> By the same power those dishes fill;
> Bless each of us and curse old GILL.[59]

But, with his admirable candor, the author is quite capable of turning the point of his satire against himself. His curse on Kentucky is broad enough to include a malison upon the poet too:

> And more accursed be myself!
> Who takes no council, mind no rules,
> And only live a jest for fools.[60]

And in another set of verses he indulges in even more bitter self-recrimination:

> HAIL Danville! hail! where Johnson shines,
> The hero of his blackguard rhymes;
> Whose limber pen and polite brains,
> Turns epic into dog'rel strains;
>
> .    .    .    .    .    .    .
>
> Each noble act by him consign'd,
> To low burlesque and dirty rhymes.[61]

Somewhat similar in tone, "The Author's Own Epitaph" is, very likely, not without some genuine biographical significance:

---

[58] *Ibid.*, p. 35.
[59] *Ibid.*, p. 13.
[60] *Ibid.*, p. 22.
[61] *Ibid.*, pp. 27-28.

UNDERNEATH this marble tomb,
In endless shades lies drunken Tom;
Here safely moor'd, dead as a log
Who got his death by drinking grog —
By whiskey grog he lost his breath,
Who would not die so sweet a death?[62]

With his facility as a satirist, however, Johnson combined
a tiresome overindulgence in sheer obscenity, for which
only the authentic comic note of many such verses as have
been noticed can atone.

Gorham Worth's *American Bards* (1819), once known as
the first volume of verse written and printed in the West,[63]
actually appeared more than a quarter of a century later
than Johnson's *Miscellany*. Nor does the weak satire of
the volume of 1819 bear any likeness to the earlier writer's
keen shafts. Worth, who himself said of his verses that
there was no approach to poetry in them, justified them on
utilitarian grounds. They were intended, he declared,

to excite a feeling of contempt for that literary affectation,
false taste, and pitiful itch for newspaper and magazine
fame, which are so strikingly exhibited by the would-be
Bards, the catch-penny authors, and conundrum wits of the
day.[64]

*American Bards* is, however, an attempt to satirize American poets in the spirit of Byron's *English Bards and
Scotch Reviewers*. Apollo, though busy with his affairs
in Britain, feels enough curiosity regarding American
bards to dispatch a lieutenant in order to secure information about them. This representative of the god, after
casually observing the South, and making only a slightly

[62] *Ibid.*, p. 34. In the original the last line ends with a period.
[63] W. H. Venable, *Beginnings of Literary Culture in the Ohio
Valley*, 1891, p. 275.
[64] Gorham Worth, *American Bards: a Modern Poem, in Three
Parts*, 1819, pp. v-vi.

successful search for poets in the Northern Atlantic states, turns toward the West:

Yet his task, he perceiv'd, he had hardly begun;
 For fame to his ear had addrest
Some tidings of Bards — of a country scarce known —
Of a people of arms — or to say all in one,
 OF AN EMPIRE ENTHRONED IN THE WEST![65]

The geographical description of the West which follows is in the extravagant style common in the conventional nature poetry of the time; but the report which Apollo's aid eventually takes back to his master is a sweeping satirical attack upon American versifiers, both Eastern and Western, among whom he finds none deserving of praise unless it be, perhaps, Selleck Osborn:

There's not one worth a — 'mong 'em all:
Unless 'tis perchance the bard of the Ode.[66]

Angus Umphraville, the author of *Missourian Lays, and Other Western Ditties* (1821), could not have been long in the West before the appearance of this "first volume of original poems ever published in Missouri."[67] Some four years earlier he had been in Baltimore and had published there, apparently when he was only nineteen years of age, a pseudo-epic on the War of 1812, together with some minor poems.[68] Though he dedicated *Missourian Lays* to William Clark, lately governor of the territory of Missouri, the author seems not to have been an established resident

---

[65] *Ibid.*, p. 21.

[66] *Ibid.*, p. 42.

[67] Angus Umphraville, *Missourian Lays, and Other Western Ditties*, 1821, p. 6.

[68] Umphraville, *The Siege of Baltimore, and the Battle of La Tranche; with Other Original Poems*, Baltimore, 1817. The several dedications which accompany the poems are also dated from Baltimore.

of St. Louis at the time; [69] and the little which he has to say about himself goes to prove that he was a poverty-stricken adventurer.[70] Like Thomas Johnson of *The Kentucky Miscellany*, he was at his best in satirical verses; and, like the earlier writer, he exhibited a taste for licentiousness. But he had little of Johnson's ability. The crudest grammatical errors disfigure his style; and, even in his best lines, as in "The Old Maid of St. Louis," he rises to nothing better than stupid blackguarding. Unlike Johnson, he admits among his satires many poems of a trite and sentimental kind and falls at times into the bombast of a serious attempt at epic style in his descriptions of Western scenery. In fact, Umphraville is noteworthy only as a literary curiosity.

But of all early Western writers, Thomas Peirce, of Cincinnati, was the best-known for satire. His first volume, *The Odes of Horace in Cincinnati* (1822), is almost entirely made up of this kind of verse. The thirty-one odes which appeared in this collection — against the will of the author, if his own statement may be credited [71] — contained personal satires, often severe, upon such persons as the mayor of Cincinnati, Professor Rafinesque, of Transylvania, Captain John Cleves Symmes, Bushrod Washington, and the members of the houses of the Ohio legislature. Some

---

[69] *Missourian Lays* was published by June, 1821 (*Mo. Gaz.*, June 6, 1821); but the name of Umphraville does not appear in John A. Paxton's work, *The St. Louis Directory and Register, Containing the Names, Professions, and Residence of All the Heads of Families and Persons in Business*, the preface of which is dated May 26, 1821.

[70] Umphraville, *Missourian Lays*, 1821, preface and p. 6. The author declares that he is compelled to print at once that he may obtain money, and he seems to imply that Clark has given or promised him aid.

[71] Thomas Peirce, *The Odes of Horace in Cincinnati; as Published in the "Western Spy and Literary Cadet," during the Year 1821*, 1822, "To the Publishers," dated Apr. 24, 1822.

of the odes, such as "To Posterity" ("The Dandy"),
"Characters at the Hotel," "City Lawyers," "City Poets,"
and "Modern Schools," are partly satires on types of people and partly personal ridicule. Peirce drew his inspiration mainly from the streets of Cincinnati, and in one of
the early odes — they were written weekly as they were
published in the newspaper — he notices the cosmopolitan
character of the people of that town and explains his purpose:

> I know not but, from time to time,
> As led by fancy, whim or rhyme,
> (I cannot say the graces)
> With Hogarth's brush, or Butler's pen,
> I may, from such a crowd of men,
> Touch off some likely faces.[72]

He apostrophizes "Professor Brickibus, M. D.," whom he
calls the "Renoun'd philosopher and sage," ironically
praising the savant's theory that America was the original
home of the human race, and approving the notion that
the Garden of Eden was located on the banks of the Mississippi.[73] He laughs at the pedantry of Rafinesque,
"ALIAS, *Professor Muscleshellorum, of Transylvania University.*" [74] He makes suggestions to Captain Symmes on
feasible methods of exploring the interior of the earth;
none of the methods heretofore discussed, he says, will avail:

> None of these can succeed. If you have the least mind
>    To examine the regions below —
> I mount my Pegassus — you jump up behind —
> And here we sail off on the wings of the wind,
>    Like an arrow discharg'd from a bow.
>
>      .   .   .   .   .   .   .
>
> The next time I take such a comical flight,
>    Dear Captain, with you for a friend,

---

[72] *Ibid.*, p. 9.

[73] *Ibid.*, pp. 17-18.

[74] *Ibid.*, pp. 22-24.

I, like my Lord Byron, a canto will write,
And you must, like Hobhouse, a volume indite
Of notes, to be placed at the end.[75]

In "The Poet's Banquet," he calls upon Western writers
to attend to the West:

Shame — to thus neglect your duty,
While such scenes remain unsung.[76]

And in his "City Poets" he follows the example of Worth
in chastising "*Ohio's Bard*," who, "with the love of death-
less glory smitten," scorned to take money for his labori-
ously written poem —

let it run its own road helter-skelter;
When lo! it took to Lethe's banks for shelter.[77]

Byron's influence, which is noticeable in "City Poets," is
perhaps also to be found in others of *The Odes of Horace*
and in the conception of the book as a whole. A later series
of satirical verses called "Billy Moody," recounting the
travels of a Yankee schoolmaster in the West, and written
in a style plainly imitative of Byron, was first published
in a Cincinnati newspaper and, it is said, later appeared in
the form of a volume.[78]

In a third publication, *The Muse of Hesperia. A Poetic
Reverie* (1823),[79] Peirce, however, turned from pure satire

---

[75] *Ibid.*, pp. 29-32.

[76] *Ibid.*, p. 75.

[77] *Ibid.*, p. 52.

[78] William T. Coggeshall, *The Poets and Poetry of the West*, 1860,
p. 37. The same authority is, however, wrong in stating that the
series was written in 1825. For the twenty-nine "chapters" of the
poem, see *The National Republican and Ohio Political Register*, Jan.
1-July 15, 1823.

[79] These verses were published as a "Philomathic Prize Poem,"
selected for this honor by the Philomathic Society of Cincinnati
College in Apr., 1822. The poem, like the others by Peirce, was
printed anonymously. (*The Muse of Hesperia*, 1823, cover and p.
v.)

to a conventional laudation of the frontier only slightly modified by passages of critical reflections somewhat in the manner of Pope and Byron and other models. The principal part of the poem is an address from the Muse of Hesperia, who reveals to the author the themes which should be the special inspiration of Western bards.

### III

The songs and ballads of the frontier country, essentially the property of the people rather than of individuals, served, no doubt, a purpose which could have been served by nothing else; and the satirical writers, although they enjoyed no such popular vogue, reflected a side of pioneer life that is of great importance in any serious estimate of the civilization of that day. Not so much can be said, however, for the bulky epics of Emmons and Genin. They had no reason for being. They were formidable only because of their length and their dullness.

Yet the pathetic devotion of Richard Emmons to an ideal wholly impossible of realization, forms one of the most striking chapters of Western literary biography. And there is perhaps even greater pathos in his belief, in later years, that he had accomplished his purpose. There is, too, something in Emmons that is more significant — he is the symbol of the blatant nationalism that was stirred into new life in the Western country by the War of 1812, and the symbol of the self-laudation of the frontiersman which masqueraded under the guise of humility. There came to him in the backwoods of Kentucky a vision, and an oracle which called him to be the laureate of this shrill-voiced, unlovely patriotism. Thenceforth his goddess was Columbia, and during his long priesthood in her service he decorated her altars with tinsel. His long struggle for recognition as the great American poet is recalled by a passage in Mrs. Trollope's book where she tells of seeing, in a museum at Philadelphia, a portrait of Emmons, to which was attached an advertisement of his longest epic, *The Fredoniad*.[80]

As early as 1822 Emmons had begun to publish, bringing out in that year a pamphlet called *Battle of the Thames; being the Seventeenth Canto of an Epic Poem, Entitled The Fredoniad*, which was intended to test public sentiment preparatory to the appearance of thirty-five other cantos.[81] In 1827 the first edition of the complete poem was printed as *The Fredoniad: or, Independence Preserved. An Epic Poem on the Late War of 1812*. The forty cantos of heroic couplets to which the work had now grown filled over twelve hundred pages bound in four volumes. This was the poet's triumphant answer to "several citizens of the Republick eminent for their literature," who had looked with indifference upon his epic when it was in the making.[82] Moreover, Emmons at once set about revising the work; and, when the second edition was issued, in 1830, he declared that he had devoted more than ten years of

[80] Frances Trollope, *Domestic Manners of the Americans*, New York, 1832, p. 217.

[81] Richard Emmons, *Battle of the Thames*, 1822, advertisement, dated from Nelson County, Ky., Sept., 1822. The author's determination to publish this single canto of 1266 lines seems to have resulted from the failure of an earlier attempt to secure subscriptions for the whole work (see, for example, proposals for publishing *The Fredoniad*, in *Mo. Gaz.*, May 16, 1821). When the complete work appeared in 1827, the poet's brother, in Boston, was the publisher. It is worthy of note that Emmons's fragment of 1822 was not the first attempt at epic poetry by a Kentuckian. Ten years earlier Anthony Hunn's *Sin and Redemption*, an episode from his long poem *The Columbiad*, was printed at Lexington. But *The Columbiad* seems never to have appeared in complete form. For an account of Hunn's epic, see *Sin and Redemption*, 1812, preface.

[82] Emmons, *The Fredoniad*, 1827, I, viii (preface, dated Great Crossing, Ky., Sept. 23, 1826).

constant labor to the monstrous poem.[83]    A third edition followed in 1832.

*The Fredoniad*, though based largely upon the history of the War of 1812, makes use of epic machinery, partly borrowed from Milton, but probably greatly influenced by Barlow's example.  The scene of the action is the universe. Within the first four cantos alone, the reader is conveyed from hell to heaven, and from heaven to Detroit, the surrender of which is the first of the purely historical events celebrated in the poem.  Almost every important action of the war, naval or military, receives attention, the Battle of New Orleans and the return of peace supplying the subject-matter of the fortieth, and last, canto.[84]

The poem begins with a description of hell and an account of the gathering of the infernal council, borrowed from Milton's picture of Pandemonium, with hell, however, shorn of its Miltonic sublimity, and Satan's hall of state transformed in a manner worthy of "Monk" Lewis:

> On fifty skeletons, of giant height,
> Fix'd is the throne, appalling to the sight! [85]

The subject of debate among Emmons's devils is the best means of bringing about Columbia's downfall.  The third canto shows a convocation of the heavenly immortals. Upon the arrival in heaven of Columbia's guardian spirit, Fredonia, bearing news of the danger which threatens her ward, the celestials are called forth from their gardens and grottoes to hear her tale.  There follows a pageant of personified abstractions moving to the council hall — Fredonia accompanied by Independence, Justice, Temper-

---

[83] *Ibid.*, third ed., 1832, p. x (preface to the second ed.).

[84] The last canto also appeared in 1827 as an independent poem under the title *An Epick Poem in Commemoration of Gen. Andrew Jackson's Victory on the Eighth of January, 1815.*

[85] Emmons, *The Fredoniad*, 1827, Canto I, ll. 780-781.

ance, Patriotism, Victory, Love, Charity, Peace, and Hope — with Washington and other great spirits of the dead marching in their wake. The poet's national feeling, which inspires almost the whole of the poem, is exhibited in his description of the musicians who accompany the procession:

> And now, behold two sons of epick song
> Are heard to sing with transport on their tongue:
> Barlow's soft numbers flow with smooth delight —
> Him, sweetly answering, swells harmonious Dwight.[86]

The venerable discoverer of America is also given a place in the celestial progress —

> Columbus next majestick treads the lawn,
> Whose noble breast three infant ships adorn.[87]

Toward the end of the canto Fame enters and informs the celestials that Columbia has declared war against Albion; and, with the opening of the fourth canto, the scene is shifted to earth, and the historical part of the action begins.

The supernatural machinery is, however, by no means abandoned. Satan raises tempests to smite the American ships at sea, and lurks in the mists that thwart the manœuvers of the American troops. Nor are the celestials inactive. One of the greatest absurdities of the poem is the action of Canto XXXIII, in the course of which the American ship "Wasp," about to go down in a storm, is snatched up into heaven with all her crew — the celestial wall opens; and the boat, now transformed to gold, silver, ivory, and silk, in a manner recalling the finest tinsel passages of the old ballads, sails in.

> Blakely in robes immortal, and his crew,
> Feel inexpressible their feeling new.[88]

---

[86] *Ibid.*, Canto III, ll. 429-432.
[87] *Ibid.*, Canto III, ll. 471-472.
[88] *Ibid.*, Canto XXXIII, ll. 922-925.

The following canto contains a vision lasting "about six hours," during which the company of the blessed, seated conveniently on the wall of heaven, witness a series of naval actions between British and Americans. The fortieth, and final, canto, besides giving an account of the Battle of New Orleans, provides the grand spectacle of Fredonia, Fame, Victory, Independence, and Peace coming down from heaven, singing a chorus of praise to Columbia.

This heavy content is nowhere relieved by either vigorous or graceful style. The heroic couplets, which Emmons probably inherited from Barlow, are without the epigrammatic quality of which they have been shown capable in stronger hands; the rimes are slipshod, the figures of speech are false, and the diction is almost entirely bad. But for its monumental bulk, if not also for its monumental badness, the verse of Emmons was unique in Western literary annals. The three editions of the epic within five years bear eloquent testimony to the state of public taste in that day. It must be remembered, however, that Timothy Flint, the chief Western critic at the time when *The Fredoniad* first appeared, regarded it as an unworthy performance. It was, he declared,

the most monstrous collection of maudlin, silly and incongruous verses, that ever were, or, we hope, ever will be put together.[89]

Another epic poem, much shorter, but exactly in Emmons's style and probably by him, was *The Battle of Bunker Hill, or the Temple of Liberty* (1839?),[90] of which no

---

[89] *The Western Monthly Review*, II, 181 (Aug., 1828).

[90] This is the date of entry as given in the tenth edition, 1859, from which I have taken the title. The proprietor in 1859 was William Emmons, who had published *The Fredoniad*. The author's reference to "my loos'd harp restrung" (Canto I, l. 3) makes the attribution to Richard Emmons more likely. The copy of this epic

less than ten editions were published within the next twenty years. It is by no means impossible that the same author was responsible for a still shorter composition, *The Battle of the Thames, October 5, 1813; from an Unpublished Poem, Entitled Tecumseh, by a Young American* (1840).[91] Unlike Richard Emmons's *Battle of the Thames* (1822), however, this poem is mainly in octosyllabics. It is, in effect, a campaign document favoring Harrison's election. *The National Jubilee, and Other Miscellaneous Poems* (1830), certainly the work of Richard Emmons, contains a selection from *The Fredoniad*, together with some bombastic patriotic verses recited by the author at a celebration of the Fourth of July and several conventional pieces on various themes.

It is only with somewhat doubtful propriety that a second epic poet, Thomas Hedges Genin, may be regarded as a Western writer; for *The Napolead*, which he published at St. Clairsville in 1833 (possibly as a result of Emmons's success), had, he says, been kept by him for seventeen years,[92] and was therefore largely written before the author's immigration to Ohio, if the date of his arrival in that state was, as has been supposed, 1817.[93] Some revision had, however, been made in Ohio; for the author was willing to admit that both sentiments and language had been emended so that the poem would not, he hoped, "corrupt the style, or morals of the reader." [94]

The story of the epic begins, as Genin explains, with the

in the Durrett Collection, University of Chicago, bears a manuscript note ascribing the work to Emmons.

[91] In the copy of this pamphlet belonging to the library of Brown University, there is a manuscript note attributing the work to William — not Richard — Emmons.

[92] Thomas H. Genin, *The Napolead, in Twelve Books*, 1833, p. v.

[93] John C. Stockbridge, *A Catalogue of the Harris Collection of American Poetry*, 1886, p. 99.

[94] Genin, *op. cit.*, p. v.

Russian campaign and ends with Elba so that Napoleon's highest qualities may be shown:

Successful campaigns abound in the life of Napoleon; but his conduct in adversity recommended him to me, as the hero of a poem. . . . A period, therefore, was selected for the action, in which the Emperor, though almost uniformly victorious in the field, was at last compelled to abdicate the throne by the force of events, and his own magnanimous regard for the happiness of his country.[95]

Like Emmons, the author of `The Napolead` made a liberal use of supernatural and allegorical machinery:

The Deity, Angels, Providence, Passions, Principles, Virtues, and Vices mostly constitute the machinery, wherein the first is represented as directing all events through the others, his subordinate agents. This machinery is well adapted to late events: The allegorical personages may be tolerated by the reason, which would reject in events so recent, the open interference of theological beings: These are never made visible to man; but communicate with him intellectually, . . .

The Deity, from the greatness of his character, is seldom introduced: In the first book, in answer to Philanthropy, he develops his views with respect to man: In the sixth, by directing Wisdom not to assist the counsels of the passions, he lays the foundation of Napoleon's disasters; and in the twelfth he is exhibited to show his regard for fortitude, and the man who is superior to fortune, that the moral grandeur of the hero may appear more conspicuous, and in his moral be seen a prospective physical triumph.[96]

Passages in the ''Analysis'' of Book I illustrate sufficiently the manner in which the supernatural and allegorical machinery is used in various parts of the poem:

The angel of Death delegates his ministers to confirm Napoleon's determination to invade Russia. Philanthropy grieved at the prospect of war, implores the Deity to pre-

95 *Ibid.*, pp. vi-vii.
96 *Ibid.*, pp. iv-v.

vent it, who refuses her request — while Napoleon raises armies preparatory to hostilities — Policy advises him how to proceed, and solicits Intrigue to aid him. . . . Then Napoleon, agreeable to the advice of Policy, demands of Alexander through his minister the adoption of the continental System in terms calculated to offend. . . . Napoleon after an interview with his wife and child proceeds to his army.[97]

The confusion of imagery and action in the poem seems to be partly due to the poet's desire to include all epic types he can cull from the literature of the past. He would neglect neither Homer nor Virgil; neither Spenser nor Milton — nor even Barlow. In accordance with epic usage he begins with an invocation to the muse:

> Sing heavenly muse, of arms, and him who mov'd
> All Europe, warring on the Russian realm,
> By federate kings constrain'd; his empire's fall,
> His passive valor midst the storms of fate,
> And moral grandeur: — Aid ye deathless powers,
> And give to immortality the song! [98]

The approximately ten thousand lines of blank verse comprised in the twelve books of *The Napolead* are heavy with a bewildering array of supernatural beings drawn indiscriminately from classic mythology, the Bible, and conventional allegory. Jove, taking a hand in the conduct of events, makes use of Uriel to send a message to Wisdom.[99] Jove's thunderbolts are intrusted to the care of Gabriel, his lieutenant.[100] At times, however, "th' Almighty sovereign" — that is, the God of the Bible — is revealed, as in Milton, omnipotent, but refusing to prevent man from working out his own doom.[101] Mars, Phoebus, Aurora, and

---

[97] *Ibid.*, p. 11.
[98] *Ibid.*, Book I, p. 11.
[99] *Ibid.*, Book VI, p. 154.
[100] *Ibid.*, Book VI, p. 164.
[101] For example, *ibid.*, Book I, p. 14.

other classical figures are mingled with a multitude of personified virtues and passions. Like Homer's gods, the allegorical personages mingle in battle, aiding or opposing the Emperor. At the end of the poem, Wisdom reports in heaven the downfall of Napoleon and entreats that his virtues be rewarded by his reinstatement on the French throne, whereupon —

> from a cloud of living gold, sublime,
> Jehovah blaz'd insufferably bright [102]

as he foretold the Emperor's fate.

Although Genin's verse is highly ornate and bombastic, a close imitation of conventional figures and phrasing saves him from the most glaring faults of Emmons. But, in spite of its lesser bulk, *The Napolead* is sufficiently wearisome and, next to *The Fredoniad*, offers, perhaps, the most tedious reading to be found in the whole range of Western poetry.

## IV

There was, before 1841, a vast amount of verse of other kinds than satire and epic, but for the most part so little marked by its Western origin that it might have been the product of almost any English-speaking community.

As early as 1801, William Littell, a Kentucky lawyer, had contributed to the newspaper press [103] a series of commonplace verses, some original, some translated, and others imitated from foreign models; and in 1814 these fugitive pieces were gathered together to form a small section in the author's *Festoons of Fancy, Consisting of Compositions Amatory, Sentimental and Humorous*. A much more famous poet in his day, and almost as early as Littell, was John Milton Harney, author of *Crystalina; a Fairy Tale*

---

[102] *Ibid.*, Book XII, p. 342.

[103] See, for example, *Ky. Gaz.*, Aug. 31, and Sept. 7, 14, and 21, 1801.

(1816), founded, the reader is told, chiefly upon super-
stitions of the Scottish Highlanders.[104]

Moses Guest had written most, but not all, of his verses
before migrating to the West. *Poems on Several Occasions*
(1823) was published with extracts from the author's
journal relating his voyages and travels, and ending with
a description of Cincinnati. Of the metrical pieces, some
had been completed as early as the period of the Revolutionary War, while others certainly belong to the time of
the author's residence in Ohio.[105] Among them are homely
jingles, acrostical praise of Washington, epigrammatic
satire on George III, and dull religious effusions. Indian
relics found near Cincinnati were the inspiration of some
blank verse. "On Viewing the Falls of Ohio," another
purely Western poem, contains, instead of the customary
tribute to the romantic beauty of the Ohio, a shrewd dis-
sertation on the commercial advantages of a canal for river
traffic. Such was the stuff of this volume of which over
twelve hundred copies are said to have been sold within
five months.[106]

*The Poetical Works of Elizabeth Margaret Chandler*,
edited by Benjamin Lundy in 1836, contains the post-
humous verse of an unpretentious Quakeress who was an
antislavery enthusiast — she was also the author of a
book of *Essays* designed to forward the cause of abolition.[107]
During her residence in Michigan — from 1830 until her

[104] John Milton Harney, *Crystalina*, 1816, preface.

[105] For evidence that Guest had arrived in Cincinnati by 1821,
see his advertisement in *Liberty Hall*, Mar. 31, 1821. His journal,
noticed above, is dated Cincinnati, May 17th, 1823 (*Poems on Several Occasions*, 1823, p. 160). For comment on the date of some
of his earlier poems, see *Poems on Several Occasions*, second ed.,
1824, "Address to the Reader."

[106] Guest, *Poems on Several Occasions*, second ed., 1824, p. iv.

[107] Elizabeth Margaret Chandler, *Essays, Philanthropic and Moral*,
1836.

death, some four years later — she wrote much of her poetry.[108] Most of her verses are sermons against slavery. Some are about the Indians. Little that she wrote, however, shows a peculiarly Western character. In general her poetry abounds in feeble, tawdry images; and it is full of platitudes and sentimentality. Yet there is in it, sometimes, a certain pleasing simplicity and gentleness which perhaps reflects the religious temperament of the author.

William Ross Wallace, perhaps for a time, in later years, the most famous of Western poets,[109] had little to say of the West beyond what was contained in the first poem in his collection called *The Battle of Tippecanoe, Triumphs of Science, and Other Poems* (1837). And, as for this first poem, it was a grandiose composition which had been recited at Battle Ground and was printed with a dedication to William Henry Harrison. "The Triumphs of Science," a long piece which also appeared as a separate publication,[110] glorifies scientific achievement, with a touch of patriotic sentiment. Among the miscellaneous poems in the volume there are some verses "On the Re-launching of the Constitution," which seem intended as a triumphant echo of Holmes's protest, and are written in the same metrical form and with the same fervid patriotism that characterize the "Old Ironsides." "Villani" tells a story of the painter of the Crucifixion in the Vatican, who, that he might produce a realistic picture, crucified his model. "Childe Harold" echoes the fame of Byron, and contains,

[108] For her life, see *The Poetical Works of Elizabeth Margaret Chandler*, 1836, "Memoir," by Benjamin Lundy, pp. 7-44.

[109] For Poe's too enthusiastic praise, see *The Works of Edgar Allan Poe*, ed. E. C. Stedman and G. E. Woodberry, 1914, VIII, 345-346.

[110] *The Triumphs of Science, a Poem, Delivered before the Whig Society of Hanover College, at their Anniversary, Wednesday Evening, Sept. 28, 1836*, 1837.

incidentally, some of Wallace's best lines.[111]  Among the other poems are one in blank verse called "The Possessions of God;" one on "Italy," suggested by Goethe's "Mignon;" "The Goblet," such praise of song and wine as was little known in the West after the days of Thomas Johnson; and the melodramatic "Dash down the Harp," with which the book ends.

Otway Curry's *The Lore of the Past* (1838), a minor performance by a writer who contributed much to the periodicals of the time, leaves the pioneer country for a pleasant, but pointless, excursion through ancient history. In James Warner Ward's *Yorick, and Other Poems,* published in the same year, the title piece, with its setting changing from East to West, is an extravagant love tale in which Byron's flippancy and sentimentality are not happily imitated.  The mood of sentimental melancholy is dominant in several of the other poems of this volume.

No doubt by far the best of those whom we may call the imitative and conventional versifiers of the pioneer period was William Davis Gallagher, most of whose poetry was included in the three numbers of *Erato* (1835-1837).  The very title was probably an echo of Percival's *Clio,* and the poems themselves are often clearly done under the inspiration of the prominent poets of the time; nevertheless they are almost, if not quite, the best verses written on the frontier.  Moreover, it is not impossible that Gallagher, in his turn, exerted some influence on Eastern writers, particularly on Poe, who was certainly well acquainted with the Western poet's work.[112]  "The Revellers," first published in 1832[113] and reprinted in *Erato, Number I,* bears

[111] See below, Chapter IX, footnote 88.

[112] Edgar Allan Poe, "A Chapter on Autography," *The Works of Edgar Allan Poe,* ed. E. C. Stedman and G. E. Woodberry, 1914, IX, 271.

[113] *The Cincinnati Mirror and Ladies' Parterre,* Jan. 21, 1832.

some striking resemblances to Poe's "The Conqueror
Worm," of eleven years later,[114] as well as to his short
story "The Masque of the Red Death," published in
1842.[115] The third and sixth stanzas of "The Revellers"
are here given as first printed:

"Cheer, comrades, cheer!" "We drink to Life,
"And we do not fear to die!"
Just then a rushing sound was heard,
As of spirits sweeping by —
And presently the latch flew up,
And the door flew open wide —
And a stranger strode within the hall,
With an air of martial pride.

. . . . . .

He struck — and the stranger's guise fell off,
And a phantom form stood there,
A grinning, and ghastly, and horrible thing,
With rotten and mildew'd hair:
And they struggled awhile, till the stranger blew
A blast of his withering breath;
And the Bacchanal fell at the phantom's feet,
And his conqueror was — DEATH!

But Gallagher's principal achievement was his nature
poetry, which is sometimes striking for its descriptive
power, as in these lines from "The Mountain Paths":

Morn on the hill-tops! Hark!
The low of kine swells up from yon green vale,
With song of meadow-lark,

---

[114] *Graham's Magazine*, XXII, 32 (Jan., 1843). It has been
suggested (J. H. Whitty, *The Complete Poems of Edgar Allan Poe*,
1911, p. 224) that Poe's poem was inspired by Spencer Wallace
Cone's "The Proud Ladye," reviewed by Poe in *Burton's Gentleman's Magazine*, VI, 294 (June, 1840). But aside from its use of
the phrase "the conqueror worm," Cone's poem bears less striking
resemblance to Poe's, I think, than does Gallagher's.

[115] *Graham's Lady's and Gentleman's Magazine*, XX, 257-259
(May, 1842).

And merry note of quail;
And the 'hip-halloo!' of the wild cow-boy,
Comes, soft and musical, and full of joy.[116]

Something of the same feeling which Lowell put into his
much later verses "To a Dandelion" is to be found in
Gallagher's poem "To an Early Spring Flower":

To me, dear art thou, herald-flower! No rich,
And gaudy coloring, hast thou; thy leaves
Have not the rainbow-brightness, nor the deep
And dazzling hue, of those which throng the earth
In summer.[117]

Perhaps, however, the most notable lines Gallagher wrote
are these, describing the change from the torrid noon of
an Ohio August to the mildness of the evening which
follows:

Flame-like, the long mid-day —
With not so much of sweet air as hath stirr'd
    The down upon the spray,
    Where rests the panting bird,
Dozing away the hot and tedious noon,
With fitful twitter, sadly out of tune.

                .   .   .   .   .   .

    Slow, now, along the plain,
Creeps the cool shade, and on the meadow's edge;
    The kine are forth again,
    The bird flits in the hedge:
Now in the molten west sinks the hot sun.
Welcome, mild Eve! — the sultry day is done.[118]

Nor are the three volumes without some more essentially
Western materials. The scenery of the backwoods and
the rapid growth of civilization there are praised with true

---

[116] William Davis Gallagher, *Erato, Number II*, 1835, p. 43.

[117] *Ibid.*, p. 44.

[118] *Ibid.*, from "August," pp. 49-50. Gallagher, who was probably familiar with Keats, may have drawn a part of the first stanza
here quoted from "Hyperion," Book I, ll. 7-10.

sectional loyalty; [119] and the well-worn theme of Indian captivity joined to a love story is reworked, with eighteenth century Kentucky as its setting.[120]

Over forty years after the three numbers of *Erato* had been published, Gallagher selected "The Mountain Paths" and "August" for republication in his *Miami Woods A Golden Wedding and Other Poems* (1881). The collection, published several decades after the close of the period with which this account is concerned, contained a significant poem, "Miami Woods," the first part of which, written in 1839, consists of contemplation and praise of the mystical quality of nature somewhat after the fashion of Wordsworth, whose influence was beginning to be felt in the West when Gallagher wrote.

Gallagher, than whom no one sought more diligently to promote the growth of a literature on the frontier, was also the compiler of *Selections from the Poetical Literature of the West*, published in 1841, just after the close of the period which is the subject of this discussion. In this anthology he includes selections from thirty-eight writers of verse, most of whom had published only in the periodicals. "Much the greater number of the persons selected from," says Gallagher, "are either western born or western educated, or both; and all of them who are now living, with a single exception, are citizens of this section of the Union." [121]  Among those from whom the largest number of selections are taken are Gallagher himself, James H. Perkins, Otway Curry, Mrs. Amelia B. Welby, Frederick W. Thomas, Thomas H. Shreve, Ephraim Peabody, and George D. Prentice.  The list is almost entirely restricted

---

[119] *Ibid.*, "Our Western Land," pp. 25-32.

[120] Gallagher, *Erato, Number III*, 1837, "Cadwallen: a Tale of the Dark and Bloody Ground," pp. 5-41.

[121] Gallagher, *Selections from the Poetical Literature of the West*, 1841, p. 7.

to writers of conventional lyrics. Doubtless it never occurred to Gallagher to include a collection of river songs and Kentucky ballads or other homely verses of the people which might today have been a treasured record. The vigorous, but unedifying, satires of Thomas Johnson and the vagaries of Umphraville were either neglected or unknown; and the racy satires of Peirce were assuredly passed over intentionally. As for the ponderous epics of Emmons and Genin, they could hardly have afforded him a quotable line. He fell back upon the makers of polite, inoffensive lyrical verses, belonging, for the most part, to a worn-out tradition of mediocrity that early poisoned the springs of native Western poetry.

## V

There remain to be noticed a group of poets who, in contrast with the writers just discussed, dealt almost wholly in Western materials, but whose manner was scarcely less conventional and imitative. They transformed the lore of the backwoods into sentimental drawing-room verse. "The west," said a contemporary critic,

is a new field for the poet, and a field filled with rich materials; but he that would use them must be a western poet; he must quit the leading-strings of the British masters, and walk abroad by himself.[122]

The poets of this group heeded only half the admonition.

Without too much insistence on the point, we may, perhaps, trace the tradition of Indian lore in Western frontier verse back to the days of the British officer Depeyster, who, while stationed on service at Detroit, at Michilimackinac, and on the shores of Lake Michigan, from about 1776 to 1785, amused himself and his companions with rimes, years later gathered into a volume for publication in Scot-

---

[122] James Hall? "Literary Notices," *The Western Monthly Magazine*, I, 335 (July, 1833).

land. "The Speech to the Lake Indians, which begins this little volume," said the author,

was (from recollection, the day after it had been [spok]en) turned into metre at the request *d'une chere compagne* [*sic*] *de voyage*, for whose amusement in that remote part of the world several songs, descriptive of the habits of the natives, were likewise composed.[123]

It is, perhaps, not without significance that, when the Western school of poetry more properly described as Indian lore romancers began to flourish, about 1819, the setting was the same Northwest which Depeyster had celebrated, and that the poets who belonged to this group were residents of the same section of the frontier. It was in that part of the West that the stream of migration had scarcely been felt until the important Indian wars were over. The settlers of that region were not, like the people of Kentucky and Ohio, embittered by the memory of fierce encounters with the savages. It was possible there to think of the Indian as a romantic figure.

In Henry Whiting's [124] *Ontwa, the Son of the Forest* (1822), what passed as the legendary material of Indian lore was wedded to the diction and octosyllabics of Sir Walter Scott. A brief introductory account of the author's voyage with an Indian guide through the Great Lakes and by way of the Fox, Wisconsin, and Mississippi Rivers to the Falls of St. Anthony, is followed by a long legend narrated by the Indian guide. The influence of Chateaubriand is strongly exhibited by the poem; and not by chance, for it is clear that there was a conscious attempt at imitating the French romancer. "With respect to the composition of ONTWA," says the author,

---

[123] A. S. Depeyster, *Miscellanies, by an Officer*, 1813, I, advertisement.

[124] The poem, though published anonymously, was at once known as Whiting's (*Detroit Gaz.*, Feb. 15, 1822).

the same remark may be applied to it which Chateaubriand applies to Atala, that "it was written in the desert, and under the huts of the savages." . . . The tradition on which the story of ONTWA is founded, unavoidably led to an apparent adoption of one of the incidents of Atala. . . . in this instance, an attempt was made to imitate its eloquent author.[125]

Over forty pages of notes, furnishing illustrations of Indian life and of Western history, accompanied the poem. *Sannillac*, another Indian tale published by the same author nine years after *Ontwa*, was, like its predecessor, a testimony to the popularity of Scott's metrical romances. Part I, following some introductory lines, begins with a description, which, with slight alteration, might be made to do service in *The Lady of the Lake*:

> On Huron's wave there stands an isle,
> Which lifts on high its tower-like pile,
>
> . . . . . .
>
> This isle — by wild tradition long
> Made theme of forest tale and song —
> In ev'ry age has caught the eye
> Of Indian, as he wander'd by,
>
> . . . . . .
>
> Gliding along this limpid sheen,
> A light and lonely bark was seen.[126]

In this bark is an Indian girl, Wona, who, like Scott's Ellen, becomes a central figure in a tale of love and adventure. The young hero, Sannillac, is the Indian counterpart of James Fitz-James, though more successful in his wooing, and with no Roderick Dhu or Malcom Græme to challenge his right. The Indian ceremonials and the occasional songs woven into the narrative are again somewhat in the manner of Scott; and so are the opening and closing

---

[125] Henry Whiting, *Ontwa*, 1822, p. v.

[126] Whiting, *Sannillac*, 1831, pp. 3 and 5.

verses, written in longer measure. But there are many
original passages and no lack of stirring incident in Whiting's poem.

Samuel Beach's *Escalala* (1824), though it did not appear until long after the author's removal to the West,
was written, partly in the East and partly in Michigan.[127]
The tragic story of a mythical Norwegian colony established among the aborigines of the Ohio Valley in the
Middle Ages, together with a description of the customs
of the savages, might almost as well have been written anywhere else as in the West. As in the case of Whiting's
poems, Scott's influence was marked.

Poems dealing with the encroachment of the white settlers upon the Indians or with characteristics of the pioneer
people, were not often published in independent form.
Henry Rowe Schoolcraft's *Transallegania, or the Groans of
Missouri* (1821) is an awkward, extravagantly fanciful
account of the ire of the King of metals when awakened by
the sounds of mighty currents of immigration surging
across the Missouri country. A council of the metals from
all the Western country is called to discuss resistance. The
clash of the stones in the debate which ensues is so great
that New Madrid (which had once been devastated by an
earthquake) sinks, and the encroaching immigrants are so
frightened that their advance is delayed, at least for a time.
Schoolcraft was also the author of a poem called "The Rise
of the West, or a Prospect of the Mississippi Valley"
(1830), published jointly with some verses apparently by
Henry Whiting. To the latter author has been ascribed a

[127] Beach had completed a first draft of the poem by 1820, apparently while living in New York. By 1822, when he was a resident of Mount Clemens, Mich., he had "remodelled parts of his
poem, carefully revised and prepared it for the press." In 1825 it
was declared by a Detroit editor that the work had "in part, been
written in this territory." For the facts here cited, see *Detroit
Gaz.*, June 14 and Sept. 13, 1822; and May 3, 1825.

poem called *The Emigrant* (1819),[128] which begins with a song of contentment —

> Thus sung the emigrated man,
> Now fixed at last in Michigan —

and continues with an account of the emigrant's success in establishing himself in the new country. *The Age of Steam* (1830), also said to be Whiting's,[129] is a humorous extravaganza originally recited at a Fourth of July celebration on board a steamboat at Detroit.

Frederick William Thomas, later known as a novelist, was the author of a Byronic imitation called *The Emigrant, or Reflections while Descending the Ohio* (1833). The poet, as he passes down the river for the first time, recalls the scenes here enacted during the Indian wars of Boone and the earliest settlers. He pauses to pay tribute to Blennerhasset, "Isle of the beautiful." He wanders wide, under Childe Harold's guidance, in his musings on the spirit of human liberty —

> A tear for Poland! many tears for her
> Who rose so nobly, and so nobly fell!
> E'en, at her broken shrine, a worshipper,
> In dust and ashes, let me say farewell!
> Farewell! brave spirits! — Earth! and can it be,
> Thy sons beheld them struggling to be free —
> Unaided, saw them in their blood downtrod —
> Nations, ye are accurst! be merciful, Oh God! [130]

Something of the darker aspects of frontier character are to be found in the title-piece of Charles A. Jones's *The Outlaw, and other Poems* (1835), the scene of which is the notorious Cave-in-Rock, on the lower Ohio. The shorter

---

[128] See MS. note on copy in the Burton Historical Collection, Public Library, Detroit.

[129] S. Austin Allibone, *A Critical Dictionary of English Literature*, 1871, III, 2699.

[130] Frederick William Thomas, *The Emigrant*, 1833, stanza lxxxi.

poems which appear in the same volume are, however, on conventional themes.  Jones's verses are not without merit, and were highly praised by a contemporary critic.[131]  Not so much can be said for *The Banks of the Ohio* (1823), a prize poem by Mrs. Lard, of Indiana,[132] in which there is attempted a rapid survey of the history of the Ohio Valley from the earliest times until the day in which the author lived.

*Harp of the West* (1839), the work of Joseph S. Welsh, another Indiana writer, affords many examples of the extremely conventional trappings characteristic of most frontier poetry which pretended to local color.  Welsh's first purpose was to teach morality and patriotism.  "If," he says,

in presenting this volume to his fellow citizens, the author can succeed in calling forth a train of moral reflections, establish one sentiment for virtuous and noble actions, or implant one patriotic feeling, founded upon a genuine love of country, — a country whose soil has been moistened by the blood of our gallant fathers — he will feel himself amply rewarded for his arduous labors.[133]

The greater part of the volume is devoted to Western themes, but the homely details of pioneer life are scarcely recognizable under the classical veneer of Welsh's style. His backwoodsman dwelt

> Where great Missouri, ponderous, deep and strong,
> Resistless pours its rapid streams along,

and his cottage

> stood,
> Embower'd in groves that kiss'd the winding flood.

---

131 *The Western Monthly Magazine*, IV, 273-275 (Oct., 1835).

132 For a biographical note, see Mrs. Lard, *The Banks of the Ohio*, 1823, p. 2.

133 Joseph S. Welsh, *Harp of the West: a Volume of Poems*, 1839, p. 10.

The homecoming of the pioneer to his cabin is described in verses which likewise recall the minor writers of the age of Pope:

Full many an eve, as homeward from the chase,
Laden with spoil, he urg'd his eager pace,
Those lovely children flew to greet their sire,
Welcom'd him home, and trimm'd the blazing fire.
With wonder heard him paint the scenes he saw
Till midnight shades around creation draw;
Then join'd the song of praise their parents sing,
And sunk with guileless hearts — on slumber's downy
    wing.[134]

As for narrative interest, in Welsh's poetry it is subordinated to the teachings of the moralist, uttered always with the same stilted formality. An adventure with the Indians, of which the author makes only a stiff, ineffective passage, serves to introduce an account of the reunion of the backwoodsman with his wife and children, whom he has rescued:

His wife unloos'd, his children clasp'd him round,
While tears of joy descending bath'd the ground.
"Receive," he cried, "my thanks, Propitious Power,
That gave me victory in this fearful hour!
Teach me no more to murmur and repine
At thy blest will and Providence divine!"
Fraught with this prayer, they trac'd their devious road,
To find once more, and bless — their distant lov'd abode.[135]

Perhaps no verse written in the West, with the possible exception of Thomas Johnson's ribald rimes, contained a truer picture of the life of the backwoodsman than did John Finley's "The Hoosier's Nest," which may also deserve the distinction of being the best-known poem produced on the frontier. Here is Finley's account of the

---

[134] For this passage and the lines quoted above, see *ibid.*, p. 70.
[135] *Ibid.*, p. 74.

reception of a traveller by the inmates of an Indiana cabin:

> The stranger stooped to enter in,
> The entrance closing with a pin;
> And manifested strong desire
> To sit down by the log-heap fire,
> Where half a dozen Hoosieroons,
> With mush and milk, tin-cups and spoons,
> White heads, bare feet and dirty faces,
> Seemed much inclined to keep their places;
> But madam, anxious to display
> Her rough but undisputed sway,
> Her offspring to the ladder led,
> And cuffed the youngsters up to bed.

And then follows what may be taken as something near a true picture of the interior familiar to a pioneer settler:

> Invited shortly to partake,
> Of venison, milk, and johnny-cake,
> The stranger made a hearty meal,
> And glances round the room would steal.
> One side was lined with divers garments,
> The other, spread with skins of varmints;
> Dried pumpkins overhead were strung,
> Where venison hams in plenty hung;
> Two rifles placed above the door,
> Three dogs lay stretched upon the floor —
> In short, the domicil was rife
> With specimens of Hoosier life.
> The host, who center'd his affections
> On game, and range and quarter sections,
> Discoursed his weary guest for hours
> Till Somnus' all-composing powers,
> Of sublunary cares bereft 'em;
> And then I come away, and left 'em.[136]

This fragmentary bit of verse, though written simply as a New Year's address for an Indianapolis paper, was not

---

[136] This and the preceding quotation are taken from Coggeshall, *op. cit.*, pp. 84-85.

only "published in a majority of the newspapers of America," but was "often quoted," we are told, "in England as a graphic specimen of backwoods literature." [137]   With its fidelity to the details of pioneer life and its disregard for conventional poetic tinsel, it was, however, far from being a characteristic "specimen of backwoods literature."   In poetry, its kind was — unfortunately, one may believe — extremely rare.   Yet there was possible, it may be argued, no higher aim for these early writers of verse than simple realism.   A higher artistic achievement was beyond their reach; none was able to fulfill Keats's prophecy of a poet in the West who should dare what no one dared and be bard completely.

---

[137] *Ibid.*, p. 83.

# CHAPTER VIII

## DRAMA

No practis'd actor here your passions charms,
Nor magic brush the vary'd scen'ry warms;
Our house, our equipage, our all but rude,
And little, 'faith, but our intentions good.

THESPIS, the father of our mimic art,
For want of better, ranted in a cart.
To him all ages still the palm resign,
And hail him founder of an art divine.
Thus when the forests of this infant world
Shall from our fertile hills be proudly hurl'd;
When commerce shall her golden wings expand,
And waft our produce to each distant land;
When wealthy cities shall extensive rise,
And lofty spires salute our western skies;
When costly theatres shall loud resound
With music, mirth, & ev'ry joyous sound;
T will be remember'd that in days of yore,
Between a ragged roof and sorry floor,
The laughing muse here for the first time sate,
And kindly deign'd to cheer our infant state.

— Prologue spoken at the opening of the Cincinnati Theatre, October 1, 1801.

## I

Before the end of the eighteenth century, amateur theatricals were known in Kentucky. At least two performances of the kind were announced at Lexington early in 1799. On the first of March in that year, the comedy of

*The Busy Body* and a farce, *Love à la mode*, were to be
presented by the students at Transylvania University; and
four days later a comedy called *He would be a Soldier* and
a farce, *All the World's a Stage*, were to be performed —
presumably by amateurs and possibly, though not likely,
by the student players — at the Court House in the same
town.[1] That these were not the first theatricals in Lexington is shown by the promise that additions would be made
to the scenery at this time. In November, plays were
again given at the Court House.[2]

But there has as yet come to light only a very slender
body of facts from which to draw a history of amateur
theatricals in Lexington for some years thereafter. Some
of the few notices which are extant suggest that the town
possessed, by about the beginning of the nineteenth century, a place commonly known as "the Theatre." Plays
were advertised to be given there in May, 1801,[3] and again
in January, 1802.[4] By November 9, 1808, a "New Theatre"
was opened in which the Thespian Society performed.[5] It
is probable that Noble Luke Usher, who was later to have
an important part in organizing a professional circuit in
Kentucky, was both owner and manager of the new establishment.[6] From this time amateur plays were given in
considerable number until the coming of what was likely
the first professional troupe of actors, in 1810. The Thes-

[1] The entertainments for both dates are advertised in *Ky. Gaz.*,
Feb. 28, 1799.

[2] *Ibid.*, Nov. 14 and 21, 1799.

[3] *Stewart's Kentucky Herald*, May 19, 1801.

[4] *Ky. Gaz.*, Jan. 1, 1802.

[5] *Ibid.*, Nov. 8, 1808. For another performance the same year,
see *ibid.*, Dec. 6, 1808.

[6] See William Dunlap, *A History of the American Theatre*, 1832,
p. 348. Dunlap states that the theatre opened in October. *Cf.* also
N. M. Ludlow, *Dramatic Life as I Found it*, 1880, p. 86.

pian Society,[7] the Military Society,[8] the Roscian Society,[9] and the students of Transylvania [10] performed during these years. After the coming of the professional troupes, however, the amateur players, if extant press notices may be taken as even a slight indication of the total number of performances, reappeared usually only at long intervals,[11] and even then were at times supported by a few strolling professionals.

Of other important towns in the West, the first to show an interest in amateur theatricals was probably Cincinnati, where the early establishment of the drama was perhaps due to the fact that a garrison was stationed there. On October 1, 1801, less than three years after the date of what seem to be the earliest extant notices of Lexington theatricals, the "Cincinnati Theatre" was opened, with the performance of O'Keefe's comic opera *The Poor Soldier*,[12] to-

[7] *Ky. Gaz.*, July 4, Aug. 1, Sept. 19 and 26, and Oct. 3, 1809; Mar. 13, Apr. 17, and July 3 and 10, 1810.

[8] *Ibid.*, May 1 and 8, and June 5, 1810.

[9] *Ibid.*, Sept. 11, 18, and 25, 1810. Probably the advertisements in the *Gazette* of Oct. 9 and 16 following are by the same players.

[10] For a performance as a benefit for charity students, see *ibid.*, Oct. 2, 1810.

[11] See *ibid.*, May 26 (play for benefit of the Lexington volunteers in War of 1812; the actors were members of the volunteer company) and June 9, 1812; Jan. 13, and Feb. 10 and 17, 1825; and Aug. 3, 1837. For a juvenile performance of *Pizarro* in a schoolhouse on Upper Street sometime after 1811, see Samuel D. M'Cullough's MS. Reminiscences of Lexington, in the Lexington Public Library.

[12] For advance notice and later account of the performance in some detail — the opening prologue, which I have quoted only in part, is given in full — see *The Western Spy*, Sept. 30 and Oct. 10, 1801. The prologue spoken at the opening apologizes for the primitive nature of the playhouse, but prophesies the future fame of this occasion. The entertainment included, besides a comic opera and a musical interlude, an original song (the words are printed *ibid.*, Oct.

gether with an unnamed "musical interlude." Probably it
was the same group of actors who, within the five months following, appeared on no less than three occasions,[13] repeat-
ing *The Poor Soldier* and giving at least one other comic
opera. Their enthusiasm for drama was, however, thwarted
by financial difficulties, so that February 19, 1802, was
announced as the last night of the season.

It does not seem possible to determine whether there were
theatricals in Cincinnati immediately succeeding this first
disastrous season; but by 1805 there was renewed activity
among amateur performers, who improvised a stage in a
stable loft. The Thespian Corps, as this organization was
called, performed a number of times from about August
to December of that year, enjoying the patronage of all
the citizens "of any taste, . . . a play, in this new
settled country, being a novelty." [14] A contemporary observer, whose chronology, however, is extremely vague,
gives an account of a debating society in existence for
some years after about 1806 or 1809, which performed
"private theatricals, the first probably got up in Cincin-

17, 1801), which was sung between the plays. Killgore and Seamons,
whose names appear in the newspaper advertisement, were, perhaps,
the managers of the company. According to Francis B. Heitman
(*Historical Register and Dictionary of the United States Army*, 1903,
I, 597), a Charles Kilgore [*sic*] of Kentucky had served as a lieutenant in the regular army during 1799 and 1800, and was honorably
discharged in June of the latter year.

13 Advertised in *The Western Spy*, Dec. 5 and 26, 1801; and Feb.
13, 1802.

14 *The Trial of Charles Vattier*, 1807, pp. 57-58, n. For other interesting references to the plays of this season, see the testimony of
witnesses, *ibid.*, pp. 57-58, 67-69, 87, 106, and 112. A few performances are here mentioned as having been given by a Mr. Smith
before the Thespian Corps was formed. For the citations here given,
I am indebted to Mr. W. H. Cathcart, of the Western Reserve Historical Society.

nati.''[15] Daniel Drake, the future ''Franklin of Cincinnati,'' is said to have appeared on one such occasion.

In 1811 professional players appeared in Cincinnati; and there is apparently no further record of amateur performers until 1814, when the members of the Cincinnati Thespian Society were urged to attend a public meeting designed to arouse sentiment for the establishment of a theatre.[16] This attempt to gain popular support for theatricals seems to have achieved some success, for not only did the society perform twice in the following February, but by the middle of March they were in possession of a new playhouse. And a few months later, after a season by professional players, the Thespians advertised further exhibitions.[17]

For another year the amateur players maintained an organized attempt at drama [18] in spite of the inroads of strolling actors. From this time, however, professional companies rapidly strengthened their hold upon the stage in Cincinnati; and amateur plays were, so far as newspaper notices show, almost a thing of the past. Later entertainments of the kind were usually attempted only as a means of raising funds for charitable, patriotic, or civic projects.[19]

[15] Edward D. Mansfield, *Memoirs of the Life and Services of Daniel Drake*, 1855, pp. 72-73.

[16] *Spirit of the West*, Dec. 13; and *Liberty Hall*, Dec. 13, 1814.

[17] For the amateur plays given during 1815, see *Liberty Hall*, Feb. 18; *Spirit of the West*, Feb. 25; and *Liberty Hall*, Mar. 14, Aug. 28, Sept. 4 and 11, and Dec. 4, 1815.

[18] For performances by ''the Thespian Corps'' advertised to be given in 1816, see *Liberty Hall*, Dec. 25, 1815; and Jan. 1, 3, 8, Mar. 18 and 25, and Apr. 1, 1816. A writer in *Liberty Hall*, for Dec. 9, 1816, urged the Thespians to attempt another winter season, but probably without result. Later in the same month a professional company appeared for a brief time.

[19] The Thespian performance of Feb. 20, 1824, in which a regular professional company assisted, was for the benefit of the Greeks,

Doubtless there also continued to be, from time to time, private performances — such theatricals as those for which Mrs. Trollope was responsible during her residence in Cincinnati — [20] but long before 1841 the conditions which had earlier accounted for the public exhibitions by nonprofessional players had ceased to exist.

The history of amateur theatricals in other important towns of the West during the pioneer period — Louisville, St. Louis, and Detroit — is obscure. In Louisville, it is altogether likely that such plays were given before 1808, about which time, we are told, a dramatic institution was formed by a company of citizens [21] (just possibly for the purpose of arranging for performances by professional actors). The fact that the professional troupe which was in the habit of appearing, not only at Louisville, but at Lexington and Frankfort as well, was known in Louisville

though the reappearance of the amateurs on Mar. 5 following was for the profit of some of the players. On Mar. 29 of the same year the Thespian Society of Newport crossed the river to play for the benefit of Symmes's fantastic project for a polar expedition; and in April the Cincinnati Thespians attempted plays to raise funds for completing the Cincinnati Theatre, a building in use by professional companies. The plays here mentioned are advertised in *Liberty Hall* for Feb. 20, Mar. 5, 23, and 26, and Apr. 9, 1824; *The National Republican and Ohio Political Register*, June 10, 1825; and *Cinc. Daily Gaz.*, Oct. 22, 1838. In June, 1825, the Thespian Corps played for the benefit of persons who had suffered on account of a fire; and in Oct., 1838, the Gentlemen Amateurs advertised a benefit for disabled firemen. Proof that a Thespian Society was active for some time in 1835 is to be found in MS. Minutes City Council (in office of the City Clerk, Cincinnati), VII, 436 (Aug. 12, 1835). According to this record, the amateurs complained that they had been fined $20 by the mayor for charging a small admission fee, and asked release from the penalty.

[20] W. H. Venable, *Beginnings of Literary Culture in the Ohio Valley*, 1891, pp. 354-355. *Cf.* also Joseph Cowell, *Thirty Years Passed among the Players in England and America*, 1844, p. 89.

[21] *The Louisville Directory*, for 1832, p. 139.

about 1814 as the Thespian Corps [22] would, however, argue
that there was at the time no amateur organization in that
town.   Yet there seems not to be conclusive evidence, and
it is possible that a dramatic entertainment given in the
autumn of 1814 was by such a company.[23]   At all events,
there are only the slightest traces of amateur theatricals
during the remainder of the pioneer period.   In 1824 a
society of young men announced that, having obtained
permission of Mr. Drake, manager of the theatre, they
would "attempt the performance of a dramatic entertainment" as a Whitsuntide fête ; [24] but we hear nothing more
of these players.   Nor is it likely that anything of importance resulted from a meeting in January, 1830, of such
young men as were in favor of forming a Thespian Association; [25] if such a society came into existence, it must
have had but little opportunity for prosperity in that year
which was remarkable in Louisville's early dramatic history for the almost continuous activity of professional
companies.   Between 1830 and 1841, among the great
number of newspaper notices of dramatic performances,
there seems to be none which proves that an amateur
theatrical society was in existence.

In St. Louis, plays were advertised to be given, probably
by amateur actors, as early as January 6, 1815, when the
Court House was to be used for the presentation of the
comedy *The School for Authors* and a farce; and other

22 *The Western Courier*, Feb. 7, 1814.

23 *Ibid.*, Aug. 29, 1814.  Except for a few fragmentary files of
various papers and for a practically complete file of *The Western
Courier* extending from Nov. 30, 1813, to Sept. 26, 1816, I have
consulted no Louisville newspapers for the period prior to July 28,
1818, from which date the excellent file of the *Public Advertiser*
(later *The Louisville Public Advertiser*) in the library of the University of Chicago affords a valuable record.

24 *Lou. Pub. Adv.*, June 5, 1824.

25 *Ibid.*, Jan. 12, 1830.

performances were announced for March 4 and 31.[26] In February, 1816, the Roscian Society exhibited plays; and on December 30 of the same year some amateurs, styling themselves the Thespian Society, were to occupy the "Theatre," which had on several occasions during the two previous months been used as a church.[27] In January, 1817, there were at least two performances by the Thespian Society.[28] The arrival, in 1818, of what was probably the first professional company in St. Louis aroused much interest in the drama; and early in the following year the Thespians announced the opening of a "New Theatre."[29] John H. Vos, who had lately been with Turner's troupe and who was the most enterprising of those interested in the "St. Louis Theatre," as this new establishment was called, succeeded so well in attracting the attention of professional players to the opening in St. Louis[30] that two such companies arrived at almost the same time and continued a ruinous rivalry until the spring of the following year.[31] The Thespians performed several times during 1820;[32] nor did the arrival of another professional company in Decem-

[26] For plays given at St. Louis in 1815, see *Mo. Gaz.*, Dec. 31, 1814; and Feb. 25 and Mar. 25, 1815.

[27] The theatrical performances are advertised *ibid.*, Feb. 10 and Dec. 28, 1816. For the use of the "Theatre" building as a church, see the same paper for Oct. 5 and 12, and Nov. 16, 1816.

[28] *Ibid.*, Jan. 11 and 18, 1817. The issue for Feb. 22, 1817, announces a grand concert of music "at the Theatre;" and the same paper for June 21 mentions a Masonic address which was to be delivered "in the building lately occupied as a theatre."

[29] *Ibid.*, Jan. 27, 1819. Another performance, to be given in the following March, is advertised *ibid.*, Mar. 10.

[30] See Vos's advertisement, *ibid.*, Mar. 31, 1819.

[31] Ludlow, *op. cit.*, pp. 184-192. Newspaper notices are lacking, but it is difficult to believe that Ludlow's detailed account of this season could have been entirely a confused memory.

[32] Thespian performances were advertised in the *Mo. Gaz.* for Feb. 2, Sept. 20, and Oct. 4 and 11, 1820.

ber [33] mark the end of the amateur period. Indeed, for a number of years after 1820, when the establishment of professional theatricals seemed assured, the Thespian exhibitions, of which, it is true, there are only scanty notices, seem to have been almost the only signs of dramatic activity. An organization styled the Thespians gave several plays in 1823; [34] the St. Louis Thespian Society was in existence in the following year; [35] and in both 1825 and 1826 the St. Louis Thespian Theatrical Association presented plays at the ''Theatre,'' on Church Street,[36] a brick house formerly occupied by the firm of Scott & Rule, and commonly known as the Old Salt-house Theatre.

From this time, however, professional theatricals were so firmly established that little more was heard of amateur companies. Yet in 1830 the regular Thespians more than once appealed to the public, and in 1832 the St. Louis Juvenile Thespians offered entertainment during what must have been an unusually dull season for theatregoers. Three years later we hear of benefit performances for rival fire companies by the adult actors and the children's company, together with at least one other performance by each group.[37] In 1837, however, with the opening of the New St. Louis Theatre by Ludlow & Smith, there began an era of such intense activity by professional players that amateur theatricals must have been carried on only with the greatest difficulty or altogether abandoned.

[33] *Ibid.*, Dec. 13, 1820.

[34] *Mo. Rep.*, Jan. 8, Feb. 5, and June 25, 1823. Entertainments of a semi-theatrical nature were given at the ''Theatre'' in July and October by a Mr. and Mrs. Dalton (*ibid.*, July 2 and Oct. 22).

[35] See *ibid.*, Sept. 6, 1824, for announcement of a business meeting of this organization.

[36] *Ibid.*, Oct. 24 and 31, 1825; Feb. 2, 1826.

[37] For amateur performances after 1826, see *St. Louis Beacon*, Oct. 21, and Nov. 4, 11, 18, and 25, 1830; *Mo. Rep.*, July 24, 1832, Feb. 24, Mar. 27, and Apr. 28, 1835; *Commercial Bulletin*, June 1, 1835.

Although the French (according to one authority) made plays in Louisiana before the English on the Atlantic coast had shown any interest in such matters,[38] this activity, if it existed, was probably confined to New Orleans, or its immediate vicinity. There seems to be no proof whatever that theatricals formed a part of the amusement of early St. Louis under either French or Spanish rule; and for Detroit, which (though isolated by its geographic position) deserves to be noticed, together with Lexington, Cincinnati, Louisville, and St. Louis, as one of the most important cultural centers of the early West, extant records show no dramatic performances before 1798, when the American soldiers were in control.[39] In that year, according to a statement made by Silas Farmer on uncertain authority, military and civic entertainments, at least some of which, it seems, were dramatic, were often given in the old council house. After passing over the record of the succeeding seventeen years in silence, the same writer tells of a theatre which was fitted up in 1816 in the upper part of a brick storehouse at the foot of Wayne Street, and stocked with scenery made by the soldiers and painted by the wives of the officers. This theatre, he asserts (without referring to any records that might confirm him), was in operation almost continuously every winter till 1830. Further vague information concerning a part of the same period is furnished by Charles Trowbridge, a citizen of Detroit during the era which he recorded, who wrote that sometime while

---

[38] John Malone, in the introduction to Oscar Wegelin's *Early American Plays*, 1900, p. vii. But according to William Dunlap, *op. cit.*, p. 348, "the French theatre of New-Orleans" was not established until 1809. It is, however, stated *ibid.*, p. 374, that "The French theatre was planted in New-Orleans as early as 1809;" and thus the possibility of an earlier date is suggested.

[39] *Cf.* Silas Farmer, *The History of Detroit and Michigan*, 1884, p. 357; and Clarence M. Burton, "Amusements of Earlier Days in Detroit," in *The City of Detroit*, 1922, II, 1405-1419.

General Macomb was in command at Detroit (1815-1821) the officers "improvised a theatre, in the upper story of a large brick storehouse belonging to the government, situated at the foot of Cass street." Both male and female parts were taken by the officers. The attendance was limited by invitation.[40] Estwick Evans, who arrived at Detroit in March, 1818, found that there was then a theatre "under the exclusive management of the military officers stationed there," who performed "for the gratuitous instruction and amusement of the public."[41] Evans, with characteristic enthusiasm, asserted that the performances he saw there were equal to the best in the country.

In 1824 there was a movement toward the founding of a Thespian Society,[42] which may or may not have been attended with some success. An ordinance of the common council passed in June, 1825, for the purpose of regulating "Theatrical and all other Exhibitions, wherein or wherefore money or any other pay or compensation is required"[43] suggests that there may have been by this time theatricals other than the private ones given by the officers; but the minutes of the council make no mention of the granting of licenses under this act until 1827, when a professional company arrived in Detroit. Not before 1837 is there indubitable evidence of renewed activity on the part of the amateurs; but on October 15 of that year there was given the opening performance of the Detroit Thespian Society, which is said to have continued its activity successfully for about four years — apparently till 1840.[44] The Thespian

40 Charles Trowbridge, *Detroit, Past and Present*, 1864, p. 14.

41 Estwick Evans, *A Pedestrious Tour*, 1819, p. 118.

42 *Detroit Gaz.*, Jan. 2, 1824. See also *ibid.*, for Jan. 9.

43 *By-laws and Ordinances of the City of Detroit, Made since the Organization of the First Common Council*, 1825, p. 52.

44 For a somewhat detailed account of this amateur society and for a reproduction of their programs for Oct. 15, and Nov. 1 and 15, 1837, see *The Detroit Tribune*, Sunday, Dec. 20, 1891, p. 11; and

theatre was a room on the upper floor of the University
Building. Among the actors, some were university students [45] and others were young men from the town. The
plays, which were given "Wednesday evenings during the
winter months," were well attended, partly, no doubt, because there was no charge for admission and because
"many straight-laced families who enjoyed a play, attended
the Thespian performances, who would not care to be seen
at the City Theatre."

Plays by amateur companies in lesser towns of the early
West were no doubt numerous. Vincennes, where a "Theatrical Association" was founded in 1814, was a center of
such activity.[46] New Harmony,[47] during the Owenite
period, was not entirely without dramatic interest. Lafayette,[48] Indianapolis,[49] Logansport,[50] Brookville,[51] and, no

_The Sunday News-Tribune_ (Detroit), Sept. 23, 1894, p. 11. Friend
Palmer, who was one of the Thespian performers, seems to have
been responsible for the preservation of some of the playbills and
probably for the details contained in the newspaper accounts here
cited.

[45] The Detroit Branch of the University of Michigan was opened
in 1838 (_Detroit Free Press_, Apr. 24 and June 2, 1838).

[46] See _The Western Sun_, Oct. 22, and Nov. 19 and 26, 1814; Jan. 7
and Mar. 25, 1815; and for later years, _passim_. These notices show
that the theatre in 1814 was "in the large room back of Mr.
Withers's Inn;" that probably the first plays seen in Vincennes were
given there on Nov. 21, 1814; that this opening season continued
irregularly till Apr. 1, 1815; and that John Ewing, G. W. Johnston,
Charles Smith, and Elihu Stout, editor of _The Western Sun_, were
managers of the amateur venture.

[47] _The New-Harmony Gazette_, Feb. 27 and Apr. 9, 1828.

[48] See Sallie Sample, MS. Early Days in Lafayette, Indiana (in
Indiana State Library), pp. 13-14.

[49] See Kate Milner Rabb, "A Hoosier Listening Post," in _The
Indianapolis Star_, Jan. 15, 1921, p. 6, col. 6.

[50] _The Logansport Herald_, Sept. 17, 1839.

[51] See Rabb, "A Hoosier Listening Post," in _The Indianapolis
Star_, Jan. 27, 1921, p. 6, col. 5.

doubt, many other Indiana towns, instituted theatricals, presumably amateur, before 1841. Dayton, Ohio; Newport and Cynthiana, Kentucky; Springfield, Illinois, and probably Chicago, were among other towns where such performances were known before 1841.[52]

## II

Perhaps a decade after amateur theatricals were first known in Lexington, straggling groups of professional players [53] crossed the Alleghenies into the frontier country. Ludlow, who came in 1815 as a member of Samuel Drake's band of adventurers, betrays in his memoirs (the most important account of the Western theatre written by a contemporary observer) not only a pardonable pride in his own achievements as a pioneer actor and manager, but a somewhat ungenerous curtness in appraising the achievements of those who had preceded him. He would not allow earlier companies a better name than irregulars or amateurs, or else he ignored them altogether.

As a matter of fact a professional troupe recruited from Montreal and Quebec had appeared in Kentucky before the end of 1810. By about the middle of December, what seems to have been the main body of this company had arrived at Lexington, where, if one may judge from a contemporary account, they received an enthusiastic welcome. "It is with sincere pleasure," wrote a contributor to the *Gazette,*

---

[52] For a Thespian performance in Dayton, see *The Gridiron* (Dayton), Nov. 21, 1822; for mention of the Thespian Society of Newport, *Liberty Hall*, Mar. 23, 1824; for Cynthiana, *Ky. Gaz.*, Nov. 14, 1836; for Springfield, *Sangamo Journal*, Dec. 3 and 24, 1836, and Jan. 14-Feb. 11, 1837, *passim.*

[53] For detailed dates and citations of newspaper notices concerning the professional companies, see the calendar at the end of this chapter (pp. 440-457).

we are at length enabled to congratulate the lovers of the
Drama, and the fashionables of the town, upon the arrival
of Mr. *Douglas*, with a company of *Theatrical performers*
from *Montreal* and *Quebec*. After an absence of eighteen
months, Mr. D. has succeeded in accomplishing the objects
of his journey, and has engaged a company sufficiently
large to form an establishment in the western country. The
citizens of Lexington and Frankfort will be gratified during the present winter with their performances, which in
addition to the usual amusements of assemblies &c. will
contribute much to dispel the gloom of the season.[54]

The tragedy of *Jane Shore* was to be given as the first performance in Lexington, sometime during the same week.
Although the new company left for Frankfort at the end
of the month,[55] it opened at Lexington again at the end of
January, 1811 — the days of performance were Wednes-
days and Saturdays [56] — and continued, in spite of the
threatened withdrawal of William Turner, Sophia Turner,
John Cipriani, and Mary Cipriani, who were among the
principal actors, until early in May. Plays were again
given, probably by the same company, in the following
June and July. In the meantime, however, Mr. and Mrs.
Turner and the Ciprianis had broken away and were attempting, with the aid of two actors named Williams and
James and with possibly some other players, an independent
season in Cincinnati, where they were perhaps the first
professional company. They seem to have performed there
twice a week for some time during May and June.[57]

[54] *Ky. Gaz.*, Dec. 18, 1810. As early as September of that year,
a "Mr. VOS, *of the Montreal Theatre*" was playing the leading
parts for the Roscian Society in Lexington.

[55] The last performance was to be on Dec. 26 (*ibid.*, Dec. 25,
1810).

[56] *Ibid.*, Jan. 29, 1811.

[57] See *Liberty Hall*, May 29, and June 5 and 12, 1811. Ludlow,
who habitually forgot or ignored the achievements of earlier players
in the West, says (*op. cit.*, p. 117), "Mr. Turner came to Cincinnati

By September, when the company reopened the Lexington Theatre, the loss of the Turners had been repaired: Vos had now become a regular member; and, besides Douglas, Mr. Kennedy, Mr. Marsh, and Mr. Jones (and, for at least part of the time, Mr. Cipriani), who are mentioned in the *Gazette*, there were added during the season Mr. and Mrs. Usher, and a Mr. Huntington, said to be from the New York and Charleston theatres. Performances were continued until November 30, the last night before the departure of the company for Frankfort. The time of the Frankfort season was doubtless regulated, as later in the case of Drake's company, to accord with the date set for the meeting of the Kentucky legislature. At all events, the conduct of the company soon began to fall into a routine. Upon the return from Frankfort, they opened the Lexington spring season of 1812 about the middle of February, continuing, possibly, as late as June. Plays were again given from October to December.

Until 1813, or for some time just preceding that year, Noble Luke Usher,[58] who owned or controlled the Lexington Theatre, had acted as manager of it; but shortly after the opening of the Lexington season of that year, he relinquished his authority as manager, at least temporarily, and

with a few actors as early as 1815.'' It is probably a typographical error that accounts for the contradictory statement on p. 405, where he says that Turner's company came to Cincinnati in 1810. It is interesting to note, however, that in the last passage cited, which is devoted to showing how James Caldwell's part in establishing the drama in the West had been overrated, he so far forgot himself as to speak of Turner's as a regular professional company. *Cf.* his statement (*op. cit.*, p. 86) that previous to the arrival of Drake's company, of which Ludlow was a member, Kentucky and Ohio had been visited only by groups of two or three strolling players, and by these only at long intervals.

[58] *Cf.* Dunlap, *op. cit.*, p. 348; and Ludlow, *op. cit.*, p. 86.

rented the property to the company.[59]    Among the actors
at this time were Mr. Kennedy, Mrs. Doige, Mrs. Turner,
Mr. Douglas, Mr. and Mrs. Thornton, Mr. Vaughan, and
Mr. and Mrs. Usher.[60]

At Louisville, where they had probably appeared at intervals since their first arrival in Kentucky, the company,
now including Mr. Usher, Mr. Douglas, Mr. Thornton, Mr.
Vaughan, Mr. Little, Mr. Ferguson, Mrs. Cipriani, Mrs.
Rivers, and possibly others,[61] occupied the theatre through
a spring season of about three months in the following year,
1814.    And it seems likely that the same company, with
possibly not more than the usual change in personnel, were
again at the Lexington Theatre within a few weeks after
closing at Louisville.

By the year 1815, which saw the arrival in the West of
Samuel Drake and his talented recruits drawn from the
Albany Theatre, a company of professional actors, doubtless loosely enough organized, had been playing in Kentucky
for five years; and in the very year of his arrival a troupe
under William Turner played both in Cincinnati and in
Lexington.    At Cincinnati, Turner's actors, heralded as
the "Pittsburgh company of Comedians, on their way to
Kentucky," occupied a theatre belonging to the Thespians.[62]    Mr. Barrett,[63] Mr. Jefferson, Mr. Morgan, and
Mrs. Turner were among the players; and so, very likely,
was Mr. Collins "of the Philadelphia and New York

---

[59] *Ky. Gaz.*, June 1, 1813.

[60] *Ibid.*, for 1813, *passim*.

[61] *The Western Courier*, Feb. to Apr., 1814, *passim*. It is clear
that as early as 1811 Louisville was included in the itinerary of the
same company which visited Lexington and Frankfort (see John
Melish, *Travels in the United States of America*, 1812, II, 186).

[62] *Liberty Hall*, Mar. 21 (or Apr. 1 — two dates, as often, are
printed; and here there is room for doubt), 1815.

[63] Possibly a newspaper misprint for Blissett.

Theatre.''[64]   From Cincinnati the company went to Lexington, where they were playing by about the middle of June.[65]   For some time after that date, Turner seems to have felt secure in his possession of the Lexington Theatre; but Luke Usher, who had succeeded his nephew, Noble Luke Usher, as the owner of the establishment, must have had long since a definite understanding with Drake.[66]

[64] *Spirit of the West*, Mar. 25, 1815.   Collins was certainly a member of the company when it was playing at Lexington a few months later.

[65] Curiously enough, a Mr. Ludlow appears as one of the players for Aug. 22 (*Ky. Gaz.*, Aug. 21, 1815).   It is, however, impossible that this was N. M. Ludlow unless the latter's account (*op. cit.*, pp. 74 ff.) in which he says the season at Pittsburg ended about Nov. 10, 1815, is in serious error.   It seems likely, on other grounds, that the author of *Dramatic Life* was not the Ludlow mentioned in the Lexington theatre advertisement.   Other actors who may have appeared in Turner's company for the first time this season were Cargill and Beale.

[66] According to Ludlow (*op. cit.*, pp. 5-8), it was in the fall of 1814 that Noble Luke Usher, formerly an actor in Philadelphia, New York, and Boston, but at this time in control of theatres at Lexington, Frankfort, and Louisville, arrived in Albany in quest of players for the circuit which he wished to establish in Kentucky.   He disclosed his purpose, says Ludlow, to Samuel Drake, at that time stage manager of the Albany Theatre, and secured the promise of the latter to form a company and bring it to the West.   On his way back to Kentucky, however, Noble Luke Usher died at a house in the Allegheny Mountains.   But Luke Usher, his uncle, into whose hands his nephew's theatres now came, began a correspondence with Drake which resulted in an understanding that the latter should become lessee of the Lexington, Frankfort, and Louisville Theatres and manage them on his own account.   Accordingly, in May, 1815, Ludlow, preceding the main company by a few days, left Albany for the first of a number of towns to the Westward where Drake wished to perform on the way to Kentucky.   The company, when it left Albany, included only eleven persons — Samuel Drake, the manager; his sons, Samuel Drake, Jr., Alexander Drake, and James Drake; his daughters, Miss Martha Drake and Miss Julia Drake (later Mrs. Dean and

At all events, Turner soon realized that his position was untenable. On June 15 Drake announced, through a Louisville paper, that he had "purchased the time which Mr. Usher had in the Kentucky theatres" and that he was about to commence a journey to the West for the express purpose of reforming the theatres there and putting the frontier drama on a firm foundation; his "itinerant friends" Vaughan and Douglas were expected to join him; and he called upon "the proprietors and trustees" "to prevent invaders from any attack on those theatres, which I now consider as mine, and which I shall open at a proper season." [67] Such was the belligerent tone characteristic of the rival managers who sought to gain control of theatricals in the pioneer West.

Turner seems now to have considered himself the victim of Usher's deception. In October, shortly after he had closed his season in Lexington, he made a public complaint and declared that he had already commenced legal action against Usher: "In consequence," he says,

of his having contracted with Mr. Usher for the Frankfort, Louisville and Lexington Theatres, he abandoned every

---

mother of Julia Dean); N. M. Ludlow, afterwards to become one of the most prominent of Western theatrical managers; Miss Fanny Denny, a novice, who was later the famous Mrs. Alexander Drake; Mr. and Mrs. Lewis (Mr. Lewis was the stage carpenter); and Joe Tracy, man of all work. Somewhat later Sol Smith, who was a boy of only fourteen when, as his first experience of drama, he saw the Drakes perform at Albany shortly before their departure for Kentucky (Sol Smith, *The Theatrical Apprenticeship*, 1846, pp. 14-15), followed in the wake of this theatrical emigration from Albany to the West. Performances in several towns along the way — especially in Pittsburg — occupied the time until the middle of November, when the company passed down the Ohio to Limestone and there secured a wagon to take them to Frankfort.

[67] *The Western Courier*, June 15, 1815; repeated June 22 and 29, and July 6. This announcement, addressed to the people of Louisville, was dated from Albany, N. Y., Apr. 27, 1815.

other prospect for the express purpose of residing with his family in Kentucky. Mr. Usher having refused him possession of the Frankfort & Louisville Theatres, he has commenced an action of damages against him, and trusts that a Jury will do HIM justice, and prove by the verdict that contracts are not to be violated with IMPUNITY.[68]

The announcement in January, 1816, that both the Lexington Theatre and Mr. Usher's home would be sold at auction may have been an echo of the disagreement between Usher and Turner.[69]  Whether or not the sale actually took place, William Turner's campaigns in Kentucky — at least in the important towns — were ended; and from this time Samuel Drake, who is said to have opened at Frankfort early in December, 1815,[70] was long supreme in Kentucky, retaining for many years his hold upon the circuit composed of Lexington, Frankfort, and Louisville.

From Frankfort, which had attracted Drake, not because of its size, but because the legislature was in session there at the time of his arrival, the company went late in the following February [71] to Louisville, where they found that

<hr />

[68] Ky. Gaz., Oct. 16, 1815.

[69] Ibid., Jan. 15, 1816.

[70] Ludlow, op. cit., p. 81.

[71] The Western Courier, Feb. 28 and Mar. 6, 1816. The date is wrongly given as about the middle of March by Ludlow (op. cit., p. 88), who, however, is usually inaccurate in his memory of dates. This fact, as well as Ludlow's jealousy of other managers and other companies, must always be kept in mind by the reader of Dramatic Life; but it would be unjust to deny the great importance of Ludlow in the early Western drama, or the value of his book in so far as it has to do with the theatrical performances in which he had a part.  Even concerning his habitual inaccuracy in dates and in his circumstantial accounts of performances of which he evidently very often had not preserved the playbills, it would be unfair to speak harshly.  When he published his book, in 1880, he was, according to his own statement, eighty-five years of age, and he was setting down a detailed record of experiences from forty to sixty-five years in the

the theatre "was not in a condition to be occupied; it was dark, dingy, and dirty." [72] Drake's first season there probably ended on May 14, 1816. [73] In the meantime, he had advertised that his theatrical corps would soon appear in Lexington; [74] and on the 21st of the same month he opened the theatre there, [75] continuing until early in July, when it was announced that the players would leave for a visit to some of the neighboring towns. [76] The company returned, however, in time to open the theatre for the fall season on the last day of September. After remaining in Lexington until near the end of November, they were off again for Frankfort, where they began their winter campaign about two weeks before the legislature met [77] and were convinced by the experiment that the town alone could not support them. During April and May of the

---

past. And he tells his readers (*op. cit.*, p. vi) that he was compelled to depend upon another for aid in the revision and reconstruction of his book, "after my eyesight became so much impaired that I could not by any means available read my own manuscript."

[72] Ludlow, *op. cit.*, p. 88.

[73] *The Western Courier*, May 9, 1816, advertises the 14th as "Positively the Last Night, *This Season*."

[74] *Ky. Gaz.*, Apr. 29, 1816.

[75] The *Ky. Gaz.*, May 20, 1816, announces the plays for the following night, and the same paper for May 27 states that Drake's company has had the house open three nights — the regular number of performances for a week. Ludlow (*op. cit.*, pp. 90-91) erroneously states that the company opened the theatre in Lexington "about the middle of June" with "Colman's" *Speed the Plough* and *Catharine and Petruchio*. The date is almost a month too late; Morton, not Colman, was the author of *Speed the Plough*; and, finally, the bill for the performance of May 21, as advertised the previous day, consisted of *The Foundling of the Forest* and *The Poor Soldier*.

[76] *Ky. Gaz.*, July 1 and 8. Ludlow (*op. cit.*, p. 91) states that the season continued till the middle of July, when the heat became too oppressive in the ill-ventilated theatre.

[77] Ludlow, *op. cit.*, p. 101.

following year, 1817, they played, it is said, in Louisville for the second time;[78] and it was at the end of this season that Ludlow, with a number of other players, withdrew from Drake's company and set out on an independent venture for Nashville, playing, along the way, in several Kentucky towns. This was the beginning of Ludlow's long career as manager or joint-manager, in which he appears as a prominent figure in theatricals at the South, reappearing from time to time at Louisville and at St. Louis, particularly in the latter place after 1836.

Drake, with the remains of the company which he had taken to Louisville, returned to Lexington, opening late in August and continuing until the second week in November. It was probably after another visit to Frankfort and to Louisville that he returned, with his company, to Lexington, about the same time in the following year; and they were there again in the fall of 1819. But the latter year was a period of uncertainty as to the future control of the Lexington Theatre. For some months, Luke Usher, who said that he had spent two thousand dollars in improving the house, sought to attract a lessee.[79] Though the Drakes were afterwards to appear at times in Lexington (and, according to Ludlow, Drake still had his old circuit of Louisville, Frankfort, and Lexington in 1826 and

---

[78] *Ibid.*, pp. 105-108. I have examined no Louisville newspapers for this period.

[79] *Ky. Gaz.*, Apr. 9-July 22, or later, 1819. I have not been able to clear up all the details of the management and ownership of the Lexington, Frankfort, and Louisville theatres at this time. Newspaper notices leave such matters in doubt; and I have not attempted to determine what facts may be had from the court records, which would, of course, supply valuable information, though some of them are certainly far from complete. As early as 1816, a Louisville paper stated that Drake was understood to have "made a purchase of Mr. Usher's right of the whole of the Kentucky Theatres" (*The Western Courier*, Feb. 7, 1816).

1828),[80] the town was visited during the next twenty years
by a number of different companies — sometimes by minor
troupes who seized upon it as their best opportunity; sometimes by companies of greater importance who turned to
it, often only for short periods, between seasons in Cincinnati and Louisville.

While Drake was establishing himself in the Kentucky
circuit, Turner, whose threats against Luke Usher must
have proved empty, seems to have made no further attempt
to retain a hold on that state. Instead, he turned in a
direction where he still had nothing to fear from rivalry.
By the end of December, 1816, a year after he had been
forced to relinquish the Kentucky circuit, he appeared
again in Cincinnati, where, as we have seen, he had taken
his company early the preceding year, and where he had
directed professional theatricals as early as 1811. Here
his company performed from December, 1816, till the middle of the following March. But, not content with having
driven his competitor out of Kentucky, Drake apparently
let it be known early in 1817 [81] that he intended to appear
in Cincinnati. Turner, who seems to have had no desire
to try his strength a second time against such a rival, is
said to have planned to descend the river to New Orleans.
Drake, however, according to a contemporary print, finally
refused to negotiate with the citizens of Cincinnati for
the erection of a new playhouse until the opprobrium of a
nightly tax on theatricals should be removed; and Turner,
learning of his rival's decision, resolved to patch up the
old theatre and return later in the year. Accordingly, in
the following June, Turner & Morgan advertised [82] for
actors to make immediate application to them in Cincinnati;

[80] Ludlow, *op. cit.*, pp. 274 and 305.
[81] *Liberty Hall*, Jan. 20, 1817.
[82] *The Reporter* (Lexington), June 25, 1817, and later.

and by the middle of July the company had again opened in the latter place.

But they were not destined to prosper. Ludlow, who closed his first season in Nashville about the end of this same July, now repaired to Cincinnati, with a companion named Phillips, to enlist recruits for his new venture in the South. According to Ludlow's own account,[83] he and Phillips found Turner with a small, ill-paid, and discontented company. Whether or not it is true, as Ludlow declares, that Turner, in financial distress, was already planning to disband his insubordinate players and return to Philadelphia, the fact is that, even though Ludlow "had in a few days nearly all the company applying" and had apparently engaged a number of them, Turner was not through. There seems to be no evidence of performances in the summer later than August 18; but in November Mrs. Turner's return to the stage was announced, and the final performance for the season in Cincinnati was to occur on the 25th of the same month. After this farewell to the Ohio Valley towns the Turners, who had had a part in what was in all likelihood the first season of professional performances in Lexington (1810-1811) and who were apparently the first professional players to appear in Cincinnati (1811), now made their way to St. Louis, where they had opened, by February 17, 1818, a season — probably the first by professionals — which continued as late as the end of July.[84] But, with this unsuccessful year,

[83] Ludlow, *op. cit.*, pp. 115-116.

[84] For advertisements of performances during this season, see *Mo. Gaz.*, Feb. 20 (nearly a column of praise for Turner's company, who had performed the tragedy of *Bertram* on the 17th); Apr. 10 and 24; July 3 and 24, 1818. There is, in the possession of the Missouri Historical Society, of St. Louis, a playbill for Apr. 9 of this year, which gives the characters in two plays performed for the benefit of Mr. Wallace. The actors set down for parts in this play were Messrs. Henry, Martin, James, Blythe, Turner, Smith, and Guthrie;

Turner's career as a manager in the West seems to have come to an end.

At St. Louis, Turner was followed by Ludlow, who now began the first of his campaigns at the North, where he had

Master Turner; and Mrs. Turner. Others whose names appear in the newspaper notices cited above are Messrs. D'Grushe, Vos, King, Peyton, and Maud; Mrs. Vos; and Miss Turner. The newspapers and the playbill seem to account definitely for only seven performances, but it is impossible to say how many others there may have been. The plays of which there is definite record were performed on different days of the week — Tuesday, Wednesday, Thursday, and Saturday — a fact which suggests that there may well have been more than one performance a week. It seems likely that the Mr. Vos who appears here was the same who belonged to the company at Lexington as early as 1810 and who was said to have come from the Montreal Theatre. Ludlow, however, bent on making the most of his claim that he himself was the first to introduce regular professional drama to St. Louis, speaks of Vos as a sign- and house-painter who was attracted by the glamour of the stage (Ludlow, *op. cit.*, p. 181); Turner, he says (*ibid.*, p. 186), had come to St. Louis thinking of engaging in his original business — bookbinding or printing, as Ludlow remembers it — but, happening upon Vos, who had chanced to arrive from Louisville about that time, he decided to try a few theatricals; the effective force in the company consisted of Mrs. Turner, Mrs. Vos, Mr. Vos, and Miss Emma Turner; and "they performed, with the aid of two amateurs found in the city, ten or twelve nights, finally giving it up, the support not being sufficient." Such was the information, says Ludlow, which he received from Vos himself. Ludlow's account is very likely correct so far as the financial results of the season are concerned, and there is at least a possibility that his report of the number of performances is fairly accurate. But he is plainly in error when he describes the company as made up of four effective players and two amateurs; for, whatever the relative numbers of the effectives and the amateurs, there are no less than sixteen actors named in the bills. It is very questionable whether the hastily assembled company brought to St. Louis nearly two years later, which consisted, by the time the theatre opened, of fifteen persons, according to Ludlow's own account (*ibid.*, p. 184), including Mr. and Mrs. Vos and Mr. King, had a better right to the name of "*regular* dramatic company."

had no important part in theatricals since he separated from
Drake in the summer of 1817. Late in March, 1819, John
H. Vos had advertised [85] for players to occupy "the St.
Louis Theatre," a new but very inadequate building re-
cently erected by the Thespian Society. In the autumn
of that year, Ludlow, who was in Nashville at the time,
began, he says, a correspondence with a Mr. Henry in St.
Louis, and later with Vos,[86] as the result of which the
Southern manager brought a company to St. Louis and
opened the theatre about the middle of December.

The difficult journey by river must have been typical of
what was experienced by many pioneers of Western drama.
As steamers were still few, the players came, for the most
part, by keel-boat, making their way in this manner down
the Cumberland, from the mouth of the Cumberland to the
mouth of the Ohio, and thence up the Mississippi to St.
Louis. Progress against the strong current of the Mississippi was painfully slow, and could only be made by the
difficult process of "cordelling," done by means of a rope
extending from the boat to the shore. The voyage from
Nashville to St. Louis required eighteen days; and Ludlow,
who, with his wife, left the keel-boat at Cape Girardeau and
waited for a steamer, found that this means of conveyance
was not much swifter, for the boat ran only by daylight,
and stopped several times each day to put out freight and
to take on wood. St. Louis proved to be, in Ludlow's esti-
mation, surprisingly primitive; and his theatrical efforts
there failed disastrously.

Drake, who seems not to have known that Ludlow had
preceded him, brought a company to St. Louis soon after
Ludlow had arrived. As the theatre was already occupied,

---

[85] *Mo. Gaz.*, Mar. 31, 1819. Certain Kentucky, Tennessee, Mississippi, and Louisiana papers were requested to copy this advertisement.

[86] Ludlow, *op. cit.*, pp. 180-181.

the Kentucky manager, who had quarters at the City Hotel, arranged with the landlord to improvise a stage in the ballroom. This place, which could be adequately heated, gave him an advantage over the players at the uncomfortable theatre; and after a few weeks, during which the two companies gave plays on alternate nights, Drake was able to bring his opponent to terms, with the result that Ludlow disbanded his troupe and engaged himself, with a few of his actors, as a member of the rival company.

But the new arrangement, which seems to have commenced about February 1, 1820, lasted only a short time; a disagreement occurred and Ludlow withdrew. Drake himself, however, presently departed with his players; whereupon Ludlow, associating himself temporarily with Vos, formed a small company and opened the theatre again, but only for a short and disastrous run. Such, if Ludlow is not in error, is the history of the St. Louis professional stage for the winter and spring seasons of 1819-1820.[87] Having disbanded his new company, Ludlow, after a brief period during which he was forced to various expedients to earn a living, returned to Tennessee.

Drake, before coming to St. Louis at the end of 1819, had played from March to June at Louisville, thenceforth the center of his activities. And he set out again for that place, according to Ludlow,[88] after he withdrew from St. Louis early in 1820. The journey was made by way of Vincennes, where the manager and some of his players performed a summer season of a number of weeks on a stage which could scarcely have contained all the members of the small company.[89]

---

[87] The whole of the above account of this season is drawn from Ludlow's narrative (ibid., pp. 180-193).

[88] Ibid., p. 192.

[89] Smith, op. cit., pp. 38-41. Cf. Ludlow, op. cit., p. 192; and Western Sun (Vincennes), May 27-June 24, 1820.

There is no evidence, however, that Drake opened the Louisville theatre after his return from St. Louis and Vincennes. Instead, he appeared, with at least part of his company, in Cincinnati. Here, there seems to have been a dearth of theatricals during the year following Turner's withdrawal to St. Louis; but before the end of 1819 interest in the drama had been revived by new rumors that Drake would attempt to erect a theatre,[90] and by the arrival of two companies of actors. Sometime during that year, a small number of players under a manager named Blanchard, it is said, performed for a few nights "in Mr. Dawson's schoolhouse on Water street;"[91] and in June and July of the same year Collins & Jones played in a makeshift theatre "in the second story of Burrows and Tunis' store, corner of Columbia and Walnut streets."[92] In the following March, with the opening of the new Cincinnati Theatre, Collins & Jones began to take an important part in Western theatricals. After a visit to Nashville,[93] Jones brought a company to St. Louis, where he opened in December (1820) and remained for only a short and unprofitable season. From St. Louis he went to Cincinnati to join Collins. The confusion of rivalries, short-lived alliances, and makeshift agreements which characterized the remaining years of the period, is illustrated by the fact that, at Cincinnati, Jones found his colleague playing with Drake's company, which had opened the theatre before the end of January, 1821.

While Drake was finishing a season at Louisville in the following autumn, Collins & Jones's company were playing at Lexington; and in November they reopened the new

[90] *Liberty Hall*, Apr. 30, 1819.

[91] Smith, *op. cit.*, p. 37.

[92] For the place used as a theatre, see Smith, *loc. cit.*

[93] Ludlow, *op. cit.*, p. 201.

Cincinnati Theatre, a feature of the entertainment being
the recitation of the celebrated prize prologue by ''Horace
in Cincinnati'' (Thomas Peirce).[94]  Here Collins & Jones
continued as late as February, 1822, and possibly until
April; and they were again at Cincinnati in May.  In the
performances at the Pavilion Theatre, Vauxhall Gardens,
which began in Cincinnati on July 4 of this year and continued into October or later, they probably had no part;
it is just possible that they kept the Cincinnati Theatre
open at the same time.

The further history of the Collins & Jones company,
which need not be followed here in detail, is remarkable for
the appearance among them, during the Lexington season
of 1822-1823, of Edwin Forrest,[95] then an obscure actor.
According to Sol Smith, Forrest was with the company
during its return visit to Cincinnati [96] after closing at Lexington; and it is certain that he appeared at Louisville during Collins & Jones's season there later in the same
spring.[97]  He was probably one of the seceding players
who, leaving Collins & Jones at Louisville, returned to
Cincinnati and opened the Globe (earlier called the Pavilion) Theatre for a disastrous summer season; at all
events, he was again seen in Cincinnati at this time.[98]  In

---

[94] For the prize prologue, see *Liberty Hall*, Nov. 24, 1821; and
Thomas Peirce, *The Odes of Horace in Cincinnati*, 1822, pp. 98-100.

[95] See *Ky. Reporter*, Jan. 27, 1823, which shows that he was to
appear as Bassanio on that night.  For the season of 1822-1823, see
*ibid.*, Dec. 16, 1822, to Feb. 17, 1823.

[96] Smith, *Theatrical Management*, 1868, p. 26.

[97] For notices of Forrest, see *Lou. Pub. Adv.*, Apr. 30 and May
7, 1823.

[98] For Forrest's fifth appearance during the season, see *Independent Press*, June 12, 1823.  *Cf.* also *ibid.*, June 26; and Smith,
*The Theatrical Apprenticeship*, 1846, p. 49, and *Theatrical Management*, 1868, p. 27.

the autumn of the same year, however, he had again joined
Collins & Jones, then at Lexington.[99] For Collins & Jones
this seems to have been the last attempt at theatrical management in the West.

Drake, meanwhile, had divided his time, for the most
part, between Louisville and the new theatres in Tennessee
and Alabama.[100] From 1824 he was able, for a number
of years, to conduct his Louisville theatre with some approach to regularity, usually keeping it open during the
first five or six months of each year. It seems probable
that at the same time he continued to retain his hold upon
the old circuit, which included, besides Louisville, both
Frankfort and Lexington.[101] Until 1833 he remained the
most important figure in Louisville theatricals; and for a
period of several years, ending, probably, in 1831, his companies were seen, at short intervals, in Cincinnati.

Long before Drake had ceased to bear an important part
in the pioneer theatre, however, new and formidable competition had to be met. None who entered the West in the
wake of Drake's expedition was more picturesque than Sol
Smith, later an eccentric chronicler of his own adventures;
but during Drake's time this newcomer offered only ineffectual rivalry. With the end of the managerial activities
of Collins & Jones, Smith, who had met them in Lexington shortly before the close of their last season (1823-1824),
organized there a company with which he soon began, at

---

[99] For Forrest, who seems to have joined the company after the
middle of September, when he was engaged "for the season," see
*Ky. Reporter*, Sept. 22, 1823; *cf.* also Smith, *The Theatrical Apprenticeship*, 1846, pp. 50-51.

[100] For Drake's excursion to the South, see Ludlow, *op. cit.*, pp.
238-244.

[101] See Ludlow, *op. cit.*, pp. 274 and 305, and Cowell, *op. cit.*, p.
87; but *cf. Daily Cinc. Gaz.*, Oct. 10, 1828, where Drake is said to be
*"Manager of the Theatres of Cincinnati, Louisville, and Frankfort,"*
with no mention of Lexington.

Cincinnati, his long career as manager in the West and South. But his first attempts were unsuccessful; and, after a change of theatres in Cincinnati had failed to improve his fortunes, he disbanded his players.

Within a short time, however, two formidable opponents, James Caldwell and N. M. Ludlow, were to invade the territory in which the passing of Turner, of Usher, and of Collins & Jones, with the temporary withdrawal of Sol Smith, had left Drake supreme.

Caldwell, who, according to Allston Brown, had commenced his career as manager at Columbus, Kentucky, in 1817,[102] but who was now proprietor and manager of the American Theatre at New Orleans, began his visits to the Northern river towns as early as 1827. In that year he brought a company to St. Louis, declaring, in the fashion common among the more ambitious of the Western and Southern managers of the day, his intention of "establishing the drama" in this town. Caldwell had, in fact, unusual ability as an organizer, which he was later to evince in his not quite successful efforts to obtain control of all the important theatres in the West, as well as in his numerous other business ventures.[103] At this time, however, he

[102] Allston Brown, *History of the American Stage*, n. d. (1870), p. 61.

[103] Some ten years later, Caldwell's activities were thus recounted by a Cincinnati paper: "Mr. CALDWELL, of New Orleans, not satisfied with owning all the Theatres between the Falls of St. Anthony, and the Balize, and managing two or three of them — with being the proprietor of a bank, and the largest bathing establishment in the Union — and with holding contracts for lighting three or four cities with Gas, has a new project on foot, . . . the formation of an 'Ocean Steam Company,' for running a line of steam packets between New Orleans and Liverpool. While he is thinking about this, he is amusing himself with a scheme for paving the streets of New Orleans with octagonal blocks of stone." (*Cinc. Daily Gaz.*, Nov. 16, 1836.)

announced a somewhat less ambitious scheme to the St. Louis public. "The Manager," he declared,

conceives that, in conjunction with New Orleans and Nash-ville, St. Louis will enable him to keep the whole of his establishment together, throughout the year, which advan-tage will afford the lovers of the Drama much better enter-tainment than they could expect, if a company were divided in the summer and fall, and then, again obliged to be collected together for the winter.[104]

Accordingly, in the summer of that year he opened the Old Salt-house Theatre, which a Thespian society had occupied before him. In still another particular he was in advance — too far in advance, perhaps — of his competitors in such primitive playhouses as the one at St. Louis: he attempted, at least during the latter part of his season, to keep the theatre open every day except Sunday. But after a few weeks this aggressively conducted season came to a close. In the following year the same manager dispatched his lieutenant, James S. Rowe, with a company to St. Louis, where the makeshift stage was again used, from July until October, when the players departed for Natchez. It is said that Caldwell returned to St. Louis in 1829, but that he withdrew early, after an unsuccessful attempt to raise subscriptions for a new theatre, appointing Charles Keemle as an agent to administer his lease on the old one.

As yet Caldwell had not come into direct conflict with Drake, whose strongholds were now Louisville and Cincin-nati. Both these places, however, were the objectives of N. M. Ludlow, who in this year, 1829, reappeared as a manager at the North. Perceiving the practicability of a combination of dramatic and equestrian companies, Lud-low had formed, by July, 1829, a connection with J. Purdy Brown, manager of a circus; and together they secured the Amphitheatre, on Sycamore Street, in Cincinnati and

104 *Mo. Rep.*, June 21, 1827.

opened there, about the middle of that month, a "DRA-
MATIC EQUESTRIAN THEATRE . . . after the
fashion of Astley's Amphitheatre, London; and several
similar establishments in the United States." Brown,
however, became dissatisfied and withdrew long before the
end of the season, leaving his partner alone to wage a
sharp contest with the Drakes, which resulted in the temporary withdrawal of the latter on August 15. Ludlow
continued performances at the Amphitheatre — a building
which had once been a bathhouse — until October 23; and
when he did close in Cincinnati it was to turn his attention to Louisville, where the Drakes had remained almost
unchallenged in their control of theatricals since their first
visit, thirteen years earlier. On October 17 Ludlow had
published his intention of erecting a temporary playhouse
at the corner of Jefferson and Third Cross Streets, to be
opened about the first of November; and in this "Melodramatic theatre" he actually began his season on November 11, 1829.[105] After a few nights he declared he would

<hr/>

[105] For the facts here cited regarding theatricals in Cincinnati and
Louisville, see *Daily Cinc. Gaz.*, July 8-Oct. 23, 1829; and *Lou. Pub.
Adv.*, Oct. 17, 1829-Mar. 22, 1830. *Cf.* Ludlow (*op. cit.*, pp. 337-
362 and 368), whose version of the events mentioned above is a
striking example of the kind of errors into which he often fell when
he trusted to his memory — as he usually did. Ludlow states (*ibid.*,
p. 340) that, as Brown's company, who were to join with Ludlow's
at Louisville, did not arrive on time, he decided to begin on his own
account and so, "about the 22d of June, 1829," opened the combined
circus and theatre which his carpenter had built, giving as the first
performance the comedy of *The Honey Moon*. As a matter of fact,
it was on Oct. 17, 1829, that he announced his intention of erecting this theatre (*Lou. Pub. Adv.*, Oct. 17, 1829), and in the same
newspaper for Nov. 3 he stated that the theatre had been built; four
days later (*ibid.*, Nov. 7, 1829) he advertised his intention to open
the theatre on Nov. 9 with the comedy of *The Honey Moon* (which
Ludlow correctly remembered as the first play performed); three
days later (*ibid.*, Nov. 10), having changed his plan, he announced

devote the place exclusively to melodramatic spectacles; and this program was apparently in accord with the popular taste, for what Ludlow at first announced as a short season previous to his departure for the South continued nearly five months. When the season finally ended, he did not go to the South, but to Cincinnati.

Caldwell had continued for some time, either by direct or indirect means, his attempt to secure control of the river towns. In the summer of 1830, Gray and Rowe, two of his agents, brought a company to St. Louis, going from that town to Nashville. In the summer of the following year,

---

that the theatre would be opened on Nov. 11 with the bill previously advertised for the 9th; and from this time plays were advertised regularly. And as his narrative advances, Ludlow falls into greater confusion. Brown, he says, had misunderstood, and had expected that the two companies would meet at Cincinnati instead of Louisville. Ludlow, therefore, according to his own account (Ludlow, *op. cit.*, p. 341), immediately advertised the last week of his performance at Louisville, and closed on July 4, 1827 (1829, of course). Thus Ludlow, clearly wrong in some of his most important statements, recites the story of a season which was, in all probability, entirely mythical. He then proceeds, however, with a record of many events of the season of July to October at Cincinnati which is substantially correct, though not so in detail. Finally, curiously enough, he turns (*ibid.*, p. 350) to a narrative, somewhat inaccurate, of the season which he in reality did perform at Louisville in the winter of 1829-1830; but he gives the date of the opening as Oct. 5 instead of Nov. 11, the correct date, and he calls the season ''my second managerial effort in Louisville'' instead of his first, as it clearly was. To the proof cited earlier in this note, it may be added that an editorial printed in the *Lou. Pub. Adv.*, Nov. 7, 1829, states that ''Mr. Ludlow is a stranger'' among the people of Louisville. For a disparaging account of Ludlow's company at this time, with, however, some praise of the manager's ability, see Cowell, *op. cit.*, p. 90. According to this English critic, the players were ''a strolling company on a *sharing scheme.*'' ''Nothing I had ever seen in the way of theatricals,'' Cowell declares, ''could be likened to this deplorable party. . . . there was not one redeeming point.'' For a reply to this criticism, see Ludlow, *op. cit.*, p. 353.

Ludlow was at the Old Salt-house, in St. Louis, in charge
of a company for Caldwell; and before the end of July he
was at Louisville on a like mission, while Caldwell himself, about the same time, defeated what seems to have
been Drake's last attempt to maintain himself in Cincinnati. Drake, who had kept his place open for only a
month, withdrew a week after the arrival of Caldwell; and
the latter remained from late in June to the middle of
October. In 1832 Caldwell's campaign at the North gave
promise of greater success. While his new theatre in Cincinnati was nearing completion, Ludlow, as his agent,
occupied the Columbia Street Theatre from late in April
to near the end of June; and Caldwell, after a month at
Louisville, appeared with his well-equipped New Orleans
company to open the New Cincinnati Theatre on July 4.[106]
His success was such that he was able to remain until the
middle of October, when the epidemic of cholera made it
necessary to close the theatre.

But in the following year, 1833, Caldwell's authority
over the companies whose movements he had heretofore
personally directed, began to disintegrate, passing to those
who had formerly been his agents. It is difficult to follow
this process in detail. According to Ludlow, it was at the
close of the New Orleans season of this year that Caldwell
announced (insincerely, as Ludlow thought) his determination to quit the stage both as actor and as manager, and
leased his theatres to his late stage manager, Richard Russell, and his late treasurer, James S. Rowe.[107] At all
events, he advertised that the Cincinnati Theatre would be
opened in June under the management of Messrs. Russell

---

106 On this occasion, Caldwell himself spoke the opening address,
a prize poem by Caroline Lee Hentz. For Mrs. Hentz, see above,
Chapter VI. The opening address was published in *Cinc. Daily
Gaz.*, for July 6, 1832.

107 Ludlow, *op. cit.*, pp. 403-404.

& Rowe;[108] and about a month later we hear that Caldwell was on his way to Europe, where he would obtain talent for the company directed by these men.[109]

Though from this time Caldwell's name does not appear in connection with theatricals under the direction of his former agents, the old policy of keeping several companies under joint control was continued. Russell & Rowe not only kept the theatre in Cincinnati open from June to November, 1833, but had a company at Louisville during a part of that time. A subordinate named Hilson had charge of the next Cincinnati season; and in 1835 another representative, F. S. Hill, acted as their agent at the same town. As early as September, 1833, Russell & Rowe were plainly acting as lessees, not as agents.[110] For some three years both Cincinnati and Louisville were frequently visited by the companies under their charge. After 1835, however, Rowe seems to have withdrawn from the river towns; and the following year, 1836, was probably the last in the Middle West for Russell, who was by this time depending largely upon agents at both Cincinnati and Louisville. Possibly the burning of the Cincinnati Theatre, which occurred in October, 1836, with the consequent readjustment of theatrical control, was responsible for Russell's withdrawal from the North. The building destroyed by the fire had belonged to Caldwell; but the losses sustained by Russell's players seem to have been great, and one of the company is said to have perished in the flames.[111]

---

108 *Cinc. Daily Gaz.*, May 7, 1833.

109 *Ibid.*, June 14, 1833.

110 In the *Daily Lou. Pub. Adv.*, Sept. 10, 1833, the opening of the City Theatre in Louisville is advertised by "RUSSELL & ROWE, Lessees of the New Orleans and Cincinnati Theatres."

111 *Cinc. Daily Gaz.*, Oct. 22, 1836, gives a somewhat detailed account of the destruction of the theatre and the losses sustained by Caldwell and the company.

In the autumn of the same year, Caldwell himself, after a long absence from the West, reappeared in Louisville, apparently for the last time as a manager.

J. Purdy Brown, whose early relations with Ludlow have already been noticed, continued, as late as 1831 and 1832, to visit both Lexington and Cincinnati with his equestrian and dramatic company. In 1837, some years after his death, a company, possibly the successor to his own, appeared at Cincinnati under the management or ownership of an O. W. Brown; and in the same year the equestrian companies, apparently, however, giving less and less attention to dramatic performances, seem to have reached the zenith of their importance — no less than four of them appeared in Cincinnati and Louisville at that time.

Such minor dramatic troupes as those of Cabell & Forrest (at Cincinnati and Louisville in 1833, and Cabell alone at Lexington the next year), Muzzy & Watson (Louisville, 1834), Forbes (Lexington, 1835), Tryon & Co. (St. Louis, 1836), Ingersoll & Dyke (Lexington, 1838), Mrs. A. Drake (Lexington, 1838), Dean (Cincinnati, 1838), Bailey & Rogers (Lexington, 1839), and Mackenzie & Jefferson (St. Louis, 1840), deserve no more than bare mention. Three important companies remain, however, to be noticed — N. M. Ludlow's (later Ludlow & Smith's), J. S. Potter's (later Potter & Waters's), and Scott & Thorne's. J. S. Potter, who was announced as manager at the Lexington Theatre in December, 1835, was, for two years, one of the most prominent men in Western theatricals, revisiting Lexington and appearing with his companies in both Louisville and Cincinnati. In January, 1837, he associated himself with Samuel Waters, formerly his stage manager, under the name of Potter & Waters. In the following April, the "Double Company," thus reorganized, opened the new theatre which they had built

at Cincinnati.   By the end of July, however, they were
at the American Theatre in Louisville; and in this town
they conducted what was very likely their last season as
managers in the West.

In Cincinnati a new era in theatricals began with the
erection, at Sycamore and Fourth Streets, of the New National Theatre, owned by Bates & Surtees and opened for
the first time by Scott & Thorne, the lessees, on July 3,
1837.[112]   Sunday performances seem to have been still unknown in the West; but, excepting Sundays, the New National was open almost every night from July 3 to November 25, when the first season closed.   In 1838 Scott &
Thorne again kept the National Theatre open for a large
part of the year and also conducted a brief season at Lexington; and in both 1839 and 1840 they continued in control at Cincinnati.   Perhaps no managers who preceded
them there had so nearly succeeded in gaining the applause of the whole community.   James Thorne, who seems
to have had direct charge of the company's interests in
Cincinnati, was the special object of popular favor.[113]

Ludlow, although he had for some years been chiefly interested in the theatres of the South, had made brief excursions into the Middle West, sometimes as a member of companies managed by others, sometimes as agent for Caldwell, and at other times as an independent manager.   And
in 1834 he began a series of seasons at St. Louis which were
soon to result in an improvement of the stage there comparable to that which Scott & Thorne brought about at

[112] For ownership of the theatre, see *Cinc. Daily Gaz.*, June 20 and
29, 1837; for lessees and account of the theatre and the opening, see
*ibid.*, same issue, and for July 3.  The prize address, by F. W. Thomas,
is printed *ibid.*, July 12.

[113] For accounts of two remarkable benefits for Thorne organized by large committees of citizens, see *Cinc. Daily Gaz.*, Nov. 1
and 2, 1838; and Mar. 20, 1840.

Cincinnati. Early in this year Ludlow conducted insignificant seasons at both Cincinnati and Louisville, but had appeared in St. Louis before the end of August and remained through the greater part of October or later. Here he found conditions still unfavorable for successful theatricals. It was, however, during this season, says Ludlow, that he received letters from Sol Smith proposing a partnership for the purpose of forming a circuit. Ludlow, leaving his company to finish the season at St. Louis, set out in September for Mobile to meet Smith. But some misunderstanding, which many years later became a point of bitter dispute between the two managers, prevented a meeting at that time, so that it was not until the following year, when Ludlow had brought his company from Mobile to St. Louis for another season at the Old Salt-house, where Smith appeared for an engagement, that terms of partnership were arranged.[114] In 1836, the first year of the joint control of Ludlow and Smith in St. Louis, this old playhouse was kept open from June (if Ludlow is correct) until October. But when it burned, in the following February,[115] a new theatre, to which nothing that St. Louis had previously known was at all comparable, was well on the way toward completion.

On July 3, 1837, the same day on which Scott & Thorne opened the New National Theatre in Cincinnati, Ludlow & Smith opened the New St. Louis Theatre, at the corner of Olive and Third Streets. Here the first season con-

[114] For Ludlow's account of these two seasons and of the beginning of his relations with Smith, see Ludlow, *op. cit.*, pp. 419-441. For brief mention of this season (the author, as throughout his book, carefully avoids the subject of his relations with Ludlow), see Smith, *Theatrical Management*, 1868, p. 121. Ludlow, it may be remarked, is almost certainly in error in stating that his St. Louis season of 1835 began "early in May." *Cf.* below, calendar.

[115] Ludlow, *op. cit.*, p. 471.

tinued till November, with performances on almost every night except Sundays. After this beginning, the managers made the St. Louis season for the first time a well-defined part of a theatrical circuit which was conducted with some regularity. They used the new establishment, says Ludlow, as a summer theatre, their winter season being New Orleans and Mobile, both open at the same time. In April or the beginning of May they concentrated the best of both companies, and continued the St. Louis season until about the first of November, with the exception of a summer vacation of the month of August.[116]

And on this plan, though not with the degree of regularity which Ludlow implies, the St. Louis seasons of the three following years, 1838-1840, were conducted, apparently without much profit, but in a manner which, with Scott & Thorne's activities in Cincinnati, gave the theatre greater prestige than it had ever before enjoyed on the froniter.

### III

The close relations which existed among the professional companies of Lexington, Cincinnati, Louisville, and St. Louis were determined by the geography of these towns. Three of them were either on or near the lower Ohio, and the other was on the Mississippi at no great distance from the mouth of the Ohio. The river highways, with such increasing facilities for travel as came with the rapid improvement of steamboats, made it hardly less certain that New Orleans, together with other Southern towns conveniently situated — such as Mobile, Natchez, and Nashville — should be linked with the Western towns farther north in some of the theatrical circuits which the pioneer managers attempted to form.

Detroit, however, with no waterway leading to the river towns, had very little contact either commercially or cul-

---

[116] *Ibid.*, p. 407.

turally with them. Its position on the Great Lakes determined that its closest relations should be with Cleveland and Buffalo. There, the drama, like everything else, came from the Eastward; and the only theatrical circuit of which Detroit formed a part before 1841 included Cleveland, but not Lexington, Cincinnati, Louisville, or St. Louis. With Cleveland left out of account — for it gave even as late as 1840 only slight promise of its future greatness and had no century-old cultural tradition to compare with that of Detroit — the theatrical history of this part of the West may be told briefly.[117]

In comparison with the river towns, Detroit was late in establishing professional theatricals. By 1825 the common council had passed an ordinance [118] regulating the licensing of theatricals, possibly intended mainly for the government of professional companies; but it is very likely that the first strolling players did not appear until 1827. In that year H. H. Fuller and a troupe of comedians arrived from Buffalo, and began their performances, probably early in June, when they were granted a license for one month at the rate of $35.[119]

We hear of a complaint lodged against Fuller on the ground that he was actually giving entertainments without

---

[117] For certain chronological details and citations of authorities omitted from the account which follows, see the calendar given below.

[118] By-laws and Ordinances of the City of Detroit, 1825, p. 52: "A Law regulating Shews, Plays, Games, Theatrical and all other Exhibitions, wherein or wherefore [sic] money or any other pay or compensation is required;" also mentioned in Journal of the Proceedings of the Common Council, n. d., p. 21 (June 27, 1825). This act was repealed on July 18 of the following year; but a law of like import, so far as it concerned the regulation of theatres, was in force in Detroit apparently throughout the period from 1827 to 1840.

[119] Journal of the Proceedings of the Common Council, n. d., p. 68 (June 4, 1827).

a license; and there was an order of the council that he should discontinue such practices under penalty of the law.[120]  A little later, however, he must have met his obligations, for he was granted permission to continue performances as late as July 13 of that year.[121]  At the close of its season in Detroit, the company, according to William S. Forrest, one of its members, sailed for Cleveland.[122]

For some years later, however, professional players rarely visited Detroit.  It is not unlikely that Friend Palmer's vague account of the first theatre which he attended there, "about 1828,"[123] actually belongs either to the previous year, when Fuller came (though Palmer's account of the building used does not agree with Forrest's description of Fuller's stage), or to May, 1829, when the council granted a certain A. Archbold a license for a theatre at the rate of $25 for two weeks, to be renewed at the option of the applicant.[124]  The *Journal* of the council, which seems to contain the only extant record of this season, does not name the place where the theatricals were to be performed, nor does it prove beyond a doubt that a theatre was actually opened.  Farmer's assertion that in the following year, 1830, a performance, apparently professional, was given in a barn belonging to the Steamboat Hotel,[125] is, like Palmer's account of 1828, very likely an error.  It may well be that the Parsons whom he mentions as manager did not actually appear in Detroit until 1833.

In 1832 the council granted one William Arnold a

[120] *Ibid.*, p. 70 (June 15, 1827).

[121] *Ibid.*, p. 72 (July 7, 1827).

[122] For an account based on Forrest's recollections, see *The Detroit Daily Tribune*, Apr. 20, 1860.

[123] Friend Palmer, *Early Days in Detroit*, n. d. (1906), p. 980.

[124] *Journal of the Proceedings of the Common Council*, n. d., p. 178 (May 15, 1829).

[125] Farmer, *op. cit.*, p. 357.

license to exhibit " 'Baby in the Woods,' etc., for one week;" [126] but it is impossible to say whether this exhibition was dramatic. Friend Palmer's conjecture that it was about 1832 when "Parson" & Dean opened a theatre over the stable at Woodworth's Hotel (the Steamboat) [127] is doubtless meant for the year 1833, when Parsons & Dean [128] arrived early in July and continued to perform until toward the end of August, though subjected to bitter attacks by a part of the press, which regarded the players as a menace to the morals of the town. A proof that professional theatricals had, up to this time, been very rare is to be found in an entry in the *Journal* of the council for the following year, 1834. It is here shown that during the nine years since the framing of an ordinance requiring license fees from various kinds of public exhibitions, little more than four hundred dollars had been received from this source, of which theatricals must have contributed only a small part. [129] By this time, however, the drama had been firmly established; and each year thereafter was to see the arrival of one or more professional companies which remained for seasons of increasing length.

In 1834 two companies came. Eberle, Powell & Co., who were licensed to perform in "the brick building on Woodward avenue adjoining the residence of Robert Smart," remained for more than a month; and at the end of July, probably shortly after the departure of this company, Dean & McKinney received a license permitting them to

---

[126] *Journal of the Proceedings of the Common Council*, n. d., p. 141 (May 23, 1832).

[127] Palmer, *op. cit.*, p. 980.

[128] Dean later appeared as a manager in Cincinnati; there seem to have been, however, no other important points of contact between the Detroit professional companies and those of the river towns.

[129] *Journal of the Proceedings of the Common Council*, n. d., p. 259 (Mar. 1, 1834).

give theatricals within the city until further notice, at the
rate of $25 a week.   In May, 1835, Dean & McKinney [130]
again received a license and doubtless opened their theatre;
and during the summer of 1836 they once more occupied
the City Theatre.   In 1837 the same men, who now announced themselves as managers of the Eagle Street
Theatre, in Buffalo, were again in the theatre at Detroit;
and early in December, McKinney opened the City Theatre
for what seems to have been the first winter season attempted in that town, and what was, very likely, McKinney's last as manager there.

On July 4, 1838, Marsh and Eaton opened the City
Theatre, but were ruined by the success of a new manager,
Henry Isherwood, who, having altered McKinstrey's old
circus and rechristened it the Detroit National Theatre,
opened it toward the Middle of August, probably closing
about the end of October — perhaps because the new theatre
could not be heated satisfactorily.   During the following
winter a manager named Blaike kept the old City Theatre
open for some time, while Isherwood performed at the
Museum, which was small and could easily be heated.
Here, however, he soon encountered opposition from a
group of citizens who protested to the council against the
continuance of theatricals on account of the increased danger of fire. [131]   He then turned to the City Theatre, remaining there from March to May.   In the following month
a new manager, W. Montgomery, after a long and bitter
altercation with the council, which at first refused him a
license, opened the National Theatre for a summer season.

The next year, 1840, the same playhouse was under the

---

130 *Ibid.*, p. 324 (May 13, 1835), occurs ''Dean and McKinstry,''
which is in all probability an error curiously influenced by the fact
that a David McKinstrey, of Detroit, was the owner of several
places used as theatres.

131 *Ibid.*, p. 535 (Feb. 26, 1839).

control of a company which Parker & Mueller brought
West by way of Cleveland. It would seem, however, that
Detroit, in this last year of the pioneer period, still offered
only meagre rewards for professional theatricals; the place
was kept open by the new managers only a month, during
June and July. At the end of this time Mueller had disappeared and Parker was asking for a public benefit to aid
him in paying the firm's debts, which had devolved entirely upon him.

## IV

Professional companies were by no means unknown in
the smaller towns, but they visited only a few such places
with any degree of regularity. From the time of the earliest itinerant performers in Kentucky, Frankfort had attracted companies playing at Lexington or Louisville.
Douglas's actors, probably the first professionals to visit
Lexington, closed their initial season there with the intention of proceeding to Frankfort; [132] and with the coming
of Drake the latter town became an important part of the
regular Kentucky circuit. Fuller, who brought to Detroit
what was, in all likelihood, the first professional troupe to
reach that part of the West, is said to have played at
Cleveland on his return to the Eastward; [133] and in later
years Cleveland and Detroit were often included in the
same itinerary.

Other towns were visited irregularly, usually by strolling
players, remnants of some company disintegrating at the
end of an unsuccessful season in a larger town, or a detach-
ment of regular players on their way overland to some
more important objective. Ludlow and his associates, for
example, played at Elizabethtown, Russellville, and Hop-
kinsville on their way from Louisville to Nashville in

[132] *Ky. Gaz.*, Dec. 25, 1810.
[133] *The Detroit Daily Tribune*, Apr. 20, 1860.

1817.[134] Smith tells of his attempts some years later at theatricals in Steubenville, Ohio, and at such small Kentucky towns as Harrodsburg Springs, Nicholasville, Versailles, Paris, Maysville, Georgetown, Shelbyville, and Richmond.[135] At Vincennes, where, as we have seen, amateur theatricals had been given as early as 1814, professional troupes sometimes stopped. Part of Drake's company appeared there in 1820 on their way from St. Louis to Louisville, playing, it is said, for eight weeks.[136] As early as 1816, Drake had planned, and probably carried out, brief visits to several of the towns in the neighborhood of Lexington during the hottest part of the summer.[137] Dean, who came to Cincinnati in 1838, had previously played both at Cleveland and at Columbus.[138] At about the same time a company of strolling players under the management of William Lindsay is said to have visited Indianapolis.[139] Mackenzie & Jefferson, when they appeared at St. Louis in 1840 with a minor troupe, were said to have been "in nearly all the principal towns in Illinois." [140] Chicago, which was already known as a place destined to quick growth and great wealth, was visited by the same company during

---

134 Ludlow, op. cit., pp. 108-110.

135 Smith, The Theatrical Apprenticeship, 1846, pp. 55 and 118-123; and Theatrical Management, 1868, p. 90.

136 Smith, The Theatrical Apprenticeship, 1846, pp. 38-41.

137 Ky. Gaz., July 8, 1816.

138 Cinc. Daily Gaz., Apr. 24, 1838. Cf. also Detroit Free Press, Feb. 22, 1838.

139 Rabb, "A Hoosier Listening Post," The Indianapolis Star, Jan. 15, 1921, p. 6, col. 6.

140 Daily Mo. Rep., Mar. 9, 1840. For an account of Abraham Lincoln's successful plea on behalf of these players against restrictions imposed by the town of Springfield, see The Autobiography of Joseph Jefferson, n. d. (1897?), p. 30. Joseph Jefferson, then a boy of ten years, accompanied his father, the junior manager of the troupe.

1839; but it is certain that the drama had, at best, gained
only a very precarious foothold there by that time.[141]

Small groups of strolling actors, however, ingeniously
turned to account many less promising places. An unusual
method of reaching the remote villages where the scanty
theatrical harvest had not already been reaped was employed by the Chapman family, who, according to a contemporary actor-manager, "established and carried into
operation that singular affair, the 'Floating Theatre,' concerning which so many anecdotes are told."[142] Few towns
of any consequence could have been entirely without first-
hand acquaintance with irregular groups of professional
players.

## V

Most of the actors who appeared as members of the Western companies were obscure, and must have gained only a
precarious income from the regular salaries and from the
not very numerous benefit nights which the manager could
allow them.[143] Forrest's rise from the mediocrity of back-

---

[141] Jefferson, *op. cit.*, pp. 21-24; and Joseph Balestier, *The Annals
of Chicago*, 1840, p. 18.

[142] Smith, *Theatrical Management*, 1868, p. 89. This eccentric
author, whose copious stores of curious anecdote are not always to
be regarded as historical fact, relates a not improbable story concerning the Chapman boat theatre: "It is said of this Floating
Theatre that it was cast loose during a performance at one of the
river towns in Indiana by some mischievous boys, and could not be
landed for half a dozen miles, the large audience being compelled to
walk back to their village." Though, as is usually the case in
Smith's books, the date is indefinite, it seems likely that the Chapman family instituted their floating theatre about 1833.

[143] For an early notice explaining the two sources of income enjoyed by the actors, see *The Western Courier*, Mar. 21, 1814.
Throughout the period individual agreements with the managers
determined the number and conditions of benefits to be allowed during a season. Though the number of benefits might seriously em-

woods theatricals was unique; and he was in the West for
so short a time that he can hardly be identified with the
Western stock companies at all.  Alexander Drake, who
came West with his father in 1815, gained much celebrity
there, and was not unknown in some Eastern cities before
his death, fifteen years later.  Julia Drake, his sister, later
Mrs. Fosdick and Mrs. Dean, won wide recognition, but was
not so closely identified with the Western stage as were
other members of her family.  Miss Denny, also a novice
in Samuel Drake's pioneer band of players, was later to
attain, as Mrs. Alexander Drake, the highest distinction
among those performers who were regarded as citizens of
the West.  She, too, had more than a local reputation.[144]
In Cincinnati and Louisville few seasons passed without
the appearance of Mrs. Drake, who was the one Western
actress who rose to the dignity of "star."

Meantime, by about 1822, prominent actors from the
East and from England began to appear in the West,
usually visiting Cincinnati and Louisville on their way to
New Orleans by the river; and soon the system of "starring," recently established in the East, was engrafted on
the system of stock company circuits, which was to remain
the most important feature of frontier theatricals.

Thomas Abthorpe Cooper appeared in 1822 [145] and re-

barrass the manager, the system probably did not afford much
profit to minor actors.

144 For an enthusiastic account of a season by Mrs. Drake in
New York, Philadelphia, and elsewhere in the East, and for her projected European début, see the *Louisville Daily Focus*, Jan. 9, 1832.
For her success on the London stage, see *Cinc. Daily Gaz.*, Apr. 10,
1833.

145 For an account of his first engagement of six nights at the
Louisville Theatre in Apr., 1822, see *Lou. Pub. Adv.*, May 4, 1822.
The theatre was invariably crowded during his stay, and his profits for
the six nights were said to be about $1200.  For Cooper's appear-
ance in Cincinnati this year, see Smith, *The Theatrical Apprenticeship*, 1846, p. 43.  At Lexington, where he was seen at the end of

turned from time to time. Junius Brutus Booth began in 1827 his visits to Western theatres, appearing at Cincinnati for the first time on December 11 of that year, as Richard III. When he returned in the following year, in the same rôle, he played, according to a contemporary account, to "the most overflowing house ever known in this place." The theatre, it was said, would have been filled had it been twice as large.[146] Cincinnati and Louisville, because of their location on the river highway, soon attracted the visits of a considerable number of distinguished players. "This has become," wrote a local dramatic critic in 1829, "the great thoroughfare for all theatrical stars traveling from New York to New Orleans."[147] The same year, 1829, saw not only the return of both Cooper and Booth to the West, but the advent there of Mlle. Celeste and Clara Fisher. Perhaps still more notable was the reappearance, at this time, of Edwin Forrest,[148] who had played there as an obscure actor some six years before. Mrs. Knight had already commenced her visits and was, for some time, to continue a favorite.

In 1831 Charles Kean made what seems to have been his

April, after his engagement at Louisville, there was much popular interest, and the box tickets were sold at auction (*Ky. Reporter,* Apr. 29, 1822).

[146] See *Daily Cinc. Gaz.,* Dec. 11, 1827; and Dec. 15 and 16, 1828. Booth's popularity in the West seems to have remained almost unchallenged as late as 1838. At Louisville, in one week of November of the latter year, he played, it was said, to more spectators than had ever before been in the City Theatre during an equal period of time. His repertoire was mostly Shakespearean. (*Lou. Pub. Adv.,* Nov. 27, 1838.)

[147] *Daily Cinc. Gaz.,* Jan. 8, 1829.

[148] Drake had expected to secure Forrest in 1828, and possibly Forrest did perform then in Cincinnati and Louisville at least (see *Daily Cinc. Gaz.,* Mar. 14; and *Lou. Pub. Adv.,* Jan. 26, 1828). For his appearance in 1829, see *Daily Cinc. Gaz.,* May 26; and *Lou. Pub. Adv.,* July 1, 1829.

only visit to the West, where he appeared with Clara Fisher in Louisville and Cincinnati.[149] During the last decade of the period James H. Hackett and Dan Marble, comedians, were frequent visitors; and Mrs. Pritchard, Miss Petrie, and Jane Placide were among the best-known actresses who came about the same time. Ellen Tree's appearance in 1838-1839 was one of the great events of Western theatricals. She was perhaps the first actress of great international repute to play at St. Louis, which was somewhat off the shortest water route from Cincinnati and Louisville to New Orleans. It was not until the remarkable season of 1839 that Forrest made his first appearance in St. Louis,[150] where he played to a large house during an engagement of twelve nights, and is said to have received $2157.[151] He had been immediately preceded by Ellen Tree [152] and was followed by Mlle. Celeste, whose popularity was so great that the seats in the front tier of boxes were disposed of, for the night of her first benefit, by lottery; and paid admissions for that night were reported to be $1149, a hundred dollars more than was ever before received in one night.[153]

The evils of the "starring" system, though evident from the first, were counterbalanced, at least partly, by the fact that theatregoers in frontier towns were in this way, and in this way alone, able to witness performances by great actors; and by the circumstance that these great actors chose very often to interpret the great plays. Shakespearean plays were favorites with most of these famous visitors, from Cooper to Ellen Tree.

[149] *Daily Lou. Pub. Adv.*, May 19-June 8, 1831; and *Cinc. Daily Gaz.*, June 13 and 15, 1831.

[150] *Daily Mo. Rep.*, May 6-20, 1839.

[151] Smith, *Theatrical Management*, 1868, p. 138.

[152] *Daily Mo. Rep.*, Apr. 22-29, 1839.

[153] *Ibid.*, May 27 and 29, 1839. *Cf.* also Smith, *Theatrical Management*, 1868, p. 138.

# VI

Not until the last decade before 1841 could the Western drama, amateur or professional, boast a playhouse that was better than primitive.[154]   In Lexington, at the end of the eighteenth century, plays were given in a room at Transylvania University or at the Court House.   It is uncertain what building was known as "the Theatre" as early as 1801; but the "New Theatre," in which plays were being given by November, 1808, was probably a room in the second story of the same building in which Drake performed in 1816 and which, it is said, had formerly been used as a brewery.[155]   About 1819 Usher, according to his own account, spent $2000 in decorating the place.   Two years later there was, however, some complaint about the discomfort to which audiences were subjected in the dark, dingy theatre.   In 1822 Collins & Jones repaired the building, making some improvements in the lighting, and providing stoves in preparation for a winter season.   By this time, and perhaps earlier, there were boxes and a gallery; and an orchestra had been secured.[156]

In later years the drama in Lexington had a number of homes, but they were mostly of a temporary nature.   In 1831 Brown built an amphitheatre for his equestrian and dramatic performances, but Drake used a room in the Masonic building for regular plays.   The erection of a new theatre was discussed, but apparently nothing was done for some time.   For a number of years a room in the Masonic Hall was the principal center of the Lexington theatricals, and at least one company used a place called

---

[154] For names of theatres and for further details, see the calendar below.

[155] Ludlow, *op. cit.*, pp. 89-90.

[156] For the facts cited above for the period 1819-1822, see *Ky. Gaz.*, Apr. 9 ff., 1819; and *Ky. Reporter*, Oct. 15, 1821, and Dec. 16, 1822.

Giron's Ball Room. In July, 1836, a "New Theatre," not yet completed, was opened; but shortly afterwards there was an attempt to sell shares for "a new joint stock Theatre," which may have been a fresh project. About the same time the Masonic Hall was destroyed by fire.[157] In 1839, however, a company of actors advertised performances "at their exhibition rooms;" and it does not seem likely that another new theatre, if projected, was brought to completion by 1840.

Cincinnati, Louisville, St. Louis, and Detroit were for many years as badly equipped for theatricals as was Lexington. The "ragged roof and sorry floor" described in the prologue at the opening, in 1801, of what was probably the first theatre in Cincinnati, were characteristic. Some years later a barn loft served the purpose of a stage for amateur drama in the same town. The "New Play-house" of the Thespians opened in 1815 was so primitive that within two years a project for the erection of a new theatre was agitated. For the time being, however, it was decided to "patch up the present *apology for a Play House*" with new boxes, scenery, and dressing rooms. In 1819 theatrical companies resorted to the use of a schoolhouse and of a room in the second story of a building used as a store.

In fact, the first playhouse worthy of the name to be erected in Cincinnati was the Cincinnati Theatre (later sometimes called the Columbia Street Theatre and the Citizens' Theatre), on Second Street, between Main and Sycamore, opened by Collins & Jones in 1820. This brick structure, forty by eighty or ninety feet, contained two tiers of boxes, a pit, and a gallery; and was designed to accommodate from six to eight hundred spectators when it should be completed — but its capacity for many years

---

[157] For the projected new joint stock theatre, and for an account of the destruction of Masonic Hall, see *Ky. Gaz.*, Aug. 29 and Sept. 1; and *Observer & Reporter*, Aug 31, 1836.

was probably not so great. The stage occupied about half
of the space. The cost of the building, which was commenced by a company of thirty or forty persons, was estimated at less than $5000; shares were sold at $150, with
the provision that the annual income on each should be
ten per cent or a season ticket.[158] Such was the playhouse
which, under various names, was in use for a long period.
Half a dozen years after its erection the place was considered a disgrace to the town. "A more uncomfortable,
dirty hole than this," wrote a contemporary critic,

never bore the name of theatre. As for its locality, a more
filthy street could not be found in town; and the mud from
the street, as a matter of course, is carried into, and
tramped upon the seats throughout the house, which are
never washed, except by the rain, pouring in torrents
through the roof.

The method of lighting the house was, according to this
writer, another means of causing discomfort to playgoers.
The sperm dripping from the candles about the boxes fell
upon people sitting in the pit.[159]

In the same town the Pavilion Theatre (later called the
Globe, and finally the City Theatre), owned by Dumilieu
& Charles, was first opened on July 4, 1822. A few weeks
later, when some alterations had been made, it was announced that, contrary to the fashion in other theatres, the
seats in the pit were here furnished with back railings to
prevent the crowd from walking over them, and to afford
added comfort to spectators seated there.[160] The Amphitheatre, the old circus building on Sycamore Street, which
Ludlow and Brown leased from a certain Woodruff, was a

[158] *Liberty Hall*, Oct. 29, 1819; *The Cincinnati Directory*, for
1819, p. 154; and Drake and Mansfield, *Cincinnati in 1826*, p. 30.
*Cf.* also Ludlow, *op. cit.*, p. 175; and *The Cincinnati Directory*, for
1834, p. 254.

[159] *Daily Cinc. Gaz.*, Jan. 8, 1829; *cf. ibid.*, Dec. 16, 1828.
[160] *Liberty Hall*, Sept. 4, 1822.

dingy place, originally built, it seems, for a bathhouse. Yet it was said to be little worse than the Columbia Street Theatre, as the old Cincinnati Theatre was now usually called; and in 1831 it was refitted by Caldwell, who had new scenery and decorations made under the direction of Mondelli, of the American Theatre at New Orleans. It would now seat about eight hundred people, one-fourth of whom could be crowded into the boxes, with room for nearly the same number in the gallery and for the remainder in the pit.

Caldwell's New Cincinnati Theatre, first opened in 1832, marked the beginning of a new era. At that time it was said to be "decidedly the most costly and elegant structure in the Western States." Its capacity of from thirteen to fifteen hundred persons — "2000 or more can probably crowd into it if the lobbies are occupied" — was much greater than that of any theatre in the West up to that time. Chandeliers and lamps took the place of the old-fashioned sperm candles. The dress circle was divided into fifteen boxes capable of seating three hundred and fifty persons — so large that small family parties were always likely to be disturbed by the entrance of strangers into these "huge cattle-pens." There were two special "stage boxes" ornamented with chandeliers of bronze and gold. The proscenium was an arch of nearly forty feet span, supported by four Doric pilasters; and each scene was thirty-two feet long and twenty-five high, the work of Mondelli. The cost of the establishment was said to be $40,000. This building, however, had been in use only four years when it was destroyed by fire.[161] For some

---

[161] For the history and description of this theatre as given above, see *Cinc. Daily Gaz.*, June 28, July 2 and 11, Aug. 4, and Oct. 5, 1832; and Oct. 22, 1836. *Cf.* also *The Cincinnati Mirror and Ladies' Parterre*, July 7, 1832; and *The Cincinnati Directory*, for 1834, pp. 254-255.

time after this catastrophe temporary quarters, such as the
Cincinnati Exchange and a room at Walnut and Pearl
Streets, were used for theatricals. In the spring of the
following year, 1837, the City Theatre, a temporary structure, was erected by Potter & Waters at the corner of
Main and Seventh Streets; but later in the same year the
New National Theatre, on Sycamore, between Third and
Fourth Streets, owned by Bates & Surtees, was opened
by Scott & Thorne. This building, which was the successor
to Caldwell's Cincinnati Theatre, was also built at a cost
of about $40,000 and seems to have been at least the equal
of that comparatively luxurious establishment.

In Louisville, an old brick building on the north side of
Jefferson Street between Third and Fourth Streets was
probably the only theatre until 1829. From about 1808
until 1818, when Drake altered it, it is said to have been
little better than a barn. In 1818, however, it was described
as a handsome building of three stories, containing a pit,
two tiers of boxes — sixteen boxes in all, says an account
of 1822 — and a gallery, and as having a total capacity of
about eight hundred persons. In 1830 this playhouse was
rebuilt by Drake as the City Theatre. The new building
was fifty-two feet in width, slightly over a hundred in
length, and about thirty-four in height, and had three
ranges of boxes, a pit, and a saloon; but it was capable of
seating only about seven hundred spectators.[162]

162 For the history and description of Louisville theatres given
above, see H. M'Murtrie, *Sketches of Louisville*, 1819, p. 126; *Lou.
Pub. Adv.*, Apr. 13, 1822, and Mar. 22-26, 1830; and *The Louisville
Directory, for the Year 1832*, p. 139. According to *The Louisville
Directory*, the old building was torn down in 1828 and a new one
built by Drake on the same spot at that time and called the City
Theatre. The theatrical notices in the press do not confirm this
statement. For comment by a British traveller on the condition of
the ''theatre at Louisville'' in 1830, see James Stuart, *Three Years
in North America*, 1833, II, 186. The house was, says Stuart, ''un-

Ludlow's Melodramatic Theatre, which he built in 1829 at the corner of Jefferson and Third Streets, was hurriedly constructed and seems to have been of a temporary nature. The following year it was altered for use as a theatre and circus; and it was probably the same structure which, in 1836, Caldwell remodeled under the name of the American Theatre, a makeshift to be used until he could realize his scheme for erecting "in the rear of the Louisville Hotel, on Market street," a structure to contain a "NEW THEATRE, ARCADE BATHS, BALL-ROOM, &c. &c." and to cost $50,000.[163] This playhouse, which was to be patterned after the New American Theatre then in process of erection in New Orleans, was never built. With a similar scheme which engaged public interest in Louisville in 1838,[164] Caldwell likely had no connection; and the new project itself seems not to have been realized before the end of the period. The Circus, near the corner of Jefferson and Third Streets, which was destroyed by fire in 1840, was probably the old building which Ludlow had erected as the Melodramatic Theatre and which Caldwell had later remodeled as the American Theatre.[165] Concerning the

der repair when I was there, but though in an unfinished state, it was opened one evening while I remained, and I had the pleasure of seeing Mrs. Drake." The playhouse which is thus referred to was almost certainly the remodeled one newly christened the City Theatre, which Drake reopened, after two postponements, on Mar. 26, 1830, with an apology for its "unfinished state" (Cf. Lou. Pub. Adv., Mar. 22-26, 1830).

[163] Lou. Pub. Adv., Oct. 26, 1835; and July 20, 1836.

[164] Ibid., Aug. 9, 1838.

[165] For accounts of the destruction of this building, on the night of Feb. 17-18, 1840, see Lou. Pub. Adv., Feb. 19, and Cinc. Daily Gaz., Feb. 20, 1840. The Louisville paper describes the place as the Circus, near the corner of Jefferson and Third, while the Cincinnati paper refers to it as the old American Theatre, which "had just been fitted up as an amphitheatre." According to the latter authority, the loss was supposed to be from $12,000 to $15,000.

Adelphi Theatre, on Fifth Street (1833), and the Pagoda Theatre, on Fifth Street between Main and Market (1837), there is little information to be had. The two may have been identical; they were, at all events, of no considerable importance in the dramatic history of Louisville.

At St. Louis, such irregular theatricals as may be traced in contemporary records were for some years performed in a building used first, it is said, as a blacksmith shop, and later as a courthouse, a church, and a theatre — so primitive was the machinery of civilization at this early frontier post. Turner, during his visit to the town, is said to have performed both in this old building and in the loft of a stable attached to the Green Tree Tavern.[166] The small frame structure, between what were later Olive and Locust Streets, opened by the Thespians in 1819 was capable of containing about three hundred people.[167] Though a foundation for a theatre to be built of brick was laid by 1821,[168] there seems to have been no other building devoted to theatricals until 1825. Drake's performances early in 1820 were in a room of the City Hotel.

In 1825, however, the Thespians fitted up a brick warehouse on Church Street which had been "formerly occupied by Messrs. Scott & Rule."[169] And this theatre, known as the Old Salt-house, was later leased and remodeled by Caldwell, and was used by Ludlow and others as late as 1836. Caldwell, with his usual enterprise, had projected, as early as 1828, a new theatre to cost $15,000, half of which sum he himself would supply. It was to be used

---

[166] *Mo. Gaz.*, 1814-1819, *passim*, as cited in the present chapter, footnotes 26 ff. *et passim*; and in the calendar printed below. See also Thomas and Wild, *The Valley of the Mississippi*, 1841, p. 24 (based on information furnished by Charles Keemle).

[167] Thomas and Wild, *op. cit.*, p. 24.

[168] John A. Paxton, "Notes on St. Louis," in *The St. Louis Directory*, 1821.

[169] *Mo. Rep.*, Oct. 24, 1825.

instead of the Old Salt-house, already regarded as inadequate.[170]　But Caldwell withdrew from St. Louis without being able to realize this project.　Although Ferrall, who visited the place about 1830, reported that this old theatre was one of the principal buildings in the town,[171] it was in fact a contemptible excuse for a playhouse.　Sometime before it was destroyed by fire, in February, 1837,[172] a successful movement was under way for the erection of a new theatre which should be comparatively magnificent. Some minor performances were given at such places as Concert Hall (1840) and the Museum (1840) ; but the New St. Louis Theatre, at the corner of Third and Olive Streets, was from the time of its opening, in July, 1837, the center of theatricals.

This theatre, according to contemporary observers,[173] was, about 1840, "undoubtedly the finest building for Dramatic purposes in the whole Valley of the Mississippi." Its front, which is described as completed (though in reality it never was), was to be copied from the Erectheum at Athens, the portico being supported by a number of imposing columns.　The building, which was seventy-three feet in width and one hundred and sixty in depth, contained a parquette and three tiers, and was capable of seating fourteen hundred persons.　The proscenium, about which were built the "stage boxes," was an imitation of the choragic monument of Lysicrates at Athens.　The stage was fifty-five feet wide and seventy-three in depth. "Square tin boxes, with large burners for spirit gas,"

---

[170] Ibid., Sept. 16, 1828.

[171] Simon Ansley Ferrall, A Ramble of Six Thousand Miles, 1832, p. 129.　Cf. the ridicule of this theatre in Mo. Rep., Oct. 7, 1834.

[172] Ludlow, op. cit., p. 471.　The project for the new theatre had made some progress as early as 1835 (Mo. Rep., Dec. 17, 1835), and bids for the construction of the building were called for a few months later (ibid., Mar. 19, 1836).

[173] Thomas and Wild, op. cit., p. 23.

formed the footlights, and lamps using the same fuel were used to light the whole auditorium. The floor of the parquette was so built that it could be removed when it was desired to transform the place into an amphitheatre for equestrian performances. The cost of the whole establishment seems to have been sixty or seventy thousand dollars, but accounts do not agree.[174]

Only meagre information is to be had regarding the buildings where Detroit theatricals were performed. The place used by the officers of the garrison for amateur exhibitions about the years 1815-1820 was government property, apparently a warehouse at the foot of Cass Street. The professional troupe which Fuller brought to Detroit in 1827 played, according to William Forrest, in the loft of "the brick barn in the rear of Uncle Ben Woodworth's Steamboat Hotel," using the stalls for dressing rooms.[175] Again, we hear of a room over a grocery store at Woodward Avenue and Atwater Street which was used for plays "about 1828." The barn belonging to the Steamboat Hotel is said to have been used again by an organized

[174] For detailed accounts from which the description given above has been drawn, see Thomas and Wild, *op. cit.*, pp. 23-24; and Ludlow, *op. cit.*, pp. 407 and 476-478. Where Ludlow does not agree with Thomas and Wild in minor details, I have, except in regard to one or two matters, preferred the account of the latter, as it was written about forty years earlier, and within about four years after the theatre was erected. As to the cost of the theatre, the *St. Louis Commercial Bulletin*, Sept. 25, 1835, states that the first estimates called for only $15,000. Ludlow, however, asserts (*op. cit.*, pp. 468-469) that it was first agreed that the expense should be $30,000, but this amount was later more than doubled. According to Thomas and Wild, the cost was $70,000. Ludlow states that the lessees were required to pay ten per cent on the investment, and were thus greatly handicapped by the increased capitalization. For a brief newspaper notice, see *Mo. Rep.*, July 10, 1837.

[175] "The First Theatrical Company in Detroit," *The Detroit Daily Tribune*, Apr. 20, 1860.

company of players in 1830; and, though this date is probably wrong, the local historian who is responsible for the tradition could scarcely have been in error regarding the place. The same building, it seems, was the scene of theatricals by Parsons & Dean about 1832 or 1833. Whatever the location of Parsons & Dean's theatre, the quarters were cramped.[176]  And the theatre of Eberle, Powell & Co. (1834), on Woodward Avenue, was likewise a makeshift.

But a change gradually came about. Though amateur performances were later to be given in the University Building, from this time more conventional housing was to be had for visiting players. The City Theatre, owned by David C. McKinstrey [177] and for some years the center of dramatic activity in Detroit, was fashioned from a brick building (at the corner of State and Farrar Streets) originally intended for a Methodist church and actually used as such for some time; but it was given the semblance of a theatre with gallery and boxes and was capable of containing about four hundred spectators. As late as 1840 it was still in use.

Another amusement place built by McKinstrey, a large frame building opposite the City Theatre, was originally intended for a circus, but probably never used as such. In 1838 it was altered and opened by Henry Isherwood as the Detroit National Theatre, which now began disastrous competition with its older rival. During the coldest part of the winter, however, this place had to be abandoned on account of the difficulty of heating; and the players were often compelled to turn to the Museum, where theatricals had been given as early as 1837. This establishment, also under the control of McKinstrey, was located in the third story of a building at Jefferson Avenue and Griswold

176 *Detroit Journal and Michigan Advertiser*, July 24, 1833.
177 *Detroit Daily Free Press*, Aug. 5, 1836.

Street. The ownership of the building was, however, in
other hands; and some of the occupants opposed the presentation of plays there because of the danger of fire. The
museum of wax figures and curiosities in this place was,
according to a certain Adair, who was for some years the
manager, a better-paying amusement than theatricals.[178]

## VII

Some light on the extent of dramatic activity in the
pioneer West and even upon the vogue of different types
of dramatic composition and the popularity of individual
dramatic authors and plays, is to be had from a study of
over seven thousand performances advertisements of which
occur in the newspaper records used as the basis of the
present chapter.[179] Though a comparatively small number

[178] The facts regarding McKinstrey's amusement places are drawn
largely from Julius P. B. MacCabe, *Directory of the City of Detroit*,
1837, pp. 28-29 and 105; and *The Sunday News-Tribune* (Detroit),
Aug. 19, 1894, p. 11. See also newspapers for 1836-1840, as cited
below in the calendar. Three slightly different spellings of McKinstrey's name occur.

[179] For the newspapers examined, see below, bibliography for
Chapter III. From these papers I have drawn notices of 7594
dramatic performances, representing approximately half that number
of nights — two plays were usually given in the course of the same
evening's entertainment. With one exception — that of a single
playbill in the possession of the Missouri Historical Society — the
data here given have been derived from those sources. Except in a
few instances, only one newspaper file for any given year was followed for each of the five towns studied. A comparatively small
amount of information, of undetermined value, has thus been disre-
garded. Such unreliable records as the recollections of contemporary
observers have here been wholly dismissed from consideration. The
detailed accounts of performances given in such books as Ludlow's
*Dramatic Life as I Found it* are too often erroneous to be given any
weight. It should be noted that for certain years — especially 1835,

of plays were the favorites which made up the programs of the bulk of the performances, there were not far from a thousand that were used at least once.[180]  Of the more than seven thousand performances noted, only fifty-one belong to the period ending with 1810, while 451 belong to the second decade, exactly fourteen hundred to the third, and 5692 to the fourth.  Some idea of the comparative dramatic activity in the various towns is to be gained from the fact that of the total number of performances recorded more than one-third belong to Cincinnati, considerably less than a third to Louisville, not quite one-fifth to St. Louis, less than one-eighth to Detroit, and slightly over one-twentieth to Lexington.

There is, of course, no very satisfactory method of classifying plays; but, of approximately 6700 performances of dramatic pieces that can be assigned with some degree of certainty to a particular category, considerably over one-third were farces of small pretense to literary value; between one-fifth and one-fourth were melodramas in which spectacle or improbable romance was the staple; only slightly more than one-eighth were tragedies or historical plays; a somewhat larger number were comedies of some pretension to literary dignity; almost one-ninth were operas, mostly comic; and the small number remaining — about a hundred — were pantomimes.[181]  During the first two decades following 1799, the ratio between the more or less dignified literary dramas — tragedies, historical plays,

and, to a lesser extent, 1839 and 1840 — newspaper records, because of the failure of the theatres to advertise regularly, are very inadequate.

[180] I have recorded 967.

[181] Of 7594 performances recorded, I have left 885 unclassified, dividing the remainder as follows: farces, 2647; melodramas, 1429; tragedies and historical plays, 871; comedies, 953; operas, 710; and pantomimes, 99.

and comedies — and the four of lower literary value — farce, opera, melodrama, and pantomime — was about one to one and a half. During the years 1821-1840, however, the less legitimate dramatic forms increased their already noticeable predominance until the proportion was one to only slightly less than three.

Of the plays which were most often seen, however, a remarkable proportion were of some literary importance. Of all dramatists, Shakespeare was not only credited with first rank in every opinion directly or indirectly expressed by Western writers, but was actually given first rank in the matter of the total number of performances of the work of any one author: of the 7594 performances recorded, 433, or more than one in eighteen, were of Shakespearean plays. The number of such performances, which was only two for the first decade of the century, increased during the latter half of the period out of proportion to the growth of drama in general, largely for the reason that prominent actors on tours, who were most numerous at that time, seldom failed to attempt some Shakespearean play.[182] Among the Western towns Louisville, according to the data here used, was first in the number of Shakespearean performances, with Cincinnati second, and St. Louis, Detroit, and Lexington following in the order named.[183] Of the individual plays, the favorites, in the order of their popularity, were *Richard III, Othello, Hamlet, The Taming of the Shrew* (invariably known as *Catharine and Petruchio*, and certainly sometimes, and probably always, the alteration of Garrick), *The Merchant of Venice, Macbeth, Romeo and*

[182] The number of Shakespearean performances (excluding doubtful ones) which I have recorded for each decade of the early nineteenth century is: first decade, 2; second, 37; third, 73; fourth, 321.

[183] The number of Shakespearean performances in each of the towns was as follows: Louisville, 150; Cincinnati, 140; St. Louis, 70; Detroit, 39; Lexington, 34.

*Juliet, Much Ado,* and *King Lear.* At least eight, and just possibly ten, others occur with less frequency.[184] *Richard III* was equalled in popularity by only one non-Shakespearean play, Kotzebue's *Die Spanier in Peru,* which was produced as adapted by Sheridan under the title of *Pizarro.*

Aside from Shakespeare, no dramatist of the Elizabethan period seems to have been known at all on the Western stage. Of the Jacobeans, John Fletcher and Philip Massinger had some popularity during the last decade before 1841, each being represented by a single play.[185] Not a play of Dryden's occurs, and the only one of Wycherley's was adapted; of Restoration playwrights, Otway and Southerne alone were known at first hand.[186]

Of early eighteenth century dramatists, Rowe was known for *Jane Shore* alone, Mrs. Centlivre for three of her comedies, and Young for *The Revenge.* Gay's *The Beggar's Opera* was performed twice; Lillo's *George Barnwell* attained some popularity; Fielding was known for his translation *The Mock Doctor,* and a burlesque called *Tom Thumb the Great,* not very popular, was doubtless his.

---

[184] The Shakespeare plays, with the number of performances of each which I have found, are: *As you Like it,* 8; *Catharine and Petruchio,* 45; *Coriolanus,* 1; *Hamlet,* 60; *Henry IV,* 10; *Julius Caesar,* 11; *King John,* 2; *King Lear,* 20; *Love's Labour's Lost* (doubtful), 2; *Macbeth,* 43; *The Merchant of Venice,* 44; *Much Ado,* 21; *Othello,* 62; *Richard II,* 1; *Richard III,* 68; *Romeo and Juliet,* 26; *The Tempest,* 10; *Twelfth Night,* 1; *The Two Gentlemen of Verona* (doubtful), 1. I have not determined which part of *Henry IV* was played. It is even possible that both parts were performed, but at different times.

[185] *Rule a Wife and Have a Wife* was played 8 times from 1829 to 1834, while *A New Way to Pay Old Debts* was performed 24 times from 1831 to 1840.

[186] *The Country Wife,* as adapted by Garrick (*The Country Girl*), was twice acted; *Venice Preserved* was performed 29 times, and *Isabella, or the Fatal Marriage,* 15.

Garrick's *The Lying Valet* was produced a number of times; and Whitehead's play of *The Roman Father*, once.[187] Many standard plays of the later eighteenth century proved popular. Home's *Douglas* and Cumberland's *The Jew* and *The West-Indian* were well known. There were frequent performances of Sheridan's *The School for Scandal*, *The Critic*, *The Rivals*, and *St. Patrick's Day*. Goldsmith, who enjoyed a wide popularity in the West as an essayist, gained some repute as a playwright, *She Stoops to Conquer* being performed more than a score of times. Mrs. Cowley and Mrs. Inchbald were each represented by a number of plays; and Holcroft's *The Road to Ruin* and *Deaf and Dumb* were known. George Colman the Younger was, however, by all odds the most popular eighteenth century dramatist. Though none of his numerous comedies, farces, melodramas, and comic operas, with perhaps two or three exceptions, could be said to have attained an unusual success, the whole number of performances of his plays amounts to two hundred and sixty.[188]

---

[187] Among the performances I have recorded for plays here cited, Rowe's *Jane Shore* appears 14 times; Mrs. Centlivre's *The Wonder! A Woman Keeps a Secret*, 15, *The Busy Body*, 7, and *A Bold Throw for a Wife*, 2. Young's *The Revenge* appears 5 times; Lillo's *George Barnwell*, 22; Fielding's *The Mock Doctor*, 7, and *Tom Thumb the Great*, 8; Garrick's *The Lying Valet*, 14, *Miss in her Teens*, 3, *The Country Girl*, 2, *The Irish Widow*, 1, *Peeping Tom at Coventry*, 1.

[188] Recorded performances of later eighteenth century plays are as follows: Home's *Douglas*, 26; Cumberland's *The Jew*, 14, *The West-Indian*, 10, *The Wheel of Fortune*, 4, and *The Carmelite*, 1; Sheridan's *The School for Scandal*, 31, *The Critic*, 18, *The Rivals*, 11, and *St. Patrick's Day*, 9; Goldsmith's *She Stoops to Conquer*, 24; Mrs. Cowley's *The Belle's Stratagem*, 19, *Who's the Dupe?* 14, *A Bold Throw for a Husband*, 8, and *Will she be Married or not?* 1; Mrs. Inchbald's *Animal Magnetism*, 24, *Wives as they were*, 22, *The Wedding Day*, 17, *The Midnight Hour*, 17, *Lovers' Vows*, 6, *The Mogul Tale*, 3, *Every one Has his Faults*, 4, *The Child of Na-*

Of the English dramatists who wrote at the beginning of the nineteenth century, only a few of any importance are to be noticed here.   There were over a hundred performances of Thomas Morton's plays, of which *Town and Country, Speed the Plough, Children in the Wood, A Roland for an Oliver*, and *A Cure for the Heartache* were the most popular.   Frederick Reynolds's *Laugh when you can* and *The Dramatist* were often played, and a few others of his pieces were known.   James Sheridan Knowles's *Virginius, William Tell*, and *The Wife* were very popular in the Western theatres.[189]   Dimond's *The Lady and the Devil, The Foundling of the Forest, The Hunter of the Alps*, and *The Broken Sword*, which were the best-known of many by that playwright, about equalled Knowles's plays in popularity.   O'Keefe's *The Poor Soldier* and Douglas Jerrold's *Black-eyed Susan* were the most popular works by these authors, each of them reaching about fifty performances. M. G. Lewis's *Timour the Tartar, Adelgitha*, and *The Castle Spectre* were successful; and at least one dramatic version of his *Ambrosio, or the Monk* was performed.[190] Maturin's *Bertram* was produced more than a score of times, and a stage version of *Melmoth, the Wanderer*, much less often.   Mrs. Shelley's fiction was represented by a

*ture*, 2, and *Such Things are*, 1; Holcroft's *The Road to Ruin*, 12, *The Two Friends*, 8, *Deaf and Dumb*, 5, and *The School for Arrogance*, 1; Colman's *The Review*, 48, *The Forty Thieves*, 42, *The Blue Devils*, 25, *The Poor Gentleman*, 21, *The Heir at Law*, 16, *The Mountaineers*, 14, *Jonathan in England*, 13, *The Iron Chest*, 13, *Ways and Means*, 12, *John Bull*, 12, *Love Laughs at Locksmiths*, 11, *Blue Beard*, 10, *Sylvester Daggerwood*, 9, *Who Wants a Guinea?* 8, *Inkle and Yarico*, 3, *We Fly by Night*, 2, and *X. Y. Z.*, 1.

[189] The tragedy of *Virginius* occurs 48 times; *William Tell*, 47; *The Wife*, 31.  Performances of several other plays by Knowles made the total 208.

[190] A play called *The Forest of Rosenwald, or the Bleeding Nun* occurs 6 times, while the title *Raymond and Agnes* occurs 5 times.

play, little seen, called *The Monster, or the Fate of Frankenstein.* Southey's *Thalaba* and "Mary, the Maid of the Inn" were not popular in dramatic form. Scott's works furnished entertainment for the Western stage in *The Lady of the Lake,* a melodrama, which occurs some thirty times; *Rob Roy* (Pocock's adaptation), with exactly fifty performances; and *Guy Mannering* (adapted by Terry), with over thirty. *The Heart of Midlothian* (Dibdin's version) and a play called *Ivanhoe, or the Jew of York,* together with several other adaptations, enjoyed scant popularity. Byron was scarcely known as a dramatist; a single performance of *Sardanapalus* appears among the recorded theatricals, and only one of *Werner.* A play by Dimond called *The Bride of Abydos,* based upon Byron's poem of that name and upon *The Corsair,* occurs thirteen times, while an equestrian drama called *Mazeppa* proved a strong attraction in the Western theatres, where the appearance of horses on the stage was a novelty which for some time excited great applause. This *Mazeppa* was played thirty-five times. A farce called *Mr. H., or Beware of a Bad Name,* probably Lamb's play which had been hissed at Drury Lane, was somewhat more fortunate upon the Western stage. Bulwer's *The Lady of Lyons* gained considerable success; and *Richelieu* and *The Sea Captain,* as well as adaptations of his novels called *The Last Days of Pompeii* and *Leila,* were performed.

American dramatists, with the single exception of John Howard Payne, were given slight attention. Payne's greatest successes were *Therese, Charles the Second, 'Twas I, or the Truth a Lie,* and *Clari.*[191] William Dunlap's adap-

---

[191] The number of performances for these four plays, in the order given above, was 43, 33, 29, and 23. *Brutus* was played 17 times; *Love in Humble Life,* 17; and the translation called *The Two Galley Slaves,* 11. The total of performances I have recorded for these and other plays by Payne is 180.

tation *Abaellino* had, it is surprising to find, only scant popularity; *The Death of André* occurs only once, and other pieces by the same author were no better known. Noah's play *The Wandering Boys* was popular; *Rip Van Winkle* and *The Spectre Bridegroom*, based on Irving's stories, had together more than fifty performances; and a very successful melodrama called *Paul Jones or the Pilot*, together with the much less successful *Mount St. Bernard or the Headsman*, *The Red Rover*, *The Wept of Wish-ton-wish*, and *The Last of the Mohicans*, reflected the fame of Cooper's novels.

Many of the successful plays used in the Western theatres were, of course, adapted from Continental novels; but few pieces of importance translated directly from French or German originals were used. *Jodolet*, announced as a translation from Corneille [192] by René Paul, a St. Louis author of French descent, kept the stage for only a few nights; and Fielding's translation of Molière in *The Mock Doctor* has already been mentioned. Hugo's *Tour de Nesle* was performed less than a score of times. But the popularity of Kotzebue during this period was as marked in the frontier theatres as on the American and European stage in general. *Die Spanier in Peru*, in Sheridan's translation called *Pizarro*, was, with its exotic and spectacular appeal, the most popular play of the whole period, receiving no less than sixty-nine performances; and *The Stranger* was only slightly less successful, occurring fifty-eight times. *Lovers' Vows*, as translated by Mrs. Inchbald, and *Reconciliation, or the Birthday* gained, however, little applause, so that the total number of performances of Kotzebue plays, including some other adaptations, bore no comparison to that of Shakespeare's and was even far below the mark

---

[192] Were it not for the newspaper statement to the contrary, it would, perhaps, be more reasonable to suppose that René Paul used not a play by Corneille, but Molière's *Les précieuses ridicules*.

set by the younger Colman. A *Faustus*, which was prob-
ably Soane and Terry's perversion of the first part of
Goethe's drama, enjoyed a small degree of popularity; and
Schiller's tragedy of *The Robbers*, even less.

In opera, more direct, though not very extensive, Continental influence was felt. *Der Freischütz* was given
several performances; and Bellini's *La sonnambula*, fewer
than half a dozen. The chief channel of Italian influence
was Rossini, the singing of whose *Il barbiere di Siviglia*, *Il
Turco in Italia*, and *L'inganno felice* by an Italian company at the American Theatre in Louisville in 1836 [193]
marked the beginning of a new era in Western music.
While these operas were being sung at the American
Theatre, the managers of the City Theatre, with no performers who could sing Rossini in the original, countered
with an English version of *Cinderella*, whereupon the
American Theatre advertised a performance of it in the
Italian original.[194] The English version of *Cinderella* was
remarkably successful in the West; and, for both Italian
and English versions, there were no fewer than sixty-one
performances.

Of the two plays almost invariably performed on the
same evening, one was usually a farce, variously denominated "farce," "afterpiece," "interlude," "petit comedy," "burletta," "extravaganza," etc. In these guises, a
large number of dramatic pieces of the slightest literary
value were admitted on the stage and were, in fact, regarded
as an almost indispensable ingredient of a theatrical enter-

---

[193] *Lou. Pub. Adv.*, Aug. 9, 12, 19, 23, and 26, and Sept. 3, 6, 8, 22,
and 30, 1836. There were a total of ten performances of these operas
during this season, and probably two of *Cinderella* in Italian — but
possibly the operas of Sept. 22 and 30 were not sung by the Italians.
The Italian Opera Company which was to have given a vocal concert
at the National Hotel in St. Louis on July 6, 1836 (*Mo. Rep.*, July
5, 1836) was the same which presently appeared in Louisville.

[194] *Lou. Pub. Adv.*, Oct. 1, 4, 6, 7, and 8, 1836.

tainment.  Many were musical, defying classification, on
the line between comic opera and farce.  Most of the compositions used in this manner were, it is true, seldom repeated; but a considerable number gained a vogue almost,
but not quite, equal to that of the best-known among the
regular dramas.  *The Spoiled Child, The Day after the
Wedding, The Rendezvous, The Irish Tutor, No Song No
Supper, The Young Widow, The Lottery Ticket, Nature
and Philosophy, The Turnpike Gate, Turn out,* and *Family
Jars* were performed from thirty-five to more than sixty
times each.  Among melodramatic spectacles or operas
which achieved a comparable degree of success were *Cherry
and Fair Star, Peter Wilkins, or the Flying Islanders,* and
such equestrian exotic pieces as *Timour the Tartar, The
Brigand,* and *El Hyder.*

Farces, melodramas, and comic operas were, in fact, the
staple of many seasons at the Western theatres.  No doubt
the exotic spectacles and the most high-colored of the
other melodramatic pieces attracted generally the largest
patronage that the regular stock companies alone could
command; but the production of these was discouraged by
the excessive expense involved ·and the time required to
provide the scenic effects.  Such minor playwrights as J.
B. Buckstone, Thomas Dibdin, W. T. Moncrieff, J. R.
Planché, and James Kenney achieved a vogue which was
surpassed only by that of a few of the more reputable authors.  Shakespeare alone triumphed over all of them de-
cisively.

## VIII

Plays on Western life awakened but little interest.  Only
a few such pieces were introduced, and they were generally
failures.  *The Lion of the West,* apparently altered from
Paulding, and *The Kentuckian, or a Trip to New York* had
together less than a dozen performances; and *Nick of the*

*Woods,* very likely Medina's adaptation of Bird's novel, was less popular than either. A number of other plays with local setting, none probably by Western authors, barely survived an initial performance or at most a second night, if the newspaper records examined may be supposed to give their entire career. *Daniel Boone, or the First Settlers of Kentucky,* advertised as a piece never before performed, was brought out in Cincinnati in 1824; *The Kentucky Rifle* was played at Louisville in 1830; and at the same place, two years later, there was a performance of *Huzzah for the Boys of the West. Main Street, Louisville* and *Life in Cincinnati, or the Valiant Earthquakes,* the latter with a title of genuine Western flavor, received a total of at least three performances in 1836 and 1837. *The Hunter of the West* was also played at Cincinnati in 1837.

Somewhat more than a score of plays definitely ascribed to Western authors must be briefly mentioned. Before the end of 1810 a certain Abram Jones, of Paris, Kentucky, had published *Love in Jeopardy, a Tragic Comedy*;[195] but there is no proof that this piece was ever performed. Alphonso Wetmore, known, some years later, for his *Gazetteer of the State of Missouri,* was also the author of *The Pedlar: a Farce in Three Acts. Written for the St. Louis Thespians, by whom it was Performed with Great Applause* (1821). Some years after this piece had appeared in print it was performed in Lexington, by the Thespian Society, and, still later, in St. Louis, by an amateur association.[196]

[195] It is advertised for sale in the *Ky. Gaz.,* Nov. 6, 1810, and later.

[196] For a performance of the play announced by the St. Louis Juvenile Thespian Association, see *Mo. Rep.,* Mar. 27, 1835. It is clear that the farce advertised as *The Pedlar* by the Lexington Thespian Society ten years earlier was also Wetmore's play (see *Ky. Gaz.,* Jan. 13, 1825).

Sol Smith, who was editor of a newspaper at Cincinnati
in 1823, wrote what was advertised as an original interlude
called *The Tailor in Distress*, in which, according to Smith's
own statement, Edwin Forrest played the part of a negro
at a theatre in that town.[197] About this time M. Smith,
the author's brother, improvised a comic piece called
*Modern Fashions*, which was, according to the same
authority, also put on at the Globe Theatre.[198]  *The Rifle,
or Presumptive Evidence*, a melodrama performed at Cincinnati in 1829, was said to have been written by a person
living in that place, who had based it upon William Leg-
gett's tale of "The Rifle," published in *The Atlantic
Souvenir*, for 1828; according to a report repeated by Sol
Smith, the author of this play was Solon Robinson, later an
Eastern editor.[199]  In 1829 there was published, presumably at Harrodsburg, Kentucky, a tragedy by G. Burton
Thompson, of Cincinnati, written, says the author, for the
purpose of punishing his enemies who had maligned him
because of his failure to pay his debts.[200]  *Loss and Gain*, a
comedy by T. Somers Nelson, was printed at St. Louis in
1835, with a dedication to the St. Louis Thespian Association.

Of greater interest, however, were a number of plays by
frontier writers which made use of the Indians and were

[197] Smith, *The Theatrical Apprenticeship*, 1846, p. 50; and *Independent Press*, July 17, 1823.

[198] Smith, *The Theatrical Apprenticeship*, 1846, p. 50. This was
doubtless the "petit comedy" of *Dandyism, or Modern Fashions* advertised (*Independent Press*, July 17, 1823) to be played at the
Globe Theatre on the same night with Sol Smith's *The Tailor in Distress*.

[199] See *Daily Cinc. Gaz.*, Jan. 22, 1829; and Smith, *Theatrical
Management*, 1868, p. 121.

[200] In his pamphlet *An Address of G. Burton Thompson, Esq. of
Cincinnati, Ohio, to the Citizens of Mercer County, Kentucky*, 1829,
p. 16, he states that this tragedy was to be published simultaneously
with the *Address*. I have found neither a copy of the play, nor a
notice of its performance.

based on historical facts, legend, or the European-made
romantic tradition. Much applause and some apparently
well deserved criticism greeted the appearance at Cincinnati, in 1832, of a thoroughly Western play, *Lamorah, or
the Western Wild,* written by Mrs. Caroline Lee Hentz,
who had, in the preceding year, gained some favorable
notice in the East, through the performance in Philadelphia
and elsewhere of her prize piece called *De Lara; or, the
Moorish Bride,* and who had already acquired, in Cincinnati, a popular reputation as an author. The strong local
interest aroused gave *Lamorah* a life of at least three
nights. A review which appeared in *The Western Monthly
Magazine* early in 1833 reveals, however, the crudity of this
"DRAMA in five acts, written in the West, and the scene
laid on the banks of the Ohio!"[201] According to the reviewer,
who had read the piece but not seen it acted, it was too
hastily written and was objectionable because of an injudi-
cious mingling of serious and farcical characters, among the
latter being a coward named Gabriel, who wears a wig to
avoid being scalped. The same critic was pleased, however, with the sentimental character of the Indian heroine,
Lamorah, who "will not yield the palm to Pocahontas"
and who was surpassed only by Atala "from having early
implanted in her bosom, the seeds of a christian education."
Such was the lack of realism in what might have been
expected to contain a genuine picture of Western pioneer
life. The Indians of Rousseau and Chateaubriand and of
romance were, in fact, more interesting to a Western playwright than the Indians of flesh and blood who had lived
on the Ohio a quarter of a century before.

Another Indian drama, *Pontiac: or the Siege of Detroit*

[201] *The Western Monthly Magazine,* I, 59-66 (Feb., 1833). This
is quoted in *The Cincinnati Mirror and Ladies' Parterre,* Feb. 2,
1833. For an additional note on Mrs. Hentz, see above, p. ix.

(1835, preface dated 1826), may or may not have been written while the author, General Alexander Macomb, was still in Detroit, where he was known for his interest in theatricals. *Tecumseh: or, the Battle of the Thames, a National Drama* (1836) was an attempt at a new literary form by Richard Emmons. Reworking the same materials which he had already put into his ponderous epic,[202] he exchanged, however, his heroic couplets for a riotous kind of prose, added several new characters, and sought to excite dramatic interest by emphasizing a love episode. Kentucky's heroes were again glorified, and it was possibly in Kentucky that the piece was performed.[203]   Lewis F. Thomas, of Cincinnati, brother of the novelist, was the author of a tragedy called *Osceola*, based on the adventures of the Indian chief of that name. It was first produced at New Orleans and was seen shortly afterwards, during the year 1837, at both Louisville and Cincinnati.[204]   In the same year there was published in New York another Western play based on Indian life, *Pocahontas: a Historical Drama, in Five Acts; with an Introductory Essay and Notes. By a Citizen of the West*. Within a short time after the piece appeared in print it was produced by strolling players and by amateurs in Indiana, the author's home,

---

[202] See above, Chapter VII.

[203] No account of the presentation of the play is given, though what seems to be the cast of actors is printed with the list of the *dramatis personae*. I am uncertain whether Emmons was at this time a resident of the West.

[204] *The Western Monthly Magazine, and Literary Journal*, I, 74 (Feb., 1837); *Lou Pub. Adv.*, Mar. 1, 2, 3, and 7, 1837; and *Cinc. Daily Gaz.*, Jan. 18 and Sept. 15, 1837. It was performed for three nights at Louisville and one night at Cincinnati. The report circulated by a Louisville paper of Jan. 7, 1837, and repeated in *Cinc. Daily Gaz.*, Jan. 12 of the same year, that *Osceola* was to be performed at the City Theatre, Louisville on Jan. 9, was probably an error (*cf. Lou. Pub. Adv.*, Jan. 9, 1837).

and was even brought out on the New York stage.[205]    The
genius of Robert Dale Owen did not, however, succeed in
making a noteworthy play by thus reshaping the old tradition of the early days of Jamestown.   It is significant that
he chose the Virginia of a legend two centuries old and not
the Wisconsin or Iowa frontier as a setting for the Indian
life he wished to picture; and, though the body of notes
which he appended shows that he had patiently explored
not only Purchas and John Halkett, but Charlevoix, Volney,
and other writers who saw something of Indian life at first
hand, he did not free himself entirely from the Rousseau-
Chateaubriand fiction.[206]

Many plays by other Western authors made, however, no
pretence of achieving local color.   Among such was Mrs.
Alexander Drake's *Leona of Athens* (1834), which, whether
through its own merit or through the remarkable popularity of this favorite actress, held the Cincinnati stage for
four nights.[207]    *Jodolet*, a translation or adaptation by
René Paul, a St. Louis writer, has already been noticed as
one of the few evidences of the influence of French drama
in the Western theatres; it received at least three or four
performances.[208]    William Ross Wallace was the author, in

[205] For a performance of the play in Indianapolis, first by a group
of strolling professionals and later by a Thespian company — making probably a total of three or four performances — see Rabb,
"A Hoosier Listening Post," in *The Indianapolis Star*, Jan. 15,
1921, p. 6, col. 6.   The information here given is based upon manuscript reminiscences by Austin H. Brown.   For a notice of the
appearance of the play on the New York stage, see Arthur Hobson
Quinn, "The Early Drama, 1756-1860," in *The Cambridge History
of American Literature*, 1917, I, 225.

[206] For a contemporary debate regarding the originality of this
play, see *The Logansport Herald*, Dec. 14, 1837-Jan. 4, 1838.

[207] For a favorable criticism of the manuscript of the play, see
*Cinc. Daily Gaz.*, Sept. 10, 1834.   For performances, see *ibid.*, Sept.
11, 12, 13, and 15, 1834.

[208] *Mo. Rep.*, Aug. 28 and 30, and Sept. 14 and 24, 1838.

the reports circulated by the contemporary prints — it is just possible that these notices were at times falsified by managers eager to make the most of local civic loyalty — were the product of pioneer playwrights. Doubtless, however, there were many dramatic pieces written and performed in the West of which we have no record. On the whole, if the short stage life of such plays as are recorded in the sources here examined may be taken as evidence, Western dramas were not successful. With three or four exceptions, they must have been financially unprofitable after a first performance. There was, however, no dearth of aspiring playwrights, whose manuscripts descended in a flood upon the harassed managers.[220]

## IX

Both as a part of dramatic performances and entirely separate from them, spectacle was regarded by the Western managers as a necessary attraction. The ordinary scenery used was of the cheapest kind, usually made for the occasion by members of the company. For exotic melodramas, however, an extraordinary expense, sometimes ruinous, was incurred. At Cincinnati, for example, the cost of producing *The Flying Dutchman* under Drake's management in 1828 was said to be about a thousand dollars; and the scenery and decorations for *The Lady of the Lake*, *The Floating Beacon*, and *The Broken Sword* caused an extravagant outlay.[221] The danger to public taste, as well as the serious risk assumed by the manager, was vainly pointed out at the time. But advice to recur to "the rich mines

---

[220] It is said that the annoyance caused by such writers early became so great that the managers found it expedient to appoint a committee to relieve them of the embarrassment of refusing the proffered manuscripts (Smith, *Theatrical Management*, 1868, pp. 251-252 and 257).

[221] *Daily Cinc. Gaz.*, Mar. 14, 1828.

of the English drama,'' [222] when followed, did not aid mate-
rially in overcoming financial difficulties; and the season,
like many others, ended in disaster.  In the following year,
however, the same director not only spent nearly a thousand
dollars in preparing for the presentation of *The Red Rover*,
but tried unsuccessfully the expedient of bringing in
''stars.'' [223]  Later the expense of staging spectacular
pieces had become still more burdensome.  In 1833 a production of *Cinderella* cost, it is said, no less than three
thousand dollars in advance of the first night.[224]

And in general the vogue of extravagant spectacle and
melodrama was perfectly in keeping with the taste of the
time.  As early as 1828 a critic complained that melodrama had driven old-fashioned comedy from the St. Louis
stage.[225]  In 1837 a Detroit editor admiringly commented
on the attractions of the local theatre as a ''rapid succession'' of ''sterling comedy, showy melo-drama, gorgeous
spectacle, broad farce, and delightful vaudeville and
ballet.'' [226]  On special occasions, transparencies, tableaux,
and like scenic devices were effective in filling the theatre.
At Lexington, in 1810, the manager advertised a special
scene representing the burning of the ''Philadelphia'' in
the bay of Tripoli.[227]  On July 4, 1818, the St. Louis
theatre was decorated with ''an elegant transparency representing the Genius of America crowning with laurels
the tomb of the Immortal Washington.'' [228]  In 1821 a
disastrous season was retrieved by Jones's company at St.
Louis when a tableau of Washington and his family was

---

222 *Ibid.*, Oct. 10, 1828.
223 *Ibid.*, Nov. 20, 1829.
224 *Cinc. Daily Gaz.*, Aug. 3, 1833.
225 *Mo. Rep.*, Aug. 26, 1828.
226 *Detroit Free Press*, Aug. 9, 1837.
227 *Ky. Gaz.*, Sept. 11, 1810.
228 *Mo. Gaz.*, July 3, 1818.

shown three nights in succession.[229]   When Gray & Rowe
visited the same town in 1830, they announced, as additional
attractions, not only a representation of the harbor of New
Orleans, showing boats moving about, but a view of Naples
with Vesuvius in eruption, and a picture of a battle between
the American and Tripolitan fleets.[230]

A variety of other spectacular devices were employed.
At Cincinnati on election night, 1822, two balloons bearing
the names of candidates for Congress, were sent up from
the neighborhood of the theatre at Vauxhall Gardens, immediately after the performance; and at another time the
stage was the scene of the presentation of a prize to the
winner of a ferry race on the Ohio.[231]   The production
of some of the equestrian dramas offered unusual opportunity for spectacle.   In *Mazeppa*, for example, the Cos-
sack hetman was exhibited bound to the back of the horse;
and, for greater effect, the wild horse might even be made
to ascend from the stage to the roof of the theatre.[232]   Such
popular marvels as experiments in "exhilarating gas" at
the close of the play were resorted to as an extra attraction.[233]   The horses, dogs, camels, and monkeys used in
exotic melodrama were at times a disgrace to Western
theatres.[234]   A "Hercules" displayed his strength to
attract an audience for drama; [235] or a tattooed man, exhibited as a modern Robinson Crusoe, performed a dance [236]
between plays.   Pugilism was at times introduced, and in

---

[229] Ludlow, *op. cit.*, pp. 213-214.

[230] *St. Louis Beacon*, Aug. 12, 1830.

[231] *Independent Press*, Oct. 8, 1822; and *Daily Cinc. Gaz.*, Aug.
1, 1829.

[232] *Cinc. Daily Gaz.*, June 28, 1834; and June 28, 1838.

[233] *Lou. Pub. Adv.*, Jan. 14, 1830.

[234] *Daily Lou. Pub. Adv.*, Dec. 20, 1832.

[235] *St. Louis Beacon*, Aug. 12, 1830.

[236] *Detroit Free Press*, July 10-14, 1837.

some cases wild animals performed on the stage.[237]  Mere
spectacles and performances of magic sometimes offered
competition for regular theatricals.  As early as 1814 there
were exhibitions of *"Arabian Transparencies or Artificial
Fireworks representing Temples, Monuments, Roman and
European* in variegated colour's."[238]  The display called
*Sodom and Gomorrah* and another representing the burning of Moscow were popular;[239] and entertainments of
magic by "Chaldean Magi" usurped the place of the
drama.[240]

## X

The conduct of the audience was a matter of concern to
managers anxious to placate the prejudice against the
theatre always kept alive by those whose religious or moral
views made them regard playing as a disreputable practice.
Negroes were usually either barred entirely or admitted
only to separate sections of the house.  Complaints were
continually heard that order was not maintained.  Threats
were made that police officers would be employed, or the
public was assured that a sufficient force of such officers
would be present to maintain good order.  Boys especially
were wont to disturb the audience when discipline was
relaxed.  At Cincinnati in 1817 public protest was made
against the behaviour of a band of youths who were in the
habit of besieging the theatre, pelting it with stones during
a performance.[241]  The patrons of the upper part of the

[237] *Lexington Intelligencer*, July 17, 1838; and *Ky. Gaz.*, Aug.
29, 1839.

[238] *The Western Courier*, Nov. 23, 1814.

[239] *Sodom and Gomorrah* was exhibited in Louisville in 1835, and
was successfully shown in St. Louis the same year (*Lou. Pub. Adv.*,
Mar.-Apr., 1835; *Mo. Rep.*, May 19 ff., 1835; and *Commercial Bulletin*, June 1, 1835).  For the representation of the burning of Moscow, see, for example, *Lou. Pub. Adv.*, Dec., 1835, *passim*.

[240] *Lou. Pub. Adv.*, Dec., 1835, *passim*.

[241] *Liberty Hall*, Jan. 20 and Mar. 31, 1817.

playhouse were often compelled to climb an outside stair-
way infested by a host of these blackguards.[242] Persons
who had places in the pit were in the habit of walking over
the seats in that section, which were commonly benches
without backs.[243] The galleries were the chief gathering
place of turbulent spirits, and in at least one case the price
of admission was said to have been increased in order to
keep out such persons.[244] Drunken men sometimes gained
admittance, and it was reported that the actors themselves
appeared on the stage while intoxicated.[245] Until near the
end of the period, apparently little or no attempt was made
to prevent the conspicuous presence at the theatre of the
women of the underworld; [246] but Ludlow sought to introduce a strict reform in this regard at the New St. Louis
Theatre in 1837.[247]

As late as 1832, when Caldwell opened a theatre in Cincinnati, the crudity of Western manners was such that he
found it necessary to admonish the public not only that
there should be no smoking in the theatre, but that the men
should not be allowed to wear their hats and that no auditor
should be permitted to disturb the general audience by
knocking with sticks or talking aloud.[248] Similar regulations were published by the managers of the theatre in
Louisville in 1833. At St. Louis, as late as 1837, it was
remarked that some men who sat in the dress circle wore

---

[242] *Independent Press*, Oct. 21, 1826.

[243] *Liberty Hall*, Sept. 4, 1822.

[244] *Mo. Rep.*, Oct. 7, 1834.

[245] *Daily Cinc. Gaz.*, Jan. 6 and 15, 1829; and *Mo. Rep.*, Oct. 7, 1828.

[246] Sometimes, however, a separate entrance for such women was provided. *Cf.* Stuart, *op. cit.*, II, 186.

[247] Ludlow, *op. cit.*, p. 478.

[248] *Cinc. Daily Gaz.*, July 4, 1832; and *Daily Lou. Pub. Adv.*, Sept. 17, 1833.

their hats during the performance.[249]   In earlier years the
capacity of the Louisville Theatre was restricted by the
fact that auditors in the pit often stood during at least a
part of the performance.[250]   Westerners were particularly
indecorous in their reception of a new performer.   "A
stranger would imagine," says an editorial writer,

that the audience were kicking their seats to atoms, or
that the building was in the act of tumbling on his devoted
head.   All manner of sounds are made, except such as
resemble the human; and the new comer stands petrified
and stunned by the confused clamor.[251]

Sometimes, too, the audience seems to have become unruly
in its demands for songs not mentioned in the bills.[252]

The Western theatres were not, however, the scenes of
continual uproar, if we may judge from the accounts of
travellers.   It is significant that usually in such narratives
no mention is made of the behaviour of the audience.   Sometimes it is commended.   A visitor from the East to St.
Louis in 1818 praised "the order and decorum uniformly
observed by the audience and the silent and respectful
attention it is accustomed to bestow on the performance."[253]   Estwick Evans, who was at Detroit the same
year, had nothing but praise for the amateur theatricals
which he saw.[254]   Patrick Shirreff, who attended the theatre
at Cincinnati in 1833, was offended only by the noisy
plaudits of the audience.[255]   On the whole, however, it must
be admitted that the famous strictures of Mrs. Trollope
were, in spite of the storm of indignant protest which they

[249] Mo. Rep., July 10, 1837.

[250] Lou. Pub. Adv., Apr. 13, 1822.

[251] Independent Press, Nov. 4, 1826.

[252] The Western Courier, Mar. 6, 1816.

[253] Mo. Gaz., Feb. 20, 1818.

[254] Evans, op. cit., p. 118.

[255] Patrick Shirreff, A Tour through North America, 1835, p. 283.

aroused, not wide of the mark. The Western theatre before 1841 was a center of culture exerting its influence under thoroughly pioneer conditions.

## XI

On the side of morals and religion, the opposition to all theatricals was continuous and bitter, but never decisive. As early as 1811 students of Transylvania and other persons debated in the public prints the question of the immoral influence of the stage in Lexington.[256]  By 1815 a similar controversy was being waged in Cincinnati, with the belligerent preacher, Joshua Lacy Wilson, as chief opponent of the drama.[257]  It was hinted that the Thespians had better be at the wars, and that drama in general was debasing. A benefit given by the players for the poor of the town was doubtless meant as a counterblast; and the partisans of the theatre asserted that Wilson, in making the quarrel a public affair, was degrading his priestly office for the sake of notoriety.

The managers, always on the defensive, seized every opportunity to placate their opponents and to gain the good will of the public. In 1819, when the building of a new theatre was proposed in Cincinnati, Drake, who desired it, pledged himself "abstemiously to preserve the purity and morality of the stage."[258]  The proscenium of the Pavilion Theatre in Cincinnati, erected in 1822, bore the motto "*The means, pleasure — the end, virtue;*" the play of *George Barnwell*, when it was performed on the eve of an execution in the same town, was announced as a lesson in morality especially for youth; Caldwell, at the opening of his Cincinnati Theatre in 1832, offered a prize valued at one hundred dollars "for the best brief History and De-

256 *Ky. Gaz.*, Mar. and Apr., 1811, *passim.*
257 *Liberty Hall* and *Spirit of the West*, Jan.-Apr., 1815, *passim.*
258 *Liberty Hall*, May 14 and June 25, 1819; and Mar. 17, 1820.

fence of the Drama.'' [259]   Benefit performances were often
made the means of enhancing the reputation of the players.
In early Lexington there was more than one such entertainment to aid in building a bridge; and there was one for
furthering the establishment of a factory and another to
raise funds for charity students at the University.[260]  There
were benefits, in various towns, for the Greeks (1824) and
the Texas Volunteers (1836) ; and, at Detroit, for the Canadian ''patriots'' (1837-1838).   There were benefits for fire
companies, for Symmes's Polar expedition, for sufferers
from fire, for orphan asylums, and for the Masons.

The controversy over theatrical morality continued, however, with but little diminution to the end of the period.
The advent of a professional company in Detroit in 1833
caused an editorial duel of unusual bitterness.[261]   In St.
Louis the same conflict of public opinion was noticeable as
early as 1821, and culminated in the withdrawal of Elijah
Lovejoy, editor of the *Observer*, in 1835.[262]

Doubtless the municipal regulation of the drama, sometimes a heavy burden upon the managers, but at other
times much less onerous, reflected the general attitude of
the various Western communities toward the moral and the
cultural value of the theatre.   It was the almost universal
practice to require some kind of license fee; and there is
abundant evidence of friction between the authorities and
the promoters of theatricals.   Though it seems that the
earliest professional companies in Lexington were not
directly taxed, it is clear that the players were expected to

[259] *Ibid.*, Sept. 4, 1822; *Daily Cinc. Gaz.*, July 23, 1829; and
*Cinc. Daily Gaz.*, June 6, 1832.

[260] *Ky. Gaz.* and *The Reporter*, 1809-1811, *passim*.

[261] *Detroit Courier*, July 17-Aug. 21, 1833; *Detroit Journal and
Michigan Advertiser*, July 24-31, 1833.

[262] *Mo. Gaz.*, Jan. 17, 1821; *St. Louis Beacon*, June 9, 1831; and
*Commercial Bulletin*, 1835, *passim*.

give a voluntary benefit for the corporation. It was for a time the policy of the manager to give a performance each year for the aid of some municipal project, so long as no tax was demanded.[263] By 1813, however, we hear of a demand upon Usher, the owner of the theatre, for a fee of five dollars for each night's performance, and of what proved to be a long drawn-out legal action in which the trustees sought to collect accumulated charges of this sort.[264] Drake, after his arrival in Kentucky, became a defendant in a similar suit.[265] Substantially the same theatrical regulations (with only slight changes in the amount of the fee) were imposed by Lexington ordinances of later years.[266]

In Cincinnati, a tax had, it seems, been levied on theatricals as early as 1806; and in 1809 an ordinance was passed which, though it tentatively fixed the charge at not more than twenty nor less than five dollars a day, provided that the council might at any time enter into a special contract and accept whatever sum seemed just.[267] There were the usual indignant protests by the actors;[268] and the

[263] *The Reporter*, May 4, 1811. For what seems to be evidence that the same practice had been followed before the amateurs made way for the professional players, see MS. Records of Lexington (minutes of the Board of Trustees, in the office of the City Clerk, Lexington), I, 300-301 (Dec. 26, 1808), where a donation from Luke Usher is mentioned.

[264] MS. Records of Lexington, II, 137-301 (Dec. 2, 1813-Mar. 27, 1816), *passim*. See also *ibid.*, III, 72.

[265] *Ibid.*, II, 375 (Sept. 20, 1817).

[266] *Ibid.*, III, 215, 230, and 234 (Feb. 6, Oct. 2, and Dec. 4, 1823); and IV, 112-113, 285, and 287 (Feb. 2, 1832; and May 7, 1834).

[267] *Proceedings of the Corporation of the Town of Cincinnati, with the Act of Incorporation*, 1814, pp. 45-46 (ordinance of Feb. 9, 1809, superseding the ordinance of Nov. 4, 1806). *Cf.* also *ibid.*, p. 47 (Sept. 25, 1813).

[268] *Liberty Hall*, Jan. 20 and Mar. 31, 1817.

fact that for a short period benefits for the corporation
were accepted instead of the regular fees [269] seems to show
that the discretionary powers of the authorities were used
to make the burden of the tax as light as possible. But in
both theory [270] and practice [271] the right of taxation was
jealously guarded. The only amelioration, in later years,
was, first, in the occasional reduction to three dollars of
the charge for each performance, and, sometime afterwards,
in the establishment of an annual rate, which was, in turn,
reduced from one hundred dollars [272] to half that amount.[273]

At Louisville, theatricals were controlled by the town
almost from the beginning. A resolution of 1809 required
a license fee of three dollars for every night of performance, while an act of some two years later gave executive
officers certain discretionary powers.[274] Although Drake
complained in 1824 that the trustees had unexpectedly
demanded a tax of five dollars a night,[275] it is clear that the
restrictions on the theatre at Louisville were, in general,
less onerous than at Cincinnati. When a city charter was
granted to Louisville, it was, indeed, stipulated that no

[269] *Ibid.*, May 31, 1820, and Mar. 28, 1821; and MS. Minutes
City Council (in office of City Clerk, Cincinnati), II, 67 and 101
(May 5, 1820; and Jan. 5, 1821).

[270] *An Act Incorporating the City of Cincinnati, and a Digest of
the Ordinances of Said City*, 1835, pp. 139-140 (ordinance of Aug.
26, 1819, and amendment of July 25, 1832). *Cf.* also *Cinc. Daily
Gaz.*, Apr. 24, 1838.

[271] MS. Minutes City Council, II, 240 (July 17, 1822)-X, 359
(Dec. 16, 1840), *passim.*

[272] *Ibid.*, VI, 81-83 (Oct. 14, 1831)ff.

[273] *Ibid.*, VII, 53 (Aug. 7, 1833) ff.

[274] MS. Record 1781-1825 Town of Louisville (minutes of the
Board of Trustees, in the office of the Clerks of the Boards of Aldermen and Councilmen, Louisville), pp. 94-95 and 112 (Nov. 10, 1809;
and Dec. 18, 1811).

[275] *Lou. Pub. Adv.*, Apr. 24, 1824.

theatrical performance might be given without license;[276] but before 1840 the charge had been reduced to five dollars a week, though such exhibitions as the circus and the animal show were still required to pay an equal amount for every day of performance.[277]

Perhaps, however, no Western town was more liberal in its regulation of drama than was St. Louis, where, even near the end of the territorial period, no special tax seems to have been imposed.[278] The ordinances in force from 1823 until after 1840 demanded, it is true, a license fee of all theatricals; but it was from the first left to the discretion of the authorities to require as much as one hundred dollars for three months or as little as five dollars for the same time.[279] And one may reasonably conjecture that in actual practice the burden which the corporation placed upon the manager was not great.

At Detroit, on the other hand, supervision of professional companies seems to have been very strict, and resulted, in some cases, in an attempt to defy the law. Moreover, the rate for licenses tended to increase rather than to diminish.[280] Among the smaller towns, it is very likely that there was little uniformity in the methods used to control the drama. It may be that a number of them had,

---

[276] *A Collection of the Acts of Virginia and Kentucky, Relative to Louisville,* 1839, p. 57.

[277] *Ibid.,* p. 154 (city ordinance in force in 1839).

[278] Ludlow, *op. cit.,* pp. 184-185. It may be added that in the MS. ordinances for the years 1809-1823 (in the Municipal Reference Library, St. Louis) there seems to be no mention of such a tax. For this and other information regarding St. Louis ordinances cited below, I am indebted to Mrs. Zay Rusk Sullens.

[279] Ordinances for 1823-1839 (improvised volume), Ordinance 19 (May 20, 1823); and *The Revised Ordinances of the City of Saint Louis,* 1836, p. 135 (ordinance approved Mar. 28, 1835).

[280] See *Journal of the Proceedings of the Common Council,* n. d., pp. 68-652 (June 4, 1827-Nov. 10, 1840), *passim.*

as was certainly the case with Vincennes, regulations flexible enough to allow immunity to "any Theatrical exhibition morally unobjectionable," [281] thus leaving the question of enforcement to be decided in individual cases.

Aside from the matter of special taxation, there were, however, a variety of causes for the long debate between Puritans and players. Flippant rejoinders by the baited actors and indecent lampoons directed by them against their enemies enlivened the contest. But, on the side of those who regarded theatricals not only as unworthy to suffer the indignity of license fees but as a positive asset to the community, perhaps the strongest argument offered was that the theatre, inadequate as it might be, was in music, in elocution, and in painting the source of the best cultural influence with which Westerners could at that time come in contact.[282]

[281] *Ordinances of the Borough of Vincennes,* 1820, p. 52 (ordinance of Mar. 9, 1819).

[282] *Cinc. Daily Gaz.,* Aug. 1, 1832.

XII

## CALENDAR OF PROFESSIONAL DRAMATIC COMPANIES

| CINCINNATI | LEXINGTON | LOUISVILLE | ST. LOUIS | DETROIT |
|---|---|---|---|---|
| | **1810**<br><br>Douglas (with company "from Montreal and Quebec"), probably in the New Theatre, later known as the Lexington Theatre, described in 1819 as being located at Water and Spring Sts. ("the Theatre" and "the Lexington Theatre" are the only playhouse names heard from 1810 to 1830, and both apparently apply to the same building), Dec. 18 (or a few days earlier)-Dec. 26, 1810.<br>*Ky. Gaz.*, Dec. 18 and 25, 1810. | | | |
| Turner, May 30 (or earlier)-June 14 (or later); *Liberty Hall*, May 29, and June 5 and 12, 1811. | **1811**<br><br>Same company, probably managed by Douglas or Usher, Jan. 30-May 4.<br>*Ky. Gaz.*, Jan. 29-Apr. 30; *The Reporter*, Mar. 23-May 4, 1811.<br><br>Same company? June 8 (or earlier)-July 4 (or later).<br>*Ky. Gaz.*, June 4-July 2, 1811.<br><br>Same company, Sept. 21-Nov. 30.<br>*Ky. Gaz.*, Sept. 10-Nov. 26; *The Reporter*, Nov. 23-30, 1811. | Douglas (or Usher), Louisville Theatre? (probably the same building—altered by Drake in 1818—used until 1829, apparently for all the theatricals, and commonly referred to simply as "the Theatre" but sometimes as "the Louisville Theatre", sometime during the year?)<br>See Melish, *op. cit.*, II, 186. | | |

| CINCINNATI | LEXINGTON | LOUISVILLE | ST. LOUIS | DETROIT |
|---|---|---|---|---|
| | **1812**<br>Same company, Feb. 18-Apr. 25 (or later). *Ky. Gaz.*, Feb. 11-Apr 21; *The Reporter*, Apr. 25, 1812.<br>Same company, Oct. 1 to early in December. *Ky. Gaz.*, Sept. 29-Dec. 1, 1812. | Same company, sometime during the year? | | |
| | **1813**<br>Same company, May 19-Sept. 4. *Ky. Gaz.*, May 18-Aug. 31, 1813.<br>Same company, Oct. 6 (or earlier)-Nov. 13 (or later). *Ky. Gaz.*, Oct. 5-Nov. 8, 1813. | Same company, sometime during the year? | | |
| | **1814**<br>Same company, or Turner? June 1 (or earlier)-June 8 (or later). *Ky. Gaz.*, May 30 and June 6, 1814. | Same company, Feb. 16-Apr. 27 (or later). *The Western Courier*, Feb. 7-Apr. 25, 1814. | | |
| **1815**<br>Turner (with "Pittsburgh company of Comedians," on their way to Kentucky"), Apr. 3-May 29 (or later). *Liberty Hall*, Mar. 21 (or Apr. 1)-May 29, 1815. | Turner, June 19 (or earlier)-Oct. 9. *Ky. Gaz.*, June 19-Oct. 9, 1815. | | | |

| CINCINNATI | LEXINGTON | LOUISVILLE | ST. LOUIS | DETROIT |
|---|---|---|---|---|
| | **1816**<br>Drake, May 21 (or a few days earlier)-July 1 (or later).<br>*Ky. Gaz.*, May 20-July 8, 1816.<br>Drake, Sept. 30-Nov. 26.<br>*Ky. Gaz.*, Sept. 23-Nov. 25, 1816. *Cf.* Ludlow, *op. cit.*, p. 99. | Drake, Feb. 26 (or 28)-May 14.<br>*The Western Courier*, Feb. 21-May 9, 1816; Ludlow, *op. cit.*, p. 88. | | |
| **1817**<br>Turner, Dec. 30 (or earlier) to about Mar. 17<br>*Liberty Hall*, Dec. 30, 1816-Mar. 17, 1817.<br>Turner, July 14 (or earlier)-Aug. 18.<br>*Liberty Hall*, July 14-Aug. 18, 1817.<br>Turner, Nov. 10 (and earlier)-Nov. 25.<br>*Liberty Hall*, Nov. 10 and 24, 1817. | Drake, Aug. 27 to second week in November.<br>*The Reporter*, Aug. 27 ff.; *Ky. Gaz.*, Aug. 23-Nov. 8, 1817. | Drake, April and May. Ludlow, *op. cit.*, pp. 105-108. | | |
| | Drake, late in August (or early in September) to Nov. 21.<br>*Ky. Gaz.*, Aug. 7-Nov. 20; *Ky. Reporter*, Nov. 18, 1818. | Drake, sometime during the summer? | **1818**<br>Turner, the "Theatre" (formerly used as a black-smith shop, and later as court house and church), and stable loft of the Green Tree Tavern, Feb. 17 (or earlier)-July 29 (or later). *Mo. Gaz.*, Feb. 20-July 24, 1818. | |

| CINCINNATI | LEXINGTON | LOUISVILLE | ST. LOUIS | DETROIT |
|---|---|---|---|---|
| Blanchard, Dawson's, School-house, Water St., sometime during the year. Smith, *The Theatrical Apprenticeship*, 1846, p. 37. | Drake (and West's equestrian and melodramatic company, from Sept. 8), about Sept. 1-10 (or later), *Ky. Gaz.*, July 23-Sept. 10, 1819. | **1819** Drake, Mar. 13 (or earlier)-June 5. *Lou. Pub. Adv.*, Mar. 20-June 12, 1819. | | |
| Collins & Jones, Burrows and Tunis's store, Columbia and Walnut Sts., June 21-July 23 (or later). *Liberty Hall*, June 25-July 23; *Lou. Pub. Adv.*, July 7, 1819; and Smith, *loc. cit.* | | | Ludlow, St. Louis Theatre, about middle of December to | |
| | | | **1820** about the end of January. Ludlow, *op. cit.*, pp. 184-188. Drake, City Hotel, late in Dec., 1819 (or early in Jan., 1820) to about the end of February? Ludlow, *op. cit.*, pp. 186-192. | |
| Collins & Jones, Cincinnati Theatre (later known as Columbia St. Theatre), Mar. 8-June 2 (or later). *Liberty Hall*, Mar. 17-May 31, 1820. | ———, Jan. 15 (or earlier)-Feb. 25 (or later; continuity of season doubtful). *Ky. Gaz.*, Jan. 14, and Feb. 11 and 25, 1820. | | Ludlow and Vos, St. Louis Theatre, March? Ludlow, *op. cit.*, p. 192. Jones, St. Louis Theatre? Dec. 13 to | |
| Drake, Cincinnati Theatre? sometime during the summer. *Liberty Hall*, Jan. 24, 1821. | | | | |

| CINCINNATI | LEXINGTON | LOUISVILLE | ST. LOUIS | DETROIT |
|---|---|---|---|---|
| Drake, Cincinnati Theatre, shortly before Jan. 24-Apr. 25 (and a few days later). *Liberty Hall*, Jan. 20-Apr. 25, 1821. *Cf.* Smith, *The Theatrical Apprenticeship*, 1846, pp. 42-43.<br>Collins & Jones, Cincinnati Theatre, Nov. 19 to | Collins & Jones, about Oct. 6-27 (or later). *Liberty Hall*, Oct. 6 and 27; *Ky. Reporter*, Oct. 15, 1821. | 1821<br>Drake, closed summer season, July 7. *Lou. Pub. Adv.*, July 7 and 14, 1821.<br>Drake, closed autumn season, Oct. 13. *Lou. Pub. Adv.*, Oct. 13, 1821. | some time in March? *Mo. Gaz.*, Dec. 13, 1820; and Ludlow, *op. cit.*, pp. 212-214. | |
| Feb. 4 (or later). *Liberty Hall*, Nov. 17, 1821-Feb. 13, 1822.<br>Collins & Jones, Cincinnati Theatre, May 11 (or earlier)-16 (or later). *Liberty Hall*, May 11-18, 1822.<br>Dumilieu & Charles, Pavilion Theatre, Vauxhall Gardens, July 4-Oct. 8 (or later), *Independent Press*, July 4-Oct. 8; *Liberty Hall*, Sept. 4-Oct. 5, 1822; and MS. Minutes City Council (in office of City Clerk, Cincinnati) II, 240 and 255 (July 17 and Oct. 3, 1822). | Collins & Jones? April. *Ky. Reporter*, Apr. 29, 1822.<br><br>Collins & Jones, Dec. 16 to | 1822<br>Drake, Jan. 14 (or earlier)-Apr. 17 (or later). *Lou. Pub. Adv.*, Jan. 19-Apr. 17, and May 4, 1822. | | |

| DETROIT | ST. LOUIS | LOUISVILLE | LEXINGTON | CINCINNATI |
|---|---|---|---|---|
| | | **1823**<br>Drake? January and later? *Lou. Pub. Adv.*, Dec. 28, 1822.<br>Collins & Jones, Apr. 16 (and earlier—probably about Apr. 1)-June 2 (or a day or two later). *Lou. Pub. Adv.*, Mar. 29-May 31, 1823.<br>Drake? July 19-26. *Lou. Pub. Adv.*, July 19-26, 1823. | Feb. 17 (and probably later in the week). *Ky. Reporter*, Dec. 16, 1822-Feb. 17, 1823.<br>Collins & Jones, July 7 (and a day or two earlier)-? (a very short season). *Ky. Reporter*, June 16 and July 7, 1823.<br>Collins & Jones? (with Pepin's equestrian company in January), Aug. 27 to | Collins & Jones? Mar. 6-14 (or later). *Liberty Hall*, Mar. 11; *Independent Press*, Mar. 13, 1823. *Cf.* Smith, *Theatrical Management*, 1868, p. 26.<br>E. Forrest and other seceders from Collins & Jones's company, Globe (earlier Pavilion Theatre), May 19 (or earlier)-July 17 (or later). *Independent Press*, May 15-July 17, 1823. |
| | | **1824**<br>Drake, Jan. 17-May 12. *Lou. Pub. Adv.*, Jan. 3-May 12, and May 22, 1824. | Jan. 7, 1824. *Ky. Reporter*, Aug. 25, 1823-Jan. 5, 1824; and MS. Records of Lexington (minutes of Town Trustees, in office of City Clerk, Lexington), III, 230 (Oct. 2, 1823). | Smith, City Theatre (earlier called Pavilion, then Globe) and Cincinnati Theatre (removed here from City Theatre by Feb. 7), Jan. 21-Mar. 19. *Liberty Hall*, Jan. 16-Mar. 19; *The Cincinnati Literary Gazette*, Feb. 7, 1824. |
| | | **1825**<br>Drake, Jan. 29 (or earlier)-May 18 (or later). *Lou. Pub. Adv.*, Jan. 29-May 18, 1825. | Drake, Aug. 29-Oct. 17 (or later). *Ky. Reporter*, Aug. 29-Oct. 17, 1825.<br>Drake, Nov. 19-? (a very short season). *Ky. Gaz.*, Nov. 18, 1825. | Dwyer, Cincinnati Theatre, for one night, in January? MS. Minutes City Council, III, 84 (Jan. 12, 1825). |

| CINCINNATI | LEXINGTON | LOUISVILLE | ST. LOUIS | DETROIT |
|---|---|---|---|---|
| | | **1826** | | |
| Drake, Cincinnati Theatre, Oct. 7 (or earlier—possibly even as early as May)-Dec. 16 (or later). *Independent Press*, Oct. 14-Dec. 16, 1826; Smith, *The Theatrical Apprenticeship*, 1846, p. 117; and MS. Minutes City Council, III, 277 and 348 (May 24 and Nov. 8, 1826). | | Drake, Feb. 4 (or earlier)-May 10. *Lou. Pub. Adv.*, Feb. 4-May 10, 1826. | | |
| | | **1827** | | |
| Drake? June 8 (or earlier).? *Ky. Gaz.*, June 8, 1827. Drake (Alexander Drake in charge, at least part of the time), Nov. 12-Dec. 17 (or later). *Daily Cinc. Gaz.*, Nov. 14-Dec. 17, 1827. | Crampton & Smiths, June 25-? *Ky. Reporter*, June 23, 1827. | Drake, Mar. 10 (or earlier)-May 19 (or later). *Lou. Weekly Pub. Adv.*, Feb. 17-May 19, 1827. | Caldwell, Old Salt-house, Church St. (formerly Scott & Rule's warehouse), July 6 (or earlier—was to have opened about the 25th of June)-Aug. 17 (or later-Aug. 16 was last night but one). *Mo. Rep.*, June 21-Aug. 16, 1827. *Cf.* Smith, *Theatrical Management*, 1868, p. 49; Thomas and Wild, *op. cit.*, pp. 24-25. | Fuller, barn attached to Steamboat Hotel, Randolph and Woodbridge Sts., about June 4 (or earlier)-July 11 (or later). *Journal of the Proceedings of the Common Council*, n. d., pp. 68, 70, and 72 (June 4 and 15, and July 7, 1827.) *Cf. The Detroit Daily Tribune*, Apr. 20, 1860. |
| | | **1828** | | |
| Drake, Cincinnati Theatre, Jan. 26 (and possibly two weeks earlier)-Mar. 17 (and probably later). *Daily Cinc. Gaz.*, Jan. 29-Mar. 19, 1828; and MS. Minutes City Council, IV, 163-164 (Feb. 13, 1828). | Drake, Aug. 27-? *Ky. Reporter*, Aug. 1828. | Drake, Jan. 2 (and earlier)-Jan. 15 (or somewhat earlier). *Lou. Pub. Adv.*, Jan. 2-16, 1828. Drake, Jan. 26-? *Lou. Pub. Adv.*, Jan. 26 and Feb. 2, 1828. | Rowe (for Caldwell), Old Salt-house, July 19-Oct. 14. *Mo. Rep.*, July 22-Oct. 14, 1828. | *Cf.* Palmer, *op. cit.*, p. 980. |

| CINCINNATI | LEXINGTON | LOUISVILLE | ST. LOUIS | DETROIT |
|---|---|---|---|---|
| Drake, Cincinnati Theatre, June 18 (or earlier)-July 21 (or later); *Daily Cinc. Gaz.*, June 20-Aug. 2, 1828.<br>Drake, Cincinnati Theatre, Oct. 25 (or earlier) to | | 1828<br>Drake, Mar. 29-? (possibly as late as June 4). *Lou. Pub. Adv.*, Mar. 29, May 28, and June 4, 1828. | | Archbold, about May 15 (or earlier)-May 29 (or later). *Journal of the Proceedings of the Common Council*, p. 178 (May 15, 1829). |
| Jan. 24.<br>*Daily Cinc. Gaz.*, Oct. 10, 1828-Jan. 24, 1829; and MS. Minutes City Council, IV, 320 (Oct. 29, 1828).<br>Drake, Cincinnati Theatre, May 25-Aug. 15. *Daily Cinc. Gaz.*, May 22-Aug. 15, 1829; and Colwell, *op. cit.*, Part II, pp. 87-90.<br>Brown and Ludlow, equestrian and dramatic company, Amphitheatre, Sycamore St., July 14 (or a day or two earlier)-Oct. 23 (Brown withdrew about the end of July).<br>*Daily Cinc. Gaz.*, July 8-Oct. 23, 1829; Ludlow, *op. cit.*, pp. 341-349; and MS. Minutes City Council, IV, 481 (June 24, 1829).<br>Drake, Columbia St. Theatre (earlier called Cincinnati Theatre), Oct. 13 to | | 1829<br>Drake, Jan. 31-July 23 (or later). *Lou. Pub. Adv.*, Jan. 28-July 22, 1829.<br>Ludlow, Melodramatic Theatre, Jefferson and Third Cross Sts., Nov. 11 to | Caldwell, sometime during this year? Thomas and Wild, *op. cit.*, pp. 24-25.<br>J. P. Brown, equestrian company, June 1-13. *St. Louis Beacon*, May 30-June 13, 1829.<br>———, June 22 and probably one other night. *St. Louis Beacon*, June 13 and 20, 1829. | |

| CINCINNATI | LEXINGTON | LOUISVILLE | ST. LOUIS | DETROIT |
|---|---|---|---|---|
| Jan. 28. *Daily Cinc. Gaz.*, Oct. 13, 1829-Jan. 28, 1830. John Carter, received license to perform at corner of Fifth and Main Sts. MS. Minutes City Council, V, 149 (Feb. 17, 1830). Ludlow, Columbia St. Theatre, Apr. 24-July 17. *Daily Cinc. Gaz.*, Apr. 21-July 17, 1830; and MS. Minutes City Council V, 191 (Apr. 14, 1830). J. P. Brown, equestrian company, Amphitheatre, Sycamore St., Sept. 24-Oct. 28 (or later). *Daily Cinc. Gaz.* (with change of title), Sept. 24-Oct. 27, 1830; and MS. Minutes City Council, V, 275 (Aug. 25, 1830). Pearman, Columbia St. Theatre, Mar. 2 (or earlier)-19 (or later). *Cinc. Daily Gaz.*, Jan. 22-Mar. 23, 1831. Drake, Cincinnati Theatre (same as Columbia St. Theatre), Apr. 11-May 2 (or later). *Cinc. Daily Gaz.*, Apr. 9-May 2, 1831. | Parsons? for Drake? Feb. 12 (and earlier)-?. *Ky. Reporter*, Feb. 10, 1830. —, May 24 (or earlier)-May 29 (or later). *Ky. Reporter*, May 19 and 26, 1830. J. P. Brown, equestrian and dramatic company, Brown's Amphitheatre, near Limestone St., Aug. 3 (or earlier)-31 (and later). *Ky. Reporter*, June 29-Aug. 31, 1831. Drake, Masonic Hall, Oct. 15-26 (and probably later). *Ky. Reporter*, Oct. 5-26, 1831. | **1830** Mar. 22 (or later). *Lou. Pub. Adv.*, Oct. 17, 1829-Mar. 22, 1830: and Cowell, *op. cit.*, p. 90. Drake, City Theatre, Jefferson St., between Third and Fourth Sts. (remodeled from the old building used by Drake since 1816 and probably used for dramatic performances by amateurs as early as 1808), Mar. 26-June 19. *Lou. Pub. Adv.* (with change of title), Mar. 22-June 19, 1830. J. P. Brown, equestrian company, Melodramatic Theatre, Nov. 9-Dec. 1 (or later), *Daily Lou. Pub. Adv.*, Nov. 9-Dec. 1, 1830. Parsons (for Drake), City Theatre, Sept. 18 to **1831** Jan. 3 (or later). *Daily Lou. Pub. Adv.*, Sept. 13, 1830-Jan. 1, 1831. Pearman? or Drake? Jan. 7-19. *Daily Lou. Pub. Adv.*, Jan. 7-19, 1831. Drake, Feb. 26-Apr. 4. *Daily Lou. Pub. Adv.*, Feb. 25-Apr. 4, 1831. | Gray & Rowe (for Caldwell?), Old Salt-house? June 12-Aug. 24. *St. Louis Beacon*, June 3-Aug. 26, 1830. Pearman, Old Salt-house? Mar. 30 (or a few days earlier)-May 13 (or later). *St. Louis Beacon*, Mar. 31-May 12, 1831. Ludlow (for Caldwell), Old Salt-house, May 19 (or a few days earlier)-July 9. *St. Louis Beacon*, May 19-July 7, 1831. | Parsons? in barn attached to Steamboat Hotel, sometime during this year? Farmer, *op. cit.*, p. 357. |

| CINCINNATI | LEXINGTON | LOUISVILLE | ST. LOUIS | DETROIT |
|---|---|---|---|---|
| Drake, Columbia St. Theatre, June 13 (or earlier)-July 8 (or later). *Cinc. Daily Gaz.*, June 8-July 8, 1831. Caldwell, Sycamore St. Theatre (sometimes called Amphitheatre), June 29-Oct. 15. *Cinc. Daily Gaz.*, June 28-Oct. 15, 1831; and MS. Minutes City Council, VI, 6-83, *passim* (June 29-Oct. 14, 1831). J. P. Brown, Amphitheatre, Nov. 8? to | | **1831** Drake, May 7-June 8 (or later). *Daily Lou. Pub. Adv.*, May 7-June 8, 1831. Ludlow? assisted for a time by J. P. Brown's equestrians? Amphitheatre, June 25 (or earlier)-July 23. *Louisville Daily Focus*, June 24-July 23; *Daily Lou. Pub. Adv.*, June 25-July 2, 1831. Ludlow (for Caldwell), City Theatre, July 25-Oct. 3. *Daily Lou. Pub. Adv.*, July 18-Oct. 3, 1831. Caldwell, City Theatre, Oct. 17-Nov. 9 and 12. *Daily Lou. Pub. Adv.*, Oct. 14-Nov. 12; and *Louisville Daily Focus*, Oct. 18-Nov. 12, 1831. | Smith, July 15 (or earlier)-23 (or perhaps two days later). *St. Louis Beacon*, July 14-21, 1831; and Smith, *Theatrical Management*, 1868, p. 72. | Arnold (possibly this show was not dramatic), about May 23 (or earlier)-May 30 (or later)—no information except dates of license. *Journal of the Proceedings of the Common Council*, p. 141 (May 23, 1832). |
| Jan. 18 (or later: both length of season and continuity of performance doubtful). *Cinc. Daily Gaz.*, Nov. 7 and 8, 1831, and Jan. 18, 1832; and MS. Minutes City Council, VI, 110 (Nov. 9, 1831). Ludlow (for Caldwell), Columbia St. Theatre, Apr. 24-June 25. *Cinc. Daily Gaz.*, Apr. 21-June 25, 1832. | J. P. Brown, dramatic and equestrian company, Brown's Amphitheatre, a few days after July 5? *Lexington Observer, and Kentucky Reporter*, July 5, 1832. | **1832** Drake, City Theatre, Jan. 5 (or a few days earlier)-June 2. *Lou. Pub. Adv.* (with change of title), Dec. 28, 1831-June 2, 1832. Caldwell, City Theatre, June 6-30. *Daily Lou. Pub. Adv.*, June 6-30, 1832. *Cf.* erroneous account in Ludlow, *op. cit.*, pp. 397-398. | | |

| CINCINNATI | LEXINGTON | LOUISVILLE | ST. LOUIS | DETROIT |
|---|---|---|---|---|
| Caldwell, New Cincinnati Theatre, July 4-Oct. 15. *Cinc. Daily Gaz.*, June 28-Oct. 23, 1832; and MS. Minutes City Council, VI, 341 (Aug. 1, 1832). | | **1832** J. P. Brown, Amphitheatre, from ? - Sept. 20. *Daily Lou. Pub. Adv.*, Sept. 20, 1832. | Robert Farrell, stage manager (possibly amateur), Old Salt-house? Sept. 25 (and probably earlier)-Oct. 2 (or later). *Mo. Rep.*, Sept. 24 and Oct. 1, 1833. | Parsons & Dean, about July 10-Aug. 16 (or later). *Detroit Courier*, July 10-Aug. 21; *Detroit Journal and Michigan Advertiser*, July 17-Aug. 14, 1833; and *Journal of the Proceedings of the Common Council*, pp. 244 and 245 (July 10 and 24, 1833). |
| Hawkins and Eldridge, equestrian and dramatic company, Amphitheatre, Jan. 26-? *Cinc. Daily Gaz.*, Jan. 24, 1833. | | ———, City Theatre, from ? to shortly before Dec. 20. *Daily Lou. Pub. Adv.*, Dec. 20, 1832. | | |
| Cabell & Forrest, Citizens' Theatre (earlier called Cincinnati Theatre and Columbia St. Theatre), Mar. 6-15 (or later). *Cinc. Daily Gaz.*, Feb. 20-Mar. 14, 1833. | | Drake, City Theatre, Dec. 29 to **1833** Apr. 29, 1833. *Daily Lou. Pub. Adv.*, Dec. 20, 1832-Apr. 29, 1833. | | |
| Russell & Rowe (for Caldwell), Cincinnati Theatre (first called New Cincinnati Theatre), June 15-Nov. 9. *Cinc. Daily Gaz.*, May 7-Nov. 9, 1833; and MS. Minutes City Council, VII, 53 (Aug. 7, 1833). | | Drake? City Theatre, May 18-? (season of only a few days, probably). *Daily Lou. Pub. Adv.*, May 18, 1833. | | |
| Hilson (for Russell & Rowe), Cincinnati Theatre, Dec. 16 to | | Cabell & Forrest, City Theatre, June 20-July 25 (or later). *Daily Lou. Pub. Adv.*, June 14-July 23, 1833. | | |
| | | Rowe? Adelphi Theatre, about July 29 (or earlier)-Aug. 12 (or later). *Daily Lou. Pub. Adv.*, July 29-Aug. 10, 1833. | | |
| | | Russell & Rowe, City Theatre, Sept. 9-Oct. 18 (or later). *Daily Lou. Pub. Adv.*, Sept. 10-Oct. 18, 1833. | | |

| CINCINNATI | LEXINGTON | LOUISVILLE | ST. LOUIS | DETROIT |
|---|---|---|---|---|
| Jan. 4, 1834. *Cinc. Daily Gaz.*, Dec. 13, 1833–Jan. 4, 1834. | Cabell, Giron's Ball Room, May 1 (or earlier)–May 15 (and probably later). | 1833 Russell & Rowe? City Theatre?–Dec. 2 (or later); possibly a continuation of the season begun Sept. 9. *Daily Lou. Pub. Adv.*, Nov. 23 and Dec. 3, 1833. | Ludlow, Old Salt-house? Aug. 29 (and earlier)–Oct. 21? (or later). | Eberle, Powell & Co., brick building on Woodward Ave. and Jefferson St., about June 11–July 16 (or later). |
| Russell & Rowe? with Hillson in charge? Cincinnati Theatre, Feb. 17–22. *Cinc. Daily Gaz.*, Feb. 17–22, 1834. | *Lexington Observer & Kentucky Reporter*, Apr. 24–May 15, 1834; and MS. Records of Lexington, IV, 287 (May 7, 1834). | 1834 Ludlow, Adelphi Theatre, Mar. 17 (or a few days earlier)–June 4. *Daily Lou. Pub. Adv.*, Mar. 12–June 4, 1834. | *Mo. Rep.*, Aug. 5 and Aug. 29–Oct. 21. *Of.* Ludlow, *op. cit.*, p. 419, for statement that he opened the theatre early in September; and see Thomas and | *Detroit Journal and Michigan Advertiser*, June 11 and 18, and July 2 and 16, 1834; *Journal of the Proceedings of the Common Council*, p. 280 (June 11, 1834); and |
| Ludlow, Columbia St. Theatre, Feb. 27–? *Cinc. Daily Gaz.*, Feb. 27, 1834. | Brown's equestrian company (only a few performances of a dramatic kind), Aug. 24 (or earlier)–Sept. 3. *Lexington Observer & Kentucky Reporter*, Aug. 27–Sept. 3, 1834. | Muzzy & Watson, Adelphi Theatre, June 21 (or earlier)–27 (or later). *Daily Lou. Pub. Adv.*, June 20–27, 1834. | Wild, *op. cit.*, p. 25, for assertion that Ludlow arrived in June. | Farrar, *op. cit.*, p. 357. |
| Russell & Rowe, Cincinnati Theatre, June 14–July 19 (or later). *Cinc. Daily Gaz.*, June 14–July 19, 1834. | | ———, City Theatre, July 21–Aug. 8 (and probably later). *Daily Lou. Pub. Adv.*, July 21–26; and *Lou. Pub. Adv.*, July 28–Aug. 8, 1834. | | Dean & McKinney, old M. E. Church building, Gratiot (or State) and Farrar Sts., about July 30–? *Detroit Journal and Michigan Advertiser*, June 25, |
| Russell & Rowe, Cincinnati Theatre? Aug. 12 (and earlier) and 13 (possibly plays were given continuously from July 19). *Cinc. Daily Gaz.*, Aug. 12–14, 1834. | | Muzzy or Ludlow? Adelphi Theatre, Aug. 8–9 (or later). *Lou. Pub. Adv.*, Aug. 8–9, 1834. | | 1834; *Journal of the Proceedings of the Common Council*, p. 289 (July 30, 1834); and Farrar, *op. cit.*, pp. 357–358. |
| Russell & Rowe, Cincinnati Theatre? Aug. 25–Nov. 8. | | Russell (& Rowe?), City Theatre, Sept. 8–Dec. 1 (or later). | | |
| *Cinc. Daily Gaz.*, Aug. 23–Nov. 8, 1834; and MS. Minutes City Council, VII, 240 (Sept. 3, 1834). | | *Lou. Pub. Adv.*, Aug. 29–Nov. 29, 1834. | | |

| CINCINNATI | LEXINGTON | LOUISVILLE | ST. LOUIS | DETROIT |
|---|---|---|---|---|
| Russell & Rowe? Cincinnati Theatre? Sept. 7 (and probably much earlier)-Sept. 9 (or later). *Cinc. Daily Gaz.*, Sept. 7-9, 1835. Hill (for Russell & Rowe), Cincinnati Theatre? Oct. 5-23 (or later). *Cinc. Daily Gaz.*, Oct. 3-23, 1835. | Forbes, Masonic Hall, July 4-18 (and later). *Ky. Gaz.*, July 4-18, 1835. J. S. Potter & Co., Masonic Hall, Dec. 7-26 (or later). *Ky. Gaz.*, Dec. 5-26, 1835. | **1835** Parsons? for Russell & Rowe? June 25 (and probably earlier)-? *Lou. Pub. Adv.*, June 25, 1835. | Ludlow, Old Salt-house, July 3-Oct. 24 (or later). *Commercial Bulletin* (with change of title), July 1-Oct. 23; *Mo. Rep.*, July 2-Oct. 3, 1835; Ludlow, *op. cit.*, pp. 435-440; Smith, *Theatrical Management*, 1868, p. 121. Ludlow (p. 435) erroneously gives the time of the opening as "early in May." | Dean & McKinney, about May 13 (or earlier)-20 (and probably later). *Journal of the Proceedings of the Common Council*, pp. 324 and 325 (May 13 and 20, 1835). |
| Potter, City Theatre (Cincinnati Theatre), Mar. 23-Apr. 16 (or a few days later). *Cinc. Daily Gaz.*, Mar. 22-Apr. 15, and May 23, 1836; and MS. Minutes City Council, VIII, 91 (Apr. 20, 1836). Parsons (for Russell & Co.), Cincinnati Theatre, May, 2-June 14. *Cinc. Daily Gaz.*, Apr. 28-June 14, 1836. Hill (for Russell, who was probably in direct charge before the end of June), Cincinnati Theatre, June 18-Oct. 20 (the theatre burned on Oct. 21). *Cinc. Daily Gaz.*, June 16-Oct. 22, 1836; and MS. Minutes City Council, VIII, 91 and 174 (Apr. 20 and Sept. 21, 1836). | Potter, New Theatre, July 11-Sept. 9 (or later). *Ky. Gaz.*, July 11-Sept. 8; and *Lexington Observer & Kentucky Reporter*, July 27-Sept. 7, 1836. Potter, New Theatre, Sept. 26-30 (or later). *Lexington Observer & Kentucky Reporter*, Sept. 28; and *Ky. Gaz.*, Sept. 29, 1836. | **1836** Potter, City Theatre, Jan. 27-Mar. 19. *Lou. Pub. Adv.*, Jan. 27-Mar. 19, 1836. Parsons (for Russell), Apr. 1?-? *Lou. Pub. Adv.*, Mar. 23, 1836. Russell (or Russell and Parsons), City Theatre? July 12 (or earlier)-Nov. 10 (continuity of performance doubtful). *Lou. Pub. Adv.*, July 12, Aug. 23, Sept. 16-17, and Oct. 1-Nov. 10, 1836. Caldwell, American Theatre (remodeled from old Melodramatic Theatre), Aug. 1-Oct. 22. *Lou. Pub. Adv.*, July 20-Oct. 22, 1836. | Tryon & Co., Jan. 6-Feb. 6 (or later). *Mo. Rep.*, Jan. 5-Feb. 6; *St. Louis Commercial Bulletin*, Jan. 6, 1836. De Prefontaine, Feb. 16. *Mo. Rep.*, Feb. 16, 1836. Ludlow & Smith, June 9?-Aug. 1 (or later). *Mo. Rep.*, June 11, 28, 30; *St. Louis Commercial Bulletin*, July 27 and Aug. 1, 1836; Ludlow, *op. cit.*, pp. 455-459. Ludlow & Smith, Aug. 29?-Oct. 1 (or later). *Mo. Rep.*, Aug. 30, Sept. 28 and 30, and Oct. 1, 1836; and Ludlow, *op. cit.*, pp. 459-463. | Dean & McKinney, City Theatre (old M. E. Church), July 28 (and earlier)-Sept. 3. *Detroit Daily Free Press*, June 15-25, July 26 and 27, and Aug. 11-Sept. 3, 1836; *Journal of the Proceedings of the Common Council*, p. 379 (May 25, 1836). Boston Arena Company, dramatic, equestrian and dramatic, Sept. 29-Oct. 1 (no plays announced). *Detroit Daily Advertiser*, Sept. 29 and 30, 1836. |

| CINCINNATI | LEXINGTON | LOUISVILLE | ST. LOUIS | DETROIT |
|---|---|---|---|---|
| Russell's company, first at the Cincinnati Exchange and later in room at corner of Walnut and Pearl Sts., Oct. 24-Nov. 11 (or later). *Cinc. Daily Gaz.*, Oct. 24-Nov. 10, 1836.<br><br>Boston Circus (gave some dramatic sketches of slight importance), Main and Seventh Sts., Dec. 8 to<br><br>Feb. 25. *Cinc. Daily Gaz.*, Dec. 6, 1836-Feb. 25? 1837.<br><br>Eagle Circus Co. (possibly entirely non-dramatic), Vine and Seventh Sts., Mar. 31-? *Cinc. Daily Gaz.*, Mar. 31 ff., 1837.<br><br>Potter & Waters, City Theatre, Main and Seventh Sts., Apr. 10-June 10. *Cinc. Daily Gaz.*, Apr. 7-June 10, 1837.<br><br>O. W. Brown & Co. (circus), Vine and Seventh Sts., June 12?-? (for season of "six nights only"). *Cinc. Daily Gaz.*, June 12, 1837. | Potter & Waters (probably only one division of the company), Lexington Theatre (same as New Theatre?), May 16-29 (or later). *Ky. Gaz.*, Apr. 20, May 18, and Aug. 3; and *Observer & Reporter*, May 27, 1837. | 1836<br>Potter (Potter & Waters from Jan. 9, 1837;. an equestrian company had a share in the performances of Jan. 13-21), City Theatre, Nov. 18 (and earlier) to<br><br>1837<br>Apr. 8. *Lou. Pub. Adv.*, Nov. 18, 1836-Apr. 7, 1837.<br>Marshall (or, according to some newspaper notices, Marschael MacGlashan), Pagoda Theatre (possibly no legitimate drama), July 26-? For the name Marshall, see *Cinc. Daily Gaz.*, Oct. 11, 1837.<br><br>Potter & Waters, American Theatre, July 24-Sept. 21 (or later). *Lou. Pub. Adv.*, July 24-Sept. 21, 1837.<br><br>———, City Theatre, Sept. 6 (and probably earlier) (continuously?) Sept. 20 (or later). *Lou. Pub. Adv.*, Sept. 5 and 19-20, 1837. | Ludlow & Smith, New St. Louis Theatre, Third and Olive Sts., July 3-Nov. 4. *Daily Mo. Rep.* (with change of title), June 29-Nov. 4, 1837; and Ludlow, *op. cit.*, pp. 477-491. | Dean & McKinney, City Theatre? May 30-Sept. 2. *Semi-weekly Free Press*, May 30 and June 2; *Detroit Free Press*, June 5-Sept. 2, 1837; and *Journal of the Proceedings of the Common Council*, p. 448 (June 13, 1837).<br><br>Dean & McKinney (or part of their company)? Museum, Sept. 6 (or earlier)-Sept. 9. *Detroit Free Press*, Sept. 6-9, 1837. |

| CINCINNATI | LEXINGTON | LOUISVILLE | ST. LOUIS | DETROIT |
|---|---|---|---|---|
| Scott & Thorne, New National Theatre (later called National Theatre, Sycamore, between Third and Fourth Sts., July 3-Nov. 25. *Cinc. Daily Gaz.*, June 20-Nov. 25, 1837; and MS. Minutes City Council, VIII, 291 and 295 (June 21 and 28, 1837).<br><br>O. W. Brown, equestrian and dramatic company, National Amphitheatre (New National Theatre temporarily altered for equestrian performances), Nov. 30 to<br><br>Feb. 3 (or later). *Cinc. Daily Gaz.*, Nov. 29, 1837-Feb. 3, 1838.<br><br>Dean (for John Young?) Pavilion Theatre, Main and Seventh Sts. (called City Theatre by Potter & Waters), Apr. 24-Oct. 27 (or later). *Cinc. Daily Gaz.*, Apr. 24-Oct. 27, 1838; and MS. Minutes City Council, VIII, 438.<br><br>Scott & Thorne, National Theatre (first called New National Theatre), May 12-July 4 (or later). *Cinc. Daily Gaz.*, May 12-July 6, 1838. | Ingersoll & Dyke, May 15 (or earlier)? (sometime before June 28). *Observer & Reporter*, May 9 and 16, 1838; and William Ross Wallace, *Leila*, 1838, dedications and advertisements.<br><br>Scott & Thorne (apparently only a part of the company) Lexington Theatre, July 2-14. *Ky. Gaz.*, June 28-July 12; and *Lexington Intelligencer*, July 3-13, 1838. | 1837<br>————, Oct. 2 (or earlier)? *Lou. Pub. Adv.*, Sept. 30-Oct. 2, 1837.<br><br>Cole (equestrian company), American Amphitheatre (American Theatre?), Nov. 1-16 (or later). *Lou. Pub. Adv.*, Nov. 1-16, 1837.<br><br>1838<br>Parsons? City Theatre, Jan. 23 (or earlier)-(continuously?) Dec. 18 (or later). Continuity of performance very doubtful. Some of the performances were given at the American Theatre, but apparently by the same company which was playing at the City Theatre. A circus assisted the dramatic company for a time in October. *Lou. Pub. Adv.*, Jan. 23-Feb. 5; May 2-24; June 16 and 20; July 14 and 28; Aug. 9 and 20; Sept. 7 and 22; Oct. 18; Nov. 26-30; Dec. 1, 14, and 18, 1838. | Matthew Field (for Ludlow & Smith), New St. Louis Theatre, Jan. 10-27. *Mo. Rep.*, Jan. 9-27, 1838; and Smith, *Theatrical Management*, 1868, p. 133.<br><br>Ludlow & Smith, New St. Louis Theatre, Feb. 6-May 30. *Mo. Rep.*, Feb. 6-May 30; and Smith, *Theatrical Management*, 1868, pp. 133-134.<br><br>Ludlow & Smith, New St. Louis Theatre, June 6-July 28. *Mo. Rep.*, June 2-July 30, 1838; and Ludlow, *op. cit.*, p. 508. | Pentland & Norris (possibly non-dramatic), about Sept. 9 (or earlier)? (time of performances very doubtful; no information except license record; possibly the company which played at the Museum, Sept. 6-9). *Journal of the Proceedings of the Common Council*, p. 465 (Sept. 9, 1837). D. D. McKinney, City Theatre, Dec. 7 to<br><br>Mar. 17. *Detroit Free Press*, Dec. 5, 1837-Mar. 17, 1838.<br><br>Marsh? (with McKinney's old company), Museum, Mar. 20-Apr. 20. *Detroit Free Press*, Mar. 20-Apr. 20, 1838; and *Journal of the Proceedings of the Common Council*, pp. 493-494 (Apr. 14, 1838).<br><br>Marsh and Eaton, City Theatre, July 4-Aug. 10 (or a few days later). *Detroit Free Press*, June 30-Aug. 10, 1838. |

| CINCINNATI | LEXINGTON | LOUISVILLE | ST. LOUIS | DETROIT |
|---|---|---|---|---|
| Scott & Thorne, National Theatre, Sept. 5 (and probably earlier—possibly the season was continuous from May 12)-Nov. 12 (or later). *Cinc. Daily Gaz.*, Sept. 4-5, Oct. 5, Nov. 1, 2, and 9, 1838; and MS. Minutes City Council, IX, 45 (July 12, 1838). | Mrs. A. Drake, Lexington Theatre, Aug. 30 (and a few days earlier)-31 (or later). *Ky. Gaz.*, Aug. 30; and *Lexington Intelligencer,* Aug. 31, 1838. | 1838 | Ludlow & Smith, New St. Louis Theatre, Aug. 9-Oct. 20. *Mo. Rep.*, July 30-Oct. 20, 1838; and Ludlow, *op. cit.*, p. 508. | H. Isherwood & Co., Detroit National Theatre, opposite the City Theatre, Aug. 13-Oct. 23 (or later). *Detroit Free Press,* July 20-Oct. 23, 1838; and *Journal of the Proceedings of the Common Council,* p. 518 (Sept. 4, 1838). Blaike, City Theatre, Nov. 10-Dec. 15 (or later). *Detroit Free Press,* Nov. 10-Dec. 15, 1838; and *Journal of the Proceedings of the Common Council,* p. 525 (Nov. 20, 1838). H. Isherwood, Museum, about Dec. 18 (or later) to |
| Scott & Thorne? National Theatre? Feb. 4 (and probably earlier)-? *Cinc. Daily Gaz.*, Feb. 2 and 4, 1839. Scott & Thorne, National Theatre? about June 5-Dec. 7 (and probably later). *Cinc. Daily Gaz.,* June 12, Nov. 30, and Dec. 6-9, 1839; and MS. Minutes City Council, X, 97-98 (Dec. 25, 1839). | Bailey & Rogers, "at their exhibition rooms," about Sept. 10?-24. *Lexington Intelligencer,* Sept. 24, 1839. | 1839 Parsons? City Theatre, Jan. 26-July 20 (or later; the continuity of performance is somewhat doubtful; and it is possible that the plays advertised for June and July were not given in the City Theatre). *Lou. Pub. Adv.,* Feb. 2 and 16; Mar. 4, 7, 14, and 20-22; May 10, 18-20, and 25; June 12; and July 16-20, 1839. | Ludlow & Smith, St. Louis Theatre (first called New St. Louis Theatre), Apr. 8-July 6. *Daily Mo. Rep.,* Apr. 5-July 6, 1839. *Cf.* Ludlow, *op. cit.*, pp. 511-514; and Smith, *Theatrical Management,* 1868, pp. 136-138. Ludlow & Smith, St. Louis Theatre, Aug. 12-Dec. 11. *Daily Mo. Rep.*, Aug. 8-Dec. 11, 1839; Ludlow, *op. cit.*, p. 514; and Smith, *Theatrical Management,* 1868, pp. 138-141. | Feb. 15 (or later). *Detroit Free Press,* Jan. 7-17 and 26, and Feb. 13 and 15, 1839; and *Journal of the Proceedings of the Common Council,* pp. 529 (Dec. 18, 1838) and 531, 535, and 536 (Jan. 8, Feb. 19 and 26, and Mar. 5, 1839). W. Isherwood, City Theatre, Feb. 27 only. *Detroit Free Press,* Feb. 26, 1839; and *Journal of the Proceedings of the Common Council,* p. 535 (Feb. 26, 1839). |

| CINCINNATI | LEXINGTON | LOUISVILLE | ST. LOUIS | DETROIT |
|---|---|---|---|---|
| | | 1839 <br> —— City Theatre, Sept. 14-Nov. 16 (or later). *Louisville Literary News-letter*, Sept. 21-Nov. 16, 1839. | | Blaike, Museum, about Mar. 5? for one night. *Journal of the Proceedings of the Common Council*, p. 536 (Mar. 5, 1839). <br> Isherwood (W.?), National Theatre, Mar. 8 (or earlier)-? <br> *Detroit Free Press*, Mar. 7, 1839. <br> W. Isherwood, City Theatre, Mar. 13 (or earlier)-May 8. <br> *Detroit Free Press*, Mar. 13-May 8, 1839; and *Journal of the Proceedings of the Common Council*, pp. 537 and 543 (Mar. 14 and Apr. 9, 1839). <br> Montgomery, National Theatre, June 19-Aug. 5 (or later). <br> *Detroit Free Press*, Apr. 3 ff., May 23 and 30, and June 19-Aug. 17, 1839; and *Journal of the Proceedings of the Common Council*, pp. 552, 554, 555, 557, and 566 (May 14, 21, and 28; and July 17, 1839). |

| CINCINNATI | LEXINGTON | LOUISVILLE | ST. LOUIS | DETROIT |
|---|---|---|---|---|
| Scott & Thorne, National Theatre, Mar. 21 (and probably earlier—possibly plays were given continuously from June, 1839)-Mar. 28 (and probably later).<br>*Cinc. Daily Gaz.*, Mar. 20 and 28, 1840.<br>Scott & Thorne? National Theatre, Aug. 31 (or earlier)-Sept. 12 (and probably later).<br>*Cinc. Daily Gaz.*, Aug. 31-Sept. 12, 1840.<br>Clark, dramatic and equestrian company, National Theatre? December?<br>MS. Minutes City Council, X, 359 (Dec. 16, 1840). | | 1840<br>———— (J. Greene, stage manager), City Theatre, Mar. 14-21 (and probably later).<br>*Lou. Pub. Adv.*, Mar. 14-21, 1840.<br>————, City Theatre, Nov. 5 (and probably earlier)-Nov. 19 (and probably later).<br>*Lou. Pub. Adv.*, Nov. 5 and 19, 1840. | Mackenzie & Jefferson, ball room at Concert Hall, Mar. 9-28.<br>*Daily Mo. Rep.*, Mar. 9-28, 1840.<br>Ludlow & Smith, St. Louis Theatre, Mar. 26-July 4.<br>*Daily Mo. Rep.*, Mar. 24-July 4, 1840. *Cf.* Ludlow, *op. cit.*, pp. 521-525.<br>Farren or Ludlow, St. Louis Theatre ? July?-July 18.<br>*Daily Mo. Rep.*, July 18, 1840.<br>Ludlow & Smith, St. Louis Theatre, Aug. 24-Oct. 29.<br>*Daily Mo. Rep.*, Aug. 24-Oct. 29, 1840. *Cf.* Ludlow, *op. cit.*, pp. 525-529.<br>Koch & Riley, Museum, Dec. 9-11 (or later).<br>*Daily Mo. Rep.*, Dec. 9-11, 1840. | Parker & Mueller, National Theatre, June 22 (or 23)-July 25 (or later).<br>*Detroit Free Press*, June 1 ff., 15 ff., and 24-July 25, 1840; and *Journal of the Proceedings of the Common Council*, p. 629 (June 23, 1840).<br>————, City Theatre, about Nov. 10?-?<br>*Journal of the Proceedings of the Common Council*, p. 652 (Nov. 10, 1840). |